Law and Morality

A Survey of Ideas, Issues, and Cases

By

Joseph L. Esposito

Law and Morality: A Survey of Ideas, Issues, and Cases

Joseph L. Esposito

This book first published 2022

Ethics International Press Ltd, UK

British Library Cataloguing in Publication Data

A catalogue record for this book is available from the British Library

Print Book ISBN: 978-1-80441-030-1

eBook ISBN: 978-1-80441-031-8

Contents

PREFACE

This book sits at the juncture of my two long careers: as an attorney specializing in federal administrative law, civil rights, employment law, and constitutional law; and as a philosopher specializing in American pragmatism. As a philosophy graduate student at New York University in the 1960s I was exposed to the emerging 'law and philosophy' conversation, inspired in large part by the philosophers who had come through the Great Depression and soon had seen the nations of Europe fall apart and into war. At that time the topic of 'law and morality' were not topics of discussion as much as matters of survival. When I later became a litigator and appellate attorney, I joined the firm of two former United States Attorneys, with a broad portfolio of representing governmental agencies and employees. From them, I learned that law, by virtue of its constitutive role in government, provided wide latitude for its interpretation and application so as to adapt to the political realities of the time. Here, I could see the ideas of the American pragmatists I studied seeping into the very roots of law in the Anglo-American tradition. So, Justice Holmes gets his due in this work.

When I taught an undergraduate course in Law and Morality and an upper-level law school class in Modern American Legal Thought, I realized that, from an student's perspective, law comes across as something formidable and 'supreme', a great and intricate labyrinth of words, rules, and precedents to be followed. But once in the actual practice of law, involving clients, evidence, and courts, law looks somewhat more uncertain and precarious, depending on the invisible intentions of lawmakers and law enforcers, the memory of witnesses, the attention of jurors, and the partiality of judges. I realized that the enterprise of law, in its practical dimensions as legislation, litigation, and enforcement, is not self-executing, nor self-certifying. Nothing of it is beyond analysis, criticism, or revision. Every part requires continual justification or reassessment to maintain its stature as legitimate authority. Attempting to understand and reconcile the relation of law and morality further complicates the picture. Legal philosophers have presented their pet ideas on that subject. Students, by contrast, must first become acquainted with a variety of ideas, issues, and examples from case law to draw out their moral implications. To study law from this perspective requires some acquaintance with areas of legal history, philosophy, religion, and the various branches of the social sciences such as politics and economics. Achieving this kind of understanding is why I wrote this book.

Acknowledgements: Many individuals influenced and contributed to the ideas that produced this book. In the area of the practice of law these include William C. Smitherman, Joel D. Sacks, Clifford B. Altfeld, James D. Whitney, and those judges, to remain unnamed, before whom I practiced, and who revealed some of the best attributes of their profession: diligent attention, sound reasoning, reflective analysis, and persuasive writing. In the area of academia, I am deeply grateful for those scholars who assisted me in thinking through issues of law and morality, or in putting together a course on that subject: Sidney Hook, Kai Nielsen, Raziel Abelson, William Barrett, James Rachels, Richard M. Martin, Ernest van den Haag, Max Fisch, Ivan Strenski, Michael Gill, Thomas Christiano, Connie Rosati, and Jane Bambauer.

INTRODUCTION

Law is a component of the coercive infrastructure of a government in a given political community, while morality provides a source of norms used to guide the applications of the law within that community. Sometime the application is successful, and sometimes not so much. If we lived as members in a great loving community of shared interests and values there would be little or no need for and intersection of law and morality. In such a utopia, if disputes were to arise, we could imagine they would be resolved in a satisfactory manner through a deep rational interrogation of the assumptions that produced the dispute in the first place. After which the disputants would go away satisfied and better informed. So, the establishment of law marks a recognition that disputes may arise that are hard to resolve, either because the disputants are not wise or honest enough to examine their own interests, or because too many interests of too many people are implicated. Historically, some sort of coercive infrastructure has been thought to be the solution to the problem of hard disputes and hard feelings. However, once the idea of coercion enters the picture, the question arises 'How much is appropriate?' and with that question arises all of the various answers the theoretical study of law (jurisprudence) provides. One answer typically given is that coercion generally is justified if it is the product of a fair system of justice, one created and enforced by people acting with impartiality according to widely recognized social norms. It is typically in the characterization of these norms that morality enters the picture. One such norm is: 'Those you make and enforce the laws must also be subject to them', popularly expressed as 'Nobody is above the law.' This norm of fairness is proposed to resist the corruption of special favors and exemptions, but *how* it accomplishes this is one of the great tasks of jurisprudence.

There have been other norms justifying the coercion requirement, such as 'Laws must reflect the intentions and will of God' or 'Laws must advance the common good'. Again, it is the deep work of jurisprudence to explain and justify why these norms should be followed. In the process of doing this work other norms will be identified and applied or rejected. Consider the norm 'The greater the harm caused the greater the punishment inflicted'. This norm usually operates in the background when attempts are made to make the punishment *fit* the crime. There is usually public consensus that premeditated murder is a graver crime than reckless killing, which is a graver crime than accidental killing. This spectrum, in turn, is governed by yet another underlying norm: 'We are more responsible for the foreseeable consequences of actions we have control over than for those we did not fully or entirely see coming'.

In general, the application of norms to law can be a bedeviling problem. It is easier to identify responsibility when someone plunges a knife into someone else than to trace a decision of an individual in a corporate boardroom that leads to gradual pollution of a waterway. Collective action and dispersive harmful consequences pose special problems for jurisprudence and for identifying and assessing the morality of law. So how do we get our hands around these multi-faceted problems that arise from the interaction of law and morality? If we try to just talk about law, we run the risk of ignoring the influence of morality; if we talk just about morality, we run the risk of leaving out how law can constrain moral options, create moral dilemmas, and even become an instrument of immorality in the name of lawful authority.

The three parts of the book – focusing on theory, method and practice – represent three approaches to characterizing this multifaceted subject. In Part One (Theory) two chapters are devoted to some general theories of the relation of law and morality, the goal being to identify concepts that subsume and govern both domains and in the process to help mark the borderlines between moral and immoral laws. In Chapter One, the ideas of American legal theorist Lon L. Fuller (1902-1978) are presented. He looks at law and morality as examples of rule and norm making activities of social actors designed to delineate acceptable and unacceptable forms of social behavior. So, to the extent that rules are by their very nature hard to formulate for all conditions, and norms hard to apply in all situations, so will these problems emerge in applications of law and morality. From his perspective, morality would be powerless to serve as a constraint on law without the constant vigilance over those involved in the creation and enforcement of it. Such vigilance requires the guidance, in his words, of the norms of the "inner morality" of law. These are norms, he argues, we must constantly return to in order to see whether we are constructing and applying laws using fair, reasonable, and proportionate rules.

Chapter Two provides several traditional theories of the relation of law and morality. Theories of 'moral law' and 'natural law' eliminate or come close to closing entirely the law-morality gap by identifying certain fundamental characteristics either of human reasoning or of 'laws of nature' that serve as a unified foundation of both law and morality. By contrast 'positive' law theories attempt to explain why law and morality must be regarded as separate enterprises, allowing that moral values (often *utilitarianism*) identifiable as *social facts* may be incorporated into law, but once there cannot be subject further to moral norms. Positivists prefer to talk about the validity of law rather than its moral goodness. If it turns out that a law is 'bad' it must be amended by using the procedures of 'good' law; it cannot be just ignored. In the case of moral and natural law, law reflects the culmination of the best of what reason has to offer because it is constructed from the same operations that make mind and nature possible in the first place. Philosophical giants like Gottfried Leibniz (1646-1716) and Immanuel Kant (1724-1804) accepted this view and set about to create a true 'scientific jurisprudence' as law's foundation. In their view a properly constructed legal system would have no need for *ad hoc* rules to fill in gaps in law coverage, nor 'courts of equity' to make new rules to fit new circumstances when applying existing law would not achieve justice. Positive law, on the other hand, unites law and morality, in the words of English philosopher and jurist, Jeremy Bentham (1748-1832), into a "vast organic whole," a project made possible not because of some appeal to a transcendent realm but because empirical research and the scientific method are capable of knowing the best strategies of action for human improvement and what specific laws should be crafted to achieve it. With their reliance on a transcendent moral order whether embodied in God as Divine lawgiver, the unchanging order of Nature, or the state itself as a permanent embodiment of moral reason, all three theories, in the end, discourage or even outlaw a moral critique of law from any other alternative than that allowed by the law itself.

In the two chapters of Part Two (Method) various strategies for reconciling law and morality problems are discussed. In Chapter Three the relation of law to morality may be looked upon from the issue of the relation between common law and statutory law. These are often considered separate *sources* of law and legal authority – laws made by legislators versus laws made by judges – but are they really? Can statutes permanently function without the need for judges to interpret them? Can constitutional interpretation be reduced to distinct and complete canons and principles? Does a legislature have the final say over the entire scope of the jurisdiction of its courts? These questions are discussed and answered in the negative. The critical point is that laws being largely made up of definitions and rules inevitably require interpretation. Language as a vehicle of communication is intimately connected with the transient nature of human experience. This means that laws by their very nature are historical creatures. Yesterday's laws require today's interpretations, because often those who created them are gone and have left behind only more words about them.

This expressive and interpretative process is the subject of Chapter Four, which reviews standards of adjudication (interpreting and applying laws to facts) in lower courts and judicial review (applying judicial decisions to law from a broader legal perspective) in higher/appellate courts. These standards are necessary but not sufficient, it will be argued, for meeting the requirements of an effective moral influence on law. No matter how air tight a theory is that the laws of a society will incorporate its moral norms, in practice it always will take judges to determine if that is the case. Rigorous and precise applications of rules by themselves do not provide that guidance or make for a good judge. Precisely written oppressive laws enacted in bad faith and with insufficient analysis by legislators and notice to the public are still capable of being enforced and interpreted with diligence and consistency. Laws 'on the page', whether as statutes or judicial rulings, must still be evaluated to see whether they perversely require the nearly impossible, have been enacted in bad faith to deceive or entrap, are coherent with other laws, and do not punish retroactively.

So, a well-formed legal system is designed to constrain bad behavior by creating procedures of accountability for the drafting and enforcing of laws, such as: open meeting laws, accurate and informative minutes of meetings, notice and opportunity for public comment, maintenance of accurate legislative and court records, accurate police reports, police conduct review procedures, freedom of information acts, etc. In the case of adjudication, where laws are applied to facts, rules of procedure and evidence are required. Chapter Four reviews such rules and their importance in producing acceptable lower court decisions. In the case of appellate review, decisions are evaluated in the broader context of the law prevailing in the jurisdiction and even beyond. Here the appellate judge has a wide variety of tools to work with: doctrines determining how much weight to give to precedent (*stare decisis*), rules of statutory interpretation, and an appeal to various judicial philosophies such as legal realism, textualism, originalism, and legal formalism, to be explained later. In this chapter each philosophy is evaluated and the question is considered whether adopting and even promoting a judicial philosophy is consistent with what have been called the 'judicial virtues' of an appellate judge: careful and sober evaluation of the record and pertinent law, as well as an honest and thorough explication of the working assumptions and personal convictions built into the final decisions, especially including the reasons why contrary judicial philosophies do not apply. These critical standards and procedures for producing good judicial decisions, it turns out, also provide opportunities for the introduction of moral norms into the law making and enforcement process.

Part Three (Practice) takes up some of topics and problems that arise when law is applied to social life. Inevitably, applications of law as enacted and applied produce unanticipated practical consequences. The five chapters in this part consider topics closer to the direct influence of law on various areas of ordinary life, and the degree to which law can and ought to impose upon them. Religion is at once deeply personal and yet also permeates may aspects of social life within communities and the nation. How law has tried to reconcile the private and social influence of religion is the subject of Chapter Five. A main difficulty is defining religion itself and the nature of the claims made in its name. Clearly it is a moral question whether the strictures of one group's religion ought to be applied to other religious groups in the same political community. The framers of the Constitution recognized this problem even though they operated largely within the Protestant orbit. Their proposed solutions involving free exercise of religious worship and non-establishment of a state religion ran headlong into their enlightenment values of a government founded on the universal rights of an autonomous citizenry. The result was that the religion clauses of the First Amendment could not cleanly harmonize private religious values with nonsectarian public life and so produced a long and contentious debate. Religious toleration and the rights of conscience, the answer favored by Madison and Jefferson, have not been embraced by those who live their faith internally but also see it as entirely the measure of what should be true and real for many others outside their faith. Our survey of religion cases reveals a history of *ad hoc* solutions to disputes among sectarian interests and between the sectarian and non-sectarian, raising questions such as whether the claims of religion can be cognizable and adjudicated by law within the existing (non-theocratic) constitutional framework, or whether they are so endemically vague as to be incapable of clear, consistent, and universal application in law?

Chapter Six considers the constellation of laws and norms that affect public communication, including laws limiting or prohibiting speech deemed harmful to individuals, as well as laws promoting speech deemed beneficial to political debate and consensus. The former are laws that prohibit what is deemed 'low value' or even 'immoral' speech; for example, obscene, pornographic, libelous, slanderous, blasphemous, sexist, and racist speech. The latter are laws and regulations of speech directed to the public, particularly during election campaigns. In reviewing free speech cases it is worthwhile to ask: what words in the First Amendment would have to be changed to make them still compatible with the complete suppression of free speech? The answer appears to be: very few, if any; for the history of the First Amendment suggests that the Constitutional guarantee of free public speech and debate is honored except when it is deemed too risky to do so.

Part of the direct moral influence of law on daily life is seen in the ways in which it sets the boundary between acceptable and unacceptable affronts to privacy and intimacy. When such violations occur, our dignity is either enhanced or diminished by what the law allows. Chapter Seven explores the reciprocal interaction between privacy, intimacy, and dignity in American law. Like the wavering protections of free speech, protections to dignity also seem to reflect shifting standards of law; the same law can support one degree of privacy today and a lesser degree tomorrow through only a slight reinterpretation of its language. An unlawful search one day may be made into a lawful search on another day, depending on surrounding circumstances. Our expectations of privacy may diminish not from an initial change in the law but from what technology makes possible subsequently. In other words, the same wording of the Fourth Amendment, such as "unreasonable searches and seizures" or "probable cause," could be made to apply in a libertarian or an autocratic state by good faith jurists who approach the disputes before them with a different view of the extent and moral value of privacy. If this is the case, then it seems that in the arena of privacy, moral norms have only a tenuous grasp on what the law requires. This chapter examines some areas of human experience where laws affect privacy, intimacy, and dignity, including laws regulating marriage, polygamy, incest, birth control, abortion, and government surveillance.

To discuss law and morality is at the same time to discuss morality and politics because the creation and administration of law is one of the primary missions of politics. The main subject of Chapter Eight is political power itself and the ways it is facilitated or thwarted by law. Superficially, law's influence on politics is made to come across as regular, authoritative, and ineluctable. On the one hand, politicians take an oath to follow the law; in the Constitution (Art. II, Sec. 3) the President "shall take care that the laws be faithfully executed." On the other hand, politicians often seek novel opportunities to bend the law or embrace strained interpretations of it for partisan gain. They pass laws affording them a partisan advantage they would oppose if their opponents did the same. The central question of this chapter, then, is whether there are norms that will ultimately constrain politics within fixed guardrails or whether political power has unlimited license to define its own legitimacy through law. Madison believed the former was possible, arguing that a properly constructed representative electoral system of divided government could be achieved when the general public has an opportunity to elect politicians who would put consensus and the common good above their own self or party interests. Yet, remarkably, in spite of this initial faith that such a system had been or was on the way to being constructed, the Constitutional guarantee (Art. IV, Sec. 4) requiring a republican form of government to the states has been all but dead letter from the start, allowing politicians to create voting eligibility rules, voting districts, and access to the ballot to achieve biased and decidedly un-republican outcomes. Also discussed in this chapter, illustrating the interaction of law and politics, include the doctrine of separation of powers, formation of the Senate, judicial selection and ideology, additional remarks on the doctrine of *stare decisis*, the amendment process, and the moral norms embedded in the Fourteenth Amendment.

Finally, Chapter Nine surveys areas of law that raise the most salient issues for law and morality: the degree to which law can trespass not merely upon privacy and dignity, but directly upon our physical bodies. Some laws are formed because they are able to affect our physical bodies and, in the process, also our minds. Breaking these 'laws of the body' means being broken ourselves in our personhood or humanity. Whenever a penal law affecting the body is drafted, lawmakers anticipate what its effect will be on the average person in terms of pain or the risk of pain. They may say that they have made the punishment 'fit' the crime, but such a claim is imprecisely compatible with a wide range of possible punishments. This process applies not only to criminal punishment, but also to civil infractions, and even to laws that regulate access to pleasure. A threshold question raised in this chapter is: To what extent, if at all, is it moral to use fear, pain, coercion, confinement, or social stigmatization to achieve the purposes of law. This is a question English philosopher and political economist, John Stuart Mill (1806-1873), urged us to consider in *On Liberty*. Mill wanted us to recognize that coercive laws of the body could be justly enacted and enforced only when measured against a presumed standard of avoiding harm to individual autonomy and dignity. With Mill's insight in mind, this chapter looks specifically at the development of laws and cases regulating suicide and dying, marriage and parenthood, birth control and sterilization, sexual experience, abortion, and criminal punishment. In the process two pervasive forms of paternalism come into view: the paternalism of laws that constrains liberty of action and experience, and the paternalism that restricts the degree to which those subject to the laws have an opportunity to change them.

Since this book is a survey of topics on law and morality, chapters are organized by topic and need not be read in the order presented.

Part One: Theory

CHAPTER 1

THE INNER AND OUTER MORALITY OF LAW

In discussing the relation between law and morality we may distinguish whether a law embodies moral values in its creation by law-making bodies, or whether once created it is interpreted and enforced morally. Suppose a system of laws are enacted to allow collective punishment of family members for crimes committed by one of their members. Then the jurisprudence surrounding such a law could easily fill several volumes and could be impressively articulated, but without addressing the question of whether other family members deserve to be punished as well. Definitions of a 'family member' would be required as well as standards for punishing them. Many threshold questions would have to be answered: Should third cousins be punished the same as first cousins? What about members living overseas or in other jurisdictions? A regime of rules and procedures would be required, raising further questions of how well the rules articulate what the law intends and how well the procedures are followed by those carrying out the law. But, in addition, we may also ask: why did legislators decide to legalize punishing family members in the first place? What was their penological philosophy and was it moral? It is always possible to raise such questions about ethical values and moral norms from outside the law.

That there was a fundamental connection between law and its surrounding norms was the insight of Lon L. Fuller when he referred to the inner and outer morality of law.[1] *Outer morality* refers to the moral content expressed directly through law. Even a 'dead letter' law that was enacted but never enforced could still express immoral values. *Inner morality*, by contrast, refers to the norms of behavior of people who create and carry out the law. It operates, for example, in the courthouse when judges, lawyers, jurors,

---

[1] Lon L. Fuller, *The Morality of Law*, 2nd ed. (New Haven: Yale University Press, 1969).

and witnesses assemble to put on a trial. It also is found in the State Houses and halls of Congress when lawmakers sift through documents, listen to constituents and lobbyists, take testimony and then draft, negotiate, and vote on laws. It operates on the cop on the beat, the preparation of reports of pretrial services and the probation department, and all the associated activities that go into managing our prison system. And it is found in the activities of the law interpreters – the professors who teach 'law' to students and write theoretical essays on law in 'law reviews' for colleagues and judges. But suppose on a given day those acting to carry out the law decided to ignore the norms they are supposed to openly follow. Police officers would use their badge to intimidate neighbors or would fabricate evidence and falsify their reports of crime. Lawyers would deliberately misinterpret the law to jurors and sway their opinion with inadmissible or even fraudulent evidence. Judges would make rulings on the basis of personal animus against one or more of the parties before them or would take bribes or spend most of their time in a profitable business of routinely fixing traffic tickets. Prison guards would extort or play favorites with those in their custody. Congressional members of the Senate Judiciary committee would suppress derogatory information about a court nominee they favored. Law professors, legal scholars and high court justices would explain the law in ways calculated to deceive in order to achieve personal or partisan political objectives. *In other words, the persistent violation of the inner moral norms of law would undermine even the best of moral codes and in a matter of time produce endemic corruption, public distrust, and eventually political chaos.*

The Ambiguity of Rules

By focusing on the norms of morality Fuller is stressing a problem that is endemic to all rule-governed activity. Laws provide rules and must be implemented in a rule-governed way. But no law can ever guarantee its faithful execution. No rule or set of rules is self-executing. There is always a question whether rules or laws apply in a given situation. The act of taking an oath involves an agreement, expressed publicly, to follow certain rules, for example of an officer to carry out the law or of a witness to tell the truth in court. But oath taking by itself is never sufficient to guarantee the faithful execution of the law; nor the uniform and consistent application of rules. If there is to be a guarantee at all it is only to be found in the degree to which laws and their rules are open to critique and modification from the social and political environment, and especially from opportunities for the public to see the laws being created and enforced and then being able to influence those processes.

So, part of the morality of law is recognizing the fact that laws and rules are expressed in language and that words are never free from the need to interpret them correctly. Even definitions of terms incorporated into a set of laws or rules are not entirely free from a need to interpret them. Part of the diligence of rulemaking is the process of anticipating where the rules would *not* apply. Examining public discussions of law, including legal arguments made to judges and juries in court, debates in legislatures, journalistic reporting, scholarly analysis of legislation and judicial opinions, and information from lobbyists and the general public create opportunities for more precise articulations of law. In theory that flow of information ought to produce well-articulated and designed laws. That at least is the stated moral aspiration. Sometimes, however, the opposite results: laws are drafted and enacted that are vague, unenforceable, or worse yet surreptitious and entrapping, while procedures implementing laws can be corrupt, empty of true accountability, or enforced in bad faith. In those instances, the morality of law requires the analysis of the meaning of words and sentences as they are articulated in the form of assertions and explanations by those who enact and enforce the law. Since rules and laws are never self-executing or self-interpreting, it can never be a valid defense to say that they 'speak for themselves', a common method of moral evasion in the realm of law. If we set something down in writing we are simultaneously establishing a commitment to explain what we are attempting to say.

Ordinarily, the interpretation of rules is attributed to the experience of those who are in the business of applying them. But even the employment of experts does not eliminate problems of misinterpretation or interpretations that still leave some doubt. In baseball, while we have relied on the umpires' visual judgment of when a ball or strike occurs as it passes over the plate we know and accept that some umpires have a wide (or a narrow) interpretation of what it means to be 'over the plate'. Even using precise visual technology to detect whether the ball is in the 'strike zone' will require the use of written rules to set quality control protocols for the device and resolve boundary disputes over the precision of its functionability. In professional football a 'catch' is made when a player "in the process of attempting to catch the ball, …secures control of the ball prior to it touching the ground, and that control is maintained during and after the ball has touched the ground. (NFL Rule Book, Rule 3, Sec. 2: "The Ball and Possession of the Ball," Art. 7.). The rule does not define an 'attempt'; nor does the rule say anything about the loss and regaining of control of the ball during the catch process. Other rules describe 'possession' as a "firm grip" and as "complete control," but leave it to the judgment of umpires or experts to decide when those words apply in practice. When troublesome applications of rules apply, they can be rewritten to minimize ambiguity. Rules may be modified for greater clarity, but only after the fact and, then, only to reduce uncertainty but never eliminate it. One way to reduce ambiguity of rules, is to provide specific examples of situations where the rules apply or do not apply; those examples would allow an interpreter to analogize them to their situation. This process of recognizing and attempting to resolve ambiguity occurs in all of the rules of sports and other games, but also is part of the interpretation of law itself.[2]

Rules that seem to be absolutely cut and dry on their face also may have uncertain application. Consider the rule of voter eligibility in the Twenty-Sixth Amendment to the U.S. Constitution: "The right of citizens of the United States, who are eighteen years of age or older, to vote shall not be denied or abridged by the United States or by any State on account of age." The rule seems clear enough on its face – nobody can vote until they are eighteen years of age. Obviously, a difficulty arises if one does not know their birthdate even though they obviously have one. To remedy this problem an attempt is made to identify every person's birthday with birth certificates containing witnesses and signatures, but ascertaining these facts is not self-evident in which case a person who is actually eighteen still

[2] Legal treatises such as the *American Law Reports*, or the various "Restatements of Law" published by the American Law Institute, compile fact-patterns from specific cases to assist attorneys in interpreting how the law in their case is likely to be interpreted by judges.

may not vote until someone in authority determines they are eligible by age. In the case of being born at the 'stroke of midnight' it is generally accepted as being born on the 'next day'. Or: consider citizens who vote electronically from east of the international dateline where they are eighteen but then travel west across the dateline when their vote is tabulated and when they are seventeen. Was their vote authorized? Was it even fraudulent? Clearly, the assumption built into the language of the Constitution is of a world where humans or their votes do not travel at high speeds over long distances.

Another illustration of the difficulty of applying voter eligibility rules involves their application to residency. Individuals may be a domiciled resident entitled to vote as long as they intend to remain so domiciled minutes after the vote is tabulated. But they may also change their minds a few minutes later and decide to move elsewhere. There are no clear rules for situations like that, though doubtless some could be formulated; as, for example, by requiring residents to remain in place for a specified time later before their vote is validated. But then more rules about applying the residency rule would be required. Many other *ad hoc* rules apply to voting. We deny to voters an opportunity to change their votes after being cast or after the results have been announced because they have changed their minds or accidentally indicated the wrong candidate. We merely assume that voters know what they want to do and have the proper eyesight and motor skills to accomplish it even though we know that campaigns are deceptive and physical errors in marking a ballot may easily exceed the margin of victory in a close election. Also, we do not interview voters to determine whether their vote is carefully considered and informed. Consent is simply imputed to the process as a whole.

Whether in sports, morality, or law an unarticulated pragmatic assumption, perhaps expressed as a 'meta-rule', is that norms and rules need only be good enough to accomplish the result desired. But the rule of pragmatic finality is coupled with another meta-rule: where a rule can be made better it should be made so. Formulating and revising rules to make them better is a concerted process of interpretation, yet ironically subjecting rules to interpretation also turns out to be a de-legitimizing process; it reveals a certain frailty, often revealed as vagueness or inconsistency in the application of the rules. To compensate for this, *ad hoc* meta-rules are introduced to bolster application of the rules and re-legitimize them. The stipulated jurisdiction of courts and the finality of their rulings (*res judicata*) are two such meta-rules, rules specifying what kind of disputes a court can hear in its location, what kind of relationship to the court the parties must have, the dollar amount in dispute, when it is too late to sue ('statutes of limitations'), and how far an appeal may go. Other examples of rule bolstering meta-rules are the various rules for interpreting the words of statutes ('statutory construction'), for example, how to distinguish 'may' (discretionary) from' shall' (compulsory), used to determine how the specific wording of laws should be applied to specific circumstances.

The Inner Morality of Law

Fuller wants us to think of law and morality as parts of a practical and continuous process of social problem-solving and adjustment. Both are systems of rules, but it is not entirely accurate to say that moral rules function as imperatives, things we ought to do, while legal rules function as commands, things we must do. Both recognize the importance of an enforcing authority of some sort. Rules in sports require governing bodies and referees. Rules of etiquette require acknowledged social authorities about proper behavior and appearance. Many social settings imply certain rules of behavior, clothing and manner. Offices and classrooms have many tacit and often articulated rules of appearance and conduct. Military organizations are a riot of such rules from morning till night. At a certain point, social offenses may cross a line and become a breach of the peace, a nuisance, a disruption of the quiet enjoyment of others, and so elevate to violations of legal rules. But it is not just at the boundary of law and morality that rules overlap. Legal concepts at the heart of law itself when carefully teased out, concepts such as agreement, promise, remedy, remorse, duty of care, due process, equal protection, and many more are infused with moral conceptions and could not function without them. Fuller wants us to recognize that moral and legal rules are not simply the results of the edicts of rule-conferring authorities. Some authorities are better than others when looked at from the perspective of their purposes and rule-making procedures, but especially in their capacity to reexamine their own purposes and procedures.

Recognizing this complex interrelationship of law and morality, Fuller has called law a "dimension of human life."[3] By this sweeping remark he suggests that wherever there are human beings there will be found laws in some form or other. Even an utterly solitary life might be the source of rules expressed in the form of habits and routines of daily life. We may even be hardwired to develop habits and routines for ourselves, though not always for obeying someone else's. Laws set the obligation to obey; but to merit obedience the very processes of law making, interpreting, and enforcing must acquire the stature of morality. Of course, it is possible for immoral persons to accidentally produce good laws or even write laws intended to be bad that turn out to have good consequences. This seldom happens, however, because law making invariably is a *power* process that easily facilitates corrupt intentions.

In spite of their evident defects should all laws be obeyed? Should you stop at a red light in the middle of a vacant desert in the middle of the night? If a baby is about to be born in the backseat should you stop under the same circumstances? If laws are designed to regulate social life by subjecting conduct to norms, do they apply at the limits of social life, for example in extreme emergencies when a natural catastrophe is about to occur? Also, do I have the same obligation to obey the laws of a foreign country as I do in my own? Treaties, international conventions, 'laws of nations', diplomatic immunities, and customs regulations help smooth out some of these issues by providing some rules and remedies for peoples who enter into foreign jurisdictions. But even living in one's own country questions may arise about the limits of obedience to law and of the jurisdiction of the courts of law. Fuller toyed with this idea in an interesting essay about a group of trapped cave explorers (spelunkers) deep underground and near starvation who draw lots to kill and eat one of their members. They bring their morality with them but, Fuller wonders, do they also bring the laws that apply to them into the cave if they are bodily inaccessible to law enforcement?[4] From the perspective of jurisdiction, they might as well be on the moon, raising the question: How

---

[3] Lon L. Fuller, *Anatomy of the Law* (New York: Praeger, 1968), 2-3.

[4] Lon L. Fuller, *The Case of the Speluncean Explorers*, 62 Harv. L Rev. 616 (1949).

can the state regulate conduct through a law if it cannot control and enforce it even if it wants to?

In the spelunker case, Fuller is raising the question of the outer limits of law. Those limits are typically defined not only by the territorial limits of a law but also by its capacity to generate effective enforcement. Fuller wants us to see laws not as cut and dried commands to obey, but as a process of social adjustment and pragmatic judgment. For example, many laws 'on the books' are only selectively enforced. Some are not enforced at all because nobody knows they have been violated, at times even by the person violating them. Other laws are known to be violated in some circumstances but not enforced because the state has more important priorities and must allocate scarce resources. Every traffic cop and police department have *de facto* rules of thumb as to what speed constitutes an enforced speeding violation, which is usually more than a few miles per hour above the actual lawful limit. And, some laws are not enforced because they are no longer deemed worthy of enforcement due to changes in cultural and moral values. In recent years, adultery rarely has been punished; so also unmarried cohabitation, fornication, or sex acts deemed 'nonstandard' by previous norms. But there is an obvious distinction between laws that are unenforced because, though many people openly violate them, law enforcement looks the other way, and laws that are unenforced as a matter of intentional policy. The legal *doctrine of desuetude* ('outdated') does the work of sorting out these distinctions. For example, laws derived from constitutional provisions (bills of attainder, emoluments clauses) are deemed never to lapse, while some penal laws may lose their teeth under the doctrine because the conduct penalized is no longer offensive or practiced.

Some laws are so poorly drafted that their violations are too hard to detect. Texas has a constitutional provision (Art. 1, § 4) prohibiting anyone from holding an office who does not "acknowledge the existence of a Supreme Being." But how supreme should this being be? In referring to "a Supreme Being" does the law allow you to select your own from among other candidates; and supreme in what sense? Would a theological disquisition be required ahead of taking the oath in order to determine whether the oath is being violated? The reasoning behind the law may be that atheists cannot be moral and cannot properly take oaths and so must be weeded out. Yet, the best evidence for this would be that atheists invariably fail in their moral duties at a higher rate than do theists who are motivated by fear of divine retribution. But has evidence for this claim ever been clearly set out? Without answers to these seldom-asked questions, it is difficult to charge someone with violating the oath provision because the facts to be elicited would be so subjective and their application potentially lawless.

To get a clearer idea of the influence of morality on law Fuller first distinguishes morality as duty and as aspiration, and then describes the essential aspirational characteristics of a good law and a good law-making process. When lawmakers are considering gambling legislation, for example, they must shuttle back and forth between the two moralities. They could draft a law that prohibits the possession or use of gambling paraphernalia (dice, cards, roulette wheels, etc.). They could also draft a law that prohibits activities directly associated with gambling, such as renting a hotel room in a Las Vegas casino; or a law prohibiting the use of the national currency or banking system to make bets. In the first case you would have a clear duty not to possess or use gambling paraphernalia for gambling purposes. But in the later examples, the duty is less specific and reflects more aspirational values. Would I have a clear duty not to stay at any hotel with casinos whether or not I gamble or intend to? And if the aspirational value of restricting gambling is to discourage the healthy practice of assessing risk through reasoned analysis, is gambling utterly devoid of such analysis? The duties in these latter cases are not as clear. Betting on chance events, whether on slot machines, card games, or horse races, for example, are not a repudiation of risk assessment. After all, bookmakers profit from gambling because gamblers do not devote all their time to carefully assessing risk. If we all became casino operators or bookmakers, individual and societal benefits from gambling proceeds would suffer because we could not rely upon people who are willing to throw their money away for a small chance at a big reward. So, gambling laws must achieve a balance of risk and reward by establishing a regulated infrastructure working in the background. Gambling paraphernalia such a dice, cards, or slot machines must meet stringent manufacturing standards, which in turn require stringent quality control and administrative standards. There must be a sound promise, backed by law, that winning bets will be paid off. The entire gambling environment requires constant vigilance in order to catch cheaters. Events that influence gambling odds, such as insider corruption and new cheating methods, must be accurately identified, disclosed and publicly reported. In other words, gambling is not a repudiation of reason but a game set up to test the capacity of reason to assess risk under uncertainty. It requires a trusted *legal* system of fairness and equal opportunity for gamblers, who would otherwise flee from a rigged system. The same kind of reasoning applies to legislation that regulates the 'gambling' in the stock market. All of these considerations ought to pass through the mind of legislators when they evaluate the purposes, scope, and sanction of such legislation, while keeping in view the social values they aspire to achieve.

Aspirational morality, then, seeks to articulate big generalities about how we ought to live in a society governed by law, and hope that legislators are able to exercise aspirational morality when drafting laws. Lawmakers must focus practically on identifying what specific conduct to punish and then hope they get the consequences right over the long run. "There is no way open to us by which we can compel a man to live the life of reason. We can only seek to exclude from his life the grosser and more obvious manifestations of chance and irrationality," observes Fuller.[5] From his perspective law and morality do not perfectly fit each other's needs even under the best of circumstances:

> If the morality of duty reaches upward beyond its proper sphere the iron hand of imposed obligation may stifle experiment, inspiration, and spontaneity. If the morality of aspiration invades the province of duty, men may begin to weigh and qualify their obligations by standards of their own and we may end with the poet tossing his wife into the river in the belief – perhaps quite justified – that he will be able to write better poetry in her absence.[6]

Given the difficulties of writing laws that can be said to balance the values of duty and aspiration, by what factors should we measure success? Draconian laws may be highly successful if every member of a terrified

---

[5] Fuller, *The Morality of Law*, xx.

[6] Ibid., 28.

population never fails to obey them. But obedience cannot be a complete measure of the success of a law. They must be constructed to be worthy of obedience. Fuller's proposal is that to be considered good, or moral, laws should have certain attributes that reflect standards of good legal practice. Here he provides eight standards that good laws should meet.

Generality: Legal rules should not be overly specific, nor too general. Laws should not apply to the specific acts of specific individuals in specific places at specific times. Such a condition would render the aspiration of 'equality under the law' impossible to achieve. Under early English law, a Bill of Attainder could be issued against an individual or small group of individuals for treason or serious criminal conduct. The fact that the person and not conduct was the object of punishment is reflected in the fact that the relatives of the 'tainted' individual also could be punished; and all family lands for generations to come could be tainted by confiscation. Attainder was an efficient and elegant device for punishing crime. It made every family member both a potential law victim and its enforcer. Since, it could not be distinguished from summary punishment and applied only to one case, it offended our sense of justice that laws be drafted to apply in a variety of situations.

Attainder was practiced and abused during the American revolutionary period as legislatures enacted either vindictive laws to confiscate property of British sympathizers, or laws conferring special benefits and monopolies to businesses and individuals who assisted in the revolution. Many framers of the Constitution saw the potential for corruption in a political system that could not distinguish a law from a direct order. It should be the business of the legislature to establish general rules and it should be up to the courts to decide which individuals fell under them, they argued. So, enacting Bills of Attainder were expressly abolished by the Constitution for both federal and state legislatures (Article 1, Sec. 9, cls. 3 and 10).

Nonetheless, in spite of the constitutional prohibition, special or private laws are routinely passes by legislatures. Historically the Supreme Court has given more deference to targeted 'special legislation' that confers benefits than to such legislation that inflicts punishment. Congress has passed many bills 'for the benefit of' specifically named individuals to be exempt from immigration laws or to receive war widows' pensions, restore political rights, or grant citizenship. Sometime these benefits are even granted in such a way as to hide the identity of the beneficiary. They may even be applied to a family or small group of people and are enacted typically to correct an injury resulting from a governmental policy or program, as opposed to public laws that apply to the public generally. Fuller considers it a matter of "linguistic convenience" whether private laws are really laws as opposed to being executive orders or exemptions from laws.[7]

Fuller expressed his generality requirement as a truism: "to subject human conduct to the control of rules, there must be rules."[8] A private law that allows an individual to get a visa by issuing one and then reducing the existing visa quota by just that one looks like a mere administrative adjustment, and not the exercise of a private law. That maneuver, however, is accepted on the assumption that such private laws would be few in number and so do little harm to congressional determination of immigration quotas. Private laws, in other words, ought to be applied sparingly so as not to undermine general public laws and the policies behind them. They are sometimes justified by arguing that if Congress has plenary authority over an area of its control, such as immigration, that authority should bring within it the capacity to make some exceptions. Here the risk of violating the norm against excessive specificity is considerable, potentially turning law into gifts of favoritism. Consider a legal system with only one public rule: *All individuals must obey all private laws.* This excessively general rule has little content since the private law that I fail to obey could be written specifically to apply to my situation by those in power. Under such a system there would be little need for a Constitution or even a judiciary. The cost of such a system, however, would be that official secrecy and corruption of those in power would go unchecked.[9]

---

[7] Ibid., 49.

[8] Ibid.

[9] In *Nixon v. Administrator of General Services*, 433 U.S. 425 (1977) the Supreme Court found the law requiring President Nixon to turn over to Congress certain papers and audio tapes was not a Bill of Attainder, but governed general conduct and norms of the Presidency itself. See also Matthew Mantel, *Private Bills and Private Laws*, 99 Law Lib. J. 87 (2007).

Promulgation: Rules should be publicly available in a timely manner. The inner morality of law requires that laws be made known to the public and not be hidden away. But is there a knowledge threshold below which something procedurally passed as law ceases to be law because it was not promulgated sufficiently? Laws passed in the middle of the night that become effective at dawn may be legal as long as notice of their future enactment was itself sufficiently promulgated. To avoid unfair surprise laws typically are enacted first after several consecutive readings and then come into effect at a later time. Adding amendments to bills at the last minute, particularly by burying them in a large 'Omnibus Bill', violates Fuller's promulgation requirement, but happens nonetheless too frequently. This requirement also points to the moral importance of a vigorous system of accurate news coverage in the public interest. Journalists who follow the legislative process and report on it assist in creating public knowledge of laws that are about to be or have been recently enacted. Without it, corrupt officials could take advantage of an implicit rule that 'ignorance of a law is no excuse for violating it'.

Prospectivity: Rules should apply only to future conduct. Generality and promulgation establish that rules be made known and that they be known as a general condition for a general kind of conduct, so that someone can understand the difference between following a rule and breaking it. But rulemaking is not always perfect and its application clearly intended. Laws and judgments contain errors, as do the decisions of administrative agencies. Sometimes a mere typo has to be fixed with no effect on the law's binding effect. However, judicial opinions may more substantially change the interpretation of a law already on the books. Internal morality, therefore, requires adequate opportunities to amend legislation, reopen judicial rulings, and seek appellate review of contested rulings. Whenever a statute is interpreted by a court in some manner different from the understanding prior to the ruling, it is possible to say that a law has been changed retroactively as if a new law has been created in its place. This is how losing parties in litigation, who have relied upon a prior incorrect interpretation of the law, now regard their situation. Losing parties will conclude that they are being unfairly subject to retroactive laws. In all of these situations *de facto* retroactive laws are clarified and reinterpreted by the judicial oversight of the legislative function or by substantial constitutional rulings of the

Supreme Court, rendering the law void or requiring that lower courts adopt the correct interpretation while it remains in effect.

However, the expressly retroactive laws referred to the Constitution (Art. I, Sec. 9, cl 3) are of a more virulent kind. They may be deliberate entrapments, an excuse for retrospective punishment, or may even have an unintended punishing effect. Consider a bank that makes loans at 12% interest to less than credit-worthy borrowers. A new law setting the highest interest rate at 10% for all new loans and all existing loans going forward will seriously impact the bank's business model which had relied on the 12% return. Suppose the new law reset the rate for existing loans since their inception, requiring the bank to rebate the overpayment. This example illustrates that retroactivity comes in degrees depending on the severity of the damage. In the case of a retroactive law now carrying the death penalty for certain previous non-capital offenses the damage is absolute and final for those already charged or convicted of them. They will now be executed under the new law. The framers of the Constitution were sensitive to these degrees of penalty because they were facing a revolutionary situation where laws that people under the colonial regime had relied upon were being changed literally overnight, and they were especially worried about retroactive criminal laws. Non-criminal laws, where the penalty of retroactivity was less severe, could still be protected against retroactivity by specific prohibitions, for example, against taking property without just compensation (Fifth Amendment) or laws against impairing contracts (Art, 1 Sec. 10, cl.1), as in the banking example above, which provide remedies against less severe retroactivity. In these provisions the framers were doing the careful balancing of state and personal interests required by the inner morality of law.[10]

Nonetheless, the struggles of the framers continue on in variously degrees in everyday life. Fuller puts it this way: "If every time a man relied on existing law in arranging his affairs, he were made secure against any change in legal rules, the whole body of our law would be ossified forever."[11] This means

---

[10] See *Calder v. Bull*, 3 U.S. 386 (1798); also, Robert G. Natelson, *Statutory Retroactivity: The Founders' View*, 39 Idaho L. Rev. 489 (2003).

[11] *The Morality of Law*, 60.

that individuals must realize that new laws may change the consequences of previous laws and so must be anticipatory participants in the law making process by petitioning their government and freely associating with others of common interest to exert influence on the process.

Clarity: Rules must be sufficiently clear to achieve their purpose. This standard is "one of the most essential ingredients of legality," Fuller observes.[12] Laws require obedience and so must convey what must be done or what must be avoided.[13] There is no provision in the Constitution requiring that laws be clear. It was drafted by skilled lawyers who assumed that clarity was necessary to accomplish what they wanted in drafting a fundamental law of the land. The aspiration of clarity requires that legislation be drafted openly and in good faith by legislators who know what they want to achieve and how to say it in words. It is linguistically possible, however, for a legislature to draft legislation with the ostensible purpose of achieving *X* but in fact is intended to achieve *Y*. After the Civil War vagrancy laws were drafted ostensibly to achieve public safety but were in fact used to justify the reintroduction of the freedmen to chattel slavery. Laws encouraging the use of speed traps and red-light cameras actually may be intended to raise revenue rather than ostensibly promote road safety. Laws enacted in bad-faith are egregious violations of inner morality, so also to a lesser degree are vague and ambiguous laws that create confusion and disrespect for the administration of justice.

As noted, law and its administration require the use of ordinary language even if some technical legal terminology (including Latin) is also introduced. Great verbiage of a judicial opinion is sometimes required to explain that a statute has a simple meaning. And then those opinions are often interpreted through a whole line of other opinions enunciating some theory or other, including higher-order theories of interpretation. When words of ordinary language are imported into law no single context is imported with them. Suppose a law is written that states: 'Collect every single red object in your house or be fined $1000'. The obvious question is: 'What counts as red for purposes of this specific law?' Consider a sign that

---

[12] Ibid., 63.

[13] See *Kolender v. Lawson*, 461 U.S. 352 (1983).

reads: 'Animals are prohibited on the premises except dogs and cats'. Is a dingo or ocelot allowed or not? Many statutory schemes include a definition of terms for this reason. Or consider the words of the Constitution (Art. 1, Sec. 2, cls. 2), which provides: "No person shall be a representative who shall not have attained to the age of twenty five years, and been seven years a citizen of the United States, and who shall not, when elected, be an inhabitant of that state in which he shall be chosen." As noted previously, when a person 'attains' an age depends on how fast he can travel relative to the motion of the earth. The problem of whether somebody is an 'inhabitant' of a state is a complicated blend of legal and factual issues. The word 'person' also embeds complex layers of common contextual understanding with some philosophical assumptions. Perhaps a robot cannot be a person, but what about an android controlled by a human brain? What about a single cell or an embryo? What about a potential being *in futuro*? A certain embryo might be reasonably considered a future King under the British rules of monarchical succession. All of these examples illustrate the need to understand that words in ordinary language are tied to interpretive contexts into which are embedded specific assumptions about what is real, what the words 'really' mean, and what values they implicate.

The law often must rely on the answers to inherently vague and functionally impossible questions, answer to questions such as 'How many people are in the United States right now?' or 'What is torture and is waterboarding an example of it?' Many terms embed subjective criteria and as a result are essentially contested. Anytime the word 'religion' is used, as we shall see in Chapter 5, it presents us with many options to be selected at the pleasure of the user. The word could mean variously beliefs in supernatural beings, a direct experience with sacred objects and places, participation in certain rituals and ceremonies, a commitment to a divinely inspired moral code, personal feelings of awe and mystery experienced in the face of nature, or an entire view of the origin of the universe. Some essentially contested language is obvious: "The right of the people to be secure in their persons, houses, papers, and effects, against unreasonable searches and seizures, shall not be violated . . ." (Fourth Amendment) or "Excessive bail shall not be required, nor excessive fines imposed, nor cruel and unusual punishments inflicted" (Eighth Amendment). Words like 'unreasonable', 'search', 'seizure', 'excessive', and 'cruel' cry out for deep analysis and elucidation. Such words are not inherently clear or self-applying, even when identified in some examples of their 'original' usage.

Which branch of government is best suited to practice the inner morality of law on the question of clarity and vagueness? Some argue that the legislature should do this because it is in the best position to know what it is trying to accomplish.[14] This view, perhaps correctly, assumes that the legislature is in the best position to acquire information, including from lobbyists, experts, the public, and especially from those most directly affected by a law. It could also be argued that courts are in the best position to analyze and digest the implications of a law by looking at the conflicts that arise between real parties affected by it. The Supreme Court has observed that when legislatures make vague criminal laws, they "abdicate their responsibilities for setting the standards of the criminal law."[15] Sloppy legislation not only affects individual constitutional rights, it also creates an imbalance in the separation of powers by requiring an over adjustment by the executive and judicial branches. A law that bans motion pictures for being 'sacrilegious' and does not provide a precise definition of what the word means leaves an appellate court with no capacity to review an application of the law. "On the basis of such a portmanteau word as 'sacrilegious'," the Supreme Court noted, "the judiciary has no standards with which to judge the validity of administrative action which necessarily involves ... subjective determinations."[16]

Consistency: Individual rules should be part of a coherent schema of rules. Simply put, this means that laws should be intelligently enacted with an overview of their content and fit within a system of laws. A system of laws should not require and forbid an action at the same time. For example, a law that authorizes a food inspector to decide when to inspect the *existing* condition of the kitchen of a restaurant and a law requiring that the inspector get the

---

[14] Jeremy Waldron, *Vagueness in Law and Language: Some Philosophical Issues*, 82 Cal. L. Rev. 509 (1994); and *The Core of the Case against Judicial Review*, 115 Yale L. J. 1346 (2006).

[15] *Smith v. Goguen*, 415 U.S. 566, 575 (1974).

[16] *Burstyn v. Wilson*, 343 U.S. 495, 532 (1952).

owner's permission before entering the premises are inconsistent. In any dispute a court would be faced with the difficulty of determining which law has priority without any advice from legislators who failed to see the potential inconsistency in the way the law is drafted and the purpose to be achieved by it. Consistency failures, Fuller argues, result from a legislative failure to think through and prioritize the purposes and consequences of an overall legislative scheme.

Consistency problems also arise when a later law seems to contradict an earlier one. The problem is often resolved by the application of 'rules of statutory construction' such as 'the later law repeals the earlier one by implication' or 'the later law amends the earlier law but only to the minimal extent possible'. An obvious meta-rule might be: 'a system of statutes should be internally consistent'. However, there is no *logical* reason for this rule. Meta-rules could just as well be formulated that require the application of an earlier law to anyone who was alive at the time it was enacted, in other words tying laws to birthdays. We already distinguish legal responsibility by age in the case of juveniles, so why not in the case of laws generally? We also allow waivers of new rules when to do otherwise would produce a hardship; in that case we say application of the old rule is 'grandfathered in'. Another actual meta-rule is: 'legislators are presumed to act rationally and purposely'. Applying this rule, courts must ferret around in inconsistent legislation to find evidence of consistency in the form of 'legislative intent'.

Some consistency meta-rules are clearly morally slanted, such as: 'ambiguities in a contract should be interpreted against the interest of the drafter of the contract'; and ambiguous criminal statutes should be interpreted to favor criminal defendants. These two rules may attempt to rebalance the advantage one party has over another: the contract drafter who provides the meaning of words, and the state with its power to punish defendants. In general, courts use meta-rules to preserve as best as possible the value of consistency until the legislature makes the necessary adjustments, while at the same time giving defendants and litigants an opportunity to resolve their live disputes. From this perspective we can see how the idea of the separation of powers within a single government was devised as a device for maintaining or reestablishing institutionally the value of consistency. The idea embodies the ancient meta-rule that for those in power 'nobody can be a judge in their own case'.

Lenity: Rules should not demand the impossible. This norm, closely tied to the previous one, counsels that only what can be done, ought to be done. Laws enacted with a high failure rate should be assumed to be enacted with perverse intentions. They must be drafted to correct bad behavior but not oppressively so. Fuller observes that if we were all Angels no difficulties in the formulation and application of rules would arise. We would all behave naturally and willingly. "The need for rules," he notes, "arises wholly out of man's selfish, quarrelsome, and disputatious nature."[17] Legislators have a narrow path to walk between ineffectual laws and draconian laws designed to produce demoralization and submission. Consider the doctrine of *respondeat superior,* ("let the master answer"), which creates vicarious liability of employers for the harms caused by their employees when acting within the scope of their employment. Although the employer is not driving the delivery van when it causes an accident, the theory goes, the employer has control over selecting the employee in the first place and should exercise care in hiring and training employees. However, a rule that employers are liable for the actions of *past* employees at any time during the life of those employees would violate the rule of lenity. The use of a 'reasonable person' standard in defining negligence, in terms of what a reasonable person would do under the circumstances, tries to strike a balance between responsibility and impossibility. If every person was measured by their own standard crimes of passion would be impossible to persecute. Police officers could never be charged with excessive force if incontrovertible claims of subjective fear were sufficient to justify any force used. The use of a 'reasonable person' standard creates individual responsibility when measured against what a reasonable person would do under the circumstances. But, of course, if the standard is set so high that no one but a very few would reasonably be able to meet it then lenity is violated; most would be punished for even the most inoffensive violations. Legislators are continually attempting to strike the right balance, often hard to calculate, between intended risk and responsibility for harm. Fuller gives this example: "A poet writes a sad poem. A rejected lover reads it and is so

---

[17] *The Morality of Law*, 55.

depressed that he commits suicide. Who 'caused' the loss of his life? Was it the poet, or the lady who jilted the deceased, or perhaps the teacher who aroused his interest in poetry?"[18] Automatic or 'strict' liability is imposed where the risk of harm is extremely high (storing dynamite in a hot basement) and where the public opportunity to detect and mitigate the harm is low. As a result, a person who innocently handles highly dangerous materials is strictly liable no matter how innocent the intentions were. Cases like this meet the lenity condition, the result is harsh but not unreasonably so as would be a law that absurdly outlaws breathing, or one that mandates urination into toilets only once a day to save water. However, we should note that there are conditions under which supposed draconian laws may be reasonable. The savagery of wartime inflicted upon the local population may require shooting intruders on sight. Fuller observes: "no hard and fast line can be drawn between extreme difficulty and impossibility."[19] Nonetheless, the inner morality of law requires a constant vigilance to determine whether that line has been crossed.

Stability: Rules should be changed deliberately and slowly over time. The harm of retroactive laws, besides the likely injustice of retroactive blame, is that they undermine reliance on a system of laws. Continually changing laws also undermines our reliance on them. The value of gradualism is articulated by saying that a law is 'settled' and that the doctrine of *stare decisis* ("to stand by things decided.") ought to apply. But how much time should lapse before a law is ready to be overturned? The presumption favoring stability has more to do with the limited fact-finding and deliberative capacities of legislatures than with any *a priori* norm that for all laws time is needed to sift through and evaluate their consequences as measured against what the legislature had intended. However, this presumption works only if legislators sincerely seek to articulate their own deep commitments and are willing to engage in debate with those who have opposing commitments. So, whenever legislators become uncritical emissaries of statutes drafted by lobbyists and outside interest groups, they enact laws that should have no claim on the virtue of stability.

---

[18] Ibid., 76.

[19] Ibid., 79.

Conformity: Implementation of rules must be rule governed. Closely tied to the previous maxim is one that requires an obligation of those who carry out the law that they do so in a manner that the law requires. Clearly, it makes no sense to articulate a set of laws constructed by following the previous seven norms, and then have those laws enforced in an arbitrary or corrupt way. Official action must be truly official and rule governed. Personal favor, bribery, prejudice, stupidity, or indifference when practiced by officials reduces laws to something of little value. As noted above, it is not enough simply to have procedural rules, since some procedural rules could themselves merely mask arbitrary and corrupt practices. It is necessary to implement and enforce a law in good faith, as the final step between the lawmaker and the public. It falls to the judiciary, Fuller observes, to be the watchdog of the correct conformity of laws on the books with law in human interaction because it is to that branch that people who suffer from discrepancies will come to complain. Again, others contend it is the legislature that should handle discrepancy problems. Unfortunately, there is no general answer to the question of which is the least corrupt branch because there is no system of creating governmental authority that is not potentially amenable to corruption. Democracy has been said to be the least bad system. Every form of government is subject to the 'bad Emperor problem' – the view that no matter how many good emperors there are, autocratic values will eventually produce some bad ones as well. The same may be said for democracy itself when corrupt motives capture the apparatus of regenerative political power – the voting system.

The Outer Morality of Law

The outer morality of law comprises the moral values that can be detected directly in laws on the books, written constitutions, rules of civil or criminal procedure, international codes, rules of professional conduct, and the like. A community which accepts as one of its moral principles 'Do not take somebody else's property' first requires some clear definitions of what constitutes private property.[20] The person who took someone else's

---

[20] *The Morality of Law*, 205.

property may dispute the physical location of a boundary line, or the entitlement of someone else to wild animals roaming the countryside, or whether a person that claims something lost has a right to its return. Laws provide practical rules of decision in these gray areas. Thus, any system of laws is a great scavenging ground for uncovering moral values and our commitment to them. Often those values are part of a moral system governed by an overarching prescription such as: 'No law may infringe upon the dignitary rights of any individual!' As far as expressing moral values outwardly, law presents them as values that must be enforced using the coercive power of the state. In that sense law looks very much like traditional religion with its emphasis on commandments and law-giving authorities. Its purpose is to impose moral norms on persons within its jurisdiction whether or not they embrace them for overtly moral reasons. The following are three briefly considered examples of laws having as their primary purpose the advancement of specific moral aims.

Trademark Law. Trademarks saturate economic life. They serve as indicators of commercial value, and help consumers rely on the products they desire by looking at the names and symbols on the packages they select. Protecting against deceptive business practices and counterfeiting is the primary mission of trademark law, the one we directly confront when we foolishly purchase a knockoff Rolex watch. Yet another, less noticed aspect of trademark law, is to keep the normal stream of commerce free of salacious and immoral references. A portion of the Lanham Act (15 U.S.C. §1052) states:

> No trademark by which the goods of the applicant may be distinguished from the goods of others shall be refused registration on the principal register on account of its nature unless it (a) Consists of or comprises immoral, deceptive, or scandalous matter; or matter which may disparage or falsely suggest a connection with persons, living or dead, institutions, beliefs, or national symbols, or bring them into contempt, or disrepute; . .

So in 1892 Congress decided to prohibit trademarks that were "offensive to public sentiments or morals."[21] That standard has been continued through the various iterations of trademark legislation. It is noteworthy

[21] H. R. Rep. No. 52-1860, at 3 (1892).

that although Congress established the requirement that trademarks not be immoral, deceptive, or scandalous it did so without providing a definition of what those terms meant. It was largely left to the federal courts to review the administrative denial of trademark protections by employing a standard that looked to the ordinary and common interpretation of words or images and then ascertain whether those shocked our ordinary sense of decency and gave offense to moral feelings.[22]

With that standard in mind, the following trademarks have been rejected: "Protect the Cooch!" (clothing), "Booby Trap" (bras), "1-800-Jack-Off" (adult phone conversations), "Cock Sucker" (rooster-shaped chocolate lollipops); "The Bearded Clam" (restaurant).[23] The trademark "Technodyke" (lesbian-oriented website) was acceptable, while "Dykesinthecity" and "Superdyke" (clothing lines) were not. What is morally acceptable in a given social time and place is easier to ascertain in some cases than in others.[24] Dictionary terms cannot always serve as evidence of what the public mind accepts or rejects. Much subjective judgment goes into determining whether terms or images are vulgar, merely titillating, scandalous or immoral *per se*. In these moral distinctions some inchoate notion that there is such a thing as a collective moral judgment is at work and that the apparatus of government through law is required to serve as a moral filter to protect the general public. It is noteworthy that the wording in §1052(a) above referring to disparaging trademarks that hold up individuals, institutions, or beliefs for contempt or disrepute is now unconstitutional.[25] The only way to make sense of the distinction between trademarks that are barred because they are immoral

---

[22] *In re Riverbank Canning Co.*, 95 F.2d 327 (C.C.P.A. 1938). A trademark for wine labeled "Madonna" and bearing a sign of the Biblical figure, was rejected.

[23] Jasmine Abdel-khalik, *Disparaging Trademarks: Who Matters*, 20 Mich. J. Race & Law. 287, notes 48-49, (2015).

[24] See Megan M. Carpenter & Kathryn T. Murphy, *Calling Bulls**t on the Lanham Act: The 2(a) Bar for Immoral, Scandalous, and Disparaging Marks*, 49 U. Louisville L. Rev. 465 (2011).

[25] *Matal v. Tam*, 137 S.Ct. 1744 (2017), holding that the musical band ("The Slants") is constitutionally protected nongovernmental "viewpoint" speech and should not have been denied registration.

or scandalous and those that are allowed even if disparaging is that in the latter case values of pluralism are seriously embraced while in the former they are not.[26]

Federal Obscenity Laws. Federal obscenity laws encompass the production and distribution of obscene or indecent materials, a prohibition against broadcasting obscene or indecent language, and the distribution of obscene or indecent materials through the mails or on cable television. (18 U.S.C. §§1460-1470). Prohibited materials include "every obscene, lewd, lascivious, indecent, filthy or vile article, matter, thing, device, or substance; and every article or thing designed, adapted, or intended for . . . any indecent or immoral use;" (18 U.S.C. §1461). Interpretation of these freighted words has been left to the courts, which defined obscenity as

> (a) whether the average person, applying contemporary community standards would find that the work, taken as a whole, appeals to the prurient interest . . .
> (b) whether the work depicts or describes, in a patently offensive way, sexual conduct specifically defined by the applicable state law, and
> (c) whether the work, taken as a whole, lacks serious literary, artistic, political, or scientific value.[27]

For broadcast communications, the FCC defines 'indecency' as "language or material that, in context, depicts or describes, in terms patently offensive as measured by contemporary community broadcast standards for the broadcast medium, sexual or excretory organs or activities." Indecent

---

[26] A clothing line associated with the values of extreme misogyny, nihilism, or violence with a brand name of FUCT (to be read as the letters F-U-C-T) became the occasion of successfully challenging the constitutionality of the "immoral or scandalous" standard, as being too vague and merely a suppression of unpopular ideas. Terms such as obscene, vulgar, or profane, were said to be better suited to the purpose of the statute. See *Iancu v. Brunetti*, 139 S. Ct. 2294 (2019). Substituting such terms, however, would not change the outer-morality policing status of the statute.

[27] *Miller v. California*, 413 U.S. 15, 16 (1973).

transmissions, however, are protected by the First Amendment between 10 p.m. and 6 a.m.[28]

One outer-morality rule of obscenity jurisprudence seems to be: 'Since federal lawmakers should not directly and explicitly legislate morality, laws affecting immoral conduct should only be local and be based on community standards'. This rule, it has been argued, motivated the original creation of our federalist system of government.[29] In what sense, however, could a standard be both about morality and only relevant to local conditions? One possible answer is to argue that cultural norms are also the best moral norms because culture is just a shorthand we give to the best practices of living a good life. Consider previous laws favoring marriage and disfavoring divorce. The conduct that leads to divorce – bad communication among spouses, infidelity, drunkenness, abuse, poor money management skills – result from character traits that produce an array of other bad consequences outside the marriage as well. Thus, the argument would go, making divorce difficult on balance places constraints on such bad behavior and opens up a space for better self-examination and interpersonal relations; whereas, easy divorce merely buries bad habits and perpetuates bad social behavior. Similarly, the older tort of 'alienation of affection', which allowed an aggrieved spouse to sue a person for breaking up the marriage, was thought to have a beneficial consequence of raising the cost of infidelity and seduction. The fact that the tort has been abolished and that no-fault divorces have come to dominate suggests to some that morality has been replaced by immorality, whereas to others it may only mean that a different view of the function of law as a guardian of moral values has been adopted in the case of divorce. Here, a judgment has been made that when the law regulates marital infidelity it also produces a violation of privacy, which itself has a set of adverse consequences for the community.

This focus on consequences has allowed the Supreme Court to uphold local laws prohibiting nude dancing, not by denying that such dancing could

---

[28] *FCC Enforcement Order*, 8 F.C.C.R at 705 n.10 (1993).

[29] Guido Calabresi and Eric S. Fish, *Federalism and Moral Disagreement*, 101 Minn. L. Rev. 1 (2016).

ever be an example of free speech, but rather because such dancing establishments produce undesirable social effects in the local area.[30] However, characterizing the morality of an act in terms of its direct social consequences can produce inner-morality violations, specifically inconsistent, arbitrary, and unreasonably punitive laws. This approach is opposed by those who say the business of nude dancing, no matter how advantageous economically or welcomed by a portion of the community, is per se immoral and that the community's laws, reflecting the inherent power of local government to regulate health, safety and public morals, should override any advantages.[31]

Civil Rights Legislation. The underlying premise in such legislation is that racism is immoral, and that civil rights laws must oppose it. However, during the passage of the 1964 Civil Rights Act and also accompanying many debates surrounding desegregation of public schools and accommodations, the argument was made that laws cannot influence an individual's personal beliefs and when they tread on them, they become counterproductive and undermine the rule of law.[32] The immorality of *de facto* racism cannot be legislated away, the argument goes. Only changes from within individuals and their local culture can affect permanent change in institutionalized racism. So, trying to ban racial segregation is analogous to the failure to ban alcohol consumption during prohibition. The counter argument is that well-crafted anti-segregation laws for schools, businesses, or public accommodations have an ameliorative effect over time and were that not the case there would be little point in drafting laws to address other persistent harms like theft, assault, or even impulsive murder.

---

[30] *City of Erie v. Pap's A. M.*, 529 U.S. 277 (2000).

[31] For an argument that morals and consequences can be harmonized see Santiago Legarre and Gregory J. Mitchell, *Secondary Effects and Public Morality*, 40 Harv. J. L. & Pub. Pol'y. 321 (2017).

[32] See Linda C. McClain, *Reshaping Public and Private Space: Public Accommodations, Neighborhoods, and Housing: The Civil Rights Act of 1964 and 'Legislating Morality': On Conscience, Prejudice, and Whether 'State Ways' Can Change 'Folkways'*. 95 B. U. L. Rev. 891 (2015).

The Interaction of Law and Morality

Using Inner Morality Norms. The inner morality of law may be looked at as operating as an organic whole. Each norm when practiced contributes to the vitality of the others; and when one is weakened the likelihood of others also failing increases. Fuller notes: "infringements of legal morality tend to become cumulative. A neglect of clarity, consistency, or publicity may beget the necessity for retroactive laws."[33] Each of the eight practices requires aggressive efforts to conform individual behavior to the aspirations of inner morality. Each is a facet of a general obligation of open and honest communication, careful implementation, and good faith enforcement among those drafting and enforcing laws. Inner morality seems to be predicated upon the assumption that there is less opportunity for bad laws when procedures are transparent. In turn, this assumption rests upon a view of society as a collection of pluralistic interests not all of which are in harmony. A society of individuals with identical interests and beliefs governed by similarly like-minded individuals may find inner morality practices tedious and superfluous.

Yet, even in such a perfectly harmonious society laws will be difficult to formulate and implement, Fuller argues, because though it may be clear as to *what* should be done, precisely *how* to do it for every situation is not easy to formulate or communicate in advance. If we then add even the slightest conflict of interest the situation becomes less manageable to be subject effectively to rules; and if conflicts of interest become pervasive, as in conflicts over wealth, resources, and well-being in all modern societies, the situation can become dire, calling for severe adherence to inner morality practices. These practices may be found and encouraged in many aspects of everyday life. Since morality and legality have in common the regulation of conduct by tacit or explicit rules, the inner morality of establishing rules for organizational order could also find application in the communications and procedures that go on within families, marriages, social organizations, homeowners' associations, colleges and universities, local and national businesses, and, of course, all the various levels of government. As the arena of communication

---

[33] *The Morality of Law*, 92.

increases so does the need to write down goals and procedural rules needed to achieve and sustain them, and in addition rules to correct misapplied or bad rules. This social rule- making activity Fuller identifies as "the enterprise of subjecting human conduct to the governance of rules."[34] As human conduct becomes more complex and interactive an enterprise of rules gradually becomes an enterprise of law.

Morality interacts with law, in Fuller' view, though the norms of inner morality. "The inner morality of law," he writes, "demands that there be rules, that they be made known, and that they be observed in practice by those charged with their administration."[35] The Nazis, he noted, required Jewish businesses to paint their store window frames a distinct color that visitors would not notice but local boycotters would. This practice was not openly enacted and published into law. Doing so would have created a national and international controversy which would have required a government explanation. "It is the virtue of a legal order conscientiously constructed and administered that it exposes to public scrutiny the rules by which it acts," Fuller notes.[36] At one time Boston police departments, he notes further, required that an inmate sign a release from all civil liability while in custody as a condition to be let out. If enacted into law and publicized government officials, who would never sign such a release for themselves or their family members, would have to explain why the laws should be applied in other cases. Also, when race laws define a 'negro' with a skin color that can be lighter than some 'whites', this is evidence that these terms are left deliberately vague to accomplish other objectives. These examples violate the inner morality norms of generality, promulgation, consistency, and clarity. They illustrate the maxim that it is better to harm someone with an elbow than with a fist because the latter is harder to explain away as an accident. So, inner morality norms put pressure on lawmakers to reveal their true intentions, and in the process, help create and enforce legal duties that better conform to moral norms.[37]

---

[34] Ibid., 130-33, 145-51.

[35] Ibid., 157.

[36] Ibid., 158, 159.

[37] Ibid., 159, 170-71.

Writing Constitutions. Another way in which morality and law interact is through the process of creating a written Constitution. Like rules, Constitutions are not self-executing. They require interpretation before they may be used as a source of authority. A Constitution, Fuller noted, "cannot lift itself unaided into legality; it cannot be law simply because it says it is."[38] It must provide bylaws for a nation, indicating its officers, terms of service, and qualifications, as well rules for adopting and amending it. But it must also contain provisions designed to convince the public that the document is worthy of being a fundamental law because it is "necessary, right, and good."[39] The only way to achieve this consent is to guarantee that those governed by it will follow the norms of inner morality.

Embedded in the American Constitution are some specific constraints that encourage inner morality practices. Already discussed are legislative prohibitions against Bills of Attainder, *ex post facto* laws, and state laws impairing the obligation of contracts. Such laws, were they to be passed, would violate the norms of generality, prospectivity, consistency, lenity, stability, and conformity. However, since the Constitution lumps all contracts together from the most trivial to the most consequential it has fallen to the branches of government to evaluate consequences and balance harms and benefits in interpreting that clause.[40] Other norm-enhancing powers include: prohibiting states from enacting a variety of laws relating to foreign relations and international trade, or waging aggressive war on its own, without first getting the approval of Congress, (Art. I, Sec.10, cls. 2 and 3); removing the President from office for "inability to discharge the powers and duties of said office" (Art II. Sec.1, cl. 6); requiring the exercise of various presidential powers "by and with the advice and consent of the Senate" (Art II. Sec.2, cl. 2) as well as the executive obligation to "take care that the laws be faithfully executed," so that the laws passed by Congress do not sit around on the desks of the Executive Branch (Art II, Sec. 3). Also: judges should only serve "during good behavior," (Art. III, Sec. 1); Congress shall make "all needful rules" for orderly territorial expansion and administration until State

---

[38] Lon L. Fuller, *Positivism and Fidelity to Law: A Reply to Professor Hart*, 71 Harv. L. Rev. 642 (1958).

[39] Ibid.

[40] See *Energy Reserves Group v. Kansas Power & Light*, 459 U.S. 400 (1983).

constitutions are drafted and ratified, and prohibit states from creating states within their boundaries. (Art IV. Sec.3, cls. 1 and 2). Also, Congress must require each state to recognize the laws and judicial rulings of other states, but will also guarantee that each state will have a representative form of government. (Art. IV, Sec. 1 and 4). The overriding objective behind many of these specific rules is that when working together they will achieve efficient results and establish an environment where laws are made, interpreted, and enforced by competent government officials who are themselves subject to criticism and removal from office.

However, in spite of these broadly expressed norms the Constitution still may fall short of realizing them when officials find ways of evading its inner morality norms. The Senate could simply withhold advice and consent, particularly for Supreme Court appointments, thus violating conformity and stability; Congress could ignore extreme Presidential inability or exaggerate it, in either case for partisan gain, thus violating clarity, consistency, stability, and conformity. Requiring good judicial behavior, making needful rules, and taking care that the laws be faithfully executed are all norms vulnerable to willful misinterpretation and bad faith reasoning. This kind of possibility has raised a concern that Fuller confuses morality with technique, making the inner morality of law nothing more than a collection of rules for how to achieve goals efficiently regardless whether they are moral or not.[41] Gangs and serial killers, to be successful, also must be careful to fit their practices to achieve their immoral objectives. Technique is open to a variety of methods and skills, whereas morality sets a dividing line beyond which no technique by itself can be justified if used for an immoral purpose. Some acts of murder are more 'humane' than others, but that is irrelevant to whether a person has committed murder under the law. A response to this argument would be that the practice of inner morality norms should not, and in fact cannot, be placed exclusively at the service of private benefit. Gang members and serial killers in carrying out their business would not embrace the norms of generality and

[41] H. L. A. Hart, *The Morality of the Law,* 78 Harv. L. Rev. 1281 (1965); see also Ronald Dworkin, *Philosophy, Morality, and Law. Observations Prompted by Professor Fuller's Novel Claim,* 113 U. Pa. L. Rev. 668 (1965).

consistency. They would not apply their coercive or deceptive procedural techniques to themselves or their allies.

Morality Requires Law. Another perspective on the interaction between morality and law was developed by British jurist Tony Honoré (1921-2019), who has argued that morality requires law in order to most meaningfully manifest its value in human life.[42] Without law, morality is diminished in scope and effectiveness, he argues. Interrogating one's own morality on an isolated desert island may not be an unworthy pursuit although the opportunities to test one's true commitments are likely to be limited. Discussing morality in groups quickly becomes more complex, nuanced, and conditional and it is in that complexity of social life that the assistance of law is required. The central core of morality, he argues, is how to coexist and cooperate with others for mutual benefit. However, morality does not always give clear answers to complex problems in everyday situations. It requires the formal apparatus created within a legal system, which is the location where gray areas are rendered sufficiently distinct and resolved according to the social and political consensus supporting the system. The legal system does not take over and substitute for morality but is subject to continued reassessment by norms of morality. Each mutually improve the other. Honoré uses the example of taxation. Most citizens accept a moral obligation to contribute to the community from which they receive some degree of security and at least some opportunity to pursue happiness. But how does each citizen determine what that contribution is and how it should be made? Voluntary contributions may seem the method most compatible with freedom. However, all the considerations each individual makes in determining the goal and amount of the contribution – public safety, child welfare, arts support, etc. – invariably leaves out a great many other considerations that also affect the value choices of individuals and the needs of a viable community. Only law can reconcile the conflict between charity and the essential needs of a community that aspires to be viable over many generations. The same reasoning applies to traffic laws. They help us respect the intentions of other drivers when we would rather go our own way unimpeded. Again, the problem is a need for coordination of the activities of many individuals against a moral obligation to avoid harming others. Also,

---

[42] Tony Honoré, *The Dependence of Morality on Law*. 13 Oxford J. Legal Stud. 2 (1993).

the general moral obligation to support one's family and loved ones is assisted by laws that establish the guarantees achieved by the enforceability of wills and trusts, spousal maintenance, and child support.

Perhaps the greatest value of law to morality is how law handles moral disputes. Some disputes are of great public consequence but difficult to resolve. Moral disputes involving alcohol and drug use, abortion, prostitution, capital punishment, and euthanasia, for example, typically end in stalemate. Reducing such intractable disputes to law allows for a testing period and an opportunity and forum to revise solutions. Honoré uses the example of slavery. Slavery is immoral because the person enslaved is seriously disadvantaged in terms of freedom, happiness, lost opportunities for achieving the satisfactions of autonomy, and is treated in an inhumane way. But what would be the moral status of a law that allows individuals to willingly relinquish their right of self-determination in exchange for freedom from starvation? Morally under no circumstances should such a choice be left to individuals, and so to bolster that value the law prohibits the choice from being made. That is a decision the community has made and enforced through law for every individual. Morality *by itself* asserts that no human could use another human exclusively as a means to an end. By that reasoning voluntary slavery would be moral as long as the slave had the capacity to use the slaveholder also as a means to happiness. Putting the issue into a form of specific law resolves these rather abstract moral disputes into an outright ban as the verdict of the community.

Hard Cases. Yet, another perspective of the interaction of law and morality is provided by American legal scholar Ronald Dworkin (1931-2013). Significantly, he was a law clerk for federal appellate judge Learned Hand at one point early in his career. Law clerks typically do research to help their judge decide the case before them by finding the best law to fit the facts and achieve justice. In appellate courts there is a high probably that the task of fitting the law to facts requires complex interpretation of the meaning and purposes of existing law, as well as an eye to how a new decision will affect the calculations and future behavior of the public. If the fit was obvious the cases very likely would have been decided in a lower court. Morality comes into contact with law, Dworkin decided, at the juncture where judges have to decide hard cases, cases typically involving a conflict over the rights and material advantages of the parties. It is a fortunate judge who can go about daily life applying the law to the facts, he argued, without much need for reflection.[43] A judge must also take into consideration the influence of prevailing morality, asking: Are the moral norms relevant and sufficient to be recognized by law? In so asking, a judge is undoubtedly aware that predecessors have asked the same question, particularly in the same area of law. So, within a legal tradition there is an ongoing dialogue about morals which requires that they be ratified or modified. Even 'conservative' judges who give great weigh to precedent are also giving great weigh to past morality.

Dworkin uses the word 'integrity' to capture the notion that a principled jurist must have the courage to do some legislating in hard cases but not so much as to upend law as a systematic enterprise of the legislating branch of government as well. A principled jurist will strive to produce consistent outcomes by giving reasons for a ruling that ratifies, amends, or rejects prior reasons for previous rulings. This is not the same thing as *stare decisis*, which simply identifies a prior decision as *the* reason for the current one. Dworkin uses as an example the famous case of *Riggs v. Palmer*.[44] In that case, Palmer, a grandson and heir to his grandfather's estate, murdered his recently married grandfather before he had an opportunity to change his will. Although the will was in effect at the time of death, the court ruled that Palmer should not be the beneficiary of a murder. Instead, it looked behind the plain meaning of the document to the implied intent of the state legislature that its will statutes not be used to reward murder. This interpretation included a moral element but also a legal element. It included the moral norm that murderers should not benefit from their crimes, a norm that also prohibits convicted sexual predators from profiting from publishing a tell-all book. But it also included a legal norm that the legislative and judicial process not be corrupted by aiding criminality. So, if the social community deems certain actions to be seriously immoral, the courts of that community's political structure are obligated to make them illegal as well. Henceforth, the Riggs result would become an 'equitable principle' and an expression of public

---

[43] Ronald Dworkin, *Law's Empire* (Cambridge, MA: Harvard University Press, 1986).
[44] Ibid., 15-20. 115 N.Y. 506 (1889).

policy against which other forms of criminal conduct could be measured. As a result of the ruling, Palmer lost his inheritance in spite of what his grandfather's will said, and all those similarly situated in the future would also because of the immorality of his actions. Dworkin concludes, "legal argument is a characteristically and pervasively moral argument."[45]

Incompatibility Problems. In the views of the interaction of law and morality proposed by Fuller, Honoré, and Dworkin, moral norms are not a set of absolutes superimposed on law in a clean, deductive fashion. Problems of fitting law and morality together inevitably arise, primarily because morality focuses on the clarity and consistency of norms, while law must also focus on promulgation, enforcement, and the legitimacy of temporal authorities. Moral issues emerge out of the questions raised in legislative debates, questions such as: Is the moral infraction weighty enough to justify using the coercive force of the law? Are the laws clear enough to give adequate notice of what constitutes their violation? Can they be uniformly enforced? Do they risk inflicting excessive punishment? In other words, does the process follow the norms of inner morality? Thus, to the extent that the process becomes well-accepted by those who must be subject to its laws, it becomes possible to say that those laws will likely embody moral norms generally accepted by the community. That is not to say that the quandaries found in morality disappear in law; in fact, the consequences of a breaking law with a clear moral mandate may be greater. There are laws that punish broken promises (perjury, fraud, forgery) that carry additional consequences. For example, such crimes will appear in a public record and can tarnish a person's reputation and career if publicly reported. This is a greater consequence than merely breaking a promise in private.

Laws have the additional burden of meeting lenity norms. They must meet burdens of proof: preponderance of evidence in the case of civil matters, and proof beyond a reasonable doubt in criminal matters. Also, law protects the interests of defendants and the accused by imposing deadlines (statutes of limitations) to bring a complaint or charge. At one time a person could not

---

[45] Ronald Dworkin, *Hart's Postscript and the Character of Political Philosophy,* 24 Oxford J. Legal Stud. 4 (2004).

be charged with murder if the victim does not die until after a year and a day. This rule has been abolished or modified, because modern medicine has developed the capability of keeping a person alive for many months, including a comatose stabbing victim who died after fifteen months.[46] From a moral perspective, a person is guilty of murder no matter how long it takes the victim to die. But since the law does not just concern itself with clean moral absolutes, it must deal with proving its case with convincing evidence in full public view with a reasonable period of time. As a result, it must create all sorts of conventions and fictions that determine when someone will become subject to it and to what degree.[47] If you openly trespass on and inhabit someone's property for a certain number of years, say, ten years, the portion inhabited now could be claimed as yours in a court of law. This view is contrary to the view that something belongs to you until you openly and willingly give it up. The traditional idea that bad acts are always knowable (theoretically by God) and always merit blame (according to God's laws) is violated every day in courts where the evidence is insufficient to convict or establish liability because the facts are not convincing enough or just too complicated to sort out by judge or jury.

Morality and the Rule of Law

Theoretical discussions of the relationship between morality and law often intersect with theories of the 'rule of law', usually capitalized as the 'Rule of Law'. The view taken by Fuller and others associated with his jurisprudence may be characterized as 'bottom-up' theories. Rule of Law from this perspective is an emergent property that results from the close coordination and practices of a variety of actors and institutions striving to achieve certain prized social objectives. Fuller has summarized these practices as inner morality norms operating in a system of law designed to perpetuate their effectiveness. If the system works properly the objectives of equal justice and

---

[46] See *Rogers v. Tennessee*, 532 U.S. 451 (2001), where the Tennessee Supreme Court abolished the year-and-a-day rule and concluded its ruling could be applied retroactively. The U.S. Supreme Court affirmed this ruling because the rule had not been relied upon in Tennessee and was 'archaic'. But see the Dissent by Associate Justice Scalia.

[47] See Lon L. Fuller, *Legal Fictions* (Stanford, CA.: Stanford University Press, 1967).

procedural fairness have a high probability of being achieved relative to any other system of law. But since these practices require mutual support and are not self-certifying, it remains a theoretical possibility that an immoral system may be able to mimic the inner morality norms and produce immoral results. Recognizing this problem Fuller wrote: "I shall have to rest on the assertion of a belief that may seem naïve, namely, that coherence and goodness have more affinity than coherence and evil."[48] Clearly, there are a lot of conditions packed into his idea of coherence, any one of which when defeated could make Fuller's claim impossible to realize. Equal justice and procedural fairness make high demands on the way knowledge is exchanged and evaluated. In the lawmaking, interpreting, and enforcing process information must be openly acquired, shared and evaluated. This cannot be accomplished with an incoherent system of justice. Incoherence, Fuller suggests, is the devil's playbook. This idea takes us to the beginning of this chapter, where all of the participants in perpetuating a legal system must know the practices the system requires, strive to accomplish them, and apply the results to themselves as well.[49] Still, the only assurance that the system will continue to operate as a Rule of Law system is that breakdowns will be identified in time and that the system is elastic enough to provide mechanisms for correcting them.

The search for a deeper foundation of the Rule of Law has led some theorists to outline a 'top down' approach. Here the aspiration is to find aspects of reality and the nature of things that when identified can serve as a source of transmission of legitimacy directly into a legal system. Traditionally, the authority of the monarch derived directly from God, and the promise the monarch made to God that he will obey the laws of God produces the basis for the Rule of Law. Other legitimation approaches are discussed in the following chapter that take up theories of moral, positive, and natural law. These approaches theoretically authenticate the Rule of Law because they could not be conceived without it. But, from a practical point of view, they suffer from the same disability as the norm-driven

---

[48] Fuller, *Positivism and Fidelity to Law,* 636.

[49] See Brian Z. Tamanaha, *The History and Elements of the Rule of Law,* Sing. J. L. S. 232, 233 (2012). ("The rule of law means that government officials and citizens are bound by and abide by the law.")

approach: they do not provide satisfying explanations for why mistakes or unintended consequences can occur in drafting laws, or in ascertaining what a law means in given hard situations, or how it should be applied and enforced. The edict of the monarch or dictator is a convenient device for establishing full authenticity and legitimacy. The problem is that the fiat system is less adaptable to changing circumstances over time than the more flexible and multi-polar norm-driven system.

Neither Rule of Law theory can provide assurance of moral outcomes. There are no ultimate guarantees since human beings are in charge of *all* aspects of the legal system, and each person must act normatively instead of privately in order for the system to have a chance to function as a Rule of Law enterprise. As legal scholar Brian Z. Tamanaha has summed it up:

> The idea of 'the rule of law, not man' has been forever dogged by the fact that laws are not self-interpreting or self-applying. The operation of law cannot be sequestered from human participation. . . . The inevitability of human participation in the application and interpretation of rules provides the opening for the reintroduction of the very weaknesses sought to be avoided by resorting to law in the first place. The indeterminacy of law and language suggest that this opening can never be shut completely.[50]

Laws outwardly expressing moral values are especially vulnerable to a failure to achieve their moral objectives by using methods that are themselves moral. Enforcing obscenity laws may produce results that are oppressive of human dignity. The same may be said for laws regulating marriage and gender relations. When legislating morality there is the risk of producing tenuous and sometimes incoherent connections between law and morality when applied in practical situations. In the process the ideal of the Rule of Law is often undermined, producing the opposite effect than that intended.

---

[50] Ibid., 244.

CHAPTER 2

MORAL LAW, POSITIVE LAW, NATURAL LAW

Fuller's view of law is that of a system of rules that does not always provide answers to the ways in which they are to be interpreted or enforced. His answer: any system of law requires an aspirational set of moral values to be used to continually monitor law's application and effect. From this perspective the authority and legitimacy of law is always open to question. Some legal theories have been proposed to eliminate this problem by arguing either (1) that law and morality share a common foundation (theories of moral or natural law), or else (2) that laws' moral authority and legitimacy is not open to question if it can be determined *as an empirical social fact* that they were official enactments of the law-making power of the government (positive law theories).

Moral Law

Gottfried Wilhelm Leibniz. Beginning in the seventeenth century some philosophers sought to construct a metaphysical theory of reality that could be at the same time a moral theory and a foundation for law. In doing so, law and morality could be unified by revealing their deep necessary interconnections. The very notion of a material amoral world was thought to be an absurdity. If humans could create mathematics and if mathematics could reveal the hidden logic of nature and events, then reality was eternally rule-governed and fully rational and complex no matter how far down one drilled. Material reality is a garden full of plants, a pond full of fishes, said Gottfried Wilhelm Leibniz.[1] At age twenty-one Leibniz was given a formidable task of reconstructing the legal system of Mainz on a new and deeper foundation, comprising a 'science of law'. This would give

---

[1] *The Monadology* (1715) § 67.

law the stature of theology in not being based on mere conjectures regarding the moral significance of contingent facts. Jurisprudence must be as rigorous as mathematical science and yet as dense with meaning and value as theology, he argued: "Theology is a particular category of jurisprudence, taken universally; that is to say, it deals with right and laws which are respected in the state, or rather in the reign of God over humans."[2] The finished work, which Leibniz used to get a position as a judge on the Mainz court, would be a judge's 'how to rule' handbook, but not in any narrow technical sense. For Leibniz, the obligation of judges was great. They had to study jurisprudence because they were under an obligation to improve their abilities to judge individuals not for their specific acts alone but for the entirety of their behavior over their entire lives, including also their eternal afterlife. This latter obligation arose from his view that humans were eternal rational substances which they shared in kind with God, though not as well-perfected as was God's own infinite capacities.

Leibniz viewed individuals as having varying capacities to understand the right course of action and having varying degrees of habitual power to maintain the right courses and resist the wrong ones. The purpose of jurisprudence, then, as the science of the right course of action, is to understand the right choices of means to ends so that a judge is able to assist less intelligent and virtuous individuals better achieve more fulfilling conditions for themselves. But right conditions do not only apply to individuals; they also apply to the societal life of individuals. Leibniz writes: "Jurisprudence is the science of actions, insofar as they are called just or unjust. Just and unjust is defined as whatever is publicly useful or harmful. Publically, that is, firstly for the world, or for God who is its rector, and secondly for mankind, and finally for the state"[3] It makes sense, then, to say that some communities embody morality more so than others. They are capable of thinking about their purposes in a systematic way; they are rational in how they approach problems and how they solve them, just as

---

[2] Gottfried Wilhelm Leibniz, *The New Method for Learning and Teaching Jurisprudence* (1667). Trans. Carmelo Massimo de Iuliis (Clark, N.J.: Talbot Publishing, 2017), 34.
[3] Ibid., 49-50. For further discussion see Christopher Johns, *The Science of Right in Leibniz's Moral and Political Philosophy* (London: Bloomsbury, 2013).

some individuals are better at using their rational faculties to achieve what is useful, pleasurable, and the persistent state of pleasure called happiness. Here we can see why Leibniz related jurisprudence to theology. He is describing on a worldly level a heaven-like condition where individuals achieve happiness to the fullest level of their capacity just as they would do in heaven should they reach there under God's judgment. The worldly judge, then, does not judge individuals for their crime but for their ability to reform themselves, a part of which is understanding what God's commandments require. The judge must not only know the law but understand its theological originations, and exercise judgment over individuals according to the norms of 'scientific' jurisprudence.[4] Leibniz probably would recoil from the modern view that a person's past bad behavior, except in certain circumstances, should not be evidence for possible current bad behavior. Past behavior is relevant because people have a tendency to act in character, he would say.

But how is such a scientific jurisprudence possible? Leibniz believed that we could not have progressed to understanding a need for a truly consistent and rational science of law without the intellectual resources that first produced mathematics and natural science. With such tangible evidence of our capacity to reason, we now should be able produce a true science of individual and communal happiness. An enlightened jurist can see that in order to create a just society, individuals must recognize that their own moral freedom to choose their course of action entails obligations not to hinder the freedom of others. So, if the laws are properly aligned, breaking them means that the virtuous cycle of freedom and restraint had been broken and that it would be the task of the judge to find the right remedy to repair it. This is done by finding the inherent moral nature of individuals as rational substances and their capacity to create a community under the inspiration of God. In each moment in our lives we are either moving on a course of action that increases the prospect of happiness individually, communally, and eternally, or else takes us farther off course. To follow the rules of God's plan is to take the better course, a course that is always linked in a harmonious way with the strivings of others pursuing

---

[4] *The New Method of Learning and Teaching*, 34-35. ("In brief, almost the whole of theology depends for the greater part on jurisprudence.")

their own happiness. To achieve this harmony, Leibniz argued, it is necessary for a good and just person to take pleasure in the happiness of others but also to feel the pain of others. When you strive to increase a just society you produce an increase in aggregate happiness for a community and as a result an increase in your own happiness.[5] The underlying condition for this justice is found in the creation of the universe as an elegant system where each part is capable of fully understanding aspects of the overall design according to its capacity to know and learn. In the human world a just society is built upon "the charity of the wise."[6] Three maxims governed interaction in that world: *harm no one, give to each his due, and live piously*. For example, if a person harms me or my state, that should not be an excuse to kill that person or his family or destroy entirely another state. Instead, I or my state should be made whole with restitution through arbitration or diplomacy not through vengeful or holy warfare. Living piously means making a commitment to strengthen moral practices in one's own life and in one's community in daily interactions with others and in perfecting one's knowledge so that future decisions will be even better informed. Law breaking, then, was an offense against morality itself and against the divine architecture of creation. We have been created, in Leibniz' view, to experience pleasure from the happiness of others, and so our idea of justice should be based on the goal of practicing and encouraging universal benevolence. This goal could only be achieved, he argued, with the creation of a commonwealth that gave priority of the public good over private self-interest and private wealth.[7]

In Leibniz' world, church and state did not function separately and so neither did church and law. His early studies in jurisprudence were

---

[5] See Alberto Artosi and Giovanni Sartor, "Leibniz as Jurist," in *The Oxford Handbook of Leibniz*, ed. Maria Rosa Antognazza (Oxford University Press, 2018), Ch. 38. See also, Patrick Riley, *The Political Writings of Leibniz* (Cambridge: Cambridge University Press, 1972), 83.

[6] For one account of Leibniz's architectonic perfectionism see *The Principles of Nature and of Grace, based on Reason* (1714). Maria Rosa Antognazza, *Leibniz: An Intellectual Biography* (Cambridge: Cambridge University Press, 2009), 259-262.

[7] See Patrick Riley, *Leibniz' Universal Jurisprudence: Justice as the Charity of the Wise*, (Cambridge, M.A.: Harvard University Press, 1996); and his "Leibniz on Justice as 'The Charity of the Wise'," *Annual Review of Law and Ethics* 8 (2000): 143-58.

sponsored by a Catholic archbishop who was also an elector of Mainz, one of the seven princes of the Holy Roman Empire. At the same time he embarked on a project of theological apologetics, attempting to demonstrate the existence of God, the immortality of the soul, and the authority of the Catholic Church.[8] With so many religious and political jurisdictions within that Empire, it was a daunting task that Leibniz eagerly took on to create a legal system that was both politically and theologically authoritative and scientifically rigorous. But with this jurisprudential theology, a whole host of questions required explanation, one being how our divinely created rational nature could make bad decisions, produce disappointing outcomes, and create conflicts among various political jurisdictions that seemed to arise everywhere. Traditionally, these questions required explanation through *Theodicy*, the task of explaining how evil could exist in a world created by a beneficent, all-powerful God. Leibniz' explanation was that political authority could only come from a wise and devote Prince, determined to realize in practice the three maxims in daily life for his subjects, while operating within a long-standing tradition of religious authorities. Any other form of government would produce consequences not authorized by God's plan for individual and communal life. For example, political authority coupled with theologically grounded judicial authority could not be established through consent of the governed; nor exclusively in what would become dominant individual nation states since moral goodness and moral benevolence were universal human capacities. Ultimately, the authority of the Prince must be established outside the legal system, by a theory of natural law and by the particular providence of God.[9]

Immanuel Kant. German philosopher, Immanuel Kant, also attempted to create a foundational unity of law and morality by means of a rational deduction from first metaphysical principles. Like Leibniz he brought philosophy to the service of jurisprudence. Kant wrote within the same reformist tradition as Leibniz. But whereas Leibniz built a system upon broad content-rich metaphysical components, and deep theological

---

[8] Antognazza, 79-82, 90. Leibniz dedicated the *New Method* to Archbishop, Johann Philippe von Schönborn.

[9] Leibniz, "The Prince," in Riley, 85-103.

commitments, Kant began his journey with a view of philosophy as a spare but powerful mental enterprise, capable of discovering deep unshakable truths. He believed that human reason had an elastic capacity for digging beneath foundations and dissecting assumptions to reveal the true groundwork of a subject, whether it be in natural science, philosophy, ethics, or law.

The breathtaking discovery of laws of physics and chemistry in the eighteenth century inspired Kant to search for similar laws governing all human action. Humans have a capacity to form positive or negative 'images' of the future and then direct their activity toward achieving or avoiding them. We think of ourselves as moving from the present into the future and away from the past. That future is always a mixture of the expected and unfamiliar. Without that capacity it would be cruel to subject human conduct to law. This temporal recognition is what it meant, Kant said, to have and live a *life*.[10] The study of morality and law, then, is a search for the specific rational conditions of human life. Here Kant postulates that individual behavior always reflects instants of general laws of practical action. Life is not a series of accidental events that just happen to someone; it is a project consisting of many intertwined planned activities all linked to an individual's desire and intent to control events. So, Kant set out to identify the common structure of all human action, rejecting the idea that human motivation is a jumble of impulses, feelings, and beliefs or that decisions are made when the strongest one at the last minute overrides all others. Rather, human action is a continual sifting of data derived from memory, feelings, and attitudes about what is happening now, followed by hypothesizing and prioritizing over future possibilities.

The fact that we have a concept of morality, Kant argues, that includes a sense of duty and obligation, a sense of what is right and wrong, and a requirement that morality conform to universal imperatives, means that when we talk about morality we are talking about something that we do not derive merely from our own personal preferences but from a

---

[10] Immanuel Kant, *The Philosophy of Law: An Exposition of the Fundamental Principles of Jurisprudence as the Science of Right*, (1887), trans. W. Hastie. Reprint: Clifton: Augustus M. Kelley, (1974), 9.

recognition of being subject to a command we cannot manipulate at will. His analysis consists of a three-stage ascent, as if ascending a mountain, where it becomes progressively easier to see where you have been and how that stance differs from where you are now. From experience we learn that certain things we thought were good turned out not to be. We also notice that some people display self-control and a rational temperament, and yet do not always use them for moral action. The one indispensable feature of morality that *no* experience can discredit, Kant says, is a *good will*. That does not mean the persons of good will cannot fall on hard times; but it does mean that they will never be deemed *bad* because of those circumstances. External consequences by themselves cannot be the measure of morality, Kant is arguing. A bad person may accidently produce a good result. The beneficial consequences of an action may be the result of insincere publicity seeking. Charity in whatever form, on the other hand, is a virtue because it manifests a good will. Every other option may deserve applause but never esteem or respect.

Kant now identifies moral action as acting from a sense of duty in conformity with a conception of some universal law applicable to everyone. This observation is not an obscure insight of philosophers, he argues; it is a guiding principle all of us use when we calculate the consequences of various strategies, but it is also a directive we rebel against when we decide to do some cheating.[11] We know, for example, that any morality entirely structured around the idea of personal happiness leads to a morass of adverse consequences we cannot rationally reconcile. Some pursuits of happiness work out; others produce disappointing results. We are then plunged into the bottomless of pit of trying to distinguish true happiness from false. Only morality derived from rational duty is truly what it is under every condition and not something that turns out to be counterfeit in practice.

The category that Kant identified as fulfilling the condition of a universal command is *law*. Contrary to what Fuller believed, laws as Kant conceives them, apply universally, unconditionally, and necessarily. They are more

---

[11] Immanuel Kant, *Fundamental Principles of the Metaphysic of Morals*, trans. Thomas K. Abbott (New York: Bobbs-Merrill, 1949), 21-22.

stringent than norms that may or may not fit the current situation; they come with a sanction and they demand obedience.[12] Kant labels such universal, unconditional, and necessary laws *categorical imperatives* – 'categorical' rather than hypothetical because they must be followed regardless of circumstances or consequences, and 'imperative' because we are left with no other choice but to obey them. Kant, however, is not saying that anything that gets to be a called a law attains such high dignity. Besides the three formal conditions, a law acquires the stature of law when it is developed by rational beings governed by "the idea of a reason possessing full power over all subjective motives."[13] The only candidate that both extinguishes subjective motives and has the status of a law as a categorical imperative is the rule that results from a three-part analysis: (1) identify the rule implied in the act you want to choose; (2) commit yourself to the universal application of that rule; and (3) examine carefully all consequences of that universal application.

Kant gives some examples. A person in despair over a series of misfortunes decides to commit suicide because he can see nothing but bad things in his future. So, that person decides to act by the following rule: 'When life will bring only misery, end it!'. However, before acting he must go to step (2), and ask whether this should be a general rule of conduct for everybody in his situation. In doing so he recognizes, in step (3), that he has the capacity to analyze the future, the very same capacity people not in despair use every day to improve their lives. In effect he is using a life-affirming capability, rational analysis, that is self-refuting and can never be universalized. The decision to end one's life reflects a value and reason to live far greater than the value misery provides as a reason to end life because rational thought is used in all aspects of living, while specific emotions, no matter how dark, inevitably dissipate. Therefore, the despairing person should not choose suicide. Consider the person who will break a promise to borrow money to pay a debt, even while recognizing that the credit system upon which he relies can only function if enough promises are kept to maintain the trust necessary for a system of borrowing and lending in the first place. Or, consider also persons who can find no

---

[12] Ibid., 34.

[13] Ibid., 37n6.

interest in self-improvement or in acts of charity to others because they are either complacent about their own circumstances or sufficiently prosperous. When such individuals universalize their conduct toward others, they can see that if others did the same, their own autonomy would diminish as well. When some people aspire to self-improvement, they create helpful social conditions that may be relied upon by those who do not; and a loss of charitable giving usually creates costs in the form of social instability to those who refrain from it.

Kant recognized that his categorical imperative was only worthy as a principle of morality if it could be shown that it was itself a rule of general applicability. Every course of action and moral choice that defeats itself if universally applied serves as a test for bad law. If you treat other people as morally inferior to you, then your version of the categorical imperative will reduce to a truism that universal application doesn't apply to them because of your moral superiority. So, the only universalizable norm that could generate a real command upon your free will is your acceptance that other people are always worthy of respect and dignity and cannot be a means to accomplishing your ends. For Kant that norm is: "rational nature exists as an end in itself."[14] In the suicide example, a rational being asserts his will only by destroying it. The promise breaker uses the trust of the credit system only by betraying it; and of course this is even more severely true anytime direct assaults on the freedom and property of others are done to enhance the freedom and autonomy of the assailant. All of these cases destroy certain values in the name of preserving them. Showing the truth of this is what Kant means by the 'metaphysics of morals'.

Under Kant's moral system all members of humanity must be treated as rational ends in themselves. This principle applies not only to individuals in their daily lives interacting with each other but is given broader expression through a common system of laws that reflect the rational insights derived from application of categorical imperatives to moral dilemmas arising in ordinary life. But treating persons as ends is not an external designation or description. It is an acknowledgment that they manifest a free and autonomous will, and further that all of humanity

---

[14] Ibid., 46.

belongs to a single rational community. Even the most unredeemable villain, Kant argues, is fully capable of membership in the rational world if he is accustomed to using his reasonable faculties and is then shown how to use them in categorical-imperative moral analysis.[15] Any theory of law in the form of jurisprudence, then, must be built upon a foundation of the values established in the metaphysics of morals. It must be a 'science of right' setting forth the commands of reason to do one's duty in the public and private arenas of life, and it must provide guidance for resolving the dilemmas arising from novel situations: "Reason commands how we ought to act, even although no example of such action were to be found."[16] Jurisprudence as a science of law fills in gaps by providing 'what if' examples for analysis of their moral implications and their relevance to law.

As a science, jurisprudence also establishes the criteria of legitimacy for legislation. In order to clearly articulate such laws legal concepts must be explicated in terms of the rights they enforce. A right abstractly considered of necessity includes a power to compel recognition of itself, and perhaps even to compel conformity of another's behavior, but the exact measure of that right must still be whether it conforms to the categorical imperative and principle of universal freedom of all autonomous individuals. Consider the legal concept of *possession*. The fact that I hold an apple in my hand does not mean it belongs to me. My claim to ownership also applies to the apple when it is not in my hand and this claim can only be based on a collateral claim compelling you not to possess my apple. However, in recognizing this collateral claim I must be willing to subject myself to it as well, not just compelling resistance by you but resistance by me with respect to your possessory claims. If we lived in a world where each of us could only use the things we immediately and physically possessed there would be little need to recognize competing claims to the same object. However we live in a world where use is transferred by physical possession, and since we cannot be certain that each person is willing to check their act of will against another's possessions, a civil state is established along with public legislative power to express the rational concept of the right of possession in all of its various forms. Even if I were

---

[15] Ibid., 71.

[16] Kant, *Philosophy of Law*, 17.

to possess something in the state of nature and declare it to be mine it would be mine not absolutely but only presumptively unless law says otherwise.[17]

We have ascended from an examination of the concept of duty to a recognition of an overarching duty to follow categorical imperatives in moral reasoning and finally to a view of humanity as a union of intelligible and free autonomous beings operating in a system of communal law manifested in the state. Throughout Kant is assuming that when reflective reasoning occurs it is working well in generating moral results that are self-authenticating.[18] A jurisprudence thoroughly founded on the "metaphysics of morals" allows no possibility of deviance when establishing the laws of the state. The state is thus thoroughly rational, thoroughly moral, and at all times legitimate. Its constitution cannot include exceptions or limitations. All claims that legitimacy of the state derive from an original contract, consent of the governed, or even from God are irrational and without foundation. Only the sovereign power can initiate reforms and decide to transfer power, as Louis XVI did during the French Revolution. For this reason, Kant sees no rationale for rebellion against the state. There are no residuary natural rights that a person takes from nature into the state. Rather, he leaves entirely behind a "wild lawless Freedom" and *acquires* a new freedom under the regulated order of the state to which he owes absolute obedience:

> Every transgression of a law only can and must be explained as arising from a Maxim of the transgressor making such wrong-doing his rule of action; for were it not committed by him as a *free* Being, it could not be imputed to him. But it is absolutely impossible to explain how any rational individual forms such a Maxim against the clear prohibition of lawgiving Reason.[19]

Every guilty defendant, then, must be found guilty for actions resulting from poor moral reasoning. By going against reason the guilty party must

---

[17] Ibid., 48-50, 61-80.

[18] For a discussion on Kant's moral self-authentication see John Rawls, *Lectures on the History of Moral Philosophy*, ed. Barbara Herman (Cambridge: Harvard University Press, 2000), 253-272.

[19] Kant, *The Philosophy of Law*, 169-70, 174-78.

also be going against the law. The fit between the two was absolutely seamless in Kant's system. There was no room within the judicial system for adjustments between law as it actually existed and law as it should be after equitable factors are considered. Making exceptions to the law under unanticipated or extreme conditions is not permitted. A servant who agrees to a fixed amount payment at the end of the year cannot complain that subsequent depreciation in the value of money reduced that payment. Law should never recognize excuses. Kant rules out the opportunity for a judge to adjust to the terms of a contract "on the basis of vague or indefinite conditions." A similar analysis applies to the excuse of breaking the law out of necessity (cannibalism on a deserted island). The fact that people will not be deterred by the law when their life is immediately in danger cannot be excused and is not relevant to a law's applicability, Kant argued.[20] His idea of the state and the role of jurisprudence could not be farther apart from the Anglo-American system that assumes human error and self-interest in the creation of law, and then provides a mechanism for adjustments to minimize their pernicious effects.

Positive Law

Legal validity. The concept of validity is part of any legal system. Legal validity involves many different kinds of human transactions, such as when a marriage is lawful, when an arrest has occurred, when a sale has been accomplished, what is needed to make a valid will, and what the difference is between an employee who quits and one who is fired. A legal system should provide clear rules for determining whether some event or activity meets a standard of validity. Ideally, the rules should be definitive: if they are not followed, they dictate invalid results. Legal positivists like to think of rules as on/off switches rather than as dimmer switches. They attempt to characterize unambiguously the defining feature of legal validity and of the matrix of human activities that authorizes it. That feature is the recognition that law, 'positive law', generally refers to the actual specific and tangible manifestation of law as found in statutes, codes, in certain rule-conferring portions of written constitutions, but also in

[20] Ibid., 50-53.

socially ascertainable moral values of society. The focus is not on what law creators say they are doing or on the general cultural influences deemed foundational to laws 'on the books' at any given time. Rather than engage in deep philosophical analysis of law and morality, legal positivists examine the content and purpose of actual legislation expressly stated and then creates jurisprudence that is based entirely on law and its tangible sources.

John Austin. Reconciling established law and morality is not part of a positivist agenda. British legal philosopher and reformer, John Austin (1790-1859),[21] who is considered a founder of the school of 'legal positivism' famously wrote: "The existence of law is one thing; its merit or demerit is another. Whether it be or be not is one enquiry; whether it be or be not conformable to an assumed standard, is a different enquiry. A law, which actually exists, is a law, though we happen to dislike it, or though it vary from the text, by which we regulate our approbation and disapprobation."[22]

Of course, Austin realized that words on a page by themselves are not all there is to law. They need to be put into practice. The words of a judge spoken from the bench are just as much a physical manifestation of law and so are the handcuffs when they are used to take a prisoner away. Besides words on a page, these also are crucial elements of positive law. So Austin created as the keystone of his jurisprudence a legal system centered on commands connected to written law, the commands of judges, legislators, the monarch, and ultimately God. In his view, a law is always a command given by a political superior to a political inferior. Also, there cannot be a command without a commitment to punish. Law and morality therefore are distinguished by the fact that morality lacks the force of a command and a sanction of punishment. Violation of moral rules, or 'laws', may result in a bad reputation or public condemnation, but if they are to be an occasion for punishment it can only be because they are part of law itself. "By the distinctive names *law* and *morality*, I denote the difference between the human sources from which the two classes respectively emanate,"

---

[21] Not to be confused with British philosopher of language John Austin (1911-1960).

[22] John Austin, *The Province of Jurisprudence Determined*, (1832), ed. W. Rumble (Cambridge: Cambridge University Press, 1995), Lecture V, p. 157.

Austin notes.[23] The commands of law always emanate from a determinative entity with sovereign power, typically a chief executive, law-making body, or law enforcement official of a governmental body, while the 'commands' of morality result from an indeterminate entity, consisting of various moralizing social groups, like religious or human rights association, or even simply from 'public opinion'. Kant may be a great authority in morality but he lacked the capacity to command and punish those who did not follow his categorical imperatives.

Yet the aspirational value of morality cannot simply be ignored; it must be reconstructed into a system of rules made useful to law. On this project, Austin imported into his jurisprudence the utilitarian moral system of Jeremy Bentham. He credited Bentham with being the first philosopher to promote individual and social happiness as a direct and objective measure of good law and foundation of jurisprudence.[24] Inspired by Bentham, Austin set about to create a robust jurisprudence that would unify law and morality into a "vast organic whole." Positive Law was to be seamlessly united with Positive Morality, by which he meant the moral values accepted as social facts in a specific community subject to legislation.[25] The unity of law and morality is only accomplished, then, when the state creates laws reflecting the actual moral values of its people. The architecture of his jurisprudence may be described as a 'chain of command' with authority flowing downward from God through the state to each particular subject. God's law (Divine Law) is the exception to Positive Law because there is no way for us mortals to be certain of the *precise* articulation of what God commands except through natural reason and revelation. We may be told to follow the Ten Commandments, but what do they command in given cases? The answer is not always clear. Honoring your parents may have meant in earlier times, 'act towards them as they wish so you can inherit their property', for example.

---

[23] John Austin, *The Province of Jurisprudence Determined: Being the First Part of a Series of Lectures on Jurisprudence, or, the Philosophy of Positive Law*, 2nd. ed. (London: J. Murray, 1861-1863), I: 113

[24] Ibid., I, 103.

[25] Austin, *The Province of Jurisprudence*, I, xxiv, 114.

The substance of Divine commands, however, can be known objectively according to Austin because God always commands what is useful and so what is observably useful must be evidence of what God commands. Furthermore, since all of mankind is capable of understanding what actions are useful and what actions are destructive, such knowledge provides empirical evidence of Divine Law. So, although God's commands are imperfectly known, there is also no question that there is among mankind "the decided predominance of good which is observable in the order of the world," and this knowledge is sufficient, as a practical matter to build a jurisprudence on a theory of utility alone.[26] Hence, since Divine Law is founded on God's plan that mankind benefit from what is useful, and since Positive Law must always take a precise form as the law of the state, all Positive Laws must be useful and beneficial; those that are not do not merit the status of laws even though they may be designated as such. In Austin's view it is inconceivable for a corrupt state to carry out the legitimate functions of a state, as God had intended. It may survive for a short time but would soon self-destruct through internal or external dissension. A given law, for example, may make a few people happy but at the expense of many others. Such a law is not genuine unless it can be shown that the increase in happiness among a few creates a longer-term benefit for the many. For example, to the question why there should be such a wide unequal distribution of property Austin answers:

> Without security for property, there were [would be] no inducement to save. Without habitual savings on the part of proprietors, there were no accumulation of capital. Without accumulation of capital, there were no fund for the payment of wages, no division of labor, no elaborate and costly machines: there were none of those helps to labor which augment its productive power, and therefore, multiply the enjoyments of every individual in the community.[27]

Government itself is the most efficient means of carrying out Divine Law, for although there is some waste and mischief in every form of government it is not inherent in government itself but rather "it is only in the ignorance

---

[26] Ibid., 78-79.

[27] Ibid., 33.

of the people, and in their consequent mental imbecility, that governments or demagogues can find the means of mischief."[28]

Under Austin's system the worldly rulers, whether individual or collectively, stand in the shoes of God. They promulgate the laws that carry out God's commands. That is also true of judges. Positive laws, being commands, cannot be interpreted or modified by judges. That is for the sovereign legislator to do. To accept the opinions of judges as judge-made law, and even more so the arguments of lawyers "is one of the foolish or *knavish fictions* with which lawyers, in every age and nation, have perplexed and darkened the simplest and clearest truths." Although a rigorous system of statutes drafted by the best legal minds ("scientific lawyers") will have its defects, a legal code is far superior to a patchwork of statutes and judicial rulings. "There can be no doubt that a complete Code is better than a body of judiciary law: or is better than a body of law partly consisting of judiciary law, and partly a statute law stuck patchwise on a body of judiciary," Austin believed.[29] Overall, Austin's command-centered legal positivism was at its core anti-democratic. A government of, by, and for the people could never be established and endure. A witness to the revolution of 1848 in Paris he became convinced that if a society gets to the point of being completely shattered it cannot be systematically rebuilt. Something else will emerge in its place for better or worse over which there will be little control by the survivors. Once morality and law are separated in theory, it is not conceivable that their connections can be rebuilt by any normative process worthy of either.

Jeremy Bentham. Legal positivism without an embedded moral perspective is compatible with any imaginable legal system that can be written down or enunciated, whether for a society of altruistic angels or one run by sadistic autocrats. If laws must be regarded as social facts, so must morality if it is to provide a backbone for jurisprudence. In the case of Austin and Bentham, the foundational social facts were identified as the individual human interests and aspirations that increase the happiness of those

---

[28] Ibid., 50.

[29] Ibid., 23; III, 382, 386. For Austin's discussion of the difference between common law and code law see Vol. II, Lecture XXXIX.

individuals. Individuals are governed by pleasure seeking and pain avoidance, Bentham argued, and any effort to live a life contrary to that principle was impractical and even impossible. By *utility* he meant "that property in any object, whereby it tends to produce benefit, advantage, pleasure, good, or happiness." The utility of a community is simply the sum of the interests of the members that compose it. Consequently, any measure of government that increases the happiness of the community is conformable to the principle of utility.

Since the principle of utility is part of what it means to be a human being, it is just as impossible to establish a proof for it as it is to require proof for why human beings must breathe air to survive. We are simply built that way, Bentham argued.[30] All efforts that may seem contrary to pleasure seeking, such as actions characterized by empathy, benevolence, altruism, asceticism, sacrifice, martyrdom or even self-mutilation, are invariably accompanied by edifying justifications of the importance of such actions to the individual, the nation, or to God. The principle of utility cuts through all of the false sentimentality in moral theory when applied to law. All legal-theory talk about the laws of nature, laws of reason, right reason, natural justice, natural equity, and good order are merely words of sentiment not scientific facts. A politician as well as a jurist uses such empty terms as a pretense to deciding difficult questions "in the manner that best pleases him, without the trouble of inquiry," Bentham argued.[31]

For Positive Law to develop into a real, usable system of jurisprudence it must be thoroughly empirical and scientific in its practices and in the responsibilities of those who make and enforce the laws. All analysis in jurisprudence must start with the application of the principle of utility to legislation. Without legislation that establishes what each person may claim as their own property, there can be no real usable ethical rules to resolve such disputes. Before the obligations and offenses of citizens to their state may be articulated and enforced, legislation must say what they are: "Without legislation there would be no such thing as a *state*: no

---

[30] Jeremy Bentham, *An Introduction to the Principles of Morals and Legislation* (Oxford: Clarendon Press, 1876), 1-7.

[31] Ibid., 16-19.

particular persons invested with powers to be exercised for the benefit of the rest." Bentham recognized this chicken-and-egg problem: how to establish the legitimacy and authority of those who set up a system of legitimacy and authority? His solution is found in the rejection of the fiction of a state of nature where all mankind moves from a state of nature to a state of government. In reality we are all born into some governing framework that includes a system of obedience which all individuals experience at birth and thereafter.[32]

The art of legislation consists of both knowing what legislation is required to carry out the principle of utility and how it should be articulated. Commands like 'thou shall not steal' are too vague to be implemented in a rigorous utility-compliant manner. Stealing may take different forms and in one context the same act may be an act of stealing and another not so. Stealing food from a few to give to the starving many could in some circumstances be justified by the principle of utility. An empirical analysis of all possible consequences of a law must be spelled out for the jurist so that the law may be effectively enforced and the proper punishment, if any, administered.[33] Punishment therefore should never be inflicted for its own sake. It should not be inflicted where no mischief has been committed, or where it will not prevent mischief again, or where it is too expensive to carry out, or where it is needless because the mischief to be avoided is easily prevented without it. "Legislation has the same center with morals, but it has not the same circumference," Bentham wrote.[34] The skill of the legislator involves knowing when to leave a problem to the natural working moral indignation, prudence and public embarrassment and when to put it under the system of punishment through law. Nonetheless, the legislator still makes the public good the foundation of his reasoning and so "to know the true good of the community is what constitutes the science of legislation; the art consists in finding the means to realize that good."[35]

---

32 Ibid., 322. See also *A Fragment on Government* (Dublin: J. Sheppard, 1776), Ch. 1.

33 Ibid., 332.

34 Jeremy Bentham, *The Theory of Legislation* (London: K. Paul, Trench, Trübner, 1908), 60.

35 Ibid., 1.

Hans Kelsen. Since Austin, legal positivism has been in a constant state of adjustment and refinement. Austrian jurist and philosopher, Hans Kelsen (1881-1973), like Bentham and Austin, regarded jurisprudence and the operations of law as an autonomous scientific enterprise, not a collection of rules derived from psychology, sociology, or economics. But rather than simply focus on the authority of laws as the expression of commands from superiors to inferiors, Kelsen regarded them as products of networks of authoritative structures. He recognized the difference between a command and obedience. No matter how much fear there is in facing up to a command, obedience will only follow if a person makes a cognitive decision to accept its authority as a norm to follow. "The norm which confers upon an act the meaning of legality or illegality is itself created by an act, which, in turn receives its legal character from yet another norm," he wrote.[36] Behind the norm of following a command is the norm that the command must be followed. The difference between killing by execution and murder is not the physical affliction, but the differing normative interpretations of the two actions. When a conversation between merchants occurs within the course of their business relationship the words they use may ripen into a contract and not simply be an exchange of information; this too results from norms embedded in such activity among such individuals acting in the regular course of their business.

Although we require interpretation when we observe the act of creation of a law – for example, the deliberations and passage of a bill in Congress – we understand immediately that the command has been created. Kelsen writes: "The difference between is and ought cannot be explained further. We are immediately aware of the difference."[37] The arm motions of a traffic officer at an intersection are signs of permissions or restrictions and are not to be interpreted as waving hello or goodbye. When a robber says "Hand over your money!" we reject the command as legal because we do not

---

[36] Hans Kelsen, *Pure Theory of Law*, trans. Max Knight, 2nd ed. (Berkeley: University of California Press, 1967), 4. See also Kelsen, *General Theory of Law and State*, trans Anders Wedberg (New York: Russsell and Russell, 1961). Following citations are to *Pure Theory*.

[37] Ibid., 5.

suppose he is an authorized agent of official state action.[38] But do we in fact have an innate cognition of an ought-command? Infants seem to require an ought-learning curve but with the results, depending upon social environment, ranging from a highly robotic to a highly rebellious set of behaviors with no recognition of validity in the process. Kelsen acknowledges that custom can generate norms, though these norms lack legal validity until authorized as official commands of government. He gives the example of a gang that puts one of its members on trial, collects evidenced testimony, and then sentences to death and executes the member. This event, he argues, is purely subjective because it lacks the authorization and validity of official state action. We would say that such a trial is legally invalid, and those who participated committed crimes. But what are we to say about a state that passes laws in its official manner that seem nonsensical or unenforceable, the kind of laws Fuller had highlighted? Laws that require what everybody must do anyway (breathe) or cannot do (live without food) are ineffective and so ought to be deemed invalid. Between those points are a wide range of legal requirements, including many unenforced/stale laws and other technical transgressions of law that are either too trivial to bother with or else ignored through prosecutorial discretion. To the legal positivist, these remain fully laws until repealed.

Unlike Bentham, who incorporated the tenets of utilitarianism directly into the system of laws, Kelsen's pure theory of law has no way to integrate law and morality. The drive to create a legal social order is focused entirely on first creating lawmaking institutions and then making laws.[39] There is no prior systematic undertaking of what morals the laws are to reflect. It makes no sense, Kelsen argues, for a society to draft immoral laws. We only judge a society's laws as immoral when it is not our society. Besides, in reality morality always presents itself with "extraordinary heterogeneity."[40] Even those who seek to impose a command theory based upon God's will are still left with the work of explaining what that will commands in so many different situations and cultures. Legal values may

---

[38] Ibid., 47-50.

[39] Ibid., 74.

[40] Ibid., 64.

reflect moral values but it is not their moral content that makes them valid. "According to a positivistic theory of law," Kelsen wrote, "the source of law can only be law."[41]

Positivist theory does not make law just one of the attributes of the state; it is the living expression of the state. States are not formed and then laws created to be executed. The state comes into being when it *defines* its legal boundaries, legal membership, and the legal powers of state legal entities. It is a contradiction to say that the state is subject to its laws because it receives commands from no other entity.[42] Positivist theory also does not recognize a norm-creating function for any legal interpretation carried on outside the state and its judicial infrastructure. Judges may interpret the law in their official capacity; not so law professors in law review articles. When judges cite law review articles they cannot do so as sources and authorities of law. The flexible view of law which gives legal force to ever changing business practices, e.g., in the Uniform Commercial Code, is lawless interpretation according to the pure theory of law.[43]

H. L. A. Hart. Although legal positivism has not been the dominant Anglo-American legal theory in recent years, English legal philosopher, H. L. A. Hart (1907-1992), has given us a revised and more nuanced form of legal positivism, first by pointing out that many laws are not direct commands ('You must never murder anyone!') but conditional ones ('If you want to sell your land, you must put the sale terms in writing and affix your signature.'); and then by arguing that positivists do not, or at least should not claim that because laws are always valid in form they require no interpretation when implemented. The legal interpretation and opinion writing of judges in their official capacity, sometimes covering hundreds of pages, do not take a law, dissolve it, and reconstitute it into a new form. The law remains valid throughout as long as the process occurs in the authorized format.[44]

---

[41] Ibid., 59-69, 233.

[42] Ibid., 279-319.

[43] Ibid., 355.

[44] H. L. A. Hart, *Positivism and the Separation of Law and Morals*, 71 Harv. L. Rev. 593 (1958).

Hart also refined the view that laws are commands from superiors to inferiors. Superiors also make laws that apply to them, and their laws live on after they are dead. In fact there are many ways in which laws do not function as commands. Procedural laws about how laws should be made and what subjects judges may legitimately consider, their 'jurisdiction', are rules more so than commands. Constitutional provisions referring to concepts such as 'due process' and 'equal protection' require dense interpretations, and so are completely unsuited as commands. Also, laws typically are not specifically directed to individuals but to the public or some subgroup of it. If laws are analogous to orders they are more like hypothetical standing orders directly applied to whoever qualifies. Laws also refer to infractions in general terms and do not always define all their terms. They are only accepted because those who obey them operate under a system of general obedience to the Rule of Law. They even accept they may be punished for breaking laws they never heard of as long as the legal system is prepared to show them their legitimacy. All of these considerations suggest that laws presuppose a set of commitments to a system of legal norms and cannot be reduced to simple commands.

In making his case, Hart argued that law operates at the intersection of two kinds of rules. The first kind are those that directly impose behavioral obligations under social pressure by imposing sanctions, whether as targeted punishment in law proper or as diffuse shame-making in custom and morality. The second group of rules monitors the functioning of the first set of rules. These are (1) rules tasked with recognizing what the rules are, where they are located, who are obligated officially to identify them, and how their identification is to be justified (rules of recognition); (2) rules empowering individuals to enforce rules and interpret and resolve rule conflicts (rules of adjudication); and (3) rules for empowering individuals to make recommendations for rule changes (rules of change). Rules of sports, indicating how the game should be played, are watched over by official rules committees who are empowered to police rules violations and make rule changes.[45] If baseball games take too long for the needs of commercial television broadcast, the rules committee may seek ways to shorten the game (e.g., reducing pitching mound conference time) without

---

[45] H. L. A. Hart, *The Concept of Law*, 2nd ed. (Oxford: Clarendon Press, 1994), 79-99.

changing the first kind of rules (how many outs per inning, how many strikes per out, how many innings per game, etc.). These latter rules are so embedded in what we understand to be baseball that changing them amounts to creating a whole new game. In the case of the legal system it is the recognition of the indispensable defining features of the system as a system of law. This recognition is an empirical fact, hence positivistic in nature, identifying what norms individuals must follow when they are part of the legal system, whether as judges, attorneys, or law enforcement officers. As a statement in positivistic jurisprudence the rule of recognition is the ultimate rule in the sense that it tells us that there are no rules behind the actual rules functioning in the operations of the legal system.[46]

Since moral values, attitudes, and judgments are part of our individual and social lives, it is understandable that they will feed into our constructions of the rule of recognition in given legal systems. But this too, positivists argue, is an empirical fact, not based on any metaphysical necessity that before you can have any legal system you must have a moral one. It also means that immoral values can be integrated in the same way. There is just no automatic sorting mechanism at work here. Consider the following secondary process rules: 'treat similar cases similarly', or 'punish similar infractions similarly'. Does this mean that all blonde defendants must be punished similarly? Hart argues that these rules generally work only because there is already "a great measure of agreement" about how they should be applied.[47] It is in that agreement that morality touches base with law. However, that connection is a contingent fact not a philosophical one, as Leibniz and Kant proposed. Hart completely denies Kant's perspective that human reason can discover moral truths and then construct a legal system to operationalize them. In fact, Hart's criticism of Austin's command theory probably derives from a different underlying assumption than the one made by Austin. Austin believed the human command system was embedded within the divine command system so it was not a problem for him to have laws continue on after all of the legislators that enacted them have long since died. God remains in his heaven keeping the command system afloat. For Hart continuity was a theoretical problem that could only be solved by embedding law in social agreements

---

[46] Ibid., 100-123.

[47] Ibid., 159, 161.

living human beings make in order to deal with the physical and biological constraints of human life.

Here Hart lists five such constraints: (1) *human vulnerability*: as biological organisms no human is immune from being attacked, killed or made vulnerable from injury or illness; (2) *approximate equality*: although there is great variation in strength, agility, and intelligence, those variations are never sufficient to create a lasting and permanent advantage; (3) *limited altruism*: human altruism can be advantageous for individual and social well-being but it is also necessarily intermittent thus requiring the creation of rules of "mutual forbearance" in order for social life to continue; (4) *limited resources*: human organisms require exchanges of energy with their environment and are not biologically self-sufficient, thereby requiring organizational and energy expenditures to compensate for these necessary transactional costs; (5) *limited understanding and strength of will*: human beings have limited capacity to comprehend and counteract all of the variety of problems that arise during their life spans.[48] These constraints have produced responses in the form of moral and legal norms and the various ways they are implemented using sanctions. It is biology and sociology, not philosophy or theology that links morality and law in Hart's scheme. A legal system as a system of mutual forbearance is born out of necessity, but that does not mean that the system always operates as an unqualified good. Highly centralized legal systems are also prone to be captured by powerful minorities to oppress majorities; they may falsely appropriate the good name of morality, and use legal interpretation for evil or corrupt purposes. These disruptions are not always quickly detected and repaired by the best reasoning or commitment to justice. Nonetheless, it is better to call something a law even if it is odious and irrationally discriminatory when it is revealed by the rule of recognition, than to risk intractable confusion and anarchy by allowing members of the group to decide on their own which laws morally demand their obedience.[49]

In a "Postscript" to *The Concept of Law* Hart argues against the claim that he fails to see an important difference among legal systems, viz., that some are

---

[48] Ibid., 194-198.

[49] Ibid., 200-212.

fairly closed and leave little room for interpretation or disagreement, while others allow disagreement and debate at each phase of the operations of law. For example, some legal systems are better suited than others to the perspective of legal positivism in the way they concentrate or disperse legal authority. In the American federal appellate system, the Supreme Court is the final authority but only as to the cases it decides to hear, leaving the rest to lower courts. Also, one district court may issue an injunction binding upon the entire nation, even though other lower courts have not taken up the issue. The analysis of legal scholars is cited as authority in judicial opinions. Supreme Court justices give public talks and write books; their selection is deeply embedded in political debate, and some are open to the results of empirical studies in fashioning their opinions. "An important function of the rule of recognition is to promote the certainty with which the law may be ascertained," Hart writes in the Postscript. What the rule of recognition will not allow is a view that participants in a legal system do not have certainty as to what the law requires. Yet, in a system of dispersed legal authority with so many opportunities outside of official action to interpret the law, it is not so easy to detect what the law is in the first place and even if the law is facially clear it is not always clear that it must be enforced as written. There are many instances when officials applying the law have their own view of how to execute their duty. Traffic officers seldom if ever pull over someone going one or two miles per hour over the speed limit even if the speed is registered electronically. Some police officers may decide that the best way to control a large unruly crowd and save lives is to inflict disproportionate force on a few leading protestors at the outset even though they are not the one's acting in the most threatening manner. Anyone who has practiced law for a long time in a certain jurisdiction learns through the grapevine about the judge's attitude, say about divorce, based on the judge's own personal experience in that area.

Another criticism of Hart is that he ignores legal principles that are not reduced to clear legal norms or rules and do not function as such. The 'principles' of the Declaration of Independence are not direct authorities for legislation but they allow legislators to be guided by them when they draft laws and explain them to the public. Moral principles embodying notions of equality and fairness often operate beneath the surface in debates over great constitutional questions. Are these principles specific factual attributes of a legal system? It is a clear legal rule that in a five-to-four Supreme Court decision the five voters win but that does not mean that the principles upon which the majority based its opinion have nullified the principles of the minority. The minority principles may live on, though without the same stature as the winning principles; they are not literally outside the law since they may be invoked in the opinions of later cases. In the process, the Justices at times accuse each other of being unfair and operating according to an incorrect view of the philosophical theory the law should follow. This confrontation seems to contradict Hart's view that "the existence and content of the law can be identified by reference to the social sources of the law (e.g. legislation, judicial decisions, social customs) without reference to morality except where the law thus identified has itself incorporated moral criteria for the identification of the law."[50]

The various theories of legal positivism force us to think deeply about the relationship between law and morality, primarily by first saying that there should not be such a relationship, and then by doing some damage control against our common reaction that the whole point of law is to institutionalize and regularize many of our core moral beliefs. We want a legal system to serve as a good approximation of our moral system, but we come up against what may be called the 'paradox of authority': a legal system must be recognized as fully authoritative and demand obedience if it is to operate as a source of legitimate coercion, but obeying legal authority is not the same thing as obeying the authority of our conscience and the moral reasoning about what is the right thing to do. The legal system cannot simultaneously accept both sources of authority, since the latter directly diminishes the former. This dissonance is not an urgent matter as

---

[50] Ibid., 269. For a few of the many reactions to Hart's positivism from a variety of perspectives, see Jules Coleman, ed. *Hart's Postscript: Essays on the Postscript to the Concept of Law* (Oxford: Oxford University Press, 2001); also E. Phillip Soper, *Legal Theory and the Obligation of a Judge: The Hart/Dworkin Debate*, 75Mich. L. Rev. 473 (1977). See also Joseph Raz, *The Authority of Law: Essays on Law and Morality* (Oxford: Clarendon Press, 1979), 51, also generally, 3-33, 147-159, and his "Authority, Law and Morality," *The Monist*, 68 (1985): 308-309; and Tom D. Campbell, ed., *Legal Positivism* (Aldershot: Dartmouth, 1999), Robert Alexy, *The Argument from Injustice: A Reply to Legal Positivism*, B. L. Paulson and S. L. Paulson, trans. (Oxford: Clarendon Press, 2002).

long as the public believes its legal system already incorporates a lot of its moral reasoning, through its many deliberative rules-making exercises that individuals do not have time to think through themselves. But these considerations do not satisfy someone who confronts a legal system that contains and enforces immoral laws according to their own moral reasoning, or who finds that the legal system's deliberative mechanisms are either ineffective or perverse.

Natural Law

The Concept of Nature. The 'moral law' perspective attempts to create a pure foundation for morality through philosophical reasoning and then sets about to build a system of law upon it. The 'positive law' perspective attempts to describe a legal system with only those moral values that are accepted and recognized as demonstrable social facts by those who have official status within the system. Natural law theory, by contrast, attempts to locate objective moral values in law not based in theology, metaphysics, or the creation of the nation state, but rather in empirically discovered manifestations in the natural world. What positive law theory did for the state, natural law theory does for human life within a natural world that includes birth, lifespans, sexuality, love and death, and familial and social attachments. Yet, overhanging this project is a question of how we understand nature as a place where actions and events are said to occur *naturally*, and that understanding is intimately linked to the latest scientific knowledge. For one thing, the very idea of something being 'natural' depends on our technological capability to observe, interrupt, and manipulate the processes of nature through experimentation. Before the nineteenth century, nature was small in time and space; species were fixed, the earth only several thousand years old, space and time consisted of objective Newtonian units applicable everywhere; the solar system was the entire universe, the very existence of atoms was still conjectural. Now the solar system is a mere speck among galaxies themselves specks in a wider universe; the workings of the human organism has turned out to be vastly more complex than Renaissance anatomists could ever have imagined; the barrier between the organic and inorganic all but disappeared in the nineteenth century, and the same may be said for the distinction between the natural and artificial since then. At the same time, the complexity and interconnections of social life create both opportunities to exercise personal autonomy and conditions that just about make it impossible to achieve.

Historically, the patterns, cycles, equilibria, and goal-driven processes of nature gave pride of place to order over disorder, perhaps, on the assumption that orderly events, especially long-range ones like acorns becoming oak trees, could only result from an intended plan by some lawgiver. The problem with this primary assumption of natural law theory, as Fuller once pointed out, is that it makes the theory vulnerable to the overthrow of yesterday's best science and theology and hence undermines the notion of natural *law* itself.[51] It is rather counterintuitive and perhaps paradoxical to speak of the conjunction of 'nature' and 'law' if the idea of nature itself has been such a changing story. As long as natural law theory identifies predictability with rule-governed activity in the observable natural world it is vulnerable to refutation when predictions turn out to be wrong or nature itself becomes seen as inherently random or probabilistic. In the seventeenth century the idea of nature assumed fixed processes of fixed entities. So, French priest and philosopher, Nicolas Malebranche (1638-1715), could write: "What we call *nature* is nothing other than the general laws which God has established to construct or to preserve his work by very simple means, by an action which is uniform, constant, perfectly worthy of an infinite wisdom and of a universal cause."[52] Subsequently, natural law theorists had to contend with our changing concept of nature and the evidence the best science may provide to sustain the central idea of its lawfulness. The following are some natural law theorists who have attempted to extract as much law from nature as the science of their time would allow.

Hugo Grotius. Dutch prodigy, polymath and legal scholar, Hugo Grotius (1583-1645), was born into an influential Protestant political family in the Netherlands during its war of independence from Spain. As a teenager he had already witnessed serious diplomatic negotiations between nations designed to advance Dutch national and economic interests. In 1625 he

---

[51] Lon L Fuller, *The Law in Quest of Itself* (Boston: Beacon Press, 1966), 102-103.
[52] Nicolas Malebranche, *Treatise of Nature and Grace*, trans. Patrick Riley (New York: Oxford University Press, 1992), 196.

published *On the Law of War and Peace* to justify the Dutch internationalist worldview founded on his view of natural law. He believed that God constructed the natural world with built-in risks and human nature with the capability of recognizing and reducing risks through social arrangements. Hence, God drives us to aggregate, and not only among individuals but states as well, potentially producing a "great society of states" governed by a law of nations. No state or nation, Grotius argued, is so powerful as never to need the aid of other nations. This insight became the foundation for his view of international law.[53]

Grotius unified law and morality in his very definition of a 'law of nature' as "a dictate of right reason, which points out that an act according as it is or is not in conformity with rational nature, has in it a quality of moral baseness or moral necessity; and that, in consequence, such an act is either forbidden or enjoined by the author of nature, God." Hence, natural laws require or forbid; they are not optional or changeable even by God. Whatever is natural is good; whatever is unnatural is bad. Self-defense is natural; hence it is good, in fact even obligatory. This dichotomy applies to states as well because "nature has given to each animal strength sufficient for self-defense and self-assistance," while our natural sociability only increases the means of self-assistance through the cooperative construction of a society as a "community of resource and effort."[54]

Grotius cited Aristotle for another natural fact: that "some men are by nature slaves, that is, are suited to slavery" in the sense that they are "so constituted that they understand better how to be ruled than to rule." Some people, in other words, are naturally disposed to follow rules than to make them for others to follow. On the social level, once a people agree to be governed by a monarch – since their natural docility allowed monarchy to take command in the first place – it would be unnatural to reverse course. Therefore, there is no inherent right of rebellion against a sovereign state for self-protection since it was for self-protection that the state was created in the first place. And if under rare and unusual circumstances, a monarch

---

[53] Hugo Grotius, *On the Law of War and Peace*, ed. Stephen C. Neff (Cambridge: Cambridge University Press, 2012), 6-7.

[54] Ibid., 28, 29, 35, 36.

subjects its citizens to imminent "atrocious cruelty" resistance is allowed though never to the point of killing the monarch. Rebellion, on the other hand, is permitted in states in which the ruler does not rule absolutely but only conditionally and then violates the conditions of authority, as, for example, when a king sells out his kingdom to a foreign enemy, or when a king violates a clearly expressed liberty right of his citizens.[55]

With these foundational issues out of the way, Grotius sets about to complete his natural law scheme. For his natural law theory of property, he argues that things that may be owned are only those that may be fully acquired and used through individual action. Some things, no matter how much effort is expended, cannot be owned, for example the oceans of the world. However, ownership is not reduced to mere possession since theft successfully carried out would acquire new ownership. Instead, the natural law includes a concept of "natural equity" which applies to those things acquired by honest labor and those things that permissibly could be taken from others which are absolutely necessary for survival. In such dire cases, "the primitive right of user revives, as if community of ownership had remained." It is by this principle that there is a natural right to use running water even if it flows through private land because the river remains common property. So also is the right to travel over open unoccupied (but owned) land and to resist by force those who try to obstruct the traveler.[56] Other natural rights include: a right to occupy and cultivate unsettled land though not a right to annex it; a right to acquire those things necessary for life such as food, clothing, and medicine "at a fair price"; under conditions of dire scarcity foreigners should not be expelled because "a common misfortune must be endured in common." Also, marriage and intermarriage should be available in all nations, although states can regulate the property rights of marriage and limit them to marriage among their own citizens. Natural law requires monogamy but also allows divorce if infrequent, in both cases to avoid "confusion of offspring." It also requires that parents take care of their young children and mature children take care of their elder parents. Parents have rights over the children and the right of the father over the mother "on account of the superiority of

---

[55] Ibid., 53, 69, 73, 75.

[56] Ibid., 97, 100.

sex." A father may pledge his son as security, lease him out as a servant, or even sell him as a slave if there is no means of supporting him and if civil law does not prohibit this.[57]

All of these natural laws are discovered, Grotius argued, through the exercise of natural reason which identifies an underlying value – survival of life, propagation of offspring, security of the community, increase in things individually or commonly valued – and then attempts to identify which habits and practices achieve those desired outcomes. However, though natural reason is capable of identifying the value to be achieved, it is not always capable of identifying the means of achieving it. For example, by natural reason we know that criminal acts should not go unpunished, but that still leaves open the question of who should inflict the punishment and how much. Grotius argues that punishment must be inflicted by someone who is morally superior and not someone equally guilty. Extreme punishment motivated by vengeance or by a desire to put on a violent public spectacle is also contrary to natural law because they are responses to uncontrollable emotions and have adverse social consequences, which reflective reason always tries to avoid. As a general rule, the moral dimension of natural law can be found in the observable connection between means and ends when both the individual and social interests of human are analyzed and balanced. Things that end badly inevitably do so as a result of a choice of unnatural means. "In a moral question," Grotius says, "things which lead to an end receive their intrinsic value from the end itself." In other words, the means *may* justify the end if the end has intrinsic value. Defending my life and property and conducting defensive warfare, for example, are justified even if the means may be highly extreme because the underlying end is the restoration of a condition of natural equality. But those are extreme cases. In most cases, the value of the end limits the means that should be taken to achieve it. There must be a natural fitness between both. A person who steals a flower pot from your front porch should not be given a life sentence even though the disregard for private property rights is the same as if he steals all your valued possessions. The bottom-line measure of natural law for Grotius is the recognition that human beings are both self-regarding and

---

[57] Ibid., 102, 103,120,124,126, 127, 146.

constructed with "an impelling desire for society, that is, for the social life – not of any and every sort, but peaceful, and organized according to the measure of his intelligence."[58] Out of this assumption he attempted to build his natural law jurisprudence.

John Locke. Grotius believed that the wild parts of the world constituted a 'state of nature' that was not a lawless jungle where might made right. As soon as habitation occurred, so did cooperation and the rudiments of society, he had argued. In a state of nature natural rights would be honored, and the best proof of this is that human life has endured and become more civilized. This too was the perspective of English philosopher and political theorist, John Locke (1632-1704). Evidence for the genuine effect of natural law can be seen in the sense of fairness among children and thieves, in a guilty conscience, in the overwhelming predictability of social action and interaction, and, of course, in the predictability of all the forms of natural life. "All things observe a fixed law of their operations and a manner of existence appropriate to their nature," he wrote.[59] For example, one important tenet of, and evidence for, natural law for Locke, like Grotius, was the recognition of a personal obligation to keep promises and not abandon them when better opportunities arise. Without such social commitments and the pervasive workings of "mutual love" among human beings, interpersonal social life could not function to the degree necessary to make the pursuit of happiness a realistic political objective.[60] Through "diligent study" of shared information and experience the best course for human advancement could be identified and selected. Self-interest by itself, Locke claimed, does not get us where we need to go to advance out happiness and well-being.[61] It is only in the inclusive interactions of public life that exclusive self-interest comes under the full constraint of natural law, he argued.

How we propagate our species was an important natural constraint in Locke's legal theory. Humans conceive of children in a personal

---

[58] Ibid., 31, 272, 326. Hugo Grotius, *Prolegomena to the Law of War and Peace*, trans. Francis W. Kelsey (New York: Liberal Arts Press, 1957), par. 6.
[59] John Locke, *Essays on the Law of Nature* (Oxford: Clarendon Press, 1954), 115, 117.
[60] Ibid., 119. John Locke, *Two Treatises of Government*, Bk. I.Ch. 2, Sec. 5.
[61] *Essays on the Law of Nature*, 187, 205f.

individualized manner: specific sexual relations followed by specific personal gestation and birth. But once born children also become subject to the natural laws governing social life and their parents become obligated to support and care for them. Children at that point are no longer the exclusive property of their parents. They come under the protection of government which should construct positive laws "made conformable to the laws of nature for the public good." For example, it is contrary to the laws of nature that the first-born male son should inherit all of his father's property (primogeniture). Each child born should not be given an artificial temporal priority. Each is an individual with unique personal traits. "The first-born has not a sole or peculiar right by any law of God and nature," Locke tells us. All children have an equal claim for nourishment and education from their father, and they have no inherent right to inherit their father's servant, since they have "no right to demand *rule* or *dominion* from him."[62]

Locke's empirical evidence for the operation of natural law in the real world – besides becoming increasingly manifest in the discoveries of science and math – was the discovery of an actual state of nature. "In the beginning all the world was America," he claimed. The new world, as he believed and as did many other white Europeans at the time, was evidence of a state of nature where natural instincts to make fair bargains and solemnly obey contracts eventually overrode the instincts for revenge and theft to became the building blocks of a great civil government founded on natural law.[63] In such a world, dominion and property were limited by the contingencies of physical and mental labor, and labor was usually rewarded by sustenance, shelter, and security. In that world, women naturally acquired authority over their children and household when their men died or left them. This was contrary to the false idea that only males could exercise dominion over their family, Locke argued, since in a state of nature every person is born "free, equal, and independent," except when subject to parental dominion, and then only temporarily.[64]

---

[62] *Two Treatises of Government*, Bk. I. Ch. 9. Sec. 92-93.

[63] Ibid., Bk II. Sec. 49.

[64] Ibid., Sec. 95.

Throughout Locke's political and legal writings, natural law is always the measure of positive law. God has given humans, he argued, sufficient intelligence to analyze and solve their problems so as improve upon the freedom and happiness originally established in the state of nature. Laws that do not enhance freedom fail the test of natural law. For example, since labor is the condition for acquiring personal property in a state of nature, no one would willingly consent to a government that disallows personal property. Governmental powers must be restricted to the mission of enhancing freedom and limiting the excesses of power. So, the laws of the Lockean Commonwealth must be established according to four legislative norms:

> First, they are to govern by promulgated established laws, not to be varied in particular cases, but to have one rule for rich and poor, for the favorite at court and the countryman at plough. Secondly, these laws also ought to be designed for no other end ultimately, but the good of the people. Thirdly, they must not raise taxes on the property of the people, without the consent of the people, given by themselves or their deputies. And this properly concerns only such governments where the legislative is always in being, or at least where the people have not reserved any part of the legislative to deputies, to be from time to time chosen by themselves. Fourthly, the legislative neither must nor can transfer the power of making laws to anybody else, or place it anywhere but where the people have.[65]

Under Locke's model we are under absolutely no obligation to obey even provisionally positive laws of a usurper or conqueror. Since they were never a party to the social contract establishing our political community, they cannot take away our freedom or our natural rights, for example, to inherit our parents' property.[66]

Locke's natural law jurisprudence hinges crucially on providing an account of the state of nature in a non-question begging way and on articulating positive law in all of its details based alone on foundational principles of natural law. It is a daunting task to explain how the supposed fitness of human reason to operate in a state of nature may also be capable of

---

[65] Ibid, Sec. 142.

[66] Ibid., Sec. 186-190.

constructing a complex nation state and legal system. Even more so is it difficult given his views that people often draw different conclusions, and reason differently, from what seems to be similar experiences and ideas. "Nothing [is] more obvious," he writes, "than that one man wholly disbelieves, what another only doubts of, and a third steadfastly believes, and firmly adheres to." Since many of us are "unavoidably given over to invincible ignorance," how can we be certain that the moral laws we identify as natural are sufficiently so to serve as a basis for our positive system of law.[67]

John Finnis. In *Natural Law and Natural Rights,* Australian legal philosopher and jurist, John Finnis (b.1940), distinguishes between natural law and *theories* of natural law.[68] The former, if natural law theories are correct, is always in operation, subjecting all of nature to its laws. The latter is a human construction with a history subject to the latest empirical knowledge. Since the eighteenth century traditional natural law theory has lost favor as our views of nature and human living changed under the influence of the scientific revolution. Again, not only has nature become vast and vastly more complex to understand, so has the workings of the human mind itself. Since the nineteenth century, the notion that our minds could reason with clarity and correct its errors has come under suspicion and with it the status of all the absolute pronouncements of philosophy and religion. Traditional natural law theories based on Aristotle, Aquinas, Grotius, and Locke were theoretical expositions of nature with only a sparse understanding of physics, chemistry, astronomy, psychology, or how we can learn about the past. Nonetheless, Finnis contends that we have a sufficient knowledge base now with which to establish a natural law theory without a full reliance on knowledge sources claimed ultimately to be based on revelation from God.[69] To the extent that he places the human capacity to reason at the foundation of his theory, he follows the traditional approach.

---

[67] John Locke, *An Essay concerning Human Understanding,* Bk. 4, Ch. 20.Sec. 1-2.

[68] John Finnis, *Natural Law and Natural Rights,* 2nd ed. (Oxford: Oxford University Press, 2011), 24-25.

[69] Ibid., 49.

His starting point is the human capacity to analyze living through time, identifying those intentions and projects that worked out and those that failed. Humans may not have the sharp instincts and specialized skills of lower animals but they have a greater capacity for second-guessing, self-assessment, redirection, and planning. We can do this, he argues, because we can reason about the practical as well as about the abstract. And when we do this we can see that there are basic practical principles which allow us to flourish when they are directed to a certain class of goods – those that are good for their own sake. Information collected under this calculating process ends up being called *morality*. The success of knowledge pursuits using practical reasoning is a basic good, a *first principle*, according to Finnis, not in terms of content alone but as an object of pursuit and achievement as well. Seeking knowledge is tied closely to curiosity, inventiveness, and our remarkable ability to formulate and test hypotheses. It could be applied equally to momentous questions of constitutional law affecting millions or to trivial daily pursuits. Exercising curiosity produces a well-informed and clear-headed person. Curiosity animated by a desire to learn never results in a muddled or stupid mind on a permanent basis. Curiosity chews away at ignorance and confusion. If human knowledge pursuits invariably ended in pessimism and despair, they would not be reasonable to pursue; they would not continually be reinforced by the satisfaction results actually bring. In an argument reminiscent of Kant, Finnis claims that his first principle needs no further justification and is self-evident because to maintain otherwise is to employ the principle itself. "Such principles of theoretical rationality are not demonstrable, for they are presupposed or deployed in anything that we would count as a demonstration," he writes.[70]

Finnis then identifies six other basic forms of good, beside knowledge (curiosity), that should be the focus of our practical endeavors: *life* (procreation, self-preservation), *play*, *aesthetic experience*, *sociability* (friendship), *practical reasonableness* (self-improvement, dignity, autonomy) and *religion* (wonderment and meaning). To vigorously and intelligently participate in the pursuit and fulfillment of these goods is to live a life in accordance with natural law "because they lay down for us the outlines of

[70] Ibid., 63-66, 69.

everything one could reasonably want to do, to have, and to be."[71] To keep from being overwhelmed or easily distracted by the demands of daily life, Finnis recommends that one way to measure our projects and rank our preferences is to look at them backwards from the time of our death. We should not bounce from one project to another; nor be easily distracted. We should choose our priorities and values carefully, reflecting upon what we want to hold onto and what new course we want to follow; and we must always conscientiously be on the lookout for decisions that destroy one or more of the seven basic goods.[72]

Like other traditional natural law theorists, Finnis also posits the inherent and stable social nature of mankind. But he does not contrast the individual and individual self-interest against a 'community' or 'society', which he regards as unfruitful abstractions. Rather, the individual interacts with many different specific groups and associations simultaneously. We are born as members of a group, our relatives, bonded together through sexual intercourse and inherited traits, sharing the same foods and dinner-table stories. Our schooling brings together another level of associations and friendships. But if these local associations are to be nurturing and promote personal flourishing, they must be free from the requirement of "unremitting toil by all of its members for material necessities." So, the primary community, the family, requires assistance from a body politic and from its laws, and this can be accomplished only if the body politic shares the same aims and values, comprising the common good, as the human groups it supports. This common good, however, is not a generalized 'public interest' in the sense that the members all have the same set of values and objectives, but the promotion of conditions that allows members to attain their own life-plans.[73]

With these preliminaries out of the way, Finnis is now prepared to set out his natural law jurisprudence. He rejects Hart's view of justice –'Treat like cases alike and different cases differently' – which still opens the door to torture in the well formulated and implemented legal regimen. Nor is

---

[71] Ibid., 86-90, 97.

[72] Ibid., 104-127.

[73] Ibid., 136-37, 141-45, 148, 152, 156.

justice something that could be spoken of from the high-altitude perspective as a general theory of justice. Instead, justice must operate on the personal level as facilitating and achieving the objectives of the seven basic goods in my life-plan. By contrast, experiencing injustice presents an obstacle to the effectiveness of practical reasoning in constructing that plan. Justice as fairness based on a mere quantitative equality in the distribution of resources does not achieve real justice, he argues:

> If redistribution means no more than that more beer is going to be consumed morosely before television sets by the relatively many, and less fine wine consumed by the relatively few at salon concerts by select musicians, then it can scarcely be said to be a demand of justice. But if redistribution means that, at the expense of the wine, etc., more people can be preserved from (non-self-inflicted) illness, educated to the point where genuine self-direction becomes possible for them, defended against the enemies of justice etc. then such redistribution is a requirement of justice.[74]

Proponents of distributive justice, in other words, must keep in mind that their aim is individual human flourishing not the flourishing of some over others, as in utilitarianism. Their purpose must be to incentivize flourishing not stifle it. The new motto should be: 'Each person counts for one and only one'. Distribution must be tailored to individual need and measured by individual merit and potential.[75]

Authority in the Finnis natural law system is not based on an *a priori* view that some must lead and others follow. It is based on a need to coordinate life plans among many striving individuals. Even a society of intelligent and motivated strivers could not flourish without compromise and some form of dispute resolution. Natural resources do not naturally distribute themselves among a population. Even a resource like breathable air requires monitoring and regulation under certain conditions (pollution). In addition, coordination of individual life activities and plans cannot be achieved as a practical matter by unanimous consent even if it were easy to get and keep. There are too many details of individual life to be accounted for. Nor can reliance on customary practices work effectively to enhance individual

---

[74] Finnis, *Natural Law*, 174.

[75] Ibid., 176-77.

flourishing. Only concentrated authority in some person or group, Finnis argues, will meet the needs of an energetic and inventive people. How this is to be done is an empirical question for political science. Whether one person rules or an assembly rules by unanimous consent what is critical is that the rest of the community as well as the assembly members themselves accept the rules as authoritative and feel obligated to follow them.[76]

What we call 'law' under this system is not a system of sanctions, a 'legal' justification for punishment, for 'breaking' the law, but a creative process of clarifying and resolving coordination issues that invariably arise in the flow of social life. A regime of law would be necessary even in a community of saints, Finnis maintains. Natural law theory, then, is built upon the concept of a person as a striver for personal flourishing, an individual seeking fulfillment through the use of empirically-based practical reasoning. So, natural law jurisprudence must be person centered: "Individuals can only be *selves* . . . if they are not made to live their lives for the convenience of others but are allowed and assisted to create a subsisting identity across a 'lifetime'." Finnis does not contemplate a community in which every member is willing to 'forgive all trespassers'. Such an utterly selfless community would have little need for punishment (retributive justice) because nobody would demand it. All would be forgiven all the time. At the same time, a community of unreflective selfish and possessive individuals requires an impersonal system of general public laws, with all of the inevitable problems of aligning justice, authority, and the punishment for the crime.[77]

So far, Finnis' hyper-rationalist natural law viewpoint takes us only so far. Individuals emerge from families and grow up in small networks of people. But their flourishing depends on conditions in a larger world that predates their families and exerts continuing pressure over their opportunities. Asking political science to sort out coordination problems would seem to work only if political scientists and economists were brilliant self-less technocrats, fixing all bridges, squelching all corruption, and providing mental-health care before damage is done. This kind of

---

[76] Ibid., 232-33, 245, 252-53.

[77] Ibid., 269, 272, 351.

high proficiency is not within the Finnis viewpoint, however. Human life, he also tells us, is deeply infected with contingency. We age and die; many of our relatives and friends also drift away and die. Aches and pains, and sickness overhang the life process throughout. When sacrifices are called for the question arises: toward what end in the grand scheme of things is all this striving and how durable is flourishing if and when it is achieved? In response, Finnis seems to think that just as the mind must posit rationality when it attempts to reject rationality, so also when we question our capacity to live meaningful and flourishing lives, we are also implicating our philosophical and theological traditions of natural law that oppose despair and provide hope that viability and even flourishing are still possible.[78]

To strengthen the influence of natural law jurisprudence on daily life, Finnis applies what he calls the *principle of subsidiarity* as a guiding presumption that "it is unjust for a higher authority to usurp the self-governing authority that lower authorities, acting in the service of their own members (groups and persons), rightly have over those members." This principle, he says, does not preclude regulation by state law to prevent concrete injustices to vulnerable individuals, but clearly only on a case-by-case and not policy basis. Thus the natural place for the growing individual is within a family surrounded by relatives and friends, and any policy that erodes that nurturing infrastructure produces injustice. Families typically ask for the common good of their members; they share assets, experiences, and guidance. But families may also be stifling and may "emaciate" the free development of some of their members.[79] Clearly, any political philosophy that sees the state as a protector of individuals against *any* associations, whether families, religious bodies, trade unions, or capitalist enterprises, cuts to the heart of the subsidiarity principle and is more likely than not to produce injustice, Finnis is saying. Any disruption or dislocation of family life violates the principle, including common capitalist practices such as downsizing, relocation to cheaper labor markets, predatory lending, and stock manipulations.

---

[78] Ibid., 372-73, 378-88, 398-403.

[79] John Finnis, "Subsidiarity's Roots and History: Some Observations," *The American Journal of Jurisprudence* 61 (2016): 133-41.

Looked at from a natural law perspective, some rulings in American courts may be seen as secular subsidiarity violations of private family life. For example: courts have held that Jehovah's Witnesses could not withhold blood transfusions on religious grounds. In those cases parents unsuccessfully argued that they had natural law rights over their children that no state could contravene;[80] or in some child custody cases, where a mother essentially abandons her child for others to raise and then some years later unsuccessfully wants the child back, her plea to assert her parental natural law rights may be overridden by the rule that the best interests of the child staying with adoptive parents are weightier.[81] Natural law theory has often been at the center of many controversies in recent years involving contraception, abortion, the rights of transgender individuals, and same-sex marriage. In many cases the argument is made that these disputes are predicated on behavior that is contrary to natural law. For example, the elements of the traditional institution of marriage, including promises of monogamy and lifetime commitments, are only meaningful, according to Finnis, if marital sex is given its original generative purpose. "No sex act can be marital unless it not only expresses the spouses' commitment in friendship but also is of a generative kind," he writes.[82] Sexual relations outside of marriage, then, would be a perversion of the natural purpose of marriage; so would be the use of contraception in marriage and even more so acts of abortion.[83]

How well does flourishing theory follow the natural *law* tradition? Is it really a natural law theory at all? It seems to modulate between two apparently irreconcilable positions. On the one hand, as natural law it claims to be grounded in a long intellectual tradition over many centuries,

---

[80] For example, *Morrison v. State*, 252 S.W.2d 97 (1952), where the court argued that the state was no less a natural creation than the family.

[81] *Stout v. Massie*, 140 W. Va. 731 (1955).

[82] John Finnis, "Natural Law: The Classical Tradition," in Jules Coleman and Scott Shapiro, eds., *The Oxford Handbook of Jurisprudence and Philosophy of Law* (Oxford: Oxford University Press, 2002), 42.

[83] See John Finnis, "Marriage: A Basic and Exigent Good," *The Monist* 91 (2008): 388-406; John Finnis, "Abortion, Natural Law, and Public Reason," in Robert P. George and Christopher Wolfe, eds., *Natural Law and Public Reason* (Washington D.C.: Georgetown University Press, 2000) 75-105.

recognized by Plato, Aristotle, Cicero, the authors of the Ten Commandments, Medieval scholastics, and the appeals to conscience and 'the light of reason' by enlightenment *philosophes*. Unanimity of insight, then, counts in favor of the theory. On the other hand, there is also pervasive and widespread disagreement about the basic ingredients of a Finnis-style natural law over many cultures and periods, especially during the scientific era of the past two centuries. Also rubbing against the grain of natural law theory are the economic doctrines of *laissez faire* capitalism and the political doctrines of inclusive liberal pluralism. Liberty and pleasure are not central to his theory, and yet widely acknowledged to be goods at least in the West. Knowledge is a basic good, yet some natural law proponents argue that public reason should include the opinions of people who are not in the best position to give good reasons for their beliefs, people who rely on culture and tradition and who resist change.[84] Also, natural law theory does not have a monopoly on the inventory of basic goods. Many other lists have been compiled by philosophers not within a natural law tradition, values that include bodily integrity, affiliation with other species, environmental concerns, leisure, hedonism, gender equality, and material well-being – all values that are difficult to fit into the natural-law scheme of things.[85] Other criticisms from a common law perspective will be discussed in the next chapter.

---

[84] Robert P George and Christopher Wolfe, "Natural Law and Public Reason," in *Natural Law and Public Reason*, 51-74.

[85] See Sabina Alkire, "The Basic Dimensions of Human Flourishing: a Comparison of Accounts," in Nigel Biggar and Rufus Black, eds., *The Revival of Natural Law: Philosophical, Theological and Ethical Responses to the Finnis-Grisez School* (Burlington: Ashgate, 2000), 73-110. Also, in the same volume see Michael Northcott, "The Moral Standing of Nature and the New Natural Law," 262-281.

Part Two: Method

CHAPTER 3

COMMON LAW AND STATUTORY LAW

Introduction

In the Anglo-American tradition laws may derive from one of two sources – from the legislature in the form of statutes and from the courts in the form of judicial opinions. Administrative bodies tasked with the articulation of rules interpreting statutes may also be thought of as sources of law, though their authority to illustrate what a statute means or refers to has been questioned. The 'common law' usually refers to the rulings and opinions of judges compiled sequentially and organized by jurisdiction. This 'body of law' is then scrutinized for patterns and theories, whether those are presented by judges themselves or by lawyers who seek to draw out from the opinions, implications helpful to their cause. The common law, then, is a continual churning and digesting of this ever-growing body of law. Legal scholars and lawyers dissect the corpus of legal opinions to identify topics, patterns, and techniques of legal reasoning, as well as explanations and rationalizations used by the judiciary to render its opinion. Statutory law, on the other hand, is drafted, enacted, amended, and either sunsetted or abolished by legislatures.

Common law and statutory law both are subject to interpretation by their creators in the process of getting to their specific legal result, the final judicial ruling or final draft of the statute. Both may be seen as methods by which the principles of jurisprudence and judicial philosophy are made to directly influence human habits and actions. In a system of divided government, the legislature and the judiciary are usually authorized to be a check on each other. Legislatures can determine the scope of jurisdiction of the judiciary and may create or abolish court systems. Judiciaries can determine the legality and constitutionality of the statutes within its jurisdiction. Statutes come and go as legislatures so determine. Legislatures also authorize externally created systems of rules assembled as organized

Codes (e.g., the Uniform Commercial Code or the Uniform Partnership Act), while judiciaries authorize the creation of procedural or evidentiary rules for the court system, which may or may not be themselves authorized or amended by fiat of a legislature (e.g., Rules of Civil Procedure or Rules of Evidence). The Administrative Procedure Act was enacted by Congress in 1946 to provide a roadmap for determining how regulations implementing statutes are created and given legitimacy. Legislatures may also adopt in whole cloth the common law of their jurisdiction, or they may adopt pieces of it. Clearly, the common law and statutory law do not exist in separate realms. Rather they may be looked upon as separate methods for effectuating values, such as economic efficiency or the proper public order, of the strongest political will at the time. Political will does not reside only in the legislative branch of government. It is reflected in the controversies surrounding the selection of judges at all levels of government. In some states, judges are chosen in partisan elections; in others, in putatively non-partisan elections, still others by judicial commissions, or appointed by the legislature or governor. The common law and statutory law comprise a multi-dimensional web of reciprocal influences pushing on each other to achieve some semblance of social equilibrium. There is no timeless formula or method for establishing the priority of one over the other; both are subject to the political winds that influence the creation of government generally.

Holmes and the Common Law

Oliver Wendell Holmes Jr. (1841-1935) was a Harvard Law Professor, legal commentator, state judge, and Supreme Court Justice. In many ways, he may be thought of a philosopher of law because he approached law not as a fixed system of authoritative rules but as a mode of human adaptation. Laws, first and foremost, were problem-solving techniques, and the only real question, for him, was whether they were doing a good job or not. To get a good idea of how he approached the law, consider a short article he published in 1918 in the *Harvard Law Review*, entitled "Natural Law." He began the article this way: "It is not enough for the knight of romance that you agree that his lady is a very nice girl – if you do not admit that she is the best that God ever made or will make, you must fight. There is in all men a demand for the superlative . . . ." What he is saying is that we have a very strong tendency to believe that our judgments are absolutely the correct ones; and that once we find the solution to a problem, we believe that solution is the best one possible. He goes on to say "certitude is not the test of certainty," meaning that our mental embrace of a solution is not the test of its certainty. "The jurists who believe in natural law," he continued, "seem to me to be in that naïve state of mind that accepts what has been familiar and accepted by them and their neighbors as something that must be accepted by all men everywhere."[1] At the time he dashed off the essay he was an Associate Justice of the U.S. Supreme Court and had already a long and illustrious career in jurisprudence in the lower courts. He fought in some of the bloodiest battles of the Civil War and was wounded several times. He was on the Massachusetts Supreme Court for twenty years before going on to the United States Supreme Court in 1902 and remained there for the next thirty years.

Holmes was exposed to the philosophy of pragmatism being advanced at the time by his friends, the philosophers Charles S. Peirce and William James. A central idea of their philosophy was that experience, language, and truth claims do not seamlessly work together; each is a prism that distorts reality to some degree. Experience is colored by memory and emotion; language is an historical tool freighted with prior use and misuse, while truth claims are typically constructed out of some uncriticized inferences and some direct experiences; and all three are continually shot through with continued doses of interpretation. Although we may express something as a superlative, as 'the best ever' or 'the most beautiful' or as 'a fundamental good', we only do so on the basis of our particular experiences and ways of thinking. We are not born with a truth- seeking faculty and an unerring way of using it correctly, a pragmatist typically argues. No matter how wonderful it seems to identify the object of a superlative, we are only describing our own feelings of certainty and deliberately excluding troubling counterexamples. Holmes looked at law in the same way. Law operates through a dense and technical expression of written language; it cannot be conducted without it. Lawyers and judges, like philosophers, are continually engaged in modifying language and adding to its vocabulary in order to accomplish their purpose. For Holmes that purpose is to

---

[1] *Natural Law,* 32 Harv. L. Rev. 40-41 (1918).

harmonize as best as possible the interest of individuals with the larger society around them. So, when he says that "property, friendship, and truth have a common root in time" he is saying that our legal concepts, our social relations, and our securest beliefs all arise from our social interactions and particular experiences – all operating within the constraints of our language and prevailing customs.[2]

One of his early projects was to compile and analyze cases for the updated editions of Chancellor James Kent's *Commentaries on American Law.* Kent (1763-1847) could be thought of as the American equivalent of the great English jurist, Sir William Blackstone (1723-1780). Both wrote voluminous legal 'commentaries', grouping judicial rulings by subject matter and then commenting on what they meant, and what their precedents and latest trends were. Kent's commentaries began in 1826, when American courts were still relying on the common law of England. As legal opinions flowed out of the court system, Holmes would read them and try to understand what judges were trying to accomplish in their rulings against the background of the analysis initially provided by Kent.

Various strains of legal theory ran through Holmes's ideas during his lifetime.[3] Some found him to be a social Darwinian, where the function of law was to protect the status of the successful and well-off. Others thought him a free market capitalist where the resolution of cases was often resolvable into a question of how to preserve as much existing wealth as possible. And some thought him to be a legal positivist in the tradition of John Austin. Often the case before him as a judge would be determined by the jurisprudence he selected at various periods of his life. As a result, Holmes was a hard jurist to pin down philosophically. But there is an overarching theme he derived from his interest in systematic German philosophical and legal thought: that law is a human activity as old as the human race itself and that it cries out for some kind of deeper theory of why it takes shape the way it does in different eras and cultures. When he

---

[2] Ibid., 40.

[3] For a brief overview of the various strains of Holmes's legal thought see Michael H. Hoffheimer, *Justice Holmes and the Natural Law* (New York: Garland Publishing, 1992), 3-26.

wrote his early paper, *The Common Law* in 1881 the influence of Austin is clearly evident in his idea that law is the way a community decides what its values should be whether or not they are objectively right or wrong. So, different standards of liability became applied throughout history simply because of changes in the standards of socially acceptable behavior. Consider the harm to property or life caused by animals. At one time animals were thought to be at fault for their 'bad' behavior and were punished accordingly. Later that notion was rejected, and fault was transferred to the person who had the greatest ability to control the problem in the future, usually the animal's owner. Eventually, the general rule emerged that fault for causing harm should be placed on those in the best position to reduce future causes of that harm. That was but a variation of a deeper and harsher rule that Holmes formulated as a result of his Civil War experience: that every society would willingly sacrifice its members if it believed its survival was at stake. In law this rule is formulated as: "Public policy sacrifices the individual to the general good."[4]

As an example of Holmes's approach, consider the long-held practice of paying the laborer after work has been performed rather before it commences. There is no other rationale for this rule other than a customary assessment about the trustworthiness of individuals, how risk should be allocated, and which party had the greater bargaining power. So, workers get paid after work is done because of the risk they may abscond and because the employer has greater bargaining power in negotiating a labor contract. Legal norms are usually evidence of such risk assessments and the many minute choices a community decides are worthy enough to ripen into custom and then into law. A society may choose from a variety of legal norms in developing its jurisprudence. It may decide to punish a wrongdoer for inflicting physical injury in different ways, calling one 'criminal' and another 'civil' and may select from a variety of various degrees of punishment. It may decide to characterize some injuries as 'breaches of contract' and decide to punish them sometimes with restitution, sometimes requiring the contract be fully performed and all consequential damages paid by the party at fault, and sometimes by allowing the party at fault to pay a monetary penalty. All of this was a far cry from old notions of paying for one's sin, especially for

---

[4] Oliver Wendell Homes Jr., *The Common Law* (Boston: Little, Brown, 1881), 48.

evil intentions. There was no point to trying to design a legal system based on eternal principles of justice or unerring intuitions, he thought. Law was always fully what it is when the legislators formulate a law to solve a legal problem before them, and then judges implement it according to their judgment that the solution works or must be modified. The legal enterprise, in other words, from start to finish is an empirical enterprise of social problem solving:

> All law is directed to conditions of things manifest to the senses. And whether it brings those conditions to pass immediately by the use of force, as when it protects a house from a mob by soldiers, or appropriates private property to public use, or hangs a man in pursuance of a judicial sentence, or whether it brings them about mediately through men's fears, its object is equally an external result.[5]

For Holmes, there is no legally meaningful category of a 'bad' law, only laws that fail to achieve their intended purpose. He was aware that moral phraseology permeated law, with notions like *fault* and *obligation* and *breach of trust*, but these were not additional standards that could be clearly applied as if from a higher court. They were just factual indications of the moral values embraced by those in charge of the law system in their specific culture.

In this spirit, Holmes wrote "The Path of the Law" (1897) to "dispel a confusion between morality and law." Law does the work, he argued, not of conveying moral values but of exerting "public force" directly over human action.[6] The function of an attorney, then, is to make sure that his client does not feel too much of that force, unless the attorney represented the public, in which case the attorney wanted the defendant to feel the fullest extent of it. So, a good attorney had to be a good predictor of what judges would actually do, given their temperament, experience, and prior rulings, rather than what they ought to do in some ideal world. That is how clients are properly served, according to Holmes. But once the practical objectives of law had been revealed, it became possible to think of future law as a shaper of future consequences. Law could become an aggressive vehicle for reform. Holmes's used his platform as editor of *The American*

---

[5] Ibid., 49.

[6] Oliver Wendell Holmes, Jr., *The Path of the Law,* 10 Harv. L. Rev. 457, 459 (1897).

Law Review, started in 1866, to begin his modernization of American law.[7] "I look forward to a time," he wrote, "when the part played by history and the explanation of dogma shall be very small, and instead of ingenious research we shall spend our energy on a study of the ends sought to be attained and the reasons for desiring them. As a step toward that ideal it seems to me that every lawyer ought to seek an understanding of economics."[8]

Holmes had been interested in the way law interacts with social status and class for many years. Before he wrote *The Common Law* he penned a brief note on the strike of 'gas stokers' in London in 1872.[9] Gas stoking kept the street gas lanterns lit at night, presenting the question of how far the public and its court system should go to sacrifice the health and well-being of a few workers in grueling labor for the safety of the community. This was the question stimulated in Holmes's mind by an account of the strike by a British barrister at the time, Henry Crompton (1836-1904).[10] Historically, under British labor law every strike was unlawful as a breach of contract between employer and employee. That law was changed to allow peaceful strikes, with a maximum penalty of three months in prison for violent or threatening striking. Thinking they had the protection of the express statutory provisions of the law recently passed by Parliament four hundred gas stokers conducted a peaceful strike. However, four were arrested and convicted of *common law* (not statutory) conspiracy to attempt to influence adversely the mind of the company owner and each was sentenced to one year at hard labor. With the prospects of the streets being lit at night London newspapers and the general public cheered. Legal scholars and reformers were aghast: a small statutory fine is imposed if one person litters, but if two agree to litter they could receive up to two years in prison with hard labor. Crompton argued that, as a general rule, laws affecting the

---

[7] See for example, *Codes and the Arrangement of the Law,* 5 Am. L. Rev. 1 (1870); *The Arrangement of Law: Privity,* 7Am. L. Rev. 46 (1872); *The Theory of Torts,* 7 Am. L. Rev. 652 (1872-1873); and an essay from one of his colleagues, Nicolas St. John Green, *Proximate and Remote Cause,* 4 Am. L. Rev. 14 (1870).

[8] "Path of the Law," 474.

[9] Anonymous Note (Holmes), *Great Britain,* 7 Am. L. Rev. 582 (July, 1873).

[10] Henry Crompton, "Class Legislation," *Fortnightly Review* 13 (February 1873): 205.

upper classes carefully restricted a court's ability to impose penalties, while laws affecting the working-class gave courts wide latitude to impose severe penalties. In the gas stokers' prosecutions, courts had continued that practice even though the statutes passed by Parliament explicitly restricted the penalties. "Is it not the most serious thing when over 600,000 of the best workmen, scattered throughout England, believe that the laws are unjust and that the judges are partial," he asked.[11] Crompton gave other examples of inconsistent legislation: laws involving fraudulent transfers of property, bribery, or adulterating food for sale, in other words, laws affecting the upper classes, were penalized with a light hand, whereas penalties for gambling, vagrancy, or work stoppages were treated as severe criminal offenses. This was "class legislation" at its worst, he argued. The result of such laws, he said, was simply to increase the disadvantage of the disadvantaged. Crompton's solution was to abolish labor laws except those regulating the employment of children and women and let the labor market adjust wages by supply and demand. Instead of using penal laws to motivate workers, labor contracts should be bargained for without restraints on labor. For example, when demand for labor is high workers should have an opportunity to sell their labor on a piece-work or daily basis so as to be free to find employers who will pay more. If workers are as unreliable as employers claim, he argued, they should not be hired in the first place. But if we are to have labor laws they should be applied and sanctioned uniformly.

Such was Crompton's argument, which Holmes thought fascinating but also containing some unsound notions of law. He agreed with Crompton in opposing a legal theory based on social Darwinism, i.e., the view that laws which disadvantage the already disadvantaged provide hard medicine but also improve society in the long run by producing grateful efficient workers who want to better themselves. We should expect, Holmes remarked, that the powerful would use a legal system to maintain their power and wealth, even if inefficiency results. What particularly annoyed him was the moral posture of both sides of the debate; each gave a moral slant to what was blatantly and simply a matter of economic class warfare. The rich justify their laws using social Darwinism; reformists

[11] Ibid., 207.

appeal to egalitarian principles of social justice. In reality, what was really at issue, he argued, was a blatant "struggle for life" over scarce resources, in which all parties seek to maximize their own interests by gaining better control of those resources. Those at the top make the laws and there is no other justification than that they have the power to do so. If there is a formula to be followed, he suggested, it is this: "All that can be expected from modern improvements is that legislation should easily and quickly, yet not too quickly, modify itself in accordance with the will of the *de facto* supreme power in the community, and that the spread of an educated sympathy should reduce the sacrifice of minorities to a minimum."[12] Besides seeking greater political power, the disadvantaged classes should turn to the courts for legal reform, Holmes advised. Judges are confronted on a daily basis with the detailed factual circumstances statutes are devised to control, while no body of legislators could fully anticipate the consequences of their legislation.

Holmes's Legacy

While on the Massachusetts Supreme Court, Holmes announced several rulings that have had long-standing impact. One involved freedom of the press, specifically the freedom of reporters and the general public to go into court houses to inspect the files of cases currently or previously under consideration. However, court records, particularly in cases like divorce or embezzlement, often contain information damaging to the reputation of some of the parties. So, should newspapers be subject to libel suits when they report information filed in these cases? Should all court records be sealed, as they are under special circumstances (as in juvenile cases)? If court records are public records, why should a newspaper be subject to libel for printing something any member of the general public can go to see at the courthouse? Holmes thought the best solution was to keep courthouses open to the general public, in spite of the potential for abuse, in order to engender public confidence in the administration of justice. "It was of vast importance to the public that the proceedings of courts of justice should be universally known," he argued.[13] Public scrutiny was a check upon possible

---

[12] "Great Britain," 583.

[13] *Cowley v. Pulsifer*, 137 Mass. 392 (1884).

political corruption if court proceedings were to be closed on a routine basis. In this case, the court had to balance personal privacy against the public access. Holmes reconfigured the issue as one between potential corruption and public's right to discover it. He asked: what is the policy the law in question encourages and what should it be?

When there is a dispute in court where both sides have meritorious arguments, Holmes looked to issues of public policy to determine which party should prevail. This does not mean that the judge has the final word on what the policy should be. It does mean that by expressly articulating policy alternatives, other judges, and then legislators, would articulate their own policy views and make the necessary adjustments to the law if needed. In this way the creation and interpretation of laws could become smarter and more open to public debate. Here are some policy rules Holmes favored while serving on the Massachusetts Supreme Court.

(1) When newspapers make damaging statements about individuals either deliberately or inadvertently and present them as facts, especially if they specifically vouch for them as true, they are liable to those individuals since the power of newspapers over public opinion creates a duty to diligently investigate and present the truth. So, newspapers, especially of wide circulation, must be circumspect when they publish derogatory information about individuals even if they do so without intending to harm anyone. They are like a person who shoots a gun into a crowd and then claims he is not at fault because he never intended to harm the person actually shot. Holmes's analysis here favored privacy over public knowledge, but subsequent Supreme Court cases changed the policy to protect the free speech of newspapers when they print falsehoods about public figures, unless they deliberately or recklessly do so.[14]

(2) When workers striking peacefully in public for a nine-hour day and higher wages are arrested, the law is simply punishing them for doing what the Constitution allows: exercising a right of free speech and

---

[14] *Burt v. Advertiser Newspaper Co.*, 154 Mass. 238 (1891); *Hanson v. Globe Newspaper Co.*, 159 Mass. 293 (Holmes dissenting). *New York Times Co. v. Sullivan*, 376 U.S. 254 (1964), *Curtis Publishing Co. v. Butts*, 388 U.S. 130 (1967).

assembly. The employer argued that the strike was injuring the operations and reputation of the business. Yet, Holmes points out, the law frequently permits injuries from purely passive behavior as when it allows someone to start a business even though it could injure other businesses, or when a large business lowers prices to drive out smaller ones. So, echoing his thoughts about the Gas-Stokers strike, he argued that disputes between business and labor really come down to "considerations of policy and of social advantage." On those grounds the law permits free competition among businesses because it is thought that the benefit of free competition exceeds the costs of destroying less competitive ones. Hence, the same standard should be used in the case of strikes. Strikers ought to be able to present their grievances to the general public on the public streets even if their employer's business may be injured. And strikers ought to be able to organize into unions for collective advantage just as businesses do, Holmes argued.[15]

(3) When someone builds a fire bomb and drives with it to within a quarter mile from the building to be bombed and then decides not to go through with the plan and turns away, is he guilty of attempted arson? In this case Holmes wanted to know whether the defendant was "near enough" to the building, when he turned away, to be guilty. He tells us that the word 'attempt' "suggests an act seemingly sufficient to accomplish the end." In other words, to call something an attempt begs the question of whether or not an actual attempt has really taken place. Is just getting up in the morning, he asked, an act taken in furtherance of the attempt? Drafting a law against 'attempt' tells us nothing about the standard that must be used to determine when an attempt is underway and when it has been renounced. Only judges are able to determine, on the facts before them presented in court, where to draw the line. No statute could provide a rule in sufficient detail to resolve this borderline issue.[16]

(4) Spoken or written words are themselves actions with legal consequence in certain contexts, such as taking oaths, issuing military commands or acknowledging obedience to them, mutually promising certain

---

[15] *Vegelahn v. Gunther*, 167 Mass. 92 (1896).

[16] *Commonwealth v. Peaslee*, 177 Mass 267 (1901).

commitments in wedding ceremonies, making agreements by shaking hands (a form of linguistic behavior). But when is speech a form of action that may be punished by law? Is a wish a form of incitement under certain circumstances? These questions cannot be answered without interpretation of the context identifying speaker, listener, and purpose. I cannot marry the bridesmaid if I say "I do" privately intending her. I cannot issue a command if I am not a superior officer. These context issues arose in a series of cases involving speech and dissent during World War I. At that time Congress passed a series of laws designed to strengthen national resolve by identifying and incarcerating opponents of the war, including the Espionage Act of 1917 and the 1918 Sedition Act. These Acts prohibited conveying false statements with an intent to interfere with military operations, promoting the success of enemies, attempting to cause insubordination among military forces, willfully obstructing the recruitment or enlistment into military service, or, in the case of the Sedition Act, prohibiting "disloyal, profane, scurrilous or abusive language about the Constitution . . . or the military or naval services, . . . the flag, . . . or the uniform of the Army or Navy." Twenty-seven socialist farmers from South Dakota who opposed the war were convicted and sentenced for up to five years in prison. Their actions consisted of petitioning the governor, who administered the draft, to call a referendum on the draft, equalize draft quotas for each county, not count volunteers in the quotas, and oppose the use of bonds to fund the war. The Supreme Court upheld the convictions, but Holmes dissented, arguing "from beginning to end the changes advocated are changes by law, not a resistance to it, the only threat being that which every citizen may utter, that if his wishes are not followed his vote will be lost." He gave two conditions under which convictions would be proper: if the communications to the governor had been aggressively propagated to the general public and if there was a sufficient wartime emergency to stifle all opposition no matter its merits. Given the almost unlimited power of government officials in cases such as this, he argued, under current conditions it is better as a policy matter to permit disruptive speech than stifle dissent.[17]

---

[17] Holmes's dissent may be found in Ronald K. L. Collins, ed., *The Fundamental Holmes: A Free Speech Chronicle and Reader* (Cambridge: Cambridge University Press,

The Interplay of Common Law and Statutory Law

The common law tradition involves a continual interaction between courts and legislatures. As Holmes's career illustrated, judges must confront hard cases brought before them. They must decide what is the exception and what is the rule. Beside examining the policy implications of a statute, common-law courts will examine whether the statute should apply to the facts of the case before them. To do this they mut look closely at the meaning the words used in the statute itself. For example, in1880 Congress passed a law prohibiting the importation of foreign labor under contract to work for a domestic corporation. The Alien Contract Labor Law prohibited "the importation and migration of foreigners and aliens under contract or agreement to perform labor or service of any kind in the United States, its territories, and the District of Columbia."[18] This prohibition seemed to be violated when a church in New York City hired an English cleric to be its rector and pastor. In arriving at its ruling that pastors were not intended by Congress to be included in the definition of laborers or service provides, a unanimous Supreme Court noted:

> It is a familiar rule that a thing may be within the letter of the statute and yet not within the statute because not within its spirit nor within the intention of its makers. This has been often asserted, and the reports are full of cases illustrating its application. This is not the substitution of the will of the judge for that of the legislator, for frequently words of general meaning are used in a statute, words broad enough to include an act in question, and yet a consideration of the whole legislation, or of the circumstances surrounding its enactment, or of the absurd results which follow from giving such broad meaning to the words, makes it unreasonable to believe that the legislator intended to include the particular act.

Note that the court's ruling here was not based on identifying an idiosyncratic interpretation of the words, 'labor' or 'service', in the statute, but of rejecting any interpretation whatsoever. Instead, the court referred

---

2010), 206-207, 216-217. The case, *Baltzer v. United States*, 248 U.S. 593 (1918), favored conviction by a 7-2 margin. However, neither the majority nor dissenting opinions were published, as the case was sent back to the lower court for a new trial.

[18] 23 Stat. 332 (1885).

to the 'spirit' behind the words and the firm conviction that if Congress had passed a law specifically penalizing the hiring of clerics from abroad it would not have received a single vote.[19]

Another interesting case illustrating the interplay of common law and statutory law, involved the death of a stevedore working in New York Harbor onboard a ship owned by his employer, an interstate railroad company. The employer argued that the Federal Employers' Liability Act (1908), which compensated railroad workers for injuries on the job, did not apply because the death occurred while unloading cargo, and the state workmen's compensation law did not either because only federal law applies to harbors. Here, the scheme of federal statutes regarding railroads and harbors left a gap in insurance coverage and so the employee's surviving family was not eligible for compensation for his death. A Supreme Court majority agreed with the employer's position, noting that by its specific wording the federal law covering workplace injuries on interstate carriers did not apply in this case because the employee was not directly working on the railroad when he was killed. The federal liability law required a "direct and substantial connection with railroad operations, and not with another kind of carriage recognized as separate and distinct from transportation on land."[20] The court majority recognized that the federal law governing harbors and sea going vessels applied to the work of stevedores. However, that law did not provide compensation for the worker's family. The majority also determined that the work of a stevedore is maritime in its nature, and although courts have required employers to pay for injuries to seamen on the high seas, they have never required compensation for their families.

Holmes dissented, arguing instead that the common law of maritime commerce is not a fixed body of law that cannot be revised except by legislation. He cited instances where *state* laws were accepted to govern injuries between seamen and their employers on the high seas. Maritime law is of murky origins, he argued, consisting of an ongoing history of practices and customs, upon which seamen and shippers have relied for

---

[19] *Church of the Holy Trinity v. United States*, 143 U.S. 457, 459, 472 (1892).
[20] *Southern Pacific Co. v. Jensen*, 244 U.S. 205, 213 (1917).

centuries. It has been the practice in the United States, as it was in England, to continually supplement maritime law as new problems and issues arise; besides, Congress has not explicitly outlawed the state compensation law in this case. Hence, it is not a gratuitous judicial action to allow New York's compensation law to apply here. Maritime law, as a common law system, is not undermined when it adapts itself to state statutory remedies that are closely linked to interstate commerce, Holmes argued, because,

> the common law is not a brooding omnipresence in the sky, but the articulate voice of some sovereign or quasi-sovereign that can be identified . . . It always is the law of some state, and if the district courts adopt the common law of torts, as they have shown a tendency to do, they thereby assume that a law not of maritime origin, and deriving its authority in that territory only from some particular state of this Union, also governs maritime torts in that territory, . . .[21]

Here Holmes argues that since the time of the nation's founding maritime law has been found to be wholly inadequate to an expanding nation and its increasingly complex transportation economy. States have been allowed to regulate the qualifications of harbor pilots as harbors filled up with shipping traffic, for example, and Congress has acquiesced by silence throughout this process.

Can Common Law and Statutory Law be Reconciled?

Legal Formalism and Legal Realism. In October 1917, Congress amended the Judiciary Act of 1789 to allow for compensating employees under state laws for death or injuries on the job in a maritime context. Rather than allow the courts to resolve the issue considered in *Jensen* by appealing to the common law, Congress asserted its statutory power and made the change itself. For Holmes this distinction did not matter as long as some source of authority made changes in the law necessary to solve emerging problems. But since Holmes left the bench a wider dispute over the relation between established principles of law, typically found in statutes, and the common law has emerged within jurisprudence. On the one side are those who argue that the reasoning behind court rulings must be based on reference

---

[21] Ibid., 222.

to some 'form' of legal content that can be identified as being within the body of law – content such as legal concepts and principles found in court rulings, the texts of statutes and Constitutions, and the texts of Treaties, Codes, and Procedural Rules if 'formally' adopted by law. [22] Excluded are 'informal' remarks by philosophers, law school professors, or even Supreme Court Justices when on the lecture circuit. Words expressed on a Twitter account by someone with legal executive authority, on the other hand, are deemed to be formal statements of law if the executive treats them as such. These are some of the ideas of *legal formalists,* so named because they imagine legal reasoning always as a deliberate collaborative and, more importantly, formal process involved in drafting, interpreting, and applying laws. In applying the law in courts, in judicial adjudications, the process involves deriving rulings from these various forms of law when applied to the facts of the case.

By contrast, the idea that laws and rules are *applied* to facts has been challenged as a vague and confusing misnomer at the heart of legal formalism. Every time a rule is successfully applied to facts those facts become incorporated into the meaning of the rule, either expanding or contracting it with reference to its prior or future applications. But there is never a tight fit between what the words mean when they are selected to make a law or legal opinion, and how they are used in applying the law subsequently to facts. At the same time, there is not a clear idea what the 'facts' of a case are. Only *relevant* facts should be considered in adjudication, but assessing relevance is both a legal process and a scientific one. Medical science, for example, is indispensable in a medical malpractice case. The same applies to assessing bodily injuries from air pollution. Before the legal system takes on the task of rectifying an injury there must be a judgment that the injury is serious enough to employ it. This judgment comes from outside the legal system, Holmes had argued, from the customs and morals of the community.[23] The articulation of 'public policy' is discoverable in law because it motivates its creation. Judges should, therefore, appeal to the values and interests of the public in deciding how to resolve a case. *Legal realism* is the view that judges ought to use the tradition of common law to

---

[22] See Frederick Schauer, *Formalism*, 97 Yale L.J. 509 (1988).

[23] "Path of the Law," 466.

modify the law when statutes no longer reflect the public interest or fail to account for new technological and economic developments.

Can these differing theories of law be reconciled? We must also ask: What kind of a dispute is this between differing theories of jurisprudence? In part it seems to be a dispute about the ways law ought to be influenced by public interests and values; and to the extent that there is dispute among these interests and values that division likely will be imported into a legal system as conflicting theories of law. The primary arena of dispute over interests and values is, of course, in the operations of government and the contests between political parties. A trend may be observed: political conservatives have tended to line up with various forms of legal formalism, while political liberals have tended to embrace the built-in pragmatism of the common-law approach. However, when theories of jurisprudence are looked at from an ideological perspective, they become merely tools for achieving political objectives. Conservative judges will employ the interpretive strategies of common law against statutes intended to achieve liberal aims; while liberal lawmakers will attempt to codify common law rulings if their legislative power allows.

Council of Revision. In the early days of the American republic, there was a recognition of the tension between statutes and the common law. This tension was aggravated by the separation of powers in the Executive, Legislative, and Judicial branches. A device was created in New York State for collaboration between the legislature and judiciary, called the *Council of Revision,* consisting of the Governor and various members of the state judiciary. The Council would work this way: Judges with knowledge of the constitution and common law history would provide their view of legislation in its drafting phase so that the final product would not be a sharp departure from precedent. (Although favored by James Madison, the Constitutional Convention (1787) rejected the formation of such a Council in federal courts, favoring instead the Presidential veto.) Had such an advisory practice continued throughout the American court system, the conflict between common law and statutory law may have diminished. Applied nationally, we might not have some states that permitted common law marriage and others not, nor states with different criteria for establishing such a marriage.

Administrative Agencies. Common law and statutory law come into conflict in the dispute over whether courts or administrative agencies are the best source of authority over the interpretation of how statutes should be applied. The Administrative Procedures Act (5 U.S.C. Sec. 551 et. seq,) establishes procedural rules for applying statutes to specific situations. The procedure includes public notice by an agency of proposed rules and an opportunity for the public to provide input to the agency (Sec. 553) regarding the impacts of the rules. The rationale for the APA is that laws as written do not, and could not, anticipate every situation where they may be reasonably applied and so it is the job of an agency with expertise in the area to make such decisions. That rationale is challenged by claiming that agencies will abuse their interpretive discretion and end up creating *de facto* new laws. When this dispute arrives in courts yet another dispute over rules arises, this time, whether courts should defer to agency rule-making because of agency expertise and because an agency, as part of the executive branch, is also tasked with carrying out the political policies of elected officials.[24] So, if there is an interpretative bias, the argument goes, it is legitimate political bias ultimately authorized by the electorate but only as long as it is reasonable. Agency political bias operates on a statute when its implications are favored in a politically advantageous way, again, but only within reasonable limits. A study of how federal agencies interpret statutes in Republican or Democratic administrations indicates that both parties will choose the interpretive scheme that produces the most advantageous policy consequences.[25] The study indicates that Republicans can be legal realists when it suits them, and Democrats can be legal formalists for the same reason.

Legal Rationalism. Casting common law and statutory law as a dual track process, and calling the distinction political in origin, however, does not make them anymore reconcilable. Another avenue may be possible, called for labeling purposes here *Legal Rationalism,* a view that legal reasoning must (1) reveal all of its critical premises, assumptions, and presuppositions, whether legal or factual; and (2) must assemble these

---

[24] *Chevron U.S.A., Inc. v. Nat. Res. Def. Council,* 467 U.S. 837 (1984).

[25] See Amy Semet, *An Empirical Examination of Agency Statutory Interpretation,* 103 Minn. L. Rev. 2257, 2316 (2019).

propositions into an argument in support of the conclusions reached. Legal rationalism might be looked at as a robust form of legal formalism, or as a rigorous form of legal realism. In plain speak, it means putting all your cards on the table. Revealing premises not only helps clarify an argument in a given case, it also sets up a contrast with previous rulings by the same or different (often deceased) judge. The virtue of consistency is satisfied not only when the same legal method of reasoning is followed, whether formalist or realist, but also when all of the factual premises are identified and reconciled within the given case and then among related cases.

A rationalist perspective regards the dichotomy between formalist and realist as overstating the differences in the legal philosophy of each. Lawmakers are politicians who by their nature are realists. They respond to the efforts of lobbyists and their constituents to correct social problems by drafting laws, with the final result being a statute or a collection of interrelated statutes. Judges are formalists because as judges they begin with a body of evidence: statutes, legislative history, oral testimony, documentary evidence, and a great body of interpretive law consisting of prior statutes and judicial opinions. Out of this inchoate mass of information they reconstruct what is presented into a sequential rational structure that supports a legal conclusion. At this point, realists may disagree with where the evidence and law take them. Supreme Court Justices may dissent or only partially agree, or the Court as a whole may decide to limit the damage by restricting its holding to the facts of this case alone. A trial judge may lessen or increase a sentence or fine in a criminal case, or monetary penalty in a civil case. But if the consequences are potentially weighty enough, as in hard cases, a trial judge may find a *rational* justification for articulating an implied right or obligation. In the case of *Riggs v. Palmer,* the New York court decided that the legislature never intended to allow a beneficiary to profit from his act of murder. But how far should courts and judges go in deciding what the *rational* course is? Perhaps, the greater departure from precedent or the plain meaning of a statute the greater the obligation to present weighty, indeed voluminous, factual evidence for a change of course, and then give legal reasons why. What statutes and common law have in common is that they both require the use of rules to draft or enforce them. Rules, in turn, cannot be divorced from identifying the purposes for which they were drafted; nor from the standards, like fairness and reasonableness, all legal actors assume the law will implement.[26]

The way the Constitution is written invites a process of legal rationalism. It is not written as an organized body of 'code law', with clear definitions of terms and short sequential sentences organized by topic and subtopic. Some passages require intensive textual interpretations and reference to surrounding norms and practices. For example, the document sets out the jurisdiction of the Supreme Court as an appellate court, except in certain enumerated kinds of cases where it serves as a trial court (Art. III, Sec. 2, cls.1 and 2). I cannot go to the Supreme Court to get a divorce or sue my neighbor for trespass. But I can go eventually to the Supreme Court if the laws of my state prohibit me from marrying someone of another race or religion. Yet, at the same time the Constitution provides that Congress may regulate the appellate jurisdiction of the Supreme Court: "the supreme court shall have appellate jurisdiction, both as to law and fact, with such exceptions, and under such regulations as the congress shall make" (Art III, Sec. 2, cl. 2). There have been many congressional efforts over the years to expand or reduce the kind of cases the court could hear and decide on, often with partisan political motivations. Legal scholars today debate the meaning of the 'exceptions and regulations' provision, some arguing that it was intended to come into play only after lower federal courts were created, and others that it was a blanket of power to Congress. Imagine if Congress denies to the Supreme Court the right to hear appeals of cases challenging a federal income tax assessment. Your only option might be: pay the tax or go to jail. Or, consider that the Constitution seems to assert a right of prisoners or detainees to appear in a public court room, except during invasion and rebellion, to challenge their detention through a 'writ of habeas corpus' (Art. I, Sec. 9, cl. 2). This provision was a tremendous improvement over a system favored by dictators that pulled somebody out of their homes in the middle of the night and secretly locked them away for good. But does this mean that Congress could not, if it wants, abolish that provision? Any answer to that question would require an elaborate argument involving textual analysis

---

[26] Brian Z. Tamanaha, *Beyond the Formalist-Realist Divide: The Role of Politics in Judging* (Princeton, N.J.: Princeton University Press, 2009), 189, 192.

and historical references, and in the end still would remain highly contested.

We are forced to deal with the Constitution because it is the fundamental law of the land. We must search for answers within its words and phrases, and because they do not very often provide ready answers, we are driven to create interpretive rules and theories to formulate and justify those answers. In the process, we are driven to confront our own social and moral values. Analyzing the *Jensen* case, we are confronted with the question of whether the deceased stevedore's family could be compensated for his death under existing state and federal law, and if not, should they be? The court was split 5-4 on these questions. Congress very soon thereafter amended the law to allow family members to be compensated. But then, we must deal with recognizing the moral consequences of not giving his family retroactive relief. Moral decisions, in any case, are unavoidable if a rational exercise of discretion is to be undertaken.[27] Although the focus in legal rationalism is largely on how judges answer hard cases, it applies also to lawmakers. Passing a law that says "No vehicles in the park" still requires a consideration whether a stroller or a moderately-sized radio-controlled toy car is a vehicle. The law implies a purpose and a purpose implies a value (peaceful enjoyment and reduced vigilance); and the word 'vehicle' implies a standard, as to size, speed, and noise. Recognizing these attributes of both lawmaking and judging, statutes and the common law, provides a basis for reconciliation.

In the following chapter, these differences between formalism, realism, and rationalism will be considered more closely from the perspective of the judicial philosophies appellate judges adopt to organize their reasoning about the cases that come to them from lower courts for review.

---

[27] The link between discretion and rational decision-making is argued by H.L.A Hart, *Discretion,* 127 Harv. L. Rev. 652, 664-665 (2013).

CHAPTER 4

THE ETHICS OF ADJUDICATION AND JUDICIAL REVIEW

In the previous chapter, we considered how the interaction of statutes, the common law, and constitutional law force consideration of moral issues in the legal system. If legal proceedings took on the deductive rigor of a mathematical proof, difficult moral questions would never arise. Discretion would be unnecessary. A critical part of those proceedings involves the deliberations of judges – *adjudication* (applying law to facts) in the case of trial judges, and *judicial review* (applying law to the result of adjudications) in the case of appellate judges. In both cases, a judge identifies relevant sources of law and exercises discretion about how to apply them to the facts under consideration. The entire process should be guided by the norms of legal rationalism, which requires a good faith review of the sources of law, and the choice of their most compelling and defensible options to resolve the case.

Adjudication

A good legal system is one that places constraints on bad behavior. It attempts this by creating accountability conditions such as open courts, open meeting laws, weekly public reports of legislative drafts and of votes on laws, accurate police reports, freedom of information acts, and of course the whole panoply of judicial writings from minute entries, to written rulings and appellate opinions – all of this overseen by legal scholars in law review articles and by the press and public generally. Yet, it remains the case that if Fuller's idea of inner morality has any salience, a legal system is only as *good* as the people who actively engage in creating, enforcing, and interpreting its laws. The norms and procedures of adjudication, he argued, both derive from the "extra-legal community" and must "maintain and develop" through legal interpretation that community.[1] The 'rule of law' results from a confluence of those reciprocal processes, making well-functioning adjudication an indispensable element of democracy itself.

Influence from the extra-legal community, however, is not always transparent or beneficial. Laws may be created with intent to accomplish something far from what a cursory reading of their short title or summary would indicate. The same applies to ballot initiatives which may be drafted to accomplish the opposite of what their publicity pamphlets say they will. Every time a police report is falsified or shaded, fair enforcement and equal protection of the law fails. These are all inner morality problems of law. Adjudication and judicial review, then, are supposed to be processes of the legal system that are designed to detect and be most resistant to prevarication and corruption. Their hierarchical and territorial structures mean that the work of state and local courts will come under close scrutiny by those who practice law in those courts. Judges in legal proceedings must, in most cases, 'show their work' to the litigants and to the court reporter, and if needed to a higher court. Each step in the process is typically governed by norms requiring explanation and justification. These are the areas of a legal system under the greatest degree of close scrutiny. The very fact that higher courts may review the work of lower courts reflects a recognition that error, misinterpretation, or outright mischievous bias are sufficient dangers to warrant the high costs of continual vigilance through appellate review. At the highest level, Supreme Court interpretations may be reviewed by later Supreme Courts, or modified by subsequent legislation or constitutional amendment. These checks upon judicial power, however, are seldom timely enough to undo completely the damage from error, misinterpretation, or judicial mischief. Ultimately, the norms of fairness, public candor, and intellectual honesty lie within the personal moral commitments individuals must embrace in carrying out their judicial functions.

Arbitration. Arbitrators are also adjudicators, in many cases developing expertise in specific areas of dispute, such as employment, labor relations,

---

[1] Lon L. Fuller, *Adjudication and the Rule of Law*, 54 Proc. Am. Soc'y Int'l L. 1, 7 (1960). ("Adjudication may profitably nurture extra-legal community and help it into being; it cannot create it.")

aviation, engineering, etc. In such cases the opportunity for bias is ever present, arising from the fact that in the case of employment arbitrations, for example, the company appears more often than each complainant before a selected arbitrator. So, without procedural safeguards the opportunity for corruption in arbitration is considerable. The Federal Arbitration Act has provisions for vacating an arbitral award if "evident partiality or corruption in the arbitrators" can be shown.[2] Arbitrators who are members of the American Arbitration Association, for example, are subject to ethical norms of impartiality, even in three-arbitrator panels where each party chooses an arbitrator and a third-party chooses the third. Full pre-appointment disclosure of any facts that might create bias or its appearance is required.[3] In many situations, arbitrators also must take an oath to be fair and impartial.

Most of the organizational components of arbitration – such as belonging to a respected arbitration association, taking an oath, following well-established evidentiary procedures, sensitivity to the anxieties of the disputants, judicial review of awards – are designed to expose partiality and make it risky and consequential to practice it. An ethical arbitrator doesn't need any of these safeguards to be a fair adjudicator. But arbitration is also a public activity that requires public confidence in impartial outcomes. The components build confidence that arbitration will not be a corrupt process producing an unfair outcome. Of course, during the past century arbitrations, particularly compulsory arbitrations, have been conducted in highly contentious political environments, being used to stop nationwide general strikes or to block efforts to enforce grossly unfair labor contracts favoring parties with dominant bargaining power. In such cases, good arbitrators are asked to use their skills to adjudicate claims already subject to unfair rules. Suppose an employment contract requires

---

[2] 9 U.S.C. § 10(a)(2).

[3] "The Code of Ethics for Arbitrators in Commercial Disputes," ("Canon II: An arbitrator should disclose any interest or relationship likely to affect impartiality or which might create an appearance of partiality.") and "Code of Professional Responsibility for Arbitrators of Labor-Management Disputes" ("Essential personal qualifications of an arbitrator include honesty, integrity, impartiality and general competence in labor relations matters.").

arbitration of the amount of a monetary penalty for an employee's breach of the contract for injuring the interest of the employer. The task of the arbitrator is (1) to identify the interest; (2) determine the injury if any, and (3) set the amount of the penalty. The arbitrator follows all the procedural rules of the profession, sifts the evidence carefully and arrives at a meticulously impartial result. *But is the result just and ethical as well?* By what standards of justice should the result be measured? Has the arbitrator identified the interest too narrowly or broadly? Has the arbitrator reasonably used or abused the arbitral power of discretion? If the actual facts of this example provide a close question for the arbitrator to answer, other examples easily could be provided that shock the conscience, reminding us that the ethics of adjudication requires impartiality in interpreting the agreement, but also fairness in recognizing the surrounding circumstances of its creation. An agreement signed at the point of a gun, obviously would not be enforceable. It is not enough to say that the rules the parties agree to will define the arbitrator's scope of discretion, because the agreement itself must be investigated for signs of duress or undue influence, as well as signs that the selection of the arbitrator was the result of corruption or collusion.

Good Trial Judges. Scale up now to judicial adjudication in the courts of law, with all of the gravitas associated with them. The organizational components here include oath taking, procedural and evidentiary rules, and rules of review by higher courts. A good judge does what a good arbitrator does and more. Judges must also preserve the public image of the judiciary and public courthouse. What makes a good judge? Surely, one who stays awake during testimony. But what about one who appeals to the common sense of a housekeeper as a sounding board; or one with such a busy trial calendar that by the end of the week makes rulings that 'even out' his rulings between plaintiffs and defendants, the way referees in sports sometimes shade their calls so as not to appear biased for one side? Such practices somehow seem not only ancillary to the process of adjudication, but also downright dishonest or even dangerous. A trial judge is supposed to examine and weigh all relevant facts and subject them to the correct legal standard in order to arrive at a factually sound and legally fair ruling. Good judges, who preside over jury trials make careful and considered rulings on the evidence to be submitted at trial and the correct instructions on the law the jury must consider in arriving at its verdict. The whole adjudicatory process must be governed by the norms sustained by the careful articulation and application of rules of procedure.[4] It is theoretically possible for virtuous judges to be rigorous and fair adjudicators in every case. However, as a practical matter, judges are frequently selected for their political biases, as we shall discuss in Chapter 8, and develop quirks and peeves the longer they sit on the bench. Every experienced litigator recognizes this, which they pass on to their clients in the process of strategizing the case.

The adjudicatory process contains some rules designed to motivate fairness by exposing partiality and corruption, making it risky to give in to their temptations. Court procedural and evidentiary rules slowly evolved over the past two centuries that were designed to minimize *ad hoc*, arbitrary, and capricious rulings, and in effect minimize one-man judicial rule. So, in New York State prior to the 1840s "each judge was himself an institution with substantial, if not really unlimited, authority to determine the rules of legal practice before his court. Also, each judge generally had the final word in controversies before him as there was little in the way of an appellate court structure."[5] In the early Republic judges typically made oral rulings, with court reporters only taking down the bottom-line outcome of the dispute.[6] The obligation to explain a ruling or enter it in written form into the canon of the common law usually came later. The origin of that obligation may simply have been the recognition that a fair result must also be a systematic result. Ideally, the same set of facts in the legal system of a given jurisdiction should produce the same result before the same judge, and if judges differ there should be some reasons why the outcomes differ. Those reasons, then, would be compiled and explained in terms of differing theories or approaches to law. What they couldn't be, however, was utterly arbitrary or a result of bald favoritism.

---

[4] Jeremy Waldron, "The Rule of Law and the Importance of Procedure," *Nomos* 50 (2011): 3-31

[5] Marc Bloustein, *A Short History of the New York State Court System*, (Albany: The New York State Library, 1987), 2.

[6] Ellen A Peters, *Brennan Lecture: Capacity and Respect: A Perspective on the Historic Role of the State Courts in the Federal System*, 73 NYU L. Rev. 1065, 1073 (1998).

The function of the judicial adjudicator takes place against a background of statutory and common law, as discussed in previous chapter. American judges must continually evaluate the meaning and intent of legislation and determine whether they should also weigh the options provided by the common-law tradition. They must also consider the constitutional jurisprudence of their court, depending upon whether they sit on a state or federal court. And to the extent that the codification of law is a factor in their jurisdiction, they must consider whether the codification regime is coherent with constitutional law or the common law tradition it was intended to supersede. All of these competing sets of rules and sources still require the fulfillment of the institutional obligation that regardless of the court system the facts and law be adjudicated in a uniform and consistent manner. Among other things, this means that final rulings be explained, in many cases written down, and appear to be a rational resolution of the issues in dispute. In judicial adjudication, the responsibility for rationality does not only fall on the judge or the jury instructions. The parties and their lawyers are expected to present reasons and principles in the form of proofs and arguments for their side of the case, if they are to respond at all. Even if they ask a judge to 'bend the rules' for them, they must give reasons for doing so. Fuller saw adjudication as the locus of rationality in law. It is the process whereby disputes over personal interests are reconciled with the shared purposes and values of the community. Out of this process, rules of procedure and jurisprudence get to be articulated and modified to changing circumstances. "Where legal rules have evolved out of the process of adjudication," Fuller wrote, "law has in effect been built on community. Uncritical proponents of extending the rule of law propose to build community on law. I cannot be done."[7] The most critical feature of the process, he believed, was the freedom of the parties to present their side of the story using proof and argument. This procedure provides a continual supply of nutrient information from the community to the courts about how well its laws are performing. (The chapters in Part Three will provide numerous illustrations of the continual tension between law and the values of the community.)

Measuring Performance. Can there be an objective standard for measuring judicial adjudicatory performance? A *legal positivist* might say that fidelity

---

[7] Lon L. Fuller, *The Forms and Limits of Adjudication*, 92 Harv. L. Rev. 353, 374 (1978).

to the law as written is the only workable standard. A good judge cannot use sympathy to bend the law to the needs of sympathetic litigants. Rather, the public purpose of the law as revealed in the intentions of the lawgivers must be effectuated. A *legal realist* might say that a good judge must strive to achieve a morally beneficial result taking into consideration the interests of litigants, of the legislative and judicial functions, and of the community generally. These conflicting theories, by themselves, raise a question whether objectivity is ever possible. Nonetheless, the emergence of procedural rules has been an indirect and practical way of measuring and even improving judicial quality. Good judges will for the most part adhere to the procedural rules applicable to their court. The emergence of efficient and workable rules of procedure in the twentieth century, not burdened by the arcane classifications and distinctions from previous centuries, was primarily motivated by a need for fairer adjudication standards and greater access to justice. Chief Justice William H Taft, who served on the Supreme Court (1921-1930) and also as U.S. President (1909-1913), for example, recommended in 1908 that the salaries of judges, as essentially government employees, be paid from the general fund of the government and not from the fees of litigants. He proposed this change to encourage the public view that the courts were not for the rich alone and that judges were not for sale.[8]

Rules of Procedure and Evidence. The American Bar Association, formed in 1878, recognized that justice and procedure, both civil and criminal, were inextricably linked with judicial performance, and were in conflict in so many state and federal courts across the nation. Its early efforts to create uniform rules of procedure for some courts and jurisdictions met with long-standing opposition from lawyers and judges who wanted to be free from procedural time limitations, for example, for preparing trials and adhering to evidentiary limitations for conducting them. Eventually the Supreme Court, though not unanimously, supported procedural reform and agreed to be bound by the new rules adopted by Congress. Learning the rules of procedure, then, became part of the curriculum of law schools. Built into the procedural rules were the adjudicatory virtues, for example, of requiring that claims be stated in clear plain wording, being able to challenge unclear statements and having time to do so, and requiring that

---

[8] William H. Taft, *Inequalities in the Administration of Justice*, 20 Green Bag 441 (1908).

claimants show their evidence ahead of time to eliminate unfair surprise at trial. The entire system was designed, in the words of one who helped design it, "as an assisting means to effective disclosure of the truth in any lawsuit."[9]

The Federal Rules of Evidence, adopted only in 1975, set up a multi-step procedure for admitting 'good' (admissible) evidence and filtering out 'bad' (inadmissible) evidence. Its purpose in a criminal context was to affix blame, if merited by consequential facts related directly to the crime being tried, and not from gratuitous prejudice. Collective guilt and guilt by association were now to be avoided. So was guilt due simply to a determination that the defendant suffered from having a bad character. The rule that potentially admissible evidence must be relevant forced a judge to run through a reasoning process. The rule (FRE 401) states that evidence is relevant if: (a) it has any tendency to make a fact more or less probable than it would be without the evidence; and (b) the fact is of consequence in determining the outcome of the case. Relevancy requires an exercise of probabilistic reasoning at both stages; candidates for relevant evidence should be "tested by the processes of legal reasoning," using "principles evolved by experience or science, applied logically to the situation at hand."[10] By this rule, relevant evidence is tied to the activity of a disciplined mind tethered to intersubjective standards of experience and science. Good adjudicators, then, must be good logicians and scientists. Their reasoning must produce sound probabilistic inferences.

To whom does a good judge owe a duty to give well-reasoned rulings – to the litigants, the public, the administration of justice, or all of the above? Should judges as triers of fact explain why some claims are accepted as factual and not others? In doing so do they then put themselves on trial? An elaborate explanation of the factual evidence and legal standards that were applied, and why other standards came up short, in a bench trial could hinder the administration of justice if it meant

---

[9] Charles E. Clark, *The Influence of Federal Procedural Reform*, 13 Law & Contemp. Probs. 144, 157 (1948).

[10] FRE 401, Notes of Advisory Committee, Pub. L. 93–595, §1, Jan. 2, 1975, 88 Stat. 1931.

that other litigants would not get to court sooner rather than later. So, ethical judges must be as rigorous as the circumstances allow, and where financial constraints adversely affect the administration of justice, they also owe a duty to the public to be advocates for a sounder but also more efficient justice system. An unethical adjudicator would tolerate a system of sham justice, incapable of achieving the values of fairness and impartiality. The real world, of course, operates somewhere between a thorough justice system and a sham one. Justice is more often achieved than not, judges and attorneys usually strive to honor and practice their ethical norms, and when the losing litigants feel sufficiently aggrieved, they have recourse to appeal. The opportunity for appellate review, then, may be seen as another check on the corruption of the adjudicator, whether judge or jury, and on an incompetent ('ineffective') attorney as well as a process for correcting honest legal errors in the lower court. Victims of corruption are more likely to complain if they have an appellate opportunity to do so, an opportunity due process and appellate jurisdiction provides.

Judicial Immunity. Since being a judge as adjudicator often carries with it the condemnation of losing litigants, judicial immunity from lawsuits for, say, condemning a man to die who was later found to be not guilty by DNA testing, must in some sense be an essential component of a practical and reasonable administration of justice. Without it, every outcome of bitter litigation would spawn an endless stream of retaliatory claims, charges, and lawsuits. Judicial immunity is one component of the finality required in any system of justice. But how far does it reach? The difficulty of the question is clearly manifest in the case of *Stump v Sparkman*.[11] On July 9, 1971, Judge Harold D. Stump of the Circuit Court of DeKalb County, Indiana was presented with a document captioned "Petition to Have Tubal Ligation Performed on Minor and Indemnity Agreement." The minor was fifteen and her mother had an attorney draft the Petition which she signed and presented to the judge who also signed it the same day as "Judge, DeKalb Circuit Court." The mother's rambling affidavit, all that the judge had before him, alleged that:

---

[11] 435 U.S. 349 (1978).

> her daughter's mentality is such that she is considered to be somewhat retarded although she is attending or has attended the public schools in DeKalb Central School System and has been passed along with other children in her age level even though she does not have what is considered normal mental capabilities and intelligence. Further, that said affiant has had problems in the home of said child as a result of said daughter leaving the home on several occasions to associate with older youth or young men and as a matter of fact having stayed overnight with said youth or men and about which incidents said affiant did not become aware of until after such incidents occurred. As a result of this behavior and the mental capabilities of said daughter, affiant believes that it is to the best interest of said child that a Tubal Ligation be performed on said minor daughter to prevent unfortunate circumstances to occur and since it is impossible for the affiant as mother of said minor child to maintain and control a continuous observation of the activities of said daughter each and every day.[12]

When the minor was sterilized, she was told that she had an appendectomy. Several years later after she married and attempted to have children, she learned she had been sterilized. She then sued her mother, the attorney who drafted the affidavit, the doctor who performed the operation, and the hospital. She also sued Judge Stump in his capacity as a state judicial officer for violating her civil rights without giving her notice of the petition and an opportunity to rebut it. The federal district court ruled against her, invoking the doctrine of judicial immunity. On appeal, the Circuit Court reversed the lower court ruling, arguing that the judge had operated outside of his jurisdiction because his signature did not reflect a judgment of a litigated case, and specifically not on Indiana law relating to sterilization, which he did not follow.[13] Additional irregularities included the fact that the petition was not filed in the clerk's office, nor given a docket number, and was executed without notice to the minor; nor did the judge appoint a guardian *ad litem*, or set the matter for hearing. It was, the Circuit Court concluded, an act of judicial tyranny plain and simple.

The general rule of judicial immunity applies in cases where a judge acted with partiality, malice, or corruption – since every losing party believes this

---

[12] Ibid., at 351 note 1.

[13] *Sparkman v. McFarlin*, 552 F.2d 172 (7th Cir. 1977), relying upon *Bradley v. Fisher*, 80 U.S. 335 (1871).

to be the case – but not if a judge acts extra-judicially. When the Circuit Court ruling reached the United States Supreme Court, there was discussion as to whether *certiorari* should be granted in such a "sordid case" which had little prospect of making good law.[14] Nonetheless, the appeal was accepted and the Circuit Court ruling was overturned. The Supreme Court decided that the judge had engaged in a "judicial act" in reviewing and signing the petition because the act was "a function normally performed by a judge" and that the mother and her attorney had come to him in the expectation that he would exercise his judicial capacity. Judges, the reasoning went, are given broad judicial powers and will only operate outside of their jurisdiction when the legislature explicitly takes it away. The fact that Indiana had enacted a set of sterilization laws and procedures did not mean that the judge acted outside of his jurisdiction when he disregarded them. Nor did the egregious adjudicative irregularities constitute a denial of jurisdiction sufficient to pierce the judge's immunity. The dissenters in the case argued that there was nothing normal about the activity of the judge, stating "a judge's approval of a mother's petition to lock her daughter in the attic would hardly be a judicial act simply because the mother had submitted her petition to the judge in his official capacity."[15] The dissenters also argued that there were no litigants, no record of proceedings from which appeal could be brought, and so no way to review the judge's decision. Hence, as a threshold matter the judge did not act judicially within his jurisdiction and that the aggrieved party should have a monetary remedy rather than merely filing an administrative complaint.

Cases after *Stump* have used a four-part 'judicial act' immunity test: (1) the act must be a normal judicial function; (2) the act must occur in open court or in chambers; (3) the act must be part of a case pending before the judge; and (4) the act must arise out of a visit to the judge in his or her judicial capacity. Absolute immunity attached to judicial behavior within those parameters. For example, it was a judicial act for a judge to award the marital home to the husband in a divorce proceeding before him on the condition that the

---

[14] Laura T. Kessler, *'A Sordid Case': Stump v. Sparkman, Judicial Immunity, and the Other Side of Reproductive Rights*, 74 Md. L. Rev. 833 (2015), arguing that *Bradley* and *Stump* have roots in post-Civil War attitudes about civil rights, race, and eugenics.
[15] *Stump*, 435 U.S. at 362, 367.

husband get a vasectomy. The husband got a vasectomy and was subsequently awarded the marital home. It was also a judicial act for a judge to award temporary custody to a father after the father had gotten his own father, also a judge in the same court system, to call the judge to obtain a custody order without giving notice to the out-of-state mother.[16] On the other hand, it is not a judicial act for a judge to order a man jailed after he came to the courthouse to make a child support payment and was confronted by the judge in plain clothes in chambers who demanded he submit to an *ad hoc* "contempt proceeding" where the judge "acted as complaining witness, prosecutor, factfinder, and judge." Also, judges' decisions made in their capacity as a courthouse employer are not judicial acts.[17] The reasoning behind the doctrine of judicial absolute immunity is that it is intended to support the core fairness values of the adjudicative process and all of the procedural safeguards that give the public confidence in the judicial system. Judges should be given absolute freedom to exercise their judgment on the facts and law of the case before them. In that spirit, judges who use their influence and prestige to fix traffic tickets and do friends favors by making important phone calls do not undermine the judicial system because those actions do not implicate a judicial proceeding within the system or violate of the epistemic virtues embodied in FRE 401.[18]

Judicial Review

Judicial Record Keeping. In *The Federalist* No. 78 Alexander Hamilton argued for an independent judiciary, with judges serving without fixed terms during good behavior. The judicial branch once established, he reasoned, would produce an impressive body of legal reasoning spanning fixed political terms and even generations of Americans. It will be a

[16] Respectively, *Scott v. Hayes,* 719 F.2d 1562 (11th Cir. 1983) and *Dykes v. Hosemann,* 776 F.2d 942 (1985).

[17] Respectively, *Harper v. Merckle,* 638 F.2d 848, 852 (5th cir.1981) and *Forrester v. White,* 484 U.S. 219 (1988).

[18] For a review of issues surrounding the current doctrine of absolute judicial immunity see Timothy M. Stengel, *Absolute Judicial Immunity Makes Absolutely No Sense: An Argument for an Exception to Judicial Immunity,* 84 Temp. L. Rev. 1071 (2012).

multigenerational body that develops a canon of legal truth. In this vein he wrote:

> To avoid an arbitrary discretion in the courts, it is indispensable that they should be bound down by strict rules and precedents, which serve to define and point out their duty in every particular case that comes before them; and it will readily be conceived from the variety of controversies which grow out of the folly and wickedness of mankind, that the records of those precedents must unavoidably swell to a very considerable bulk, and must demand long and laborious study to acquire a competent knowledge of them.

The claim that strict rules and precedents create duties assumes a unified collegiality of the judicial branch, with each member able to review the opinions of others readily available in court libraries. The sound analysis on a particular question from one judge shortens the work of another confronting a similar question so that records not only unavoidably swell but they become the authoritative source material for further legal analysis and interpretation.

Today we regard Hamilton's view as commonplace. But in the early Republic written opinions in most lower and higher courts were handed down to the parties and their attorneys but not systematically published and preserved. That practice provided an advantage to attorneys and law firms with frequent business before a given court. Increasingly, however, publication of opinions by official recorders came to be seen as an essential component of equal access to justice. In fact the whole doctrine of *stare decisis* required a heightened obligation to write a reasoned opinion, at least in the case of final judgments, and have them distributed to the legal community and public. Appellate rulings returning cases to the lower court for further action without written reason-giving analysis would leave the lower court without any instruction on how to proceed. Written and reported reasoned opinions not only increase the likelihood that justice will be consistent, but also inform those who are considering the likelihood of recovery should they decide to sue under similar facts. In spite of these clear advantages, the need for written opinions has always been debated, some finding them necessary and even constitutionally required, others finding them a waste of judicial resources given that the parties of interest typically know the outcome and no longer care that much about the reasons for it.[19]

Nonetheless, Hamilton's observation remains essential to an independently functioning judiciary. If all of the written opinions and state and federal reporters were to disappear, so would the judiciary as a counterbalancing weight in a political system of checks and balances. He could not have anticipated the modern practice where the overwhelming percentage of federal appellate court opinions and rulings, disposing of cases on the merits, are unpublished and unavailable to be cited as precedent. Even still, statistics maintained by the federal court system indicate that most unpublished opinions and orders are still "reasoned," i.e., "opinions and orders which expound the law as applied to the facts of the case and detail the judicial reasons upon which the judgment is based."[20] A much smaller percentage of reasoned opinions are published. This outcome suggests that Hamilton's task for the federal judiciary has been fairly well achieved. The compromise seems to be: novel and precedential opinions are disseminated widely, while the litigants in cases with pedestrian facts also get the explanations they require. However, when unpublished opinions cannot be cited by court rule in subsequent litigation attorneys may be unfairly constrained in using arguments that have been persuasive in previous cases. Such a practice has been called anachronistic in light of new technological capabilities to store and transmit information, as well as an unconstitutional restraint on the speech of attorneys to advocate for their clients.[21]

Measuring Judicial Quality. Although judicial record keeping provides a basis for evaluating the quality of judicial review, other measures have been identified. Judicial quality at the state appellate level also might be measured using the metrics of productivity, opinion quality, and

---

[19] Max Radin, *The Requirement of Written Opinions,* 18 Cal. L. Rev. 486 (1930).

[20] See statistics available at http://www.uscourts.gov/statistics-reports/analysis-reports.

[21] J. Lyn Entrikin Goering, *Legal Fiction of the 'Unpublished' Kind: The Surreal Paradox of No-Citation Rules and the Ethical Duty of Candor,* 1 Seton Hall Cir. Rev. 27 (2005); and Marla Brooke Tusk, *No-Citation Rules as a Prior Restraint on Attorney Speech,* 103 Colum. L. Rev. 1202 (2003).

independence from partisan and political influence.[22] Writing one published opinion a year, however brilliant, would little serve the interests of the courts as a public dispute resolution forum. Opinion quality of a decision also might be measured by the number of times other court systems cite and follow it, or law reviews respect it for its reasoning. The ability to handle novel problems with novel solutions might be another factor to consider in assessing judicial quality. The great jurists of the past, like Holmes and Supreme Court Justice, Joseph Story (1779-1845), are often praised for their ability to cut legal trails through the otherwise intractable legal underbrush. The number of times a judge's argument has been questioned or cited with disapproval has been taken as a measure of lesser competence.[23] There is also evidence that state appellate judges produce higher quality opinions when they have more time to write them, but also that pay is not a strong correlate to performance.[24] Evidently, judges are not in it for the money; professional values and a commitment to the values of appellate review seem to be greater motivators of performance; and appellate judges generally do not attempt to monetize their skills while still on the bench, but instead strive to produce sound and persuasive arguments.

Quantitative citation studies also turn up *ideology* as an identifiable factor in assessing the quality of judicial review. For example, "judges appointed by Democrats cite those appointed by Republicans more negatively than they cite those appointed by Democrats, and the opposite is true."[25] But such studies seem to indicate that ideology is less a factor than deference to within-circuit precedent. So, how much weight should be given to ideology? How much does the political process involving judicial selection influence the work of individual appellate judges? In theory a good appellate judge is supposed to review the relevant facts in

---

[22] Stephen J. Choi, Mitu Gulati and Eric A. Posner, *Measuring Judges and Justice: Judicial Evaluations and Information Forcing: Ranking State High Courts and their Judges*, 58 Duke L. J. 1313 (2009).

[23] Robert Anderson IV, *Distinguishing Judges: An Empirical Ranking of Judicial Quality in the United States Courts of Appeals*, 76 Mo. L. Rev. 315 (2011).

[24] Elliott Ash, and W. Bentley MacLeod, *Intrinsic Motivation in Public Service: Theory and Evidence from State Supreme Courts*, 58 J. L. & Econ. 863 (2015).

[25] Anderson IV, *Distinguishing Judges*, 373.

the record of the lower court and interpret their significance in light of the correct law to be applied. Appellate judges cannot insist, in a traffic accident case, that the traffic light must have been green when the record states it was red or states that the evidence is inconclusive. To assert factual claims with little plausible evidence in their favor is the making of a bad appellate judge. Unfortunately, measuring the quality of judicial review does not come down to identifying the correct facts at issue in the case and then 'applying the facts to the law' as is simplistically claimed. Facts and law reciprocally influence each other. Facts are relevant only if the law gives them legal significance. The relevance of the color of a traffic light is given legal significance because of the traffic law that asserts 'stop on red, go on green'. In most cases brought to a higher court there is already a dispute over which facts have legal significance. Here judges who pervasively disagree about which facts have legal significance, and provide reasons why, and then apply *those* facts to the law may still be good judges. Put this way, we can say that a disagreement over which facts have legal significance, is a disagreement over jurisprudence, over judicial philosophy and ideology. Some good judges consider that the identification of legal facts must be determined by legislation, others by the wording of the Constitution, while others consider the courts the proper forum to identify or adopt them in light of their own reasoned view of the best interests of the community. Each follows a judicial philosophy; each is an 'activist' in terms of what their own philosophy requires of them.

Judicial Philosophies. What, then, are those philosophies and is there a way to assess or even think about the question of which are better than others? Judicial activism is a viewpoint attribute; an activist ruling is simply one that is unsupported by the judicial philosophy embraced by the person making the charge. Its contrast is not judicial restraint or modesty because restraint can be seen as activist from the viewpoint of someone who regards a result as falling short of what the law or constitution requires. The following are some judicial examples considered by some as 'activist':

> ... overruling actions by other federal branches or state governments, failing to follow textual meaning, departing from history or tradition, issuing maximalist and not minimalist holdings, using broad remedial powers, basing decisions upon partisan preferences, failing to follow an originalist

> view of the Constitution, issuing an opinion inconsistent with prior precedent, exercising power beyond a court's jurisdiction, creating new rights or theories, altering prior doctrines or interpretations, establishing substantive policy, and failing to use an accepted interpretative methodology.[26]

Each element expresses a judicial philosophy that embraces a set of normative beliefs about how a legal system ought to function and be structured in a political community. Many are backward looking, considering a body of law legitimate due to its historical pedigree. Appellate reasoning, the argument goes, is legitimate when it conforms to norms established by foundational authorities manifesting their intent in foundational documents. All subsequent legitimate reasoning must reflect and derive from that body of law. From this perspective judicial review is simply adjudication on a broader scale; anything else is illegitimate *ad hoc* reasoning, a departure from what is constitutionally permissible. A contrary view is that historical pedigree is largely an unhistorical mirage, given the many disputes among founders, merely intended to legitimize *contemporary* ideas, principles, and values.

These contrasting views of judicial philosophy are what lie behind the popular accusatory political debate over 'activist' judges. Among legal scholars and within the judiciary itself, debate centers on adopting the appropriate legal philosophy. Everybody in the debate agrees that history is central, some finding it more adequate than others in determining how to resolve cases. Everybody also agrees that the debate requires a commitment to some judicial philosophy in order to explain disagreements over the scope of judicial review. Nobody believes that appellate review standards should be randomly selected based on moods, emotions, or time of day. Everybody assumes that the commitment to a judicial philosophy defines their role as judge and the reasons why they rule the way they do. In the nineteenth century, the emergence of a judicial philosophy as a justifying framework for judicial review came more clearly into view. Holmes's emphasis on jurisprudence was primarily responsible for this trend. Nowadays, evidence of a judicial philosophy is directly woven into

---

[26] Corey Rayburn Yung, *Flexing Judicial Muscle: An Empirical Study of Judicial Activism in the Federal Courts,* 105 Nw. U. L. Rev. 1, 10 (2011).

some opinions, publicly debated among legal scholars, and is even publicly embraced by some judges as their preferred philosophical stance. Like the 'activism' debate the judicial philosophy debate is more philosophical than judicial. Each side accuses the other of adopting the judicial philosophy that justifies the outcomes they prefer. However, at least on the public level, there is little evidence that a judicial philosophy is openly adopted as an insincere Machiavellian maneuver. If anything, a sincere desire to discover legitimate foundations and fully interrogate presuppositions seems more of a motivating factor in arriving at a judicial philosophy after a journey of careful study.

Judicial philosophies have been placed on a spectrum from realist pragmatism (consequentialism, instrumentalism) to formalism (textualist, strict constructionist, originalist).[27] They can be 'discovered' by legal scholars in the course of studying the history of law, but they may also be adopted in the course of becoming an appellate judge. A good appellate judge might wonder whether or not to adopt a specific judicial philosophy for all cases, or select realism for some and textualism for others. Some judges do adapt their philosophies over time to cases that come before them especially through their interactions with fellow judges on the same court. Realists can become formalists and vice versa. The interesting question is: by what criteria? In considering this question, it is good to keep in mind the ways in which each overlaps and embraces values their opponents also adopt. Legal realists and legal pragmatists, on the one hand, and formalists, textualists, and originalists, on the other, each make commitments to the importance of determining and weighing the relevance of historical data; each is committed to the view that sound legal reasoning requires a deductive structure; each agrees to at least some degree of restraint and *stare decisis* so as to avoid being so out of step with social and political reality as to instigate outright revolt and destruction of the very institutions they cherish as jurists; and each embraces many of the intellectual virtues of 'formalist' reasoning. Such virtues in relation to judicial review have been described this way: "'judicial virtues' include both the human virtues

[27] Lawrence B. Solum, *Jurocracy and Distrust: Reconsidering the Federal Judicial Appointments Process: Judicial Selection: Ideology versus Character*, 26 Cardozo L. Rev. 659 (2005).

that are relevant to judging and any particular virtues that are associated with the social role of judges."[28] For example, all individuals who take on the role of a judge must be habitually temperate and sober, have the courage to reveal their working assumptions and convictions, be diligent and assiduous, know their subject matter and have the skill to express effectively the results of their deliberations. These traits apply to judges in law as well as to judges in dog shows, and to art or land appraisers. In addition to these virtues, appellate judges have additional duties by virtue of their oath and role in a constitutional judiciary: they must make decisions after careful assessment of how those decisions may affect the norms and traditions of their community and nation. In making such an assessment they must be able to say whether the case before them provides compelling reasons for a change in positive law, and if so, how that change should be accomplished (whether by courts or legislatures). This latter duty requires good practical reasoning in the form of locating the best workable resolution of conflicting interests that improves the situation over time.[29] But judicial problem solving does not exist in a vacuum. It is a process within a body of laws, customs, and norms. Knowing which to give precedence to is the corundum of judging. Knowing when to adopt *stare decisis* and when to reject it is part of the weighing that a good and wise judge must make. Asserting abstractly that the 'rule of law' must be followed, may on balance be the default position, but only until it no longer is. How helpful is a judicial philosophy at that point? Each proponent adopts a global judicial philosophy as a way of authorizing a set of preferred outcomes for cases before the court. Formalists consider their philosophy ideologically and politically neutral, but so do realists. No judge wants to be thought of as merely a feather blowing in the wind. Most judges adopt and prize their philosophy as an expression of the work of the virtues described above. The four predominant legal philosophies, discussed below, are: Legal Formalism, Textualism, Legal Realism, and Legal Process.

---

[28] Lawrence B. Solum, *Empirical Measures of Judicial Performance: A Tournament of Virtue*, 32 Fla. St. U. L. Rev. 1365, 1368 (2005).

[29] Ibid., 1376-88.

Legal Formalism. First, legal formalists insist that when phrases like 'the law' and 'the body of law' are used, a specific set of texts, and sentences within texts, are being referred to. It makes no sense to think of the law as a set of casual remarks that range across all human linguistic activity. The law is a demarcating process with an inside and outside. Studying law from this view involves entering a closed system of rules and norms that mutually reinforce themselves. Law is created to serve as a specific set of tools used to regulate social life and set the permissible limits of what should be expected and relied upon. So, those who makes laws and draft a constitution deserve the greatest deference possible. They have constructed the sentences we must now read and interpret according to their intentions. Formalism relies on a picture of legal language as a network of interconnected meanings expressing clear intentions. Law sentences are not created randomly or on a whim; they are not flecks of poetry designed to inspire conduct. They are norms generated by sophisticated language users with specialized knowledge of the law, who have thought long and hard about how their laws should be used and interpreted. So, the best way to be a formalist is to read texts carefully and use them to resolve cases to the greatest extent possible.

Formalists see in a legal system a concerted, coordinated, and coherent human effort to achieve justice through justification of preferred norms. The task of the judge is to identify those preferred norms and explain to the disputants why they are to be preferred in their case. This can only be done by appealing to the language of the legal system that embodies them. Justifications from outside the system almost by definition are improper because they were not contemplated by the system makers when the system was constructed and have not been ratified as 'the law' ever since. In that sense, following the law and not personal or policy preference is always the rational thing to do. Formalists believe that every case has a correct and unique legal solution, at least as the best solution among lesser competitors. Anything less, they argue, is legislating from the bench. But what gives them confidence they are right? One plausible answer is that formalists have adopted a view of human society and history as a problem-solving process. Humans make mistakes, but then correct and learn from them. They design political and social structures and then try to implement them, but when design defects arise, they can identify them and take corrective action. Humans are rational animals, and one of their greatest problems-solving devices is the creation of a legal system. Law is the storehouse of many past exercises of rational intelligence only made possible because the world itself operates by rational norms, norms where means and ends fit together. In this view, formalists embrace the rationalist tradition of western philosophy from Aristotle to Aquinas to Kant and Hegel. The law's rationality has been called "immanently intelligible," meaning that it can be understood "self-sufficiently without recourse to something external that would pose the problem of intelligibility afresh."[30]

As suggested by references to the self-sufficiency of correct legal reasoning, formalists seem to believe that there ought to be a logical structure in judicial opinions, moving smoothly from premises to conclusion with each step containing clearly identifiable terms and relations. However, legal opinion writing often displays many dense narrative and rhetorical attributes that may hide fallacies of inference studied in a basic logic course. That is because the construction of the categories and terms subject to deductive inference sometimes derive from vague policy considerations and do not have rigid meanings.[31] Also, the very stylistic practice of opinion writing, with its incessant interruptions with 'authoritative' quotations from prior cases, of not entirely clear relevance, and its heavily conversational tone, makes the formalist task of uncovering the rational kernel truly daunting. Formalists place great weight on the ability of words to have distinct meanings and referents. If something can be articulated for purposes of conversation, they seem to assume, it can be articulated clearly for purposes of law. The meaning of words, they contend, can be worked out by an analysis of their context and history. Meaning does not drift over time as long as it is carefully tracked. This view seems at odds with what we know about how language functions among contemporaries and over long periods of time. For example, the Constitutional debates, as chronicled by Madison especially, are couched in succinct words memorializing

---

[30] Ernest J. Weinrib, *Legal Formalism: On the Immanent Rationality of Law,* 97 Yale L. J. 949, 963 (1988).

[31] Lucille A. Jewel, *Old-School Rhetoric and New-School Cognitive Science: The Enduring Power of Logocentric Categories,* 13 J. Ass'n Legal Writing Directors 39 (2016).

excerpts of conversations among the delegates. Debate was nonstop, and when the work of the drafting committee was provided and voted upon, the vote was the only evidence of agreement on the meaning of the provisions in the draft. In fact, at the time it was openly acknowledged that delegates came away from the convention with their own private reservations about what they had voted upon. In that context in what sense could the text of the final draft of the Constitution be ultimately authoritative?

Formalists also seem to argue that their preferred judicial philosophy requires a specific and preferred system of law. From their perspective, American law for much of its history has been corrupted by so many extraneous non-formalist and non-textualist practices that our only true recourse is to dismantle and rebuild the system entirely from the ground up. But how can this be done using purely formalist practices? One option is to abandon one's textualist judicial philosophy and *stare decisis* in favor of a short-term pragmatic counterrevolution that overturns non-textualist decisions and then starts from scratch on a pure textualist foundation. Another difficulty involves the idea that the formalist reconstructions of law will require some degree of legislative deference, especially where legislation is also predicated on non-formalist theories. But how much deference can the law command? In the previous chapter, we noted that the Constitution grants to Congress considerable power over the jurisdiction of the federal courts. Formalists might contend that a current law is constitutionally illegitimate, but does their strict judicial philosophy provide an answer for changing it? If the Constitution contains unconstitutional provisions, it could be amended, and an illegitimate law may be stricken from the books and replaced by a legitimate one, all by the votes of the people or their representatives. Formalists, on the other hand, seem to place great hope in the outcomes of rational debate by jurists to correct the misdirections of law by getting legislators to understand how to draft unambiguous laws and laws that do not import values from outside those enshrined in the existing legal system they operate under.

When a formalist critique of a statute or constitutional provision produces an unsatisfactory result, either because of intractable ambiguity or the likelihood of a very unpopular result, formalists typically argue that the remedy is not with the courts but with the legislative branch to rewrite or vacate the law. In many cases, this is an effective process where the interpretation of statutes is at issue. A deeper problem, however, arises with constitutional wording. The Constitution's amendment provision (Art. V), spelling out the methods for amending the Constitution, is silent on the question of whether the Constitution may be amended unconstitutionally. Obviously, not following the amending procedures or obtaining results through fraud and corruption would likely be considered an illegitimate process, bringing down with it any proposed amendments. But what about procedurally sound amendments that drastically change the Bill of Rights? Could an amendment strike out most of Article II and replace it with a system of autocracy? Could an amendment authorize a state press or a state religion? These borderline questions are difficult to negotiate within an entirely formalist framework. By accepting an amendment process the framers seemed to have assumed the existence of durable human attributes that would never abandon the ideals of republican government. These include the capacity of human beings to reason well, to plan effective means to achieving well-thought-out objectives, and to successfully convince each other to choose the best options to solve the problems before them. But that capacity is not a natural and inevitable outcome of human association. Dictators and autocrats can exert disproportionate influence. People may be taken in by lies and confusions of language during the amending process.

Madison was well aware that ongoing public deliberation is essential for clarifying and overcoming the deficiencies of language. In *The Federalist* No. 37 he struggled with the problem of curtailing future mischief by drafting a well-written Constitution. However, all new laws, he argued, no matter how well written and deliberated upon initially still encounter the problem of unsure application under new circumstances, particularly complex laws as typically found in a growing representative republic. The problem, Madison thought, exists at the very heart of the use of language. Even in Great Britain, with its ancient legal traditions, there were still many problems to resolve among conflicts of common law and statutory law, maritime law, ecclesiastical law, and corporate law. He writes: "no language is so copious as to supply words and phrases for every complex idea, or so correct as not to include many equivocally denoting different ideas." Even the Almighty, Madison notes, has difficulty conveying meaning in "the cloudy medium" of language. He in effect is saying that a formalist and textualist reliance upon constitutional wording, while critically important as a first step in constitutional analysis, may not take us all the way. Sometimes it is necessary to look behind the Constitution in order to glean what the whole point of it was in the first place, and then with that in view to craft a solution based on that understanding, all the while preserving as much of the existing constitutional order as possible.

Textualism. Textualists argue that if the words of a statue or constitutional clause have a plain meaning they should be accepted for that meaning in interpreting the text. The surrounding debates and legislative history in the drafting phase may be consulted to shed light on that meaning and perhaps even provide evidence of a more nuanced meaning. A more recent form of textualism ('new textualism') argues that legislative history should not be considered because doing so leads into a morass of interpretations of the possible intent and purpose of the statute, which then leads into questions of policy that textualists consider out of bounds for judges to consider.[32] Instead, they argue, the very process of using words by mature language users implies that words have a plain and public meaning, otherwise they could not serve as vehicles of communication in the first place. But statutes are historical creatures containing words that may change in meaning over time. Textualists select the meaning of a term at the time the statute is enacted, by consulting a dictionary or other uses of the term or phrase in legal writings. They do recognize that sometimes the wording of a statute is hammered out in the legislative process by politicians with different points of view and agendas; sometimes the end result is a compromise when put down on the page. So, textualists, especially 'new textualists', do not want to look behind the legislating process, and instead will look at the end result and try to discern its plain meaning as the best measure of what the legislators had intended. Reasonable people may disagree of the use of a specific term since the dictionary, or several of them, can give a variety of options. For example, could a government agency use its statutory authority to 'modify' its regulations? That depends on the meaning of

[32] William N. Eskridge, Jr., *The New Textualism,* 37 UCLA L. Rev. 621(1990).

'modify', which could mean small, incremental changes or broader, major changes. The text by itself provides no clear answer.[33]

Sometime the 'plain meaning' is not completely evident, but the immediate surrounding legislative context of what is meant may be. This strategy, however, seems to undermine the rationale of textualism. For example, the question of whether tobacco is a 'drug' that could be regulated like other chemical substances commonly understood as 'drugs' was answered in the negative. The reason given was that Congress regulated tobacco in other legislation and in a different way, so as to manifest its intent by implication that tobacco was not to be treated as an FDA drug.[34] But if the meaning of words is governed by the intent of legislators doesn't that require that textualists explore the values and policy implications of a statute? Another illustration: Does discrimination in employment "because of sex" include discrimination because of sexual orientation and transgender status? The meaning of 'sex' when the Civil Rights Act was passed in 1964 commonly meant *gender,* male and female. Recent sexual characteristics were not openly part of the legislative process at that time. But would these characteristics, at the time, have been connected with the idea of gender in the minds of legislators? Would the status of being gay or transgender have been entirely separated from the status of being a man or a woman in the mind of an employer? A textualist does not provide a clear answer.[35]

Textualism, as judicial philosophy, may just come down to an emphasis that meaning and the reference range of words matter deeply in legal interpretation. When laws are drafted, attention is paid to the meaning of words, but that by itself is not sufficient to foreclose an inquiry into the purposes of the law or to its unintended effects over time.

Originalism. Originalism is a judicial philosophy that gives precedence to the original meaning of constitutional words, phrases, and clauses. Textualism

---

[33] *MCI Telecommunications Corp. American Telephone & Telegraph Co.*, 512 U.S. 218 (1994); 47 U.S.C Sec. 203(b)(2).

[34] *Food and Drug Administration v. Brown & Williamson Tobacco Corp.* 529 U.S. 120 (2000).

[35] *Bostock v. Clayton Cty.*, 140 S.Ct. 1731 (2020).

is the preferred method of interpretation for originalists. However, the problems of establishing the correct interpretation that apply to both formalism and textualism apply also to originalism. Traditional originalism based correct interpretation on the words of the framers and state ratifiers. Many words were used in the discussion and drafting of the Constitution, beginning with Madison's contemporaneous notes of the drafting process, and many more chronicles of the state convention debates and the many polemics published during ratification in the contest between Federalists and Antifederalists. All of these words provide material for interpretation. In addition, some of the framers went on to become members of Congress and in that capacity their words gave additional interpretive weight and nuance to the words of the Constitution. The same considerations would apply regarding the drafting of the Fourteenth Amendment where the scope of the meaning of its words have been subject to subsequent debate. An interesting aspect of the ongoing debate between legal realists who believe in a 'living constitution' and originalists is whether the framers themselves, particularly Madison, would have adopted originalism as the appropriate judicial philosophy to describe what they had intended in drafting the Constitution. The *Federalist Papers*, for example, was a political document printed in a series of newspaper articles designed to change the minds of a skeptical public in favor of a national government. On the surface the articles appear to present a canonical and neutral interpretation of the new Constitution. In reality after they left the Convention many of the delegates were aware that different interpretations could be given to some of its provisions and that not all votes on them were unanimous. At that time an original interpretation would have seemed absurd.

Originalism, as a specifically identifiable judicial philosophy, seems to have originated around 1980 in response to rulings of the Warren court. Soon after, originalists began to think that the hallmark of correct constitutional interpretation was not the psychological state of mind of the framers and other state debaters, but the broader public understanding of words used in ordinary language with fairly fixed meaning those framers and debaters adopted. That maneuver opened up the arena of interpretation by delving into the historical context of social practices and popular beliefs when the Constitution was framed and ratified by "we the people." Even with this wider spectrum of resources, originalists still found their judicial philosophy unnecessarily constraining for use in judicial review. The originalist method could filter out as unconstitutional cases based on un-originalist analysis, but originalist judges wanted to do more than send the defective cases back to Congress, particularly to a Congress by political orientation predisposed to prefer realist jurisprudence. As a result, a new interpretive brand of originalism emerged, focused upon the purposes and underlying principles involved in drafting a basic law. Behind the constitutional text originalists found a distinct political philosophy. Discovering what that was is thought to be necessary to supplement textual analysis. This brand of originalism has been characterized as 'new' or 'framework' originalism.[36] In other words, the true originalism of both the framers and the public was that the Constitution would be a framework through which inevitable change would be filtered and adapted to the way of life Americans chose by adopting that Constitution. So, when originalists advocate original meaning, that does not mean that they advocate returning to the values and customs of eighteenth-century America. New originalist reform means reconstructing American society according to the principles they identify as having motivated the structure of the Constitution in the first place as reflected in the Bill of Rights, separation of powers, due process restraints on state government, etc. For example, framework originalism recognizes that there are limits on state power over individuals as enunciated in the Ninth and Tenth Amendments. It also recognizes that the notion of courts creating laws out of whole cloth is not a historically accurate picture. Rather, courts will refrain from creating new rights or oppose long-standing practices unless the political arena has been broiling already for some time and then only in a gradual and limited way.

The Second Amendment has been an object of originalist analysis.[37] The amendment reads: "A well regulated militia, being necessary to the security of a free state, the right of the people to keep and bear arms, shall not be infringed." The rationale of the amendment, from an originalist perspective, seems to be: If 'the people' could not 'keep' arms in their

---

[36] Jack M. Balkin, *Living Originalism,* (Cambridge, MA.: Harvard University Press, 2011). See also Randy Barnett, *An Originalism for Nonoriginalists,* 45 Loy. L. Rev. 611 (1999).

[37] *District of Columbia v. Heller,* 554 U.S. 570 (2008).

homes, and then 'bear' them into the public domain as militia duty calls, then a condition for a well-regulated militia would not be possible, and nor would the security of a free state. Therefore, by implication individuals had to have a pre-existing individual right to possess firearms. The amendment, then, assumes, an individual right to keep and bear arms. An originalist also assumes that the language of the amendment was meant to be understood by the people. So, the 'arms' referred to meant those commonly used at the time. But they were not limited to those commonly used in 1791, when the amendment was ratified. The Constitution was understood by its framers to be written for future generations as well, and so would apply prospectively. We could now assume that it was meant to include "all instruments that constitute bearable arms, even those that were not in existence at the time of the founding."[38]

As the *Heller* opinion itself reveals, the originalist/textual analysis requires supplemental evidence, usually provided by reference to a great body of historical evidence, not all of it in harmony with the originalist theory of the case. Some historical evidence corroborated it, some not, in efforts to answer the questions: which arms, which people, and for what purposes? Servants and laborers, for example, were not allowed to bear arms on Sundays at the time, and negroes never.[39] Did 'the people' contain hidden exceptions? Some states specified in their constitutions that arms could only be used to defend the state and not for self-defense. But, allowing arms to be 'kept' suggested they be kept at home rather than in an armory, and this suggests that self-defense was implied as a permissible use for self-defense. Yet a natural right of self-defense could not be implied in the Constitution since at the time felons, the mentally ill, and slaves, a group most likely to need to keep and bear arms for self-defense, could not by law exercise that right. Retrospective analysis of words by originalists, then, seems to require some degree of mind reading into the prospective understanding and intentions of the framers. They lived in a world where, as *Heller* itself points out, there were a variety of public experiences and regulatory responses to firearms. Must we simply assume that they would have allowed possession of military-grade weapons today, and the ban of

---

[38] Ibid., 582.

[39] Ibid., 581.

weapons from felons and the mentally ill? Is it necessary to make any assumptions at all about what the framers thought the future would bring? To be relevant today, originalist analysis cannot proceed without making such assumptions. After all, we are being commanded not to infringe on a right, not on a norm. If the command is operative upon us, and we have chosen our arms and the people who can exercise the right in conformity with the Second Amendment, it must be because we believe that is what the framers would have intended if they had been able to see into the future. That, of course, is a question originalism, by the constraints of its own doctrine, cannot answer.

Legal Realism. Legal realism, sometimes identified as legal pragmatism, consequentialism, or instrumentalism insists that the formalist model breaks down when it does not provide satisfactory answers to disputes under adjudication.[40] Realism accepts the scholarly virtues of close reading and the study of the operations of words (theoretical lexicography, semantics). But it denies, as did Madison, that the construction of language accurately mirrors the ideas of those who produce our written laws. Debates using words as commonly understood may produce a product that is agreed upon, but that does not mean that there is only one interpretation of what was agreed upon. As we have seen, a Constitution may include the terms "cruel and unusual punishment," and it is possible to look at examples of punishment at the time the Constitution was ratified that were accepted by the general populace. However, the use of those terms in the Eighth Amendment is not descriptive; it is normative. It does not answer the question of whether constitutional contemporaries made the moral judgments *we* should follow. It does not tell us what cruel and unusual punishment *is*; it only tells us that we *ought* not to inflict it upon anyone, whatever it is in practice. It does not tell us that one form of pain infliction is to be preferred to another. It may only be saying that we ought not to produce excessive suffering, even if this is done, as in the case of waterboarding or injecting terror-inducing psychotropic drugs, in a manner that results

[40] For an anthology of classics in legal realism see William W. Fisher III, Morton J. Horwitz, and Thomas A. Reed, eds., *American Legal Realism* (New York: Oxford University Press, 1993).

in little or no bodily injury. So, the amendment leaves us to make our own moral and ethical judgments whether we like to or not.

As we have seen already, legal realism is historically associated with Justice Holmes Jr. and his program to reform law in order to solve problems of a rapidly expanding industrial society, particularly through property and tort law. As economic conditions change, the realist argues, so must the law adapt to them by creating rights and duties, such as vicarious liability and the duty to warn of dangerous conditions, that were not needed in simpler times. Holmes's friend, British political theorist and economist, Harold J. Laski (1893-1950), argued that the rationale for imposing vicarious liability upon an employer is simply to advance the policy that the law must promote social solidarity.[41] The realist steps back and sees behind the law the implementation of certain social purposes, and sees judicial review as a step in correcting or better realizing those purposes. Carrying out the duties of that step means understanding the full breath of those purposes and how the current dispute affects them. Judges, in other words, must *judge*; they must decide hard cases with difficult trade-offs. Their authority, they believe, comes from the Constitution as well as from the legislature. So, the realist sees continuity between interpreting and making law. When novel and borderline cases make interpretation difficult realism authorizes some judicial lawmaking. Realist legal scholar Karl N. Llewellyn (1893-1962) employed principles of realist jurisprudence to draft the Uniform Commercial Code in order to make commerce flow more smoothly by filling in gaps in commercial transactions that were too detailed for statutory law to bother with or even anticipate. The realist regards many concepts in law such as *corporate entity, property rights, fair valve, due process, title, conspiracy, malice,* and *proximate cause* as in need of continual elucidation under changing social and economic conditions. They are not words dropped from heaven with self-evident meanings functioning as "solving words," with uses often producing circular and question-begging arguments. Circularity is broken only by looking beyond the text to the policy behind it: "'Social policy' will be comprehended not as an emergency factor in legal argument but rather as the gravitational field that gives weight to any rule or precedent, whether it be in constitutional law,

---

[41] Harold J Laski, *The Basis of Vicarious Liability,* 26 Yale L. J. 105, 121(1917).

and the law of trademarks, or in the most technical details of legal procedure."[42]

Legal Process. Legal process theorists rejected the either/or approach of both the formalist and realist views of adjudication and judicial review. They argued that legislators and especially jurists are constrained by their institutional roles to do a deep content analysis of the materials of their task, whether it be drafting statutes or rendering opinions. Neither is free to simply articulate the desirability of their preferred outcomes and provide some reasons in their favor. Both legislators and judges experience burdens placed upon them by both legal and cultural precedent and by the specific dispute or problem before them. American legal scholar, Herbert Wechsler (1909-2000), is closely associated with the theory. During 1945-1946 he advised the International Military Tribunal in Nürnberg, Germany created to try Nazi war crimes. Some argued that the evidence against captured individuals was fairly easy to establish with a few witnesses, and that executions should follow promptly. Others, like Wechsler, claimed that the tribunal should not be just another exercise in 'victor's justice', but should provide a rigorous investigation of facts and, more importantly, establish procedural and substantive standards for administering justice in the trials. A critical part of the process would be the articulation of standards of criminality applicable to military conduct against combatants and civilians. This task first required identification of universal standards of human rights. Without a reference to human rights all war killing could be justified as expedient in the moment. Whatever standards were established (e.g., not killing children), then, had to be met by all participants in the war. Hypocrisy would be outlawed in the work of the Tribunal. Hypocrisy in law typically means applying double standards and selective prosecution. Wechsler wrote: "Shocking it was to give support to Hitler's regime, and repulsive to men of our persuasion, but measured, as it should be, by the standards we would apply to ourselves, more was required to establish complicity in the criminal conspiracy alleged."[43] Nor would blanket assertions of collective

---

[42] Felix S. Cohen, *"Transcendental Nonsense and the Functional Approach,"* 35 Colum. L. Rev. 809, 820, 834 (1935).

[43] Herbert Wechsler, "The Issues of the Nuremberg Trial," *Political Science Quarterly*, 62 (1947): 20.

guilt be applied. The culpability of each defendant had to be established by particularized evidence applicable only to that individual.

So, Legal Process adjudication required: (1) the identification of neutrally applied principles, not *ad hoc* standards to fit the circumstances under review. Judges had to be prepared to apply them in other situations under the general rubric: similar cases should be treated similarly. (2) Explanations should not rely on slogans and jargon. When sources of law are being considered they should be explicitly identified. If common-law principles are to be used this should be openly disclosed and explained. If statutes are to be used, their underlying rationale should be identified and any distinguishing factors noted. And if the opinion requires a reference to underlying values not specifically enshrined in law, those values also should be brought to the forefront and defended. (3) Judges and their courts should be respectful of their role within the established judicial system. If a trial court or state appellate court wants to make sweeping arguments, its judges cannot pretend to argue, stylistically and substantively, as if they were Supreme Court Justices; they must be mindful of their own role as a link in a chain of reasoning and precedent, and if they are prepared to challenge prevailing constitutional principles, they must do more than simply provide more attractive alternatives; they must show why settled precedent is inadequate in the case before them. And finally, (4) courts should exercise judicial restraint and not take on questions that should be resolved better in other branches of government, such as through mediation and arbitration, and with expanded fact-finding opportunities.[44]

Wechsler points out that identifying neutrally-applied standards is a particular challenge when it comes to constitutional interpretation and adjudication. Even seemingly black-and-white rules, as noted previously, such as the minimum age for qualification for public office, could require interpretation in applying the rule. The difficulty is greater when applying the broader language of the Constitution, especially found in the Bill of Rights. The problem, then, is to find ways to subject broad language to the discipline of legal-process reasoning, and to do so in a way that does not

---

[44] See Henry M. Hart Jr., and Albert M. Sacks, *The Legal Process: Basic Problems in the Making and Application of Law* (Westbury, N.Y.: Foundation Press, 1994).

invite the accusation of hypocrisy and double standards. For starters, if the goal is to treat similar cases similarly, that must apply also to the parties in the case. Some must not be favored over others. Neutral principles must apply alike to segregationists, communists, corporations, and the indigent. In "Toward Neutral Principles of Constitutional Law," Wechsler gives examples of constitutional analysis that ran off the rails throughout our history. Jefferson set the tone when he purchased the Louisiana territory after presenting a political philosophy and constitutional interpretation that prohibited him from doing so. Abolitionists were perfectly happy to break federal law in assisting fugitive slaves, but then attacked South Carolina for breaking federal law by rejecting federal tariffs. Wechsler notes that the Constitution contains many passages that raise questions not easily resolved by references to other passages. Should the wife who murders her husband, an active-duty service member, on a military base be tried before a military tribunal or a civilian court? Does the Double Jeopardy Clause prohibit a person convicted of second-degree murder but acquitted of first-degree murder, from being retried for first-degree murder after his conviction was reversed on appeal? The best approach to such difficult cases is to attempt to formulate a workable set of principles that both sides of the dispute may embrace, and if not that at least a set of principles not based exclusively on the facts of the case.

When a Supreme Court determines the outcome of a case, without articulating clearly the principles upon which their opinion is based, and then uses that case as precedent for other cases *not directly on point*, a process of constitutional drift begins. Specific terms acquire vague usages and constitutional analysis becomes more *ad hoc* and unauthoritative. Wechsler gives as an example, the Supreme Court case of *Joseph Burstyn v. Wilson* (1952) which overturned a New York law banning distribution of 'sacrilegious' films, as a First Amendment free speech violation disparaging religion. The court distinguished such films from films deemed obscene, but then went on to apply the *Burstyn* case to obscenity cases, without explaining why the court majority believed these different cases should be treated similarly. Also, in *Shelley v. Kraemer* (1948) the Supreme Court ruled that state courts could not enforce racially discriminatory deed restrictions that attach to real property because the state, through its court system, would be violating the equal protection section (Sec. 1) of the Fourteenth Amendment. Typically, such deed restrictions are contracts between private individuals. A potential buyer could simply choose not buy a house with such deed restrictions, or a seller could willingly sell their home, as was the case here, to a non-Caucasian. However, since the restrictions applied equally to other homes in the area, another homeowner not a party to the transaction sued to cancel the sale. In so doing, the state court system itself was implicated in the discriminatory actions by being the means of their enforcement, and the Supreme Court rejected the use of the courts in this way. But suppose private land owners, Wechsler argued, agree among themselves that they will only use the courts to enforce trespass actions against African-Americans and not white individuals. That's their business as to whom to bring to court, so why isn't that blatant act of race discrimination also a violation of the Fourteenth Amendment?[45] Another example can be given: many settlement agreements have a provision that prohibits disclosure of its terms by the parties to it. Why isn't that a violation of the First Amendment free speech clause? For Wechsler, *Burstyn* and *Kraemer* are examples of failures to identify underlying principles and explain how they may or may not be reconciled with supposedly related cases.

Legal Process theorists like to point out that the lack of rigor in constitutional analysis may be a necessary consequence of the uncertain and unpredictable ways the three branches of government interact. This difficulty, then, encourages sloppy reasoning, and a recourse to simplistic models of legal reasoning. The Constitution itself also is implicated in this uncertainty. It provides, in language that is not entirely clear, that Congress has the power through legislation to confer, expand, or withhold the jurisdiction of federal courts (Art. III, Sec. 2, cl. 2). The question arises: how could the Supreme Court have sole appellate authority to say what the law is, if Congress has the authority to say what kind of appellate cases the court had jurisdiction to consider? This issue was raised by American legal scholar, Henry M. Hart Jr. (1904-1969), another proponent of Legal Process theory. Suppose Congress passed a

---

[45] Herbert Wechsler, *Toward Neutral Principles of Constitutional Law,* 73 Harv. L. Rev. 10-35, 20, 29 (1959). *Joseph Burstyn Inc. v. Wilson,* 343 U.S. 495 (1952). *Shelley v. Kraemer* 334 U.S. 1 (1948).

law that banned ownership of handguns and also deprived the Supreme Court of jurisdiction to hear appeals of that law. What would become of the Second Amendment? Or, suppose Congress imposed a year of hard labor under federal custody before undocumented immigrants or asylum seekers could qualify to receive a very brief administrative proceeding to adjudicate any and all claims before being deported? Under such a regime a non-citizen would typically file a habeas corpus action. The Constitution states that the privilege of habeas corpus "shall not be suspended" by the legislative branch (Art. I, Sec. 9, cl.2) unless public safety requires it during invasion or rebellion. Its preamble states that "we the people of the United States . . . do ordain and establish this Constitution for the United States." Are non-citizens people of the United States, and if not do they lack a right to make a habeas corpus appeal? Does this mean that if non-citizens are not people of the United States, they do not enjoy the privilege of asserting habeas corpus rights? Could Congress use its power over the jurisdiction of the federal courts to eliminate or curtail habeas corpus appeals by non-citizens in the country? When applied to non-citizens the right to a writ of habeas corpus in the courts and Congress has ebbed and flowed with the political tides.[46] In raising such questions, Hart wants to point out that when the Constitution does not provide clear answers, the only recourse to maintaining a stable constitutional regime is for courts to write sound opinions based on principles the public will embrace. Those principles must be articulated by showing their relation to those used in previous arguments and why the current candidates are superior. This 'reasoned elaboration' strengthens the stature of the judicial system as an individual branch of government and makes it more difficult politically for Congress to want to tamper with its jurisdiction.

Opponents of Legal Process theory argue that in law there are no uncontested 'neutral' principles and so no way of applying them neutrally. A deep dive into the foundations of jurisprudence, the argument goes, invariably takes us to the adoption of certain contested

---

[46] Henry M. Hart Jr., *The Power of Congress to Limit the Jurisdiction of Federal Courts: An Exercise in Dialectic,* 66 Harv. L. Rev. 1362, 1396, 1399, 1401. (Efforts to amend the Constitution to decouple its jurisdiction from Congress have not succeeded.)

political values over others.[47] Wechsler seems to acknowledge this when he demands that court opinions must fully display all reasons and values constituting the decision. But could the courts really function well with such a high degree of candor? Is some degree of subterfuge, masking, and 'political correctness' needed when courts must consider so many delicate issues involving economic, ethnic, sexual, and racial interests? An argument can be made that law requires the use of certain simplifying 'myths' because on balance embracing them produces more good results than bad. So, polygamy could be outlawed among Mormons on non-religious grounds because courts do not want to be in the business of regulating religious beliefs. Courts will develop hyperfine and scholastic-sounding theories justifying the separation of powers even though no such 'separation' is explicitly articulated in our constitutional system. And they will bend over backwards to avoid describing the precise conditions justifying torture for fear of creating slippery slopes.[48] Even well-drafted statutes may create expectations and commitments courts do not want to embrace. Some courts will send a message that they must be rewritten, while others will rewrite them by reinterpreting them. One virtue of common law is that its core language is vague enough to allow the kinds of adjustments Holmes was adept in pulling off while still embracing the myth that it remains an enduring legitimate source of authority in law. Another is that common law reasoning requires a more thorough going explanation of what the common law at issue is in the first place, a process that is more value-laden and revelatory than the language of statutory interpretation.

Adopting a Judicial Philosophy. In evaluating the moral and ethical dimensions of a judge's commitment to a judicial philosophy it is important to recognize: (1) the extent to which judges become versed in the many issues involved in the debates over the selection of an appropriate judicial philosophy, and (2) the degree to which judges make a public commitment

---

[47] This is the argument of Thurman Arnold in *Prof. Hart's Theology*, 73 Harv. L. Rev. 1298-1317 1960). See also Richard H. Fallon, Jr., *The Ideologies of Federal Courts Law*, 74 Va. L. Rev. 1141-1251(1988).

[48] This is argued by Guido Calabresi, *A Common Law for the Age of Statutes* (Cambridge: Harvard University Press, 1982).

to a judicial philosophy as the 'correct' one. These two issues are interconnected. A judge who adopts, say, legal realism should become well-versed at the same time in the strong points of legal formalism and originalism. And should a judge become a public advocate for a position through essays and speeches (as prominently did Justices Holmes and Scalia for their point of view) they must also bring their knowledge of the full range of issues pro and con involved in adopting their judicial philosophy into the public debate. Thus, a judge who claims to be only and always a pure textualist or unabashed consequentialist runs the risk of becoming merely an ideological instrument for political ideologues who are confident that the philosophy adopted will always deliver the results they desire. Adopting a specific judicial philosophy as the *only* correct method of judicial review, outside the context of a case before the court, is evidence that a judge is very likely operating in bad faith and is in violation of his oath of office. That oath does not only contain a commitment to impartiality, but also a commitment to "do equal right to the poor and to the rich." This latter promise is morally substantive and not every judicial philosophy can be said to achieve that right equitably. So, adopting a judicial philosophy *a priori* runs the risk of delegitimizing much of American statutory and constitutional law. For some philosophical purists that may be a desirable outcome. They may want to uproot entirely the common law system and replace it with a judicial code applicable everywhere American courts have jurisdiction. They may want to eliminate the case law system of American legal education and replace it with the study of code treatises or foundational first principles of constitutional analysis as they see them to be. Were this to occur, the long tradition of discursive scholarly legal analysis expressed, for example, in Law Review articles also would decline because there would be fewer issues to contest or ways of doing so.

A good appellate judge, then, who adopts a rationale of a certain judicial philosophy within a written opinion should be under an obligation to explain why the analysis of competitors should be ruled out. Furthermore, a good appellate judge who publicly advances a specific judicial philosophy is under a greater obligation to avoid engaging in sloppy or simplistic rhetoric or make overblown promises about the validity of that philosophy because such public display has clear political implications. It is simplistic to argue that the role of the judge is to *interpret* and not *make* law when, in fact, rules of interpretation can be a disguise for making law.[49] Judges who advance and become associated with a specific judicial philosophy as a means of effectuating legal reform step into the shoes of politicians and become political reformers as well. This they may do since they are both citizens and resources, but they must do so candidly and sincerely. As it turns out certain philosophies are better at masking political motivations because they make it easier for judges to more plausibly tell 'noble lies' about their own impartiality.[50] A judicial philosophy may be embraced because it provides cover for ideological bias and produces the results its advocates wanted in the first place. Without a need to refute the conclusions of a contrary philosophy, judges are free to write their opinions without the threat of being subject to close counterfactual questioning and argument that, ironically, is the hallmark of their own courtroom practice.

Perhaps, only the Legal Process approach, in spite of the criticisms already noted, comes closest to exposing the motivations and assumptions of a judge. Wechsler, for example, wanted a deep interrogation of norms of interpretation as well as of their selective use in deriving a legal result. Methodological candor should govern every step of judicial review: judges should not argue from 'original intent' when they know the argument is historically inconclusive; they should not overpromise the salutary effects of their preferred method of interpretation; they should not acknowledge that meanings are fixed if there is evidence to the contrary; and they should strive to explain why in some cases they give greater weight to precedent than in others.[51] These intellectual virtues will help make a judge good in the work of judging but good also in the work of serving the Constitution, the representative republic, and the public generally.

---

[49] See William N. Eskridge, Jr., *The New Textualism and Normative Canons, Reading Law: The Interpretation of Legal Texts,* 113 Colum. L. Rev. 531 (2013); and Charlie D. Stewart, *The Rhetorical Canons of Construction: New Textualism's Rhetoric Problem,* 116 Mich. L. Rev. 1485 (2018).

[50] Jason Iuliano, *The Supreme Court's Noble Lie,* 51 U.C. Davis L. Rev. 911 (2018).

[51] See Kent Greenawalt, *The Enduring Significance of Neutral Principles,* 78 Colum. L. Rev. 982, 1005-1006 (1978).

Part Three: Practice

The central importance and purpose of law, and its relation to morality and social norms, is not what the legal theoreticians say about it; nor about the ways in which the law becomes established, whether by statute or judicial opinion; and nor in its most salient manner in the processes where it undergoes a stress test in the trial and appellate courts. Rather, its greatest influence by far is its vitally important function in broadly affecting and regulating the lives of those subject to it. Part III covers some of the applications of law at ground level where it exerts influence and structures priorities upon the enduring components of social life: religion, communication, privacy, politics, and in all the various ways we may or may not be able to live our lives under its coercive regime.

CHAPTER 5

LAW AND RELIGION

The word 'religion' is both familiar and vague. Since it is used in many contexts, the context is important for understanding its meaning. In referring to religion many people often are referring to their own religion or to their own understanding of what religions are when speaking of the 'religions of the world'. However, there is no clear consensus among scholars of religion as to what they are studying or even how their subject should be studied. This difficulty in defining what a religion is may be found in popular culture as well as in law. One person's religion may be another person's cult or philosophy. But the definitional problems may be even more difficult to solve if ideas we hold today about what a religion is were not contemplated by the framers and ratifiers of the Constitution when they drafted the First Amendment.[1] An originalist argument, for example, assumes that when they used that term, they limited their understanding to an external set of familiar beliefs comprising a creed or dogma, and not to an internal set of experiences and feelings engendered by those beliefs. If so, originalists must seem to claim, a religion would fall out of the original constitutional protection when the expressed beliefs changed; and nor could an old dogma be modified by a new interpretation without an external change of creed.

In this chapter we will examine possible answers to five questions: (1) What is religion? (2) What were some founders' views of religion? (3) How have the courts treated the subject since the founding era? (4) Is it possible for

---

[1] See Lee J. Strang, *The Meaning of 'Religion' in the First Amendment*, 40 Duq. L. Rev. 181 (2002) (arguing that the word 'religion' referred to a belief in one God, to whom we owed duties, and who established a system of rewards and punishments in the afterlife). See also Kent Greenawalt, *Religion and the Constitution, Free Exercise and Fairness* (Princeton, N.J.: Princeton University Press, 2009): 133-64. Consider the treatment by the court of Fulan Gong, in *Zhang Jingrong v. Chinese Anti-Cult World Alliance*, 311 F. Supp. 3d 514 (2018).

the law to *legally* recognize ('cognize') religion? And (5) *should* the law cognize religion? The broader question is: to what extent does American law establish a clear and consistent line of constitutionality between religion and the state, as the First Amendment seems to set out; or does the whole religion question come down to a patchwork of *ad hoc* responses to the latest sectarian pressure groups of the day.

Defining 'Religion'

Scholars who study religion, and who typically provide expert testimony in court about whether or not a certain belief system is a 'religion', provide various answers to the question of how to define religion: (1) religion is a set of rituals, behaviors, and beliefs that help individuals adjust to fearful uncertainties like death or react to awe-inspiring improbable events (often characterized as miracles or numinous experiences), resulting in a *present* sense of comfort and hope predicated upon a belief in a *future* guarantee of fulfillment, salvation and/or transcendence to an elevated dimension of conscious life; (2) an authoritative set of symbols and practices designed to bind individuals to an authoritative social system such as a church, synagogue, ministry, order, and the like; (3) a theoretical construct of Western liberal ecumenical ideology usually expressed as 'comparative' or 'global' religion; (4) a pre-scientific method of generating inferences from which to establish explanations of natural events under sparse knowledge conditions; (5) the pseudo-empirical results of the practice of using language outside its empirical reference range; (6) a belief system that assumes the existence of conscious supernatural agents influencing and operating upon the creatures of natural life; and (7) the vehicle whether as belief and/or practice through which God or some sustaining and perhaps transcendent Natural Order of Things reveals knowledge and moral teachings of right living and perhaps even destiny to human beings.[2]

---

[2] For various approaches to religion see Benjamin Beit-Hallahmi, *Psychological Perspectives on Religion and Religiosity* (New York: Routledge, 2015); Enzo Pace, *Religion as Communication: God's Talk* (Burlington, VT.: Ashgate, 2011); Timothy Fitzgerald, *The Ideology of Religious Studies* (Oxford: Oxford University Press, 2000); Mark Juergensmeyer and Wade Clark Roof, eds., *Encyclopedia of Global Religion*

The first five definitions explain religion as an entirely natural human activity, whether or not recognized by believers and practitioners to be as such. The sixth posits the actual or possible existence of non-human and probably non-caring thinking beings, such as a deistic God, or intelligent extraterrestrials, etc. Finally, the seventh is the stance of the overwhelming number of traditional believers, who claim that religious faith is the recognition of divine activity that articulates and communicates rules for human knowledge and conduct, a view articulated by Catholic theologian and Dominican friar, Thomas Aquinas (1225-1274), in his *Summa Theologica*: "Faith has not that research of natural reason which demonstrates what is believed, but a research into those things whereby a man is *induced to believe*, for instance that such things have been uttered by God and confirmed by miracles."[3] Unlike non-believing humans or angelic demons with a capacity for faith but who pridefully seek its justification, faith that brings salvation must always be unquestioned. This view is sometimes called *fideism*.

Religious belief typically includes assumptions about the sources of legitimate knowledge and authority, making it easy for people with different assumptions to talk past each other. Religious discussion, then, often leads to a realization that your faith entails your affirmative disbelief in mine. Talk about religion also embeds assumptions derived from culture and historical context, typically being linked to ethnicity and nationality. Thus, defining it and even formulating a method of studying it is a persistent problem for those who study religion, and who realize how easy it is to fall into an ideological or ambiguous use of the term. As a result,

---

(Thousand Oaks, CA.: Sage, 2012); Frans Wijsen and Kocku von Stuckrad, eds., *Making Religion: Theory and Practice in the Discursive Study of Religion* (Leiden: Brill, 2016); Russell T. McCutcheon, *Studying Religion: An Introduction* (London: Equinox, 2007); Ivan Strenski, *Understanding Theories of Religion: An Introduction* (Malden, MA.: Wiley Blackwell, 2015); René Gothóni, *Words Matter: Hermeneutics in the Study of Religions* (New York: Peter Lang, 2011); Carl Olson, *The Allure of Decadent Thinking: Religious Studies and the Challenge of Postmodernism* (New York: Oxford University Press, 2013).

[3] St. Thomas Aquinas, *Summa Theologica,* trans. Fathers of the English Dominican Province, 2nd. ed. (New York: Cosimo, 2007), Q.2 Art. 2, Pt. II-II, p. 1174. (Emphasis mine.)

many religious scholars worry about the possibility of even making accurate characterizations of a religion without first having to embrace some form of it.[4]

The term 'religion' itself has roots ('*religio*') that go back to ancient Rome where the term seems to be tied to pious feelings, and rituals paying respect to ancestors. Religion, typically as described by Roman politician and lawyer, Marcus Tullius Cicero (106 BCE-43 BCE), also was an attribute of the state itself. Good governance meant that the religion component was working properly as intended; it was harmonizing social life and creating public solidarity. Early and Medieval Christianity, by contrast, increasingly looked upon religion as a personal commitment to overcome Original Sin by providing a sacramental journey to salvation. With the Reformation came appeals to conscience that could not be countermanded by any worldly institution, whether an established church or a state. However, the Greco-Roman notion of religion as the glue of the state did not fully disappear. French political theorist, Alexis de Tocqueville) (1805-1859), thought religion to be the source of all morality in the modern nation state. A public faith was required, especially in a democratic state of many sovereign citizens. The truthfulness of religion was less important than its usefulness; in the abstract 'religion' could be something that many different sects and faiths could have in common, while religious debate over doctrinal minutia was unresolvable and itself a danger to good governance.[5]

The modern popular use of 'religion', as opposed to its use by many scholars today, is reflected in expressions like 'a religion', 'the Christian religion', 'the religions of the world', 'organized religion', or even 'system

---

[4] Gregory W. Dawes and James Maclaurin, eds., *A New Science of Religion* (New York: Routledge, 2013), 18. Also see Pascal Boyer, "Explaining Religious Concepts," in William W. McCorkle and Dimitris Xygalatas, eds., *Mental Culture: Classical Social theory and the Cognitive Science of Religion* (Bristol, CT.: Acumen, 2013); Aaron Rizzieri, *Pragmatic Encroachment, Religious Belief and Practice* (Basingstoke: Palgrave Macmillan, 2013); J. L. Schellenberg, *Prolegomena to a Philosophy of Religion* (Ithaca: Cornell University Press, 2005).

[5] Attila K Molnar, "The Construction of the Early Notion of Religion in Early Modern Europe," *Method and Theory in the Study of Religion*, Vol 14 No. 1 (2002): 47-60.

of religion' as used by Thomas Jefferson when he wrote in the early 1780s that earth "is inhabited by a thousand millions of people. That these profess probably a thousand different systems of religion. That ours [Christianity] is but one of that thousand."[6] Today, as in Jefferson's time, the notion of religion is closely tied to group identity as something to belong to; and since the founding era it has been considered a constitutionally protected social activity. There has never been a formal obligation to be a member of a religious association. The framers made sure that membership in any religion was not a job qualification for holding public office in the United States. This separation of religion from state power may be based on the view that, whatever else religion may be as a social activity, it is ultimately something to be "expressed and experienced in the lives of *individuals*."[7]

But those who study religion also know that they must study both its inner and outer dimensions because mature individuals usually are part of a culture, and since culture is part of an historical period, scholars should also study religions historically. Many, if not most, religions have sustained histories, so that it is often possible to trace their lineage as if a migration of people and their ideas across space and time. Nonetheless, religious continuity requires that religions be continually adopted and be given meaning exclusively by living individuals. So, it makes sense to say that religion is "a complex and emergent phenomenon and, therefore, must be studied with multiple methodologies, none of which exhausts the meaning of the phenomenon"; and also, that there can be no trans-historical essence of religion because any definition of religion is itself "the historical product of discursive processes."[8]

Some scholars of religion, however, do not divide religion into its inner and outer expressions, but consider it an early form of natural reasoning. Cognitive science of religion (CSR) maintains that religion is the result of a natural cognitive activity, a branch on the same tree of knowledge as

---

[6] Thomas Jefferson, *Writings* (New York: Literary Classics of the United States, 1984), 286.

[7] Meredith B. McGuire, *Lived Religion: Faith and Practice in Everyday Life* (Oxford: Oxford University Press, 2008), 3. (emphasis added).

[8] William Grassie, *The New Sciences of Religion: Exploring Spirituality from the Outside In and Bottom Up* (New York: Palgrave Macmillan, 2010), 4.

natural science, but whereas science developed a habit of inference making closely tied to hypothetical testing and experimentation, religion generated vivid explanatory inferences that were not well tested but easier to explain and disseminate widely. For example, beliefs in heaven or hell were closely tied to decisions about how consequential moral conduct should be. But rather than go down that thorny philosophical road, it was easier to convey such decisions in starker terms of punishment and reward. CSR theorists frequently point out the gap between official dogmas and how individuals process their own theology – usually with little or no concern for blatant inconsistencies in daily life.[9]

Cognitive anthropologist, Pascal Boyer, gives CSR an evolutionary perspective. He describes religion as a product of normal cognitive activity by a mind that requires little leaps of faith in order to make sense of, and control, a world that vastly overpowers it. The principle hypothetical vehicle that makes some inferences and hypotheses 'religious' is that they explain by postulating supernatural agents with the power and cognitive ability to control and change events. We have a built-in mental gadget, CSR theorists call a Hyperactive Agency Detection Device that makes it perfectly plausible that Mickey Mouse could be both a mouse, wear clothes, and talk. However, not all such agents are the perfectly well-honed perfect beings of theological monotheism; some make mistakes, others are forgetful and these too can explain misery or misfortune. In Boyer's view, a person can be 'religious' in attributing events to supernatural agents without having any faith that what these agents do can matter to us or that we can do anything about it in return. In fact, he argues, we can have a religion without 'faith', without a need to believe. Prayers and rituals are efforts to engage such agents. The ceremony of marriage is not only the symbolic act of the father 'giving' his daughter to his future son-in-law; it also calls upon God to bear eternal witness to the transaction. In advanced Western monotheism, Boyer's supernatural agents are typically highly interested parties; they stand in judgment over every moment of our lives, are moral law givers, see all and never forget. It would seem, then, that in these Abrahamic religions there is strong motivation to embed religion in

[9] D. Jason Slone, *Theological Incorrectness: Why Religious People Believe What They Shouldn't* (New York: Oxford University Press, 2004).

law, since we are able to more easily encourage a public belief in the specific operation of divine agency when we regard human life as subject to divine laws. In that form, Divine imperatives take the shape of legal imperatives; law is more effective as an expression of God's will and more efficient than continual prayers of intercession and highly infrequent bolts of lightning from above.[10]

From this brief survey one point emerges clearly: that *there is no settled view* of 'religion' among scholars who study it. Instead, they discriminate its many aspects – cultural, historical, cognitive, institutional, expressive, emotive, and deeply personal – none of which entirely exhaust the subject.

Madison and Jefferson

The American founding fathers, reflecting the interests of the general public, thought a lot about religion and wondered what its place should be in their new society. They struggled with the idea of religion with as much sophistication as today's scholars do. The early Republic has been called a "laboratory for the pluralization of knowledge about religions and for the negotiation of shifting views on religion's place within 'public' and 'private' spheres."[11] In the first half of the nineteenth century Americans learned something of Buddhism, Hinduism, Islam, Taoism, and Confucianism, eventually setting the table for a book like that of American philosopher and psychologist, William James (1842-1910), titled appropriately *The Varieties of Religious Experience: A Study in Human Nature* (1902). The Constitution provided that there be no 'religious' test for qualification for federal office (Art VI, Sec. 3.). It also makes one reference to 'religion': "Congress shall make no law respecting an establishment of religion, or prohibiting the free exercise thereof" (First Amendment). We know from this sentence alone that the framers thought of religion as something capable of being externalized (established) and internalized

---

[10] Pascal Boyer, *Religion Explained: The Evolutionary Origins of Religious Thought* (New York: Basic Books, 2001), 172-180, 300.

[11] Leigh E. Schmidt, "A History of All Religions," *Journal of the Early Republic,* 22 (2004): 328.

(exercised). But what did the framers mean when they used the words *religion* and *religious*?

Did they simply mean, in reference to their American contemporaries, 'your religion and mine'? Or did religion refer specifically to allegiance only to Protestant Christianity generally, or even only to its mainline established churches, or could various sects also be included as smaller variants within Protestant Christianity? In 1785 Madison and Jefferson opposed a Virginia bill to provide taxpayer money for religious instruction by ministers. The bill adopted the ancient Roman justification of religion as a necessity for the health of society by creating a religious community in Virginia guided by religious educators:

> Whereas the general diffusion of Christian knowledge hath a natural tendency to correct the morals of men, restrain their vices, and preserve the peace of society; which cannot be effected without a competent provision for learned teachers, who may be thereby enabled to devote their time and attention to the duty of instructing such citizens, . . . it is judged that such provision may be made by the Legislature, without counteracting the liberal principle heretofore adopted and intended to be preserved by abolishing all distinctions of pre-eminence amongst the different societies or communities of Christians.[12]

The bill assumed there was such a thing as generic, non-denominational "Christian knowledge" that could be articulated and taught in a non-denominational manner to an already existing Christian populace. The bill also asserted as a bedrock "liberal principle" that no Christian sect would be favored by state funding.

Madison, however, doubted that real neutrality was possible in the legislative process. For the state to pay teachers of Christian knowledge it must inevitably choose sides in doctrinal disputes and interpretations, and, of course, exclude non-Christian teachers of non-Christian religions. In the "Memorial and Remonstrance against Religious Assessments," written anonymously and only acknowledged by him thirty-one years later, he wrote:

---

[12] "A Bill Establishing a Provision for Teachers of the Christian Religion," (1784).

> The Religion then of every man must be left to the conviction and conscience of every man; and it is the right of every man to exercise it as these may dictate. This right is in its nature an unalienable right. It is unalienable, because the opinions of men, depending only on the evidence contemplated by their own minds cannot follow the dictates of other men: it is unalienable also, because what is here a right towards men, is a duty towards the Creator. It is the duty of every man to render to the Creator such homage and such only as he believes to be acceptable to him.[13]

In the "Remonstrance," Madison also argued that established churches do not have a good historical record in maintaining "the purity and efficacy of Religion," producing instead "pride and indolence in the Clergy, ignorance and servility in the laity, in both, superstition, bigotry and persecution." By inevitably favoring the more entrenched and influential religions, Virginia would no longer be a place of asylum "to the persecuted and oppressed of every Nation and Religion."[14] Not surprisingly, during the Constitutional Convention Madison would argue (on June 6, 1787) that 'Religion itself may become a motive to persecution and oppression'.

But what did Madison include in "every . . . Religion" and why did he seem to say that religion *itself* could become oppressive? He may have used 'religion' in two senses, the internal and external, without clearly distinguishing them. Religious duty, he argued, has priority over the claims of civil society: "in matters of religion, no man's right is abridged by the institution of Civil Society," he wrote.[15] Internally, religious duty is a state of mind and feeling belonging to an individual who alone can determine what that duty should be and how it should be carried out. Externally, there are also rights belonging to "matters of religion" that may not be interfered with by the state. These matters, presumably, pertained to the visual and practical manifestations of religion in society, to the churches, prayer books, hymns, vestments, clergymen, and overt rituals.

Madison may have seen no serious conflict between these two senses. Religion could be experienced internally as reflection and devotion, or

---

[13] James Madison, *The Writings of James Madison*, ed. Gaillard Hunt (New York: G. P. Putnam, 1901), II: 184.

[14] Ibid., 187-88.

[15] Ibid., 185.

externally as social participation in ritual or public prayer. He may have realized that there is no way to pragmatically disentangle these two forms of religion. Spirituality seeks and is nourished by fellowship expressed socially. Besides, the states had been engaged in a variety of official and institutional forms of religious discrimination, favoring some, disfavoring others. So, why did the framers think it important enough to add a religious test prohibition? In the course of the Virginia bill controversy, Madison had made two arguments: a practical political one and a philosophical one. Established religions, he claimed, *inevitably* lead to political authoritarianism in their effort to save men's souls in ways incompatible with a free society. But more importantly and philosophically, no individual could submit to the authority of sacred writings, the sayings of prophets, or the truth claims of living preachers and teachers, without first *weighing evidence pro and con regarding those claims.* That is the force of the word "cannot" when Madison writes: "the opinions of men, depending only on the evidence contemplated by their own minds *cannot* follow the dictates of other men."[16] We have an unavoidable duty of inquiry to evaluate and test the claims of religious advocates; no one else can do this for us. Even if we accept our parents' religion we do so because we judge their satisfaction with it. But we cannot blindly defer to authority in all of its forms without first identifying some traits that are worthy of being considered authoritative. By relying on vague or unsound sources, and uncritical thinking, Madison saw this problem of religious authority as undermining its role in law and government. "If religion be not within [the] cognizance of civil government, how can its legal establishment be said to be necessary to civil government?"[17] There was an unavoidable barrier, then, for established religion, based on its recourse to revelation and tradition, to serve as guidance for government in a free society premised upon republican principles. In that respect Madison was entirely a man of the Enlightenment.

Jefferson's fear of the corrosive effect of sectarian thinking on the capacity for self-governance is illustrated by his scissors and paste removal of all mention of miracles in his copies of the Bible, leaving behind only the moral sayings of Jesus. Nonetheless, he followed Locke in wanting something

---

[16] Madison, *Writings*, 184.

[17] Ibid., 188.

approximating a national religion that unified the American people around common moral values and a respect for science and the values of inquiry, a religion devoid of the pessimistic pronouncements found, for example, in Calvinism. To be avoided was the fanaticism found in the night meetings of Richmond, where women "attended by their priests and sometimes by a hen-pecked husband, . . . pour forth the effusions of their love to Jesus, in terms as amatory and carnal, as their modesty would permit them to use to a mere earthly lover."

The better model, Jefferson suggested, could be found in Charlottesville where religious practices only contained a "small spice" of fanaticism:

> We have four sects, but without either church or meeting-house. The courthouse is the common temple, one Sunday in the month to each. Here, the Episcopalian and Presbyterian, Methodist and Baptist, meet together, join in hymning their Maker, listen with attention and devotion to each other's preachers, and all mix in society with perfect harmony. It is not so in the districts where Presbyterianism prevails undividedly. There ambition and tyranny would tolerate no rival if they had power.[18]

The purpose of the "no religious test," then, seems to have been to erect an absolute barrier to religious autocracy in government, both for pragmatic and philosophical reasons. Even if with personal reservations that no Jew, Muslim, Deist, or atheist likely would ever gain public office as a practical reality in a Christian nation, the explicit *no*-test provision is a blanket rejection of ever devising an acceptable test for official religious orthodoxy in a free society. Even if the provision pertained merely to oaths or affirmations, as is sometimes claimed, it is directed against federal officials, prohibiting them from even attempting to place religious wording in an oath or affirmation of office. At the time, some state oaths were being used to protect their official state religions, requiring allegiance to specific religious beliefs, such as a belief in the Holy Trinity or in the New Testament as the revealed word of God. The no-test provision seems to recognize that referring to religious doctrine in the act that creates official governmental power would likely become yet another source of religious and political controversy, this time in the very heart of official duty. Even

---

[18] Jefferson, *Writings*, 1462. Letter to Dr. Thomas Cooper, November 2, 1822.

bland assertions of belief would be controversial to some sect or another. Conflicting interpretations of this or that line of scripture were plentiful. Whole sects were built around them. And what would the previous oath become if a new party came into office with a different religious orientation? If the wording of oaths embedded religious dogma, could religious apostasy become a source of delegitimizing office holders during their tenures, thus undemocratically erasing from history whole administrations? "The people in power were always right, and everybody else wrong. If you admit the least difference, the door to persecution is opened," argued James Iredell (1751-1799), one of the first Justices of the Supreme Court, in 1788 at the North Carolina Ratifying Convention.[19]

The First Amendment religion clause may be seen as a second attempt to call a truce over religious discord in the new republic. It may also be thought of as an attempt to remove religion as a tool of party politics, which Madison was beginning to see as an ever-increasing source of political discord. Baptists were horsewhipped in Virginia for preaching. Maryland Catholics and Protestants were continually echoing the English religious wars. Efforts were made for a while to dampen sectarian controversies by requiring only that a person in government asset there is a God, that God must be publicly worshiped, and that it was the duty of every man to tell the truth in a court of law as if standing before God. However, this form of theism was too rich for some and to bland for others. Eventually, the long experiment in state-support of an official religion, begun in the first colonies two centuries earlier, ended in 1833 when Massachusetts was the final state to disestablish its state religion.

Religion in the Courts

In looking back to the founding era, we must keep in mind: (1) that the establishment and free exercise clauses of the First Amendment did not apply to the states until 1940; and (2) when conflicts between faith and civic duty, religion and law, emerged mainly *ad hoc* religious exemptions were

---

[19] "Debate of the North Carolina Ratifying Convention," (July 30, 1788) in Philip B. Kurland and Ralph Lerner, eds., *The Founders' Constitution* (Chicago: University of Chicago Press, 1987), 5: 90.

created. Exemptions to worship and believe, however, from the beginning were never freely granted. They had to pass through a filter that weighed the various competing *institutional* interests of church and state. In the process, questions of fairness and equality invariably arose. The default position was that individuals had a right to worship God according to the dictates of their conscience as long as that exercise did not disturb public peace or adversely affect other individuals. Some states encumbered free exercise doctrinally: Maryland and Delaware required that free exercise protections applied only to Christian worship, while most states at the time, required that God be worshipped, and left it to believer to choose the manner.

Prior to Independence, swearing oaths, fighting wars, and paying taxes for religious support were the main sources of disputes between religious and civic duty. Citing the Bible (*Matthew* 5:33-37), Quakers refused to take any oath; so, states enacted laws to allow them to swear by affirmation to tell the truth but not by calling God as your witness. Quakers and Mennonites also refused to bear arms, so some states allowed payment of a fine, providing a substitute person, or requiring other useful service. But Catholics were not given an exemption against a New Orleans ordinance banning open casket funerals in churches for reasons of public health.[20] Nor was a man found guilty of manslaughter who appealed his conviction because an opponent of capital punishment was removed as a juror before trial. A Pennsylvania court ruled that, since a unanimous verdict was needed for conviction, to require a death penalty opponent to serve as a juror would effectively abolish the death penalty in any case where the defendant is lucky to get such a juror.[21] A religious exemption was denied to a Jewish plaintiff, who claimed a right not to appear in court on a Saturday, because allowing such a precedent would subject the court calendar to private religious scruples. "There are no duties half so sacred as those which the citizen owes to the laws," the court concluded.[22] Similar objections were made against Sabbatarians who opposed laws prohibiting work on Sunday except for charity or necessity. The court argued that such laws were applied neutrally to all and were required for efficient

---

[20] *Permoli v. Municipality No. 1,* 44 U.S. 588 (1845).

[21] *Commonwealth v Lesher,* 17 Serg. & Rawle 155 (Pa. 1828).

[22] *Philips v Gratz,* 2 Pen. & W. 412 (1831).

commerce. Religious liberty merely meant freedom of religion from state mandates, for example a law *requiring* Sabbatarians to work on Saturday.[23]

In the Sabbatarian cases, courts initially reasoned that a chosen day of rest was necessary for economic efficiency and that Sunday was chosen for nonsectarian reasons.[24] However, the suspicion that Sunday laws had Christian motivation behind them increased during the nineteenth century. Why were such laws always about Sunday, a California court asked, if the rationale was that there should be one day a week for social rest? Religious motivation could not hide behind the claim that the laws were merely neutral economic regulations. Nor did the claim that such laws did not prohibit worship on other days – Muslims on Fridays, Jews and Sabbatarians on Saturdays – take into consideration the restrictions imposed on Sunday work, thereby requiring that Sabbatarians and non-Christians bear the burden of having two days off a week.[25] But all pretenses were dropped in a New York ruling mandating Sunday as the day off because "the Christian religion is the religion of the people, as distinguished from the false religions of the world."[26]

In the later part of the nineteenth century, public schools were often the focus of religion court cases. In a Vermont case, several parents claimed their free exercise was violated when their children, some sixty in a number, were expelled from public school because they went to a Roman Catholic religious service instead of class. The court found no violation because the school attendance rules were not expressly intended to disrupt religious service or interfere with the rights of conscience. Religious freedom only meant being able to embrace a religious doctrine, not being allowed to carry out all religious activities in public, the court reasoned. Furthermore, no divine authority was quoted authorizing church attendance on the specific day at issue; so it was a personal choice of the parents since many Catholics in the village had gone about their business as any other day. The court also asked whether a Catholic sheriff could suspend his official duty in serving a

---

[23] *Specht v. Commonwealth*, 8 Pa. 312 (1848).

[24] *Hiram Bloom v. Cornelius Richards*, 2 Ohio St. 387 (1853).

[25] *Ex parte Newman*, 9 Cal. 502 (1858).

[26] *Lindenmuller v People*, 33 Barb. 548 (1861).

subpoena, or a Catholic juror in not attending trial, in order to attend church services.[27] A Wisconsin court in 1890 ruled that reading the King James Bible, designated as a 'textbook' by the school district, in public school was a prohibited "sectarian" activity in violation of the state constitution, regardless of whether children are permitted to withdraw from the school room during the readings. The court took judicial notice that there would be numerous religious sects demanding accommodation, each designated as 'Christian', with many different and conflicting doctrines, including disputes over predestination, eternal punishment, apostolic succession, authority of priesthood, the sufficiency of holy Scripture for faith, the nature and efficacy of the sacraments, whether the Bible is in all respects literally true, and the nature or the divinity of Christ.[28]

Bible-reading or hymn singing in public school was a continual source of legal controversy in the early twentieth century. In a few cases, the practices were upheld based on the view that when the First Amendment was drafted Bible reading was prevalent in the public schools and so it was never the intent of the framers that states could not continue that practice. However, many states' constitutions had provisions similar to the establishment and free exercise provisions in the federal Constitution. Opponents of the practice, often Catholics, argued that compulsory education meant compulsory attendance at *de facto* Protestant religious ceremonies. Many courts agreed, arguing that the Bible is not a doctrinally neutral document but a sacred writing within a denominational tradition, and more broadly within a tradition of Christianity when contrasted with Judaism for example. As a result, Bible reading and hymn singing in public school constituted a form of worship.[29]

In the twentieth century courts increasingly had to decide whether religious activity in public schools was constitutionally lawful, and if so in what form. In Iowa a public school board dominated by Catholics rented a

---

[27] *Ferriter v Tyler*, 48 Vt. 444 (1876).

[28] *State ex rel Weiss v District Board of School District No. 8 of the City of Edgerton* 76 Wis. 177 (1890).

[29] *People ex rel. Ring v. Board of Education of District 24*, 245 Ill. 334 (1910); for contrary views see *Wilkerson v City of Rome*, 152 Ga. 762 (1922), *Vollmar v. Stanley* 81 Colo. 276 (1927) and *Kaplan v. Independent School District of Virginia* 171 Minn. 142 (1927).

portion of a Catholic school ostensibly to save money, and employed one of the nuns as a teacher. However, the rent was never paid nor demanded, and Catholic religious teaching, using religious textbooks, continued in the 'public' section of the building. The court recognized that the school board, with the majority support of the district's Catholics, was using public money for Catholic instruction. It also rejected the idea that the instruction was merely generically religious: "There is no such thing as a universally accepted religion, and differences of opinion and thought along these lines have developed an almost numberless variety of churches, societies, and other voluntary organizations, each dedicated to the promotion of the peculiar views of its adherents."[30] In the course of analyzing these school Bible cases, courts often had to decide what constitutes a *religion*. Giving a spiritual reading as a psychic medium for a fee was not a religious activity because it did not specifically refer to a divinity, and did not invoke reverence, worship, and obedience to the mandate of a supernatural being, an Oklahoma court concluded.[31] Jehovah's Witnesses pupils, who were expelled for refusing to recite the Pledge of Allegiance in class because they considered it a form of idolatry, did not engage in constitutionally protected religious activity because there was nothing religious about the pledge.[32] Almost at once a federal court disagreed, saying that the Jehovah's Witnesses showed all the signs of being a genuine religion.[33]

In the 1930s religious discrimination cases began using the Fourteenth Amendment guarantee of the equal protection, due process, and privileges and immunities clauses against state laws. A California law requiring students in state colleges to take a course in military sciences was upheld because it was a universal duty of all citizens to defend their government against all enemies regardless of religious conviction.[34] However, in another Jehovah's Witnesses case the Supreme Court decided that the First Amendment's free exercise and establishment clauses, coupled with the

---

[30] *Knowlton v. Baumhover* 182 Iowa 691 (1918).

[31] *McMasters v. State* 207 P. 566 (1922).

[32] *Nicholls v. Lynn,* 297 Mas. 65 (1937); also *Bleich v. Board of Public Instruction* 139 Fla. 43 (1939).

[33] *Minersville School Dist. v. Gobitis* 103 F.2d 683 (3rd Cir 1939).

[34] *Hamilton v. University of California* 293 U.S. 245 (1934).

state restrictions in the Fourteenth Amendment, restricted *state* laws encumbering religion. The Witnesses could not be restricted from going door to door, even in a largely Catholic neighborhood, with pamphlets calling the Papacy an instrument of Satan. In order to impose restrictions on religious activity, the state had to clearly identify specific conduct constituting a clear and present danger to the public.[35]

Under the Fourteenth Amendment standard it became necessary for federal courts to weigh the religious component in any state law affecting the public. If the law had a broad public purpose that also benefitted a religious group but not going so far as to establish a religious preference, it might very well be constitutional. For example, child welfare laws requiring vaccinations or attendance at school, if applied neutrally, would override religious objections to them. Such laws, it was argued, had a religiously neutral broad social purpose in promoting healthy productive citizens as part of an overriding foundation of a democratic society.[36] Reimbursing parochial school children for the cost of bus transportation also met the constitutional test because the expenditure did not involve classroom teaching, applied to any religious school, and promoted safe transportation to all of the public.[37] However, public benefit was not a factor in a case involving a New York State program allowing public school students to attend religious instruction during the school day. The program was entirely for the benefit of the religious students, who left their public classroom for religious instruction elsewhere. No public funds were involved and there were provisions for determining attendance of religious classes. Promoting religious values was the explicit reason for the ruling. In the words of Justice William O. Douglas:

> We are a religious people whose institutions presuppose a Supreme Being. We guarantee the freedom to worship as one chooses. We make room for as wide a variety of beliefs and creeds as the spiritual needs of man deem necessary. We sponsor an attitude on the part of government that shows no

---

[35] *Cantwell v. Connecticut*, 310 U.S. 296 (1940); see also *Murdock v. Pennsylvania*, 319 U.S. 105 (1943).

[36] *Prince v. Massachusetts*, 321 U.S. 158 (1944).

[37] *Everson v. Board of Education*, 330 U.S. 1 (1947). This case incorporated the establishment clause into the Fourteenth Amendment.

> partiality to any one group and that lets each flourish according to the zeal of its adherents and the appeal of its dogma.[38]

In the nineteen fifties and early sixties Sunday closing laws were also placed under Fourteenth Amendment scrutiny. These laws were a hodgepodge of exemptions and exceptions. Bakeries could be open on Sunday, ostensibly to provide fresh bread, but also other pastry goods. Businesses associated with recreation received exemptions, such as live bait shops for noncommercial fishing, and auto rentals, but also transactions deemed necessary, such as drugstores, newspaper deliveries, and sales of perishable items like milk and cheese and ice cream. Some commercial activities were restricted to operating before 11 AM, while others selling tobacco and liquor only in the afternoon. Professional sports were licensed to be played between 1:30 PM and 6:30 PM, amateur sports between 2:00 PM and 6:30 PM. However, kosher supermarkets which were closed from sundown Friday to sundown Saturday, only had the option of being open from Saturday night until 10:00 AM Sunday rather than all day Sunday. Their owners complained unsuccessfully that the weekend hours are insufficient for a viable business, that fresh meat should not wait to be sold between Friday night and Monday morning, and that the restrictions impacted on their kosher diet, and therefore upon their religion.[39]

Seventh-day Adventists also treated Saturday as the Sabbath, a day of rest and reflection. However, when they refused to work on Saturday and were fired, they were disqualified from receiving unemployment benefits. Traditional economic reasons were given by employers for why this law must be upheld: they should not be in the business of juggling and responding to the religious schedules of their employees, and should not be in the business of determining the authenticity of the religious rules or the sincerity of their employees in following them.

Furthermore, judging the degree of orthodoxy or sincerity of beliefs as part of an individual's 'spiritual life' was not the business of the courts because

---

[38] *Zorach v. Clauson,* 343 U.S. 306 (1952).

[39] *Gallagher v. Crown Kosher Supermarket of Massachusetts,* 366 U.S. 617 (1961); also *McGowan v. Maryland,* 366 U.S. 420 (1961).

religious truth claims could not be readily and efficiently ascertained using the traditional adjudicatory function of courts.[40] The issue of adjudicating religious truth claims, however, did arise in a 1944 case involving a claim of mail fraud for distributing religious literature through the Postal Service.[41] In that case two leaders of a new religious movement distributed literature claiming its text had been dictated by Jesus. A central issue in the case was whether the defendants sincerely believed what the literature asserted. If they did, then they did not have an intent to defraud. The case turned on the distinction between the truth of someone's belief and their good faith belief in the truth of their belief. The court majority decided that the distinction could not be readily established in a court of law. Since the First Amendment protects the free exercise of religion, including having religious beliefs, to interrogate the truth status of a religious belief would entirely gut the protection, the majority argued: "The miracles of the New Testament, the Divinity of Christ, life after death, the power of prayer are deep in the religious convictions of many. If one could be sent to jail because a jury in a hostile environment found those teachings false, little indeed would be left of religious freedom." The dissent argued that by conflating truth and sincerity any belief could be justified on religious ground.[42]

In reality, of course, courts cannot entirely avoid looking at the cognitive content of a religious belief. Religious claims must not only be validated in terms of the sincerity of the believer; they must in some sense be recognized as falling under the subject matter of religious truth claims. This kind of examination typically occurs in cases where the *content* of prayer in the public school is litigated. Consider what has been proposed as a generic public-school prayer: "Almighty God, we acknowledge our dependence upon Thee, and we beg Thy blessings upon us, our parents, our teachers

---

[40] *Sherbert v. Verner,* 374 U.S. 398 (1963).

[41] *United States v. Ballard,* 322 U.S. 78 (1944).

[42] See *Jones v. Wolfe,* 443 U.S. 595 (1979) (Sectarian disputes among church members over ownership of church property are to be determined in secular courts using "neutral principles of law," not religious doctrine.) See also Jared A. Goldstein, *Is There a 'Religious Question' Doctrine? Judicial Authority to Examine Religious Practices and Beliefs,* 54 Cath. U. L.Rev. 497 (2005).

and our Country."[43] A lot of theology is packed into this wording, especially words like 'almighty', 'dependence', and 'blessing'. Asking students to recite such a prayer clearly shapes the contours of their religious expression and commitment.

The content of religious truth claims is also at issue in conscientious objection cases. These claims were litigated once more during the Vietnam War, as they had been in prior war times. To meet the "conscientious" exemption, at one time Congress required an explicit allegiance to a "supreme being" as a component of such objection, but now atheists may qualify as well. The objection should relate to war killing in general, not to a specific war, and must reflect evidence of deep and sustained inquiry and moral self-examination. By that standard, conscientious objection had a lot in common with moral and philosophical reflection about the value and purpose of life. So, in a philosophical moment the Supreme Court observed: "Few would quarrel, we think, with the proposition that in no field of human endeavor has the tool of language proved so inadequate in the communication of ideas as it has in dealing with the fundamental questions of man's predicament in life, in death or in final judgment and retribution." Conscientious convictions would be allowed as long as they reflect moral seriousness analogous to the convictions of theists, but not those based on political, sociological or economic claims.[44]

The issue of religious versus secular content arises in establishment as well as in free exercise cases. Getting a tax payer subsidy to ride a bus to parochial school was deemed devoid of religious content and had a strong public safety rationale. But what about supplying non- religious textbooks to parochial schools? This too was acceptable as long as the students requested the books and the state retained ownership of them.[45] But as one dissenter argued, how will a history of the Crusades be treated in a history textbook suitable to a Catholic School? And what if the state picked up the

---

[43] *Engel v. Vitale*, 370 U.S. 421 (1962) The dissent in this case argued that such a prayer was no different from putting "in God we trust" on our currency, or pledging allegiance to a nation "under God."

[44] *United States v. Seeger*, 380 U.S. 163 (1965); see also *Welsh v. United States*, 398 U.S. 333 (1970).

[45] *Board of Education of Central School District No. 1 v. Allen*, 392 U.S. 236 (1968).

costs of heating private schools on the theory, following the bus subsidy case, that all the nation's children need to be kept warm during the winter? Many school expenses such as sports programs are not essentially religious. Does government support of these nonsectarian components violate the establishment clause by giving the government a say in how the funds should be used and then sanctioning the religious institution for violations. The "Lemon Test" permitting such support is: first, the statute must have a secular legislative purpose; second, its principal or primary effect must be one that neither advances nor inhibits religion; third, the statute must not foster an excessive government entanglement with religion.[46]

More recently, that test has been interpreted to allow for the transfer of money in the form of vouchers through the tax system to sectarian schools for payment of tuition and not just for non-religious text books. Theoretically, the state only serves as a disinterested clearinghouse for payments that are deemed to flow directly from taxpayers to non-public school students. In the case where the intent of the legislation is to help poorer students go to private schools its purpose is also deemed secular even if the outcome is that over 90% choose to attend parochial schools. This was deemed an incidental effect: "The incidental advancement of a religious mission, or the perceived endorsement of a religious message, is reasonably attributable to the individual aid recipients not the government, whose role ends with the disbursement of benefits."[47] This rationale was extended to allow a religious school to apply for and obtain taxpayer funds to refurbish a school playground. No religion was being established, the court majority reasoned, and to automatically disqualify religious applicants from receiving a benefit that improves the health and safety of children places an impermissible burden on their free exercise.[48]

Prior to the application of the Fourteenth Amendment to free exercise state cases, public school attendance was generally considered a civic duty, like

---

[46] *Lemon v. Kurtzman*, 403 U.S. 602 (1971).

[47] *Zelman v. Simmons-Harris*, 536 U.S. 639 (2002).

[48] *Trinity Lutheran Church of Columbia, Inc. v. Comer*, 137 S. Ct. 2012, 2030 (2017). The dissent saw no difference between the playground grant and a state grant for construction materials used to build an altar.

the duty of a Catholic sheriff to serve a subpoena when 'on duty', or of a juror to attend trial on holy days. But how far does compulsory attendance go? The Old Order Amish refused to follow state compulsory attendance laws, choosing instead to withdraw their children after age thirteen in order to protect them from modern cultural influences and socialization. Their sincerely held beliefs, the court decided, to remain apart from the world was essential to their religious world view, a view that included a belief that parents should shape their children's future even for the years beyond emancipation. The Amish parents at trial called experts to testify on the linkage between education and the religious culture the parents desired for themselves and their children. No experts were called to establish alternative views of the best interest of the children. Instead, the dissenters only argued that at least some of the children's religious liberty interests could be impaired by foreclosing from them an opportunity to complete their high school edu.cation.[49]

These questions are part of a larger question: how does free religious exercise and long- standing tradition interact in a current pluralistic society? Religious exercise is always an activity of living human beings, while religious tradition transcends those specific individuals. But is accommodating 'religion', then, more than simply satisfying the interests of specific living individuals; is it also accommodating their historic religion as a separate matter, and if so must a court first know what that religion is apart from its specific adherents that come to court? This legal difficulty arises with such traditions as the celebration of Christmas in the public square.

Christian heritage, for example, is evident in the fact that nativity paintings going back centuries are found throughout our national museums. A tradition is no less a tradition if nobody complains, but it becomes a factor to be weighed when there are complaints that a religion is being established under the guise of a national holiday. Should the framers' recognition of religion as they personally understood the word be an important factor in how the First Amendment should be interpreted today? Did they intend that the First Amendment apply to religion *generally,* not to some religions and not others? Often constitutional arguments today are brought by religious claimants in the name of religions unknown to the framers.

Seldom is an argument brought in the name of religion generally. So, a sleight-of-hand move appears to be made when defending nativity scenes in the public square as a constitutionally permissible tradition because they have been religiously meaningful to the dead, while at the same time denying any necessarily specific and offensive meaning to the living.[49] Usually the religious nature of holiday decorations is minimized by giving many religions equal space in the public arena. In such cases, the decorations are often said to be a celebration of American pluralism and tolerance. The same argument is made for opening prayers during public convocations, although the actual practice often indicates a bias towards a preferred religion that is justified by reference to the "longstanding traditions" and "historical practices and understanding" of the favored religion.[50]

Much of traditional First Amendment jurisprudence of religion toggles between its inner and outer senses. The message given is that courts should not engage in theological disputes, and ought to be agnostic towards religious content and practice.[51] In recent years Congress has attempted to provide a methodology for giving constitutional weight to religious interests in the form of the Religious Freedom Restoration Act (RFRA) of 1993.[52] The rationale underlying the act is that government must have very weighty reasons for impairing religious exercise. It is not sufficient for a government to ban a religious sacramental ritual that includes a hallucinogenic drug, for example, simply because that substance is listed

---

[49] See this issue play out in *Lynch v. Donnelly*, 465U.S. 668 (1984). Also see opposing interpretations, one the "passive" Ten Commandments monument case erected at the Texas State Capitol, *Van Orden v. Perry*, 545 U.S. 77 (2005), and a Ten Commandments courthouse display, *McCreary County v. ACLU*, 545 U.S. 844 (2005).

[50] *County of Allegheny v. America Civil Liberties Union*, 492 U.S. 573 (1989). See the dissent in *Lee v. Weisman*, 505 U.S. 577 (1992) and in *Santa Fe Independent School District v. Doe*, 530 U.S. 290 (2000); also, *Town of Greece v. Galloway*, 134 S.Ct. 1811 (2014).

[51] *Thornton v. Caldor*, 472 U.S. 703 (1985).

[52] 42 U.S.C. § 2000bb through 42 U.S.C. § 2000bb-4. In 1997 the Supreme Court ruled that RFRA applied only to the federal government, *City of Boerne v. Flores*, 521 U.S. 507 (1997). As a result, some states have enacted their own RFRA versions.

as a controlled substance. Once religious claimants allege that a government restriction places a substantial burden on their religious exercise, the government has the burden of showing a compelling interest in retaining the restriction and that the restriction is the least restrictive means of protecting that interest.

Under the RFRA system it is for the courts to decide what a substantial burden is, not the religious claimant. When reclaimed water containing 0.0001% human excrement was used to create snow on a sacred mountain in Arizona, RFRA did not protect the Indian tribe's free exercise claim. The religious burden, the appellate court decided, was merely on the claimant's "subjective spiritual experience." "[R]especting religious credos is one thing; requiring the government to change its conduct to avoid any perceived slight to them is quite another," the court noted.[53] In this case, the religious claims of the Navajo nation were deemed insufficiently substantial to merit protection. But what constitutes a substantial burden? Particularly in the case of religion precision matters greatly. Beliefs are not just conjectures. Stories must be canonical. Miracles are not just likely to have happened; they are intended necessities. Dietary restrictions are not just nutritional advice. It is not for non-believers to say what a substantial burden is to a believer, and yet the court system is not an ecclesiastical court. It makes religious evaluations while rejecting theological reasoning. This was the difficulty in the case involving employers who refused to provide contraception through an employer health plan because it offended their conscience that federal law makes their company vicariously liable for thwarting conception and killing embryos. They argued that their religious beliefs make them complicit in the wrongdoing of others, a belief that improperly embroils courts in a "difficult and important question of religion and moral philosophy, namely, the circumstances under which it is wrong for a person to perform an act that is innocent in itself but that has the effect of enabling or facilitating the commission of an immoral act by another."[54] So, religious beliefs about snow quality were thought to be insubstantially religious, while beliefs about the moral implications of employer health plans were not.

---

[53] *Navajo Nation v. U.S. Forest Service*, 535 F.3d 1058, 1063 (2008).

[54] *Burwell v. Hobby Lobby Stores*, 134 S.Ct. 2751 (2014).

When federal courts engage in RFRA balancing they must decide how free 'free exercise' should be. In doing so they must inevitably become entangled in characterizing religious creeds and interests. They must decide whose interests have sufficient weight against the state. Is it the interest of any believer of a religion, of the claimants in court, or officials of the religion? Yet, why should the government be in any position to tell anyone what their interpretation of their religion is and how they should express it? Madison feared that possible entanglement of church and state. If I am to be protected from the customs laws when I desire to import hoasca (a herbal tea used in religious ceremony) from the Amazon rainforest, do my First Amendment protections really just come down to the size of the religion I belong to and its historical and institutional dominance in culture?[55]

Can Law Cognize Religion?

There are some claims the law cannot adjudicate. I cannot sue my neighbor for continually losing to him in poker if he is not cheating; and even if he is cheating, I would have to allege circumstances of serious fraud, an intent to harm me, and serious damage even to keep my case in court. If I buy some beach-front property, I cannot sue the seller and agent over the number of grains of sand on my portion of the beach even if there was a stated number promised in the sale agreement. There are some issues courts cannot take up as a practical matter, the primary reason being that the facts at issue are not empirically and practically ascertainable.

Cognizable harms should be concrete and particularized, actual or imminent, not conjectural or hypothetical. It would be hard to sue my neighbor for lowering my property values because of the way he dresses in public on the theory that no buyer would want to be his neighbor. It may also be difficult to sue him because he has painted his house black. But such a lawsuit would be cognizable if the color he chose violated the covenants of our Homeowners Association. The source of the injury in these cases results from a certain psychological condition that is hard to locate

---

[55] *Gonzales v. O Centro Espirita Beneficente Uniao do Vegetal*, 546 U.S. 418 (2006).

empirically. They are often relegated to subjective matters of taste and opinion. For this reason, courts have sometimes characterized these psychological injuries as 'generalized' or 'too abstract'.[56]

As a rule, generalized psychological injuries are not cognizable. Exceptions have been carved out but only under carefully circumscribed conditions. Psychic injuries include aesthetic injuries (the way your neighbor dresses or paints his house); group-membership injuries, often called dignitary or stigmatic injuries, typically as articulated by concerned bystanders because they see the person(s) actually harmed to be much like themselves with the harm stigmatizing them as well; or anxiety injuries, fear of the future because of some present dereliction of duty by those charged with keeping order.[57] Our question, then, is: where do the claims of religious disputes fit in? Economic injuries ('wallet injuries') are quantifiable if the offending events are locatable in space and time. Psychological injuries conjoined with hard-to-locate events are themselves hard to locate. We currently have no way of measuring them precisely in terms of place, time, and intensity. They are generally listed under the more amorphous categories of beliefs, attitudes, and feelings. Thus, measuring the *sincerity* of a belief presents a double difficulty: we cannot be certain what the actual belief of an actual claimant is, and we cannot identify the duration and intensity of the psychic harm done to that belief.

As we have seen from the previous sections, our idea of what constitutes a 'religion' within our legal system has expanded since the founding era. Religion in America is not a rote recitation of a creed. There is now a recognition that being religious does not mean exclusively adhering to an identifiable long-standing orthodox tradition. Federal law has defined a religious exercise as "any exercise of religion, *whether or not* compelled by, or central to, a system of religious belief."[58] As has always been the case in the past, religions are adaptive and people with compelling spiritual insights continually desire to innovate to make them more relevant and

---

[56] *Hein v. Freedom from Religion Foundation*, 551 U.S. 587 (2007).

[57] Rachel Bayefsky, *Psychological Harm and Constitutional Standing*, 81 Brook. L. Rev. 1555 (2016).

[58] 42 U.S.C § 2000cc-5(7)(A) (emphasis added).

salient. Before we can get to any interpretation of the religion clauses in the First Amendment, we must decide that we are talking about religion. But to do this we need criteria. Early efforts at general standards accepted by courts postulated a universal acceptance that a supreme being must be acknowledged, worshiped, and followed. More recently, criteria also included having a moral conscience and a commitment to human values such as dignity, tolerance, and equality. But these general prescriptions do not get us far. Theologically they are sparse and they may include notions from metaphysics, philosophy, and humanism, not typically identified as uniquely religious.

As we have seen, an additional question when litigating religious constitutional claims is to decide whether it is the specific parties' religion that is before the court or whether the parties merely represent a religion *per se* that is before the court. In the first case, the parties' avowal of their beliefs is all that matters; in the second case, the parties must establish their case through authoritative testimony of some sort. Distinguishing these tasks is not easy. A person may hold a sincere religious belief, and consider that belief part of an established religion, and yet be mistaken. In such a case the court would have no recourse but to evaluate the sincerity of belief in terms of its authenticity when measured against the tradition claimed by that person. The court undertook this kind of inquiry in deciding the Amish school case (*Yoder*), an inquiry different from that of examining the truth of Amish beliefs by secular standards. Fortunately, the plaintiffs in that case manifested their belief in nearly every observable moment of the day and expert testimony confirmed that congruence between individual actions and doctrinal orthodoxy. But many other cases, such as those involving time off for religious holidays, or indirect payments to parochial schools, judges are justifiably hesitant to authenticate sincerity and religiosity.

The rise of RFRA has intensified the issue of authentication. How is the prison system to know whether a particular grooming practice is required by a particular religion when trying to determine the sincerity of a claimant? Unless a court confronts the problem of determining the factuality and authenticity of religious beliefs, determining that a belief is sincerely held involves a judicial leap of faith about what goes on in a person's psyche. Of course, courts do this kind of evaluation every day, as when evaluating witnesses' trustworthiness or the intent behind words or behavior. In those cases, an examination of surrounding facts and circumstances, through fact and expert testimony coupled with the considered judgment of judge or jury, allows adjudication to proceed to a final reasoned result. But no such process occurs with religious claims where sincerely is determined *ad hoc* to be either self-certifying or in no need of justification. Claimants come to the court with stigmatizing and dignitary claims that are difficult to cognize unless, in rare cases, their evident lies betray them.

There is, of course, external evidence that the concept of religion is difficult for courts to cognize, the evidence provided by scholars and theoreticians of religion, who study religion as a social and psychological phenomenon. In such studies, these scholars, as we have seen, notoriously disagree about the very subject matter of their study and the proper way to study it. Religion shows up in various university departments sometimes as textual studies within area studies, as part of history, ethnography, anthropology, 'philosophy of religion', 'religious studies', 'sociology of religion', 'comparative religion', 'phenomenology of religion', as well, of course, as theological studies within divinity schools. What is clearly understood now is that when the framers used the word 'religion' they were using it as a deeply historical and contextualized notion, whether they realized it or not. From a comparative perspective, religious traditions are not easily categorized as separate systems of thought. Much overlap occurs among theological traditions and those traditions overlap with metaphysical and philosophical traditions.[59] Religion is the name given to a variety of different historically complex dimensions, consisting of myths, rituals, doctrines, ethical norms, social structures and organizations, emotions and experiences, and aesthetic features.[60] Underlying these dimensions are certain features of cognition that give life and salience to religion: *spontaneous thinking* (jumping to conclusions from confusing event to satisfying solution), *wishful thinking* (the ability of certain hopeful thought-predictions to produce positive emotions), and *schematic thinking* (the satisfaction of embracing a certain

---

[59] Francis X. Clooney, *Comparative Theology: Deep Learning Across Religious Borders* (Malden, MA: Wiley-Blackwell, 2010).

[60] Ivan Strenski, *Understanding Theories of Religion: An Introduction* (Chichester, West Sussex: Wiley Blackwell, 2015), 251.

belief because it tells us that everything is in its place and will remain so). Beliefs would not 'work' without these mental capacities; yet there is no clear demarcation between those that are 'religious' and those that are not.

There is also internal evidence of religion, as religious *experience*, that makes it difficult to cognize legally. Religion is meaningful to individuals for individual reasons. That is why Christians are not impressed with the argument that if they had been born and raised in India, they would be Hindus. The fine points of theology or official doctrine are not as important as the internal evidence of spiritual fulfilment frequently experienced. What is important is that their beliefs be cherished and have an enveloping effect. Such beliefs must be reciprocally informed by their religious experiences and practices while also serving to cognitively frame those experiences and practices. At the individual level religions are meaningful precisely because they are utterly private, subjective, and unique.[61] Typically, religious claimants allege that they speak for themselves and others similarly situated. In that sense they appear to be no different from secular claimants. The difficulty, however, is determining precisely wherein the similarity exists. If some Catholics choose to keep their children out of school for certain liturgical holidays, it is a disturbing fact to a court that others do not make that choice and still remain Catholic.

Should Law Cognize Religion?

Assuming for the sake of argument that religion is a manageable concept within jurisprudence and legal procedure, should it be? Religion is an area of high interest, but so is pleasurable reading and sexuality. The question is: Does it manifest legally protected interests? The framers thought so and compelled us to think so also. But the main thrust of their view is that the law should not tread on individual religious experience and nor should it undergird its social establishment. The First Amendment presents only a conditional and cautionary protection of religious interests, and that is the way the courts have treated the subject. Religion is protected except when a court decides it should not be, either because it is not deemed sufficiently

[61] Caroline Franks Davis, *The Evidential Force of Religious Experience* (New York: Oxford University Press, 1999).

'official', or when the claimant's sincerity is in question, or when the demands are too burdensome for the general public to bear. The framers also recognized what modern scholars can clearly see, that religion is a potent instrument of authority, power, and social identity. "The history of religion demonstrates the way in which a *political* theory of power and government has emerged in the guise of *theology*. Only, power was disguised in the claim that it comes from God," wrote one.[62] These studies suggest that courts cannot be indifferent to the question of whether religious claimants also seek to adjust the relations of authority and power within their society, government, and nation, so as to bring them more in line with their own religious values and goals. We always should be prepared to ask: Is there a 'sovereignty' subtext that ought to be expressed, explained, and defended?[63]

There is an uneasy relation between law, religion, politics, and power, which is implicated whenever law is tasked to provide a remedy for religious complaints. The sovereignty of religion is not the sovereignty of law or politics as commonly understood. Insofar as law involves rules of conduct, what we ought to do, involving religion in any traditional sense in the legal process of establishing rules is problematic. The law operates to free religious conduct from sanctions by creating exemptions from rules. Its authority comes from the First Amendment. But that amendment also limits the power of a religion to extend its power by creating rules for other religions and people. That is the conformity non-Sabbatarians tried to inflict upon Sabbatarians; but it is also the rule that the secular capitalist economy inflicts upon all religious people who want their faith broadly to govern the rules of the workplace or economy.

---

[62] Bulent Diken, *God, Politics, Economy: Social theory and the Paradoxes of Religion* (New York: Routledge, 2015), 2. See also Ivan Strenski, *Why Politics Can't Be Freed from Religion* (Maiden, MA.: Wiley-Blackwell, 2010); Clifford Geertz, *Available light: Anthropological Reflections on Philosophical Topics* (Princeton, N.J.: Princeton University Press, 2000), Ch. VIII; Stephen S. Bush, *Visions of Religion: Experience, Meaning, and Power* (New York: Oxford University Press, 2014).

[63] For a general discussion on this topic see B. Jessie Hill, *Kingdom without End? The Inevitable Expansion of Religious Sovereignty Claims,* 20 Lewis & Clark L. Rev. 1177 (2016- 2017).

Religious rules for living cannot be enforced and authorized independently of the way laws are made and enforced in the secular legal system. God's commands cannot override those of the courts; otherwise, all fault and harm could be easily excused by someone saying 'I'm following the will of God'. This was noticed by Plato in his *Euthyphro*, when he asked whether piety is to be desired because of its own quality or because the gods approve it. Ultimately, the default position for most theists is the command theory of law: Divine commands must undergird all legitimate human law. Under this theory what is commanded is lawful and that command is always good.[64] However, philosophers since Plato have pointed out an inferential fallacy in simply equating what God commands with what he ought to command, arguing instead that first we establish our values and then we attribute their legitimacy to God. Ronald Dworkin notes that most of the human values articulated within religion are embraced by atheists as well and that there is little pragmatic difference between values of secular humanists and those of theists. What are those values? He argues they are the ones acknowledged in Supreme Court rulings favoring conscientious objection, values not closely tied to a specific theology but following from a general recognition of the high value of the most intimate and personal choices a person may make regarding their aspirations to live a life according to their firm convictions.[65]

There is an additional gap that complicates the relation between law and religion: a gap between the processes that create law and the intentions of those who believe that the law they have created reflects the commands of God. Lawmaking, in spite of its ritualistic appeals to God for inspiration at crucial moments – famously Franklin's appeal for Divine inspiration during the Constitutional Convention – is not carried out as itself a religious ceremony. Once our representatives finish the prayer before getting down to business all that is left is the business. The Supreme Court

---

[64] A notable exception is Blackstone in his *Commentaries,* who notes: "God himself cannot make right wrong or wrong right. Right and wrong are as eternal as the Deity." (Philadelphia: R. Welsh, 1915), Vol. 1. Sec 2, 39-40.

[65] Ronald Dworkin, *Religion without God* (Cambridge, MA.; Harvard University Press, 2013). On Divine command theory see James F. Harris, *Analytic Philosophy of Religion* (Dordrecht : Springer Netherlands, 2002), Ch. VIII.

has ruled that clergy may serve in Congress or in any political office because there is no reason to believe they will not serve the general public interest or violate their oath of office.[66] The significance of this decision is that notions of fairness, deliberative procedures, drafting skills, and all of the techniques of doing research and making arguments as building blocks of law making can be accomplished outside of any religious setting.

An argument may be made that divine command theory is no different from any other legal and moral system that asserts we should follow the dictates of wise leaders, children should obey their parents, adults must obey lawful police and judicial commands, and that we ought to follow our doctor's advice. God, then, would just be a wise leader with unparalleled expertise whose commands are worthy of respect and obedience. Unlike other experts, however, God's expertise is usually established through third parties in the form of religious ministers of God's message. The framers distrusted these messengers. Madison, as we have seen, did not want to outsource our consent and obedience to them. God by definition is the source who appears and speaks through a glass 'darkly', not face to face, unlike lawmakers who speak in public and set down in writing their laws and the legislative testimony they rely upon in drafting them. Looking to European history, they concluded that any political and legal system based entirely upon obedience creates a great opportunity for political corruption. The establishment clause itself is based on the premise that established religions are likely to become morally risky ventures over time and so should not be interwoven with a representative government.

When law and religion interact, politics is also likely to be operating in the background. Some religions are explicitly engaged socially, especially if their members identify political success with their own religious fulfillment. These politically engaged members use politics to achieve their religious objectives, whether it is a heavenly kingdom on earth or a bulwark against evil or heresy. Politics, however, also uses religion

> to promote a new vertical sociability, splitting society into pure/impure human beings, loyal/disloyal citizens, friends/enemies (on the inside and on the outside). It also tends to reconstruct the myth of the origins of a nation

---

[66] *McDaniel v. Paty*, 435 U.S. 618 (1978).

> and of national identity, applying a sort of dual standard of citizenship to those who do not share the same history and certain linguistic, religious and cultural values.[67]

Religion may seek political power and, as a result, those seeking political power may also seek out religion for political uses.

Paradoxically, support for law cognizing religion may come from a nonreligious sector, evolutionary psychology. Within the context of that discipline, which studies ways in which brains develop adaptive cognitive mechanisms, religion is thought to manifest a variety of successful adaptive mechanisms and strategies. In a word, adopting a religion makes life more survivable and even better to live. That in any case is the theory, and if correct then the evolutionary psychology of religion provides an argument for some religious laws.[68] What better way, after all, to embed successful psychological habits evolved from religious thought and practice than into law? It may also be argued, however, that the characteristics that are said to make religion adaptive are not uniquely religious. Religion achieves social cohesion and solidarity against adversity, but so do military or ethnic organizations and patriotic values, and may do so at a higher social cost relative to other means of social solidarity. Also, as an adaptive mechanism, religion may be parasitic upon an already successful infrastructure of cognitive adaptations that focus more on *what* and *how* questions (science) than on *who* and *why* questions (religion). Religions sometimes take credit for predicting and even causing successful outcomes that are themselves decisively the results of other factors, as when Constantine attributed the

---

[67] Patrick Michel and Enzo Pace, eds., *Annual Review of the Sociology of Religion.* Volume 2, Religion and Politics (Leiden; Boston: Brill, 2011) pp. ix-x; Luigi Berzano and Ole Preben Riis, eds., *Annual Review of the Sociology of Religion*, Volume 3: New Methods in the Sociology of Religion, (Leiden: Brill, 2012).

[68] John S. Wilkins and Paul E. Griffith, "Evolutionary Debunking Arguments in Three Domains: Fact, Value, and Religion," in Gregory W. Dawes and James Maclaurin, eds., *A New Science of Religion,* (New York: Routledge, 2012), 133-146; also Patrick McNamara, ed., *Where God and Science Meet: How Brain and Evolutionary Studies Alter Our Understanding of Religion* (Westport, Conn.: Praeger, 2006); and D. Jason Sloan and James A. Van Slyke, eds., *The Attraction of Religion: A New Evolutionary Psychology of Religion* (New York: Bloomsbury, 2015).

military defeat of his enemies at the battle of the Milvian Bridge to his adoption of Christianity. The Roman Emperor was practicing an ancient form of inferential thought, similar to explaining the weather in terms of the moods or intentions of the gods. Even if such easier 'fast' thinking provides psychological comfort, it is only partially instrumental in military success which also requires 'slow' thinking that provides trained warriors, good equipment, and strategic planning.[69] The Popes guaranteed eternal salvation to those who fought in the Crusades, but they also raised money for provisioning and fighting the battles.

The confluence of cognitive science, social psychology, and evolutionary theory depict religion as a continually adapting strategy for attaining meaning and mental stability in an uncertain and changing world. Religion attempts to explain things that are initially hard to accept, like death, and the loss of learning and experience it brings. But religion is not only a result of fast thinking, it also creates structures that perpetuate such habits of mind. Rituals, ministers with official sacramental power, canonical writings, sacred places and structures, the appropriation of history as a special and personal story of believers, all contribute to the institutionalization of a religion. The evolutionary perspective, then, produces a further conclusion: as religions compete to survive, their institutional forms expand; they become more centralized and orthodox, with the result that religious institutions "not only dictate and control social relationships and correct forms of practice but also foster group identity and draw coalitional boundaries that become costly to cross."[70] From this perspective, allowing religion to become embedded in civil law is not just an expression of religious liberty, but contributes to its becoming more established politically as well.

There is much room for debate over the real efficacy of religion when protected by law. Does it only work if religion remains largely an autonomous realm *within* pluralistic liberal secular institutions? What are we to make of the real pragmatic effects of pacifists and martyrs who serve

---

[69] See Daniel Kahneman, *Thinking, Fast and Slow* (New York: Farrar, Straus and Giroux, 2013).

[70] Todd Tremlin, *Minds and Gods: The Cognitive Foundations of Religion* (New York: Oxford University Press, 2006), 193.

as models for educators and the general public? Is religion most effective in terms of its own goals and values if it stands apart from the public and serves instead as a model of incorruptibility? If there is a religion-law balance sheet, how should it be constructed and what are its factors? When religion and the religious seek to redress grievances through law is it possible that the inner character of religion will diminish, and its outer form becomes more socially generic, as yet just another interest group; or, on the other hand, will the religious perspective become a bottomless wish list of detailed religious demands upon secular society that the law could never satisfy without a radical transformation of itself?[71] In other words, does the freedom to flourish in a pluralistic tolerant society create opportunities for religions to revert to the sectarian warfare the framers hoped to avoid?[72]

Before we decide that law and the courts should cognize religion, we should first answer the following questions: (1) Is a definition of religion sufficiently clear to allow for meaningful constitutional analysis of the First Amendment religion clauses? (2) Are religious studies scholars able to, and will continue to, provide updated definitions of religion that are relevant and useful in interpreting these clauses? (3) Is First Amendment religion jurisprudence fatally flawed in the sense that it was conceived and structured using presuppositions about the meaning of religion that may no longer be applicable? An argument has been made that religious freedom under the American constitutional system is impossible.[73] Here are some of the components of that argument: (1) Historically and culturally,

---

[71] Daniel O. Conkle, *Different Religions, Different Politics: Evaluating the Role of Competing Religious Traditions in American Politics and Law,* 10 J. Law and Religion. 1(1993- 1994).

[72] See the dissent of Justice Sotomayer, regarding the framers: "To us, their debates may seem abstract and this history remote. That is only because we live in a society that has long benefited from decisions made in response to these now centuries-old arguments, a society that those not so fortunate fought hard to build." *Trinity Lutheran,* 137 S.Ct. at 2035.

[73] Winnifred Fallers Sullivan, *The Impossibility of Religious Freedom* (Princeton, N.J.: Princeton University Press, 2005), 10, 100-109, 143, 155-59. See also Thomas J. Curry, *Farewell to Christendom: The Future of Church and State in America* (Oxford: Oxford University Press, 2001), arguing that as intended by the framers' courts should not have jurisdiction over claims from religion for protection by government.

religion and law have not existed in separate well- defined regions but have been intertwined and embedded together. (2) Religion as embedded in our politics and law has its own religious roots, so that when serving as a supposed neutral arbiter for religious rights under the First Amendment judges easily may become subtle advocates for their favorite religions or attempt to extract and preserve the socially valued sectarian core of 'religion' as an essential component of a nonsectarian society. The result is a jurisprudence that is theoretically incoherent, and rulings that do not reach the fragile and complex nature of individual religious expression. (3) As actually litigated RFRA is really just tool in the battle between certain religions and modernity, rather than a way of protecting individual religious expression. Hence, (4) free expression may be better served if courts did not pick winners and losers under the guise of protecting an abstract ideal called 'religious freedom'.

An illustration of this difficulty is found in rulings about conscientious objection considered above. Historically, the exemption went to those associated with traditionally pacifist churches like the Amish and Mennonites. More recently the exemption was broadened into areas approaching philosophy and traditional humanism, but with the added (*ad hoc*) restriction that all wars must be opposed, not particular ones. Another problem is found in the nature of the expert testimony requested by courts in religion cases. Religious studies, as we have seen, can be approached from an inner and outer perspective, from a scientific and from a humanistic perspective. Given that profound division, how is evidence to be weighed about the internal sincerity of the claimant's religious expression, or about the external coherence of that expression with the 'official' or orthodox view of the claimant's religion? How is a religion as 'lived' by individuals to be weighed against a standard summary of the tenets and exemplars of their religious institution? Should courts extend judicial cognizance to individuals or institutions? If the latter, then there is no need to reach the particularized psychology of the believer. In the school cases, whether injecting religion in the public system (prayer and Bible reading cases) or giving public financial support to parochial schools (bus and textbook subsidies, third party tuition transfers) the individual emerges as a member of an institution with the institution as the real party of interest in the litigation.

So, if there are difficulties in giving judicial cognizance to 'religion', did the framers make a mistake, though a quite understandable one, in adding religion to the First Amendment? The Bill of Rights protects many other activities in common with those found in religious practice, including freedom of speech and of association. The Constitution in its entirety was expressly designed to "secure the blessings of Liberty." This highly generic purpose includes a wide variety of expressions: writing a poem, painting a picture, voicing your opinion, redressing grievances to politicians, carrying out scientific research. Some of these things are very important to some people, and to others they are only of a passing matter of concern. When the expressions of some become of urgent concern to others, especially in ways that threaten social and political accord, the law usually steps in to resolve the disputes. Nonetheless, religion does not coexist well with these other forms of expression. Its values, historically at least, are not compatible with pluralism and tolerance because it typically claims a "right to transcendent fidelity to a life outside the state and outside oneself."[74]

Conclusion

Our survey of religion cases has indicated an initial suspicion of religious orthodoxy reflected in the ideas of Madison and Jefferson followed by a pluralistic legal acceptance of unorthodox religions, and now a third phase in the form of a sophisticated penetration by well-established orthodox religions into hitherto well-established non-sectarian public institutions such as commerce and government. It is hard to say that the same Constitution has been in effect over that period. The Constitution accords special status to 'religion'; it bans an official national religion imposed by government, and also laws that restrict religious practices wherever found among the public. Yet, it does not officially define religion because to do so would be contradictory to its purpose. It assumes that the distinction between the sectarian and non- sectarian is an empirically meaningful one, and must remain so, in any liberal democratic society that embraces the rights of individual conscience. The establishment and free exercise clauses, however, overlook a third possibility: the recognition of a one true faith

---

[74] Sullivan, 158.

demanded by the vast majority of Americans. Even if the public willingly embraced one religion and urged government to recognize it in its laws, the First Amendment would prohibit this. Its entire legal infrastructure requires that self-identified members of a religion exercise restraint in exerting their influence on government, and yet at the same time it allows that influence as a matter of free exercise.

Religious jurisprudence presents a conundrum for law that is, perhaps, best resolved in the way Fuller would suggest: by the resolution of religious issues in the law using a variety of *ad hoc* rules, without foundations or internal consistency, designed to be the best workable solution of the moment, given the amorphous nature of the subject and the many competing interests in what should remain an essentially non-sectarian legal system.

CHAPTER 6

FREE SPEECH AND PUBLIC CONSENSUS

The Limits of Free Speech

Seditious Libel. In the early Republic speech was free but its consequences could be costly to the speaker. The Pennsylvania constitution in 1790 guaranteed a free press as a check on government officials. But that freedom did not shield authors or publishers from the consequences of putting before the public false or even true but dangerous views.[1] The constitution stated: "The free communication of thoughts and opinions is one of the invaluable rights of man; and every citizen may freely speak, write and print on any subject, *being responsible for the abuse of that liberty.*" (Art. IX Sec. 7, emphasis added.) Being a newspaper editor could be a dangerous occupation. For example, publications could be sanctioned for including materials "meant to delude and defame, subjecting the perpetrator to a charge of libel."[2] Although the American Revolution had eliminated official government censors of the press or the requirement that licenses to publish first be obtained, the sanction of vaguely worded libelous consequences still functioned as a *de facto* prior restraint. The general view was: "Every man may publish what he pleases; but, it is at his peril, if he publishes anything which violates the rights of another, or interrupts the peace and order of society."[3] Public peace, order, and dignity were standards against which libel would be measured. Under the English system as propounded by Blackstone, seditious libel could be charged even against true statements, since the crime of libel was its tendency to disrupt public tranquility, while false statements were merely

---

[1] Seth F. Kreimer, The Pennsylvania Constitution's Protection of Free Expression, 5 U. Pa. J. Const. L. 12 (2002).

[2] *Respublica v. Oswald,* 1 U.S. 319 (1788).

[3] Ibid., 329.

additional aggravating factors.[4] The First Amendment was enacted in 1791 against a backdrop of the English system of personal and seditious libel. It would take more than a century for the courts to make the changes to First Amendment jurisprudence that we know today.

The Sedition Act passed by Congress in 1798 made it a federal offense:

> To write, print, utter or publish, or cause it to be done, or assist in it, any false, scandalous, and malicious writing against the government of the United States, or either House of Congress, or the President, with intent to defame, or bring either into contempt or disrepute, or to excite against either the hatred of the people of the United States, or to stir up sedition, or to excite unlawful combinations against the government, or to resist it, or to aid or encourage hostile designs of foreign nations.

Clearly, by the standard set by British libel law and the Sedition Act, any controversial political speech could be construed as sedition *per se.* In his book *The Prospect Before Us* (1800) publisher James Callender (1758-1803) was prosecuted, fined and jailed, for libeling President John Adams by writing, among other things, "that the president is a professed aristocrat, and that he has proved serviceable to the British interest."[5] When Jefferson was elected President, he too became an object of political broadsides, but now an important threshold was established: *There could be no libel for true statements*. The rationale for this turn was, as first argued by Alexander Hamilton and later fully endorsed by Chancellor Kent: "And what can be a more important circumstance than the truth of the charge, to determine the goodness of the motive in making it?[6]

The libel standard postulated a bright line between truth and error over questions of fact, but was difficult to apply in practice because most political debates contained both factual claims and policy evaluations and opinions. Politicians who charge their opponents in a public speech with nepotism and corruption, commit libel if they do not include *all* the facts

---

[4] Blackstone, *Commentaries,* (Philadelphia: R. Welsh, 1902), IV, Ch. XI, (Of Offences against the Public Peace), Par. 13, p. 150.

[5] *United States. v. Callender,* 25 F. Cas. 239 (1800).

[6] *Reports of Criminal Law Cases,* (New York: Gould and Banks, 1825), III, 346; *People v. Croswell,* 3 Johns. Cas. 337 (1804).

upon which the charge is made.[7] Accusing judges and lawyers of corruption also subjected publishers to contempt for libel.[8] Religious claims that did not conform to the beliefs of Christian orthodoxy could also be libelous. In the first half of the nineteenth century some Americans experimented with pantheism, transcendentalism, and Swedenborgianism. Abner Kneeland professed a pantheistic God in nature and for that was charged with "willfully blaspheming the holy name of God." The court concluded that such blasphemy was prohibited by the Constitution, since it had been written by God-fearing men, not pantheists.[9]

Political Dissent. Although eventually even false statements could be protected as long as they were not maliciously intended, it was the context of the speech that ultimately determined its protection. The more speech challenged government policy and prevalent political and cultural norms, especially those involving dominant religious and economic values, the more it was likely to be curtailed and penalized. During the Civil War critics of the war in and out of Congress were tried and punished as traitors. The speeches of labor activist Mary Harris ("Mother") Jones (1837-1930), and other union organizers were considered direct threats to the property rights of business owners rather than commentaries on the political state of affairs.[10] Although free speech and press were important enough to the founders to be added to their state and federal constitutions, precisely because they affected ideas and behavior, those very same practices could also be penalized when they were effective in doing so.[11] For example, in the Mother Jones case, the fact that she gave a speech endorsing a strike

---

[7] *Lewis v. Few*, 5 Johns. 1(N.Y. (N.Y., 1809). See also *Ryckman v. Delavan*, 25 Wend. 186 (N.Y. 1840), *White v Nicholls*, 44 U.S. 266 (1845), and *Aldrich v. The Press Printing Co.*, 9 Minn. 133 (1864), and *Sweeney v. Baker*, 13 W. Va. 158 (1878). See also Wendell R. Bird, *Press and Speech under Assault: The Early Supreme Court Justices and the Sedition Act of 1798* (New York: Oxford University Press, 2016).

[8] *Illinois v. Wilson*, 64 Ill. 195 (1872).

[9] *Commonwealth v. Kneeland*, 37 Mass. 206 (1838).

[10] See *United States ex rel. Guaranty Trust Co. of New York v. Haggerty*, 116 F. 510 (W.Va. 1902), involving union organizing of miners.

[11] The paradoxical nature of free-speech protections is developed in Sam Lebovic, *Free Speech and Unfree News: The Paradox of Press Freedom in America* (Cambridge, M.A.: Harvard University Press, 2016), 2.

that miners could see and hear, because the rally was situated in an open field near their homes, was a factor in the court's decision that she abused her right of free speech. By listening to her words, striking miners would be induced to keep striking and even convince others to leave work in violation of an injunction to return to work. The court noted: "the noise and confusion created by the meeting could be heard distinctly at the mouth of the mines . . . As a result of this meeting, quite a number of miners left their work, and other persons who were employed to take their places were prevented from doing so by this agitation and excitement."[12]

It is important to keep in mind that when Mother Jones was speaking in 1902, states and their agencies including their courts could restrain speech and the press because the First Amendment guarantees did not apply to them. Nonetheless, the view that free expression should be measured by its adverse social and economic consequences raised troubling questions. Should a speech many people could hear and be influenced by be less free than one given to an intimate group? And, if a non-inflammatory well-reasoned speech produces an inflammatory effect and is also penalized, how is the original and oft-stated value of public debate served? This intermingling of content and consequence required a delicate sifting by courts and legislatures, since all spoken and written words are themselves actions intended to produce thought and action. When a speech is classified as rhetorical the speaker's blame is diminished, but only as long as the context is not a tinder box.[13] Conversely, even reciting a single line of poetry could start a revolution if conditions are ripe for change. So, is there a bottom line to our free speech heritage? May we say that, practically speaking, our First Amendment right to free speech and press is a right to communicate freely as long as doing so does not subject the speaker to the coercion of the law? We should be free under most conditions to publish Euclid's works on geometry, but we can imagine circumstances where mathematics could be deemed subversive, as it was when Jesuits banned proofs using infinitesimals in the early seventeenth century. Even the

---

[12] Guaranty Trust Co., 520.

[13] See *State v. Townley*, 140 Minn. 413 (1918), a typical wartime case where an anti-war pamphlet was deemed to be purely rhetorical.

supposedly neutral act of publishing the daily transcript of Congressional deliberations was held suspect in the early Republic.

The debate over America's role in World War I became the catalyst for testing the limits of the consequential measure of free expression. In the famous *Abrams* case, a Supreme Court majority determined that publication of pamphlets containing "disloyal, profane, scurrilous, or abusive language" about the federal government, flag, or armed forces was effective in convincing others to hold similar opinions, and so violated of the Espionage Act of 1917. The publications called President Woodrow Wilson a coward and criticized him for invading Russia for the only purpose of suppressing the Bolshevik revolution. One read: "Workers in the ammunition factories, you are producing bullets, bayonets, cannon, to murder not only the Germans, but also your dearest, best, who are in Russia and are fighting for freedom." In order to establish a link between content and consequence, and to meet the threshold of criminal intent, the court concluded: "Men must be held to have intended, and to be accountable for, the effects which their acts were likely to produce."[14] But, in his dissent, Holmes noted that the Espionage Act only banned speech or publication that was *specifically* intended "to cripple or hinder the United States in the prosecution of the war."[15] He pointed out that someone could be in favor of the overall objectives of the war and still be critical of the choice of equipment being manufactured. Such a person, for example, would be a patriot if bad government allocation decisions in fact needed curtailing. The 'war' referred to in the Espionage Act was the war against Germany, not Russia, which came later. But Holmes wanted to make an even larger point: people could debate tactics and policies endlessly. However, in that debate the Espionage Act allowed the government to blame just about any critical speech for the bad things that happened in the war effort. This loose interpretation, he argued, was directly contrary to the default position of the First Amendment as a prohibition *against* federal government censorship. All speakers want to change minds and induce future conduct; otherwise, why bother to print pamphlets or write speeches. The First Amendment accepts that risk because its framers believed that public

[14] *Abrams v. United States*, 250 U.S. 616, 621 (1919).

[15] Ibid, 626 (emphasis added).

debate was on balance a public good, even if risky at times, especially on matters of high controversy where so much was at stake and so much needed to be said.

In *Abrams*, Holmes realized that he was directly attacking the long tradition of retroactive punishment for seditious libel when he wrote: "I wholly disagree with the argument of the Government that the First Amendment left the common law as to seditious libel in force. History seems to me against the notion."[16] Only an emergency of the moment involving great *imminent* danger of *serious* harm to the nation would justify such harsh punishment, he argued.[17]

The Brandeis Test. The philosophy underlying the imminent danger standard was later expanded and articulated by Justice Louis Brandeis (1856-1941) in *Whitney v. California* (1927). In that case the defendants were members, or wanted to become members of the Communist Party, an association outlawed because of its advocacy of violent revolution. Merely joining or supporting the party was already a full-blown danger, the majority argued, because "united and joint action involves even greater danger to the public peace and security than the isolated utterances and acts of individuals."[18] Brandeis, however, was not sure the connection was all that clear. The assumption behind a clear and present danger standard, he argued, is that there is no time to debate the issues raised in a speech deemed dangerous for its ideas. This assumption may be teased out this way: (1) the protection of speech is invariably a protection of controversial ideas and policies either because they are unpopular or against established political authority; (2) such ideas are invariably deemed dangerous to the status quo by their very articulation and dissemination regardless of context; (3) but if context is disregarded, then the blanket suppression of dangerous ideas would also be justified because by their very content and

---

[16] Ibid., 630.

[17] *Schenck v. United States*, 249 U.S. 47 (1919), and *Debs v. United States*, 249 U.S. 211 (1919); and his dissent in *Gitlow v. New York*, 268 U.S. 652, 673 (1925). ("Every idea is an incitement.").

[18] *Whitney v. California*, 274 U.S. 357, 371 (1927). For later developments see the Alien Registration Act, (Smith Act), 54 Stat. 670, 18 U.S.C. § 2385 (1940); and *Dennis v. United States*, 341 U.S. 494 (1951).

articulation they would be considered *per se* dangerous; (4) but if (3) is accepted the First Amendment guarantees would be unnecessary because they would only allow and protect uncontroversial ideas, which do not need protection; (5) however, since the framers honored free expression in a Bill of Rights, they must have assumed that dangerous ideas, except when articulated in very rare circumstances, needed protection as well; (6) so, our constitutional guarantees of free expression require an examination of context to identify those elements justifying their restriction; but (7) only one such restricting circumstance may be found: *speech, especially government and legal argument that punishes speech, that destroys the opportunity for further speech; debate that cuts off further debate.* So, if the threat is real and imminent, it is already too late to respond to it by limiting free expression. In all other less imminent contexts, free expression in all of its forms should be allowed to go forward.

In the *Whitney* case Brandeis argued: (a) Our founders believed that liberty, as a social condition of free thought and expression, was both a means and an end; (b) free speech and its amplifiers (free press and free assembly) create the environment for the discovery and dissemination of political truth; (c) without free speech thought and discussion would not be stimulated, hope would atrophy, and humans would become passive citizens; (d) without hope the opportunity for repression increases, followed by resentment, hatred and eventually tyranny; (e) history shows that the best way to accelerate tyranny is for governing authorities to stimulate hatred against unpopular minorities; (f) hence, by adding a Bill of Rights to the Constitution and giving the First Amendment pride of place, the founders were signaling that fear of possible consequences by itself is insufficient to justify suppression of free speech; the danger must be determined to be imminent by articulable reasons; the speech practiced must rise to the level of clear incitement, and, most importantly, *it must be determined that there is no longer an opportunity for further discussion of underlying issues;* (g) however, determining that there is no longer an opportunity for further discussion may only occur in an *environment* where speech and assembly are freely permitted to challenge the emergency and question the rationale for their abridgement; (h) so finally, the practices of "effective democracy," including (by implication) the deliberative and fact-finding practices of public trials, are the best safeguards for free speech, for without them any form of speech may be cast as violent and insidious libel against the state and public order.

Four decades later the Supreme Court, following the Brandeis analysis, decided that even advocating violence remained protected speech. The speech must be directed to inciting imminent lawless action and is likely to produce that result given the context.[19] In *Brandenburg* a state statute that prohibited advocating violence was used to convict the leader of a Ku Klux Klan, who gave a speech at a rally that included the words: "but if our President, our Congress, our Supreme Court, continues to suppress the white, Caucasian race, it's possible that there might have to be some revengeance taken." The assembly also included firearms, but there was no call to imminent action.

To sum up this survey, our First Amendment jurisprudence, and the long history of constitutional limits on free speech, seem to suggest that there is no expressed constitutional norm that protects not only free expression but also the opportunity for sustained debate; there is no bright line free-speech test, hence no constitutional *guarantee* of its exercise. Determining when rhetorical advocacy of violent overthrow becomes part of an unlawful planning process is all but impossible for a court to apply in any consistent manner.[20] On these close questions, as Brandeis suggests, the default position should go to freedom of expression and continued debate, especially in political areas and in troubling times. The First Amendment was, after all, crafted by political dissenters to support the values of political dissent. Yet, our history does not consistently reflect that perspective.

Speech That Harms

Purpose and Function of Speech. Up to now we have emphasized First Amendment issues that pit individual liberties against state control of the political order. Propaganda, obscenity, hate speech, black lies, and ridicule

---

[19] *Brandenburg v. Ohio*, 395 U.S. 444, 446 (1969).

[20] This thorny distinction is approached and avoided in *Communist Party of Indiana v. Whitcomb*, 414 U.S. 441 (1974).

are also characterizations of speech in a contested but usually non-political context. Most of us are harmed by words at times and are nearly always emotionally affected by them. It is an affront to be told to "Shut up"! Language is not simply an expressive vehicle of feeling and cognition; it is an essential *component* of feeling and cognition themselves. Without language it is impossible to understand how life could be understood emotionally or practically. Without it we could not even be able to speak about people when they are not around. Emotions, even fits of rage, almost immediately call up self-reflection and a desire to communicate to self and to others about what is happening to us. Again, religion focuses on the written word ('scripture') and spoken word (prayer, incantations, recitation of creeds, confessions, words of contrition). Take these away and we have only vague wonderment at best with no named 'objects' to focus our wonder upon or communicate with others about. The stock in trade of philosophy, of course, is the analysis of words and how they are created and used to serve an evident purpose of helping us adjust our lives when faced with problems of desire, purpose, and meaning. In all of these instances, speech could never be neatly divided into its 'ordinary' uses, fully and legitimately protected constitutionally, and its unlawful or unconstitutional uses.

Besides being an obstacle to state repression, then, the First Amendment also recognizes this intimacy of language and social life; it tells us that we should let others speak and assemble even if we detest what they are saying, and if we resist them, we must give weighty reasons for going so. At this level, constitutional analysis seeks to achieve a balance of individual liberty and social harmony. Besides guarding us against imminent political violence and revolution, it also protects us from damaging lies. A self-professed First Amendment 'absolutist' argues that words by themselves can never harm. But that viewpoint overlooks the extent to which human beings primarily relate to and evaluate each other through language and other symbolic forms of communication. Language is used for communication, but also to influence and control. Its use is critical in politics as well as in courtship, advertising, journalism, literature, and law. Consider a simple example: police are giving chase to a suspect running north. You see him running north and tell them he is running south. Your words by themselves may provide evidence of intent to obstruct justice leading to a criminal conviction. The words of oaths are more than speech in oath taking ceremonies; so are the words of vows. They *accomplish* the specific act of loyalty for which the oath is taken.

Interpretation and Social Effects. Because language is so deeply embedded in the social arena to which law and the First Amendment applies, it is difficult to circumscribe where the free arena of speech ought to begin and end. If some people are offended by obscene, sexist, racist, or blasphemous language it is not simply their personal reaction to other people's viewpoints that is at issue. Their reaction is usually shared by many others similarly situated, making offensive communication socially divisive as well. Must or should the First Amendment care about such social effects? Reactions to offensive speech are not simply cognitive observations. Expressions deemed pornographic are feared for their potential to alter the sexual feelings, behavior, and attitudes of adolescents. Racist expressions are feared because they call up the wide array of attitudes and practices encompassed by the legal phrase 'badges and incidents of slavery' and more importantly manifest behavior that threatens to turn back the clock to a time when slavery itself was accepted as normal.[21] Similar observations apply to all of the many disputes and wars over religious dogma, especially for religions built upon literal historical claims regarding sacred persons, places and words that are easier to contest over time.

We have seen that politically ineffectual protest may escape punishment even in wartime. What are the permissible limits of free speech protected by the First Amendment that do not rise to a level threatening any serious public interest? The answer seems to be that convenient social propriety sets the standard. Historically, exceptions to free speech have included:

> the lewd and obscene, the profane, the libelous, and the insulting or "fighting" words – those which by their very utterance inflict injury or tend to incite an immediate breach of the peace. It has been well observed that such utterances are no essential part of any exposition of ideas, and are of such slight social value as a step to truth that any benefit that may be derived

---

[21] The expression 'badges and incidents of slavery' referred to the range of expressive actions prohibited by the Thirteenth Amendment. See *The Civil Rights Cases*, 109 U.S. 3, 20 (1883).

> from them is clearly outweighed by the social interest in order and morality.[22]

By this standard, the First Amendment is a safeguard of morality that changes with the times and always must be interpreted contextually. This means that the same speech may be free today and proscribed tomorrow because of changed circumstances. Nonetheless, as interpreted, the Amendment suggests a useful maxim: *Weigh carefully the costs to social order and the benefits to promoting further inquiry before establishing blanket legal prohibitions to speech; and in unresolved areas of controversy opt for the benefits.* This may be the truest value across time of the First Amendment. So, flag burning as protest is protected (even though offensive to national pride but still largely ineffective in changing the course of a war and may even be counterproductive due to the backlash it creates), while flag burning as arson never is (because of its low value as speech and its immediate danger to public order).

Consider the following city ordinance prohibiting cross burning: "Whoever places on public or private property a symbol, object, appellation, characterization or graffiti, including, but not limited to, a burning cross or Nazi swastika, which one knows or has reasonable grounds to know arouses anger, alarm or resentment in others on the basis of race, color, creed, religion or gender commits disorderly conduct and shall be guilty of a misdemeanor."[23] The drafters of this ordinance had in mind what they intended to prohibit, but their wordy draft included expressions such as "but not limited to" or "on the basis of" that could allow conduct or consequences that have little or nothing to do with the kind of bias against groups they sought to curtail. The Supreme Court majority in that case, however, did not attack the ordinance as overbroad, but instead took the position that cross burning on the front lawn of an African-American home was simply a form of free speech, merely conveying racists ideas and sentiments, and were not 'fighting words' which are prohibited because they are a threat to social order. In the calculus of risk, the court may have included a view that burning crosses lit on just one or a few occasions do

---

[22] *Chaplinsky v. New Hampshire*, 315 U.S. 568, 572 (1942).
[23] *R.A.V. v. City of St. Paul*, 505 U.S. 377, 379 (1992).

not generally burn down neighborhoods or cause intended victims to move away. Moreover, like protest flag burning, they are more often seen as counterproductive acts of futility. The harms of hurt feelings, anger, and even suppressed rage generated by such racist imagery were not sufficient, so the majority argued, to justify regulation without any further compelling state interest. Even burning a cross at a political rally on private property, presumably among like-minded people, probably would be an expression of free speech as well.[24]

The lesson to be taken from this cross-burning case is that without the realistic prospect of imminent danger, offensive speech must remain uncensored by state law. But would such an anti-bias law remain unconstitutional in a world of constant racial strife, or political warfare among party militias of the kind last seen in Weimar, Germany in the early Twentieth Century? The government should not take sides over the *content* of speech, but should it stand by and let disputes devolve from accusations to threats to physical harm? The words and symbols themselves become unlawful only in special carved-out cases, such as in a clear incitement to violence, child pornography, fraud, obscenity, defamation, libel, or lying under oath or to government officials. In such cases, the words regardless of actual consequences get no First Amendment protection. These offenses are thought to be serious enough because they harm the public order and a common public sense of decency and privacy, use deception for profit, damage public reputation, or undermine the values of a search for truth in a judicial process.

In the *St. Paul* case, the Supreme Court decided that the ordinance was unconstitutional because it prohibited cross burning, but did not say *why* that conduct was so offensive. If the ordinance had read, as in a subsequent case, "any such burning of a cross shall be *prima facie* evidence of an intent to intimidate a person or group of persons," the cross burning itself would be direct evidence of intimidation.[25] The earlier case abstractly

---

[24] Ibid., 402n4, 414.

[25] See *Virginia v. Black*, 538 U.S. 343, 399-400 (2002). In his dissent Justice Thomas writes: "Yet, here, the plurality strikes down the statute because one day an individual might wish to burn a cross, but might do so without an intent to intimidate anyone."

distinguishes between content and intent, whereas in reality they are intertwined. There are no non-contextual linguistic activities; all use of language is intentional. Congress cannot, for example, criminalize lying about having received the Congressional Medal of Honor regardless of circumstance, whether it be shouted from the rooftops or barely whispered.[26] Nor could government prohibit all access to violent video games because of the perceived harm to children, who also habitually play them. Such a blanket law, given its purpose, ignores other depicted forms of violence (e.g. in comic books or on television), and does not provide for exceptions for parents who find no danger in exposing their children to such games.[27]

Trying to make sense of First Amendment jurisprudence regarding the constitutional limits of speech is no easy task. The distinction between low-value and high-value speech (e.g., *Chaplinsky*), or between speech content and speaker intent, as sorting devices, provide many opportunities to abridge speech, and to do so in a manner that does not clearly reveal the constitutional principles relied upon. We may only be safe to say that on the question of speech that harms, the First Amendment is, for better or worse, a sociological norm of boundless flexibility ultimately grounded in a pragmatic understanding of the many different ways in which speech functions among the public.

Political Expression and Debate

Amplification Issues. We have seen that speech is not free if it invites punishment. Conversation is conditionally free as long as it avoids sanctions. That is the negative power of expressive speech. But amplification turns

---

[26] *United States v. Alvarez*, 567 U.S. 709 (2012). The plurality view is that the "remedy for speech that is false is speech that is true," while the dissenters argue that it is already against the law to wear military metals not awarded to you, and that claiming credit for receiving the Medal of Honor, is a great affront and cheapens the sacrifice of those who have meritoriously received it.

[27] *Brown v. Entertainment Merchants Ass'n*, 564 U.S. 786 (2011). See also *United States v. Stevens*, 559 U.S. 460 (2010), holding that a law prohibiting depictions of animal cruelty is unconstitutional as overbroad.

conversation into speech and creates its own positive power. If everyone in the world had to listen to me for a few minutes a day my words, no matter how humdrum, would have maximal potential power to influence. So, the function of constitutionally interesting speech is not only to communicate but to convince. In 1938 someone tuning into Orson Well's radio broadcast, presented as breaking news, would have reasonably believed that Martians were invading the earth. However, actual panic did not occur because the audience was small and unsure of what to do in any case.[28] What this tells us is that for amplified speech to be truly powerful it must be presented in a broad context of supporting, enduring, and self-reinforcing messages; and to create this speech infrastructure requires money and organization. Without money, one's freedom of speech reverts to mere rumor or conversation. Conversation is important, as in traditional classroom education, but its influence is diffuse over time. Speech that is amplified in a context that strongly motivates interest and action is what politicians and advertisers desire most. To say that the press should be free and individuals free to assemble, says very little about the values that should be encouraged and preserved by such guarantees. We saw that at the outset of the Republic, where speech was associated with the value of knowledge acquisition and dissemination, but that value was easily curtailed by more conservative interests in the years ahead.

Corruption and Lies. Given the background of seditious libel, the framers of the First Amendment could not have believed that free expression and exchange of ideas among individuals by themselves were sufficiently potent to challenge tyranny and entrenched orthodoxy. Those practices just as easily could be used to sustain political corruption and autocratic practices. Human beings not only have a capacity to lie; they have a very agile capacity even at a very young age to justify their lies when caught. Madison recognized that "liberty is to faction what air is to fire," meaning that free expression can be used to disseminate political lies as well as truths. So, a political system founded upon a right to free speech could be highly durable but also highly combustible. Free speech at the service of political factions would easily obscure "the rights of other citizens, or . . .

---

[28] See A. Brad Schwartz, *Broadcast Hysteria: Orson Welles's War of the Worlds and the Art of Fake News* (New York: Hill and Wang, 2015).

the permanent and aggregate interests of the community."[29] Madison's solution was that factional corruption was mostly a local problem that could not gain a foothold on the wider federal level. "The influence of factious leaders," he wrote, "may kindle a flame within their particular states, but will be unable to spread a general conflagration through the other states."[30] The subsequent efficiency of amplified speech through mass media clearly has refuted that prediction. Only a Constitution enumerating the rights of speech consumers, or the permanent and aggregate interests of the community, and not just speakers, would provide a way to resist the corrupting influence of political speech; and then only if a broad public consensus from the community at large was determined to enforce those norms against it. As written, the Constitution provided neither.

Radio Act and Fairness Doctrine. For example, although results of voting in elections could be regarded as a means of expressing consensus, the mechanics of voting have always been itself a politically contested process. The object was always to get your supporters to vote and to dissuade, as much as feasible, support for your opponent. The object of political campaigning was and continues to be to convince as many voters as possible of the merits of your platform's programs, regardless of whether those programs were sincerely intended projects or their merits clearly justified.[31] It is not surprising, then, that when radio transmission became a powerful new means of speech amplification, around 1920, its political implications were quickly identified. By 1927 there were 733 broadcasting stations in the country; the potential for transforming political debate was immense. The Radio Act of 1927 regulated the licensing of frequencies, prohibited monopolistic practices, and required equal time for opposing political viewpoints. At the time the bill was being drafted, one senator said: "Give me control of the character of the matter that goes out over our broadcasting

---

[29] Madison, *The Federalist*, No.10.

[30] Ibid.

[31] For an account of the long-contested history of voting in America see Alexander Keyssar, *The Right to Vote: The Contested History of Democracy in the United States* (New York: Basic Books, 2000).

stations and I will mold the views of the next generation."[32] However, it was a consensus of Congress and of both parties at the time that the radio waves should not be owned outright, but only used subject to licensing conditions established through legislation. The only vested interest preserved would be the public interest. Some degree of fair play in the Act would be established by requiring equal debate time and expressly prohibiting restrictions on free speech over the airwaves except in the case of obscene, indecent, or profane language. The Radio Act was superseded in 1934 by the Communications Act, which interpreted equal time to mean equal opportunity of access, equal rates, and a bulk rate discount. Wealthy candidates, as a result, could buy more airtime and take advantage of bulk rates purchases.

Federal regulation of the airwaves was based on an assumption that they primarily served the publics' right to hear and learn rather than exclusively the broadcaster's right to speak. Some broadcasters advanced political views as thinly disguised editorials or sneaked in partisan viewpoints as 'news'.[33] As a result, a Commission was created to digest the implications of the exploding mass-market communications of free speech. Freedom of speech could no longer simply be focused on the issuer of communication, but also on the effects of that communication on individuals and on the community at large. Free speakers and press publishers had a duty not only to speak freely, but also sincerely in their endeavor to express their own opinions and in the case of the press with as much objectivity as reasonably possible:

> [S]ince the claim of the right of free expression is based on the duty of a man to his thought, then when this duty is ignored or rejected – as when the issuer is a liar, an editorial prostitute whose political judgments can be bought, a malicious inflamer of unjust hatred – the ground for his claim of right is nonexistent. In the absence of accepted moral duties there are no moral rights.[34]

---

[32] Charlotte Twight, "What Congressmen Knew and When They Knew It: Further Evidence on the Origins of U.S. Broadcasting Regulation," *Public Choice* 95 (1998): 247-276.

[33] The Mayflower Doctrine Scuttled, 59 Yale L. J. 759 (Mar., 1950).

[34] *A Free and Responsible Press: A General Report on Mass Communication: Newspapers, Radio, Motion Pictures, Magazines, and Books* (Chicago: University of Chicago Press, 1947), 120.

The Commission proposed a tripartite investigatory system comprising private business, public consumers of information, and government agencies to continually evaluate how well mass communication was serving the needs of a democratic public. No one sector would have a monopoly on the truth, but a continual dialogue among the three could at least weed out virulent propaganda that when unchecked leads to "malicious pressures, threats and bribes, broken windows and broken heads."[35]

However, the Commission would face a serious obstacle in achieving its goals: the conflict between advertising and fair presentation. Commercially driven mass communication by its nature is highly competitive. Although the public at large may have access to a variety of sources of information, soon including television, there were only so many hours in the day to listen to or view mass media and always only one station at a time. Attracting listeners and viewers through advertising conflicted with an obligation of setting aside equal time for candidates, or time for individuals to respond to attacks against them on public issues. Fairness would eventually become a subordinate value to mass communicators, and conflicted with the government-imposed duty to use the airwaves in the public interest, as described by the Supreme Court in 1969:

> There is a twofold duty laid down by the FCC's decisions . . . The broadcaster must give adequate coverage to public issues, and coverage must be fair in that it accurately reflects the opposing views. This must be done at the broadcaster's own expense if sponsorship is unavailable. Moreover, the duty must be met by programming obtained at the licensee's own initiative if available from no other source.[36]

Since political news coverage was exempt from an equal time requirement, broadcasters could simply increase that coverage if they wanted to. This remedy, however, did not address the problem of slanted coverage presented as 'news'. Some argued that the public was safe without a fairness doctrine imposed by government, since journalists who generate

---

[35] Ibid., 114.

[36] Red Lion Broadcasting Co. v Federal Communications Commission, 395 U.S. 367, 377 (1969).

the news stories would bring with them a degree of integrity that guarantees objectivity.[37] Others argued that were Madison and Jefferson alive today, they would oppose the doctrine as contrary to the spirit of free expression. The doctrine itself also became an affirmative political tool when members of the general public, who considered news coverage to be unfair, used it to bring complaints to the FCC demanding time to respond. Some Democrats and some Republicans lined up on both sides of the reform-or-abolish issue. Some journalists and TV news anchors testified to Congress that the regulations affected their ability to inform the public. Some experts testified that spectrum scarcity was no longer a problem in light of new technologies such as cable and satellite transmission. In addition, broadcasters argued they faced high compliance costs when it came time for license renewals. Finally, evidence emerged that the FCC renewal process could be commandeered by the executive branch to put pressure on unfriendly journalists and broadcasters.[38]

Those who opposed repeal of the fairness doctrine made several arguments: (1) Restriction of free speech was acknowledged at the time the Constitution was drafted, and has been many times since then, as for example, by the imposition of 'time-place-manner' speech restrictions (e.g., on door-to-door solicitations, playing loud speakers at night, etc.), so there is nothing impermissible about the doctrine itself. (2) The values of the 'equal time' and 'personal attack' rules are not based on whether the opportunities to use the spectrum are limited. Those values could still stand on their own even with plentiful means of mass communication since an increase in the means of transmission does not guarantee the kind of fact-intensive debate required for an informed public. (3) The bureaucratic burdens placed upon broadcasters from consumer and audience complaints rarely resulted in license revocations. Public complaints that certain broadcasts were racist or communistic or un-American generally, reflected the turbulence of the nineteen sixties going forward, and in

---

[37] See Jerome L Wilson, "The Fairness Doctrine: Big Brother in the Newsroom," *American Bar Association Journal* 61 (1975): 1492-94; arguing that the constitutional guarantee of a free press should be expanded to include radio and television as well.
[38] Craig R. Smith, "The Campaign to Repeal the Fairness Doctrine," *Rhetoric and Public Affairs* 2 (1999): 481-505.

response the FCC gave great leeway to broadcasters in its interpretation and application of the fairness doctrine. What really undermined the doctrine, and the reason why it needed to be preserved, was the endemic conflict between public interest and commercial interest.[39]

In the 1980s the FCC itself saw the doctrine as working a disservice to the informational needs of the public, while courts increasingly saw the distinction between an unregulated press media and a regulated electronic media as untenable.[40] At the same time, the fairness doctrine itself was directly attacked as a regulatory overreach without statutory authority. A transactional marketplace model between broadcasters and the public was thought to be more responsive to the public needs than the doctrine's commission and compliance model, and that view won the day.[41]

Money and Political Campaigns. Once political campaigns became a source of advertising revenue, regulating advertising content was replaced by regulating advertising spending. The Federal Election Campaign Acts of 1971 and 1974 placed contribution and spending limits on campaigns and established the Federal Election Commission (FEC) to police reporting of spending by or on behalf of candidates. In 1976 the Supreme Court found that campaign spending needed to be measured against the primary objectives of the First Amendment, namely, to ensure uninhibited, robust, and wide-ranging political debate and promote that debate through

---

[39] See Mark Floyd, *'Red Lion' Confusions,* 60 Admin. L. Rev. 869 (2008).

[40] Telecommunications Research & Action Center v. FCC, 801 F.2d 501 (1986); Syracuse Peace Council v. FCC, 867 F.2d 654 (1989).

[41] Mark S. Fowler & Daniel L. Brenner, *A Marketplace Approach to Broadcast Regulation,* 60 Tex. L. Rev. 207 (1982). On the continuing debate over the value of a fairness doctrine see Colin Vandell, *Words Signifying Nothing? The Evolution of 315(a) in an Age of Deregulation and its Effect on Television News Coverage of Presidential Elections,* 27 Hastings Comm. & Ent. L.J. 443 (2005); Andrew V. Moshirnia and Aaron T. Dozeman, *In All Fairness: Using Political Broadcast Access Doctrine to Tailor Public Campaign Fund Matching,* 48 U. Mich. J.L. Reform 641 (2015) (advocating matching public funds with private funds); Michael Kent Curtis & Eugene D. Mazo, *Campaign Finance and the Ecology of Democratic Speech,* 103 Ky. L. J. 529 (2014-2015) (advocating a new fairness doctrine).

political associations and parties. Money and speech were intimately connected in the new communication marketplace, the Court reasoned: "A restriction on the amount of money a person or group can spend on political communication during a campaign necessarily reduces the quantity of expression by restricting the number of issues discussed, the depth of their exploration, and the size of the audience reached. This is because virtually every means of communicating ideas in today's mass society requires the expenditure of money."[42] Nonetheless, some limitations were deemed necessary in order to avoid corruption or its outright appearance. Political campaigns should not become a battle of millionaires sponsoring their own candidates. Limitations on spending to advance the issues *associated with,* but not given directly to, a candidate, were lifted because, it was believed, of the lessened opportunity for buying political influence. The *Buckley* ruling, however, failed to digest the full implication of equating money with speech. The difficult quantitative analysis of the fairness doctrine in terms of calculating equal time was replaced with a still more difficult qualitative measure of the appropriate influence of money and its sources on free speech. Should money given directly from the pockets of candidates as campaign contributions be restricted at all? After all, who can speak better for the candidate than the candidate? However, at the same time imposing some limits on candidate contributions seemed to be reasonable in leveling the playing field for less wealthy candidates to compete, but doing so would bring into question the simple equation of money and speech. With more money to spend, millionaire candidates would have a bigger megaphone to use. Also, in political campaigns not all money turns into speech or the means of amplifying it. Some is used to pay staff and transportation. Judicious campaigns may get more communicative bang for the buck than profligate ones. But the biggest problem would remain: making campaign contributions to an entity that supports a candidate could still have a corrupting influence as well.[43]

In spite of such questions, the underlying assumption of *Buckley* was that money is not so much of a corrupting influence as to outweigh the values

---

[42] *Buckley v. Valeo,* 424 U.S. 1, 19 (1976).

[43] See Justice Byron White's dissent in *Buckley*. Ibid., 262ff.

of greater open democratic debate. That same assumption was used in a ruling that corporations (e.g., banks) and businesses generally could spend money to affect the outcome of a voter referendum since candidate corruption "simply is not present in a popular vote on a public issue." [44] This conclusion raises the question of whether the concept of 'corporate speech' is a category mistake insofar as it considers characteristics of individuals comprising a corporation as a characteristic of the corporation itself. Individuals directly speak or like groups speak through their representative, but who speaks for a corporation? The easy answer seems to be that its board members, officers, managers, employees, or shareholders, or some combination of these, speak for their corporation when doing so in their official corporate capacity. But what is *corporate capacity*? The corporation is thought to be perpetual; its 'voice' does not change merely because shareholders die or sell their shares of stock, or a manager or board member resigns. It is created by incorporators as a legal business tool to shield liability, raise and invest money, and facilitate economic transactions at a distance. In no way do the positions taken, say, for or against a referendum issue, reflect specifically the positions taken by those acting on behalf of the corporation. Nonetheless, the corporate position on a political question officially authorized by a vote of a board of directors still comes down to the judgment of specific individuals. Protecting corporate speech *per se* is a departure from the traditional view that free speech could only apply to *individual* persons:

> Indeed, what some have considered to be the principal function of the First Amendment, the use of communication as a means of self-expression, self-realization, and self-fulfillment, is not at all furthered by corporate speech. It is clear that the communications of profitmaking corporations are not "an integral part of the development of ideas, of mental exploration and of the affirmation of self." They do not represent a manifestation of *individual* freedom or choice.[45]

Although speaking in a corporate capacity is always the speech of individuals, its effect differs from traditional speech in two respects. Corporations exert leverage on traditional voters through their 'public

---

[44] *First National Bank v. Bellotti*, 435 U.S. 765, 789-91 (1978).

[45] Ibid., 804-805 (emphasis added).

relations' (typically good will and advertising) and wealth generation (sales of products and stock), while that leverage is achieved using anonymous corporate representatives who are not personally accountable to explain or justify their message.[46]

Speakerless Speech. However, the special market-power risk identified in *Austin* was thought insufficient in *Citizens United* to penalize any speech simply by virtue of a "speaker's corporate identity."[47] Instead, disclaimer and disclosure notifications were thought sufficient to keep such speech below the corrupting threshold. This ruling applied not only to traditional corporations set up to sell merchandise or services, but also to those specifically set up to advance political ideas and policies. The corporation in *Citizens United* marketed a politically motivated documentary, using in part funds from for-profit corporations, which it wanted to make available to the public through cable subscription. It challenged the regulatory campaign finance scheme because of its complexity and built-in compliance costs, which the court majority considered a *de facto* prior restraint on speech.[48] Regulations of speech, in other words, had a chilling effect on speech because of the costs incurred in meeting them. However, by attributing to impersonal corporations the values embodied in the free speech of a human speaker – the expression of an individual mind and will with all of the risks and implications that entails – an opportunity for accountability of what is said is lost. When individuals speak their claims may be immediately challenged and put to the test of doubt and counter example. The source of the claims is transparent; exposure to the risk of refutation is established whether or not willingly embraced. However, evading accountability for what is said, by denial or prevarication, a long tradition in politics, is even more easily accomplished when the speaker is officially anonymous.[49]

A contrary view may be that when any corporation speaks, rather than achieving anonymity, anyone associated with it in the public mind

---

[46] *Austin v. Michigan Chamber of Commerce,* 494 U.S. 652, 658-659 (1990).

[47] *Citizens United v. Federal Election Commission,* 558 U.S. 310, 318 (2010). For some critical commentary see Robert Post, *Citizens Divided: Campaign Finance Reform and the Constitution* (Cambridge: Harvard University Press, 2014).

[48] *Citizens United,* 558 U.S. at 335.

[49] Ibid., 391-92.

becomes accountable for its assertions. This would be true if each associate runs the personal risk of being shown to be wrong. The individual speaker always carries that risk simply by virtue of the readily identifiable continuity of the speaker over time. He or she will be asked to account for past claims and explain why they should be accepted, modified, or rejected at some later point. Speakers with "corporate identity," however, are seldom held to that risk. They are merely mouth pieces, in most cases, while individuals merely associated with the corporation are not even thought to be held accountable as individuals. So, the conflation of individuals, associations, and corporations in *Citizens United* all regarded as *speakers,* as transmitters of ideas and arguments, captures an important aspect of free speech. Some speakers are rich; others are poor of each type, but all are equal in the eyes of the law.[50] But each cannot be regarded as equal from the receiving end of speech, the viewer, listener, or reader. Here the responsive side of communication is greatly truncated in corporate speech and from a practical point of view perhaps even obliterated. This is a distinction the *Citizens United* majority apparently found theoretically uninteresting. One suppressed premise of their view is that all important ideas will get debated because the opportunity and means will remain intact in an age of great media proliferation. Another is: that mass media controlled by large highly profitable media companies will never be so large as to make the public lose confidence in their ability to change democratic outcomes if necessary.[51]

The *Citizens United* majority looked to disclosure of the sources of campaign contributions as the exclusive anticorruption remedy: "The First Amendment protects political speech; and disclosure permits citizens and shareholders to react to the speech of corporate entities in a proper way. This transparency enables the electorate to make informed decisions and give proper weight to different speakers and messages."[52] This conclusion, however, assumes that there is a 'proper way' to react to speech and that the function of speech is to inform rather than to obfuscate or deflect. The rosy expectation of *Citizens United* is that the First Amendment by its very

---

[50] Ibid., 340-60.

[51] Ibid., 366.

[52] Ibid., 371.

language prevents such demagoguery. Some framers thought the Constitution was merely a parchment barrier to corruption unless free speech and press provided real opportunities for the evaluation of the character and trustworthiness of individual politicians. However, the more these opportunities are diminished by speech that goes without effective challenge and rebuttal, the less the First Amendment serves its restorative function as originally understood. Listening and viewing and reading from many sources are important, but so is the capacity of the public to debate and digest the information received. Remarkably, the value of evaluation as a means to public consensus is recognized in the opinion itself: "The right of citizens to inquire, to hear, to speak, and to use information to reach consensus is a precondition to enlightened self-government and a necessary means to protect it."[53] However, speaker-less corporate speech provides little or no opportunity for this kind of questioning and dialogue.

Speech and Unfettered Debate. The Supreme Court has taken the position that more opportunities for speech mean greater opportunity for the public to assess its trustworthiness, and to engage in a more meaningful political debate. Here the assumption seems to be: the opportunity for specific speech effectively to corrupt diminishes as the overall opportunities for more speech generally increase. So, anything that opens the spectrum and flow of information further, especially the use of money to build messaging and the platforms that carry them, becomes a needed component in enforcing the values of the First Amendment in the modern era. But this stated aspirational norm runs headlong into the value that more speech from more voices is better than less and fewer. This conflict is seen in the arena of public funding of campaigns for candidates with less money than other candidates. The Supreme Court has ruled that it was unconstitutional for public money to be used to support candidates who have less money because by creating increased opportunity for candidates with less money it diminished the opportunity for candidates with more money to speak louder?[54] Public financing also is said to create an unfair advantage because candidates with less money do not have to convince donors that their candidacy deserves their support; and it can reduce the influence of

---

[53] Ibid., 339.

[54] See *Arizona Free Enterprise Club's Freedom Club PAC v. Bennett*, 564 U.S. 721 (2011).

independent expenditure groups because candidates with matching funds did not need to rely upon them as much. Here the court majority openly admits that presenting views with less risk of rebuttal is one of the advantages of outspending your opponent: "All else being equal, an advertisement supporting the election of a candidate that goes without a response is often more effective than an advertisement that is directly controverted."[55] At the same time, the majority continues to argue, rather incoherently, that the primary value of political speech on public issues is the "unfettered interchange of ideas" that is "uninhibited, robust, and wide-open."[56] Effective speech, however, the kind politicians prize most, presents a message that goes unchallenged when their opponents do not have sufficient money to respond effectively. This speech is not the same thing as speech that makes a good argument in response to efforts of opponents to challenge and rebut it.

The Problem of Public Consensus

Unchallenged Speech. Historically, democratic consensus always has been achieved through a haphazard and often error prone political process. The bad effects of our national crises – our wars, civil war and regional disputes, our boom/bust economic cycles, our various hysterical 'scares', coupled with our exaggerated self-congratulations, and our foundational and imperial myths – have been cushioned by our land size, ocean borders, small population, dynamic cultural pluralism, and division of power. However, the risk of bad consequences of speech that goes unchallenged, and the bad decisions of politicians and uninformed voters that results from it, has also increased with the proficiency with which our political disputes and the misinformation surrounding them are communicated. In retrospect, the fairness doctrine and the elaborate FEC regulatory regimen could not keep up with the pace of technological change.

Political consensus is the glue that sustains a democracy. It is what keeps the losing party from changing the rules to remain in power *post hoc* or the winning party from banning the losing power or making it just about

[55] Ibid., 747.

[56] Ibid., 750, 755.

impossible for it to compete. Consensus can only be effective when there is agreement about who has won and who has lost an election. There must be agreement about the criteria to be used to determine an accurate vote count, and in the case of the presidency, how to determine the legitimate votes of the electoral college. And there must be agreement that the courts are the proper venues to resolve close questions. So, at a minimum, maintaining a legal system according to the norms of the inner morality of law, 'playing by the rules' generally speaking, is what would be necessary to achieve and nurture that consensus. We also should not be over-confident that the First Amendment is sufficient to undergird the continuing practice of those norms of truth-seeking and fair play in politics. There is a danger in believing that the First Amendment ought to have little to say about how freedom of speech and the press ought to be exercised; or that the danger of controlling the market place of ideas is greater than the danger of its abuses. A *laissez faire* theory of the First Amendment means that "the degree to which speech is protected cannot turn on a legislative or judicial determination that particular speech is useful to the democratic process. The First Amendment does not contemplate such 'ad hoc balancing of relative social costs and benefits'."[57] This view overlooks the persistent balancing that, in fact, does go on in free speech jurisprudence. The First Amendment, as we have seen, in its entirety is always a sociological measure of our nation's cultural and political health. Balancing must occur in every free speech case. When the solution is uncontroversial, according to prevailing cultural norms, the balancing of interests recedes into the background. In campaign finance cases it is always necessary to ask whether minimalist safeguards, such as donor disclosure requirements, are effective enough to propagate reasoned debate into the system. Are they effective enough in combatting the use of anonymous 'dark money' in politics?[58] These balancing questions are made further difficult by our political disagreements over how much democracy the Constitution requires. Political liberals tend to want robust regulation of campaign dollars; conservatives up to now want less, but also gladly accept restrictions on foreign money to preserve another democratic ideal: not

---

[57] See *McCutcheon,* 572 U.S. at 206; and *Stevens,* 559 U.S. at 470.

[58] On dark money in politics see, for example, Michael R. Siebecker , *Political Insider Trading,* 85 Fordham L. Rev. 2717 (2017).

putting our national sovereignty at risk at the ballot box. The problem conservatives on the high court rightly point to is the inconsistency of requiring the First Amendment to promote a robust democracy, where that robust democracy amounts to majoritarian rule, which the First Amendment cannot blindly follow. The only alternative is to proceed with a clear understanding that all balancing of interests is political, to say why, and to measure the result, perhaps, by the norms Justice Brandeis attempted to articulate in *Whitney*.

Accountable Speech. Also, to reiterate, we should recognize that the First Amendment is not about 'speech', but about human speakers expressing claims, making arguments, and proposing plans.[59] If political discussion consisted entirely of testable empirical claims, or of logical formalisms, the speaker's identity would matter little. In reality, political discussion consists of normative claims, vague and largely untestable globalized policy predictions, and overt or covert rhetorical efforts to manipulate public opinion and emotion. It is a rich salad requiring deep digestion and sufficient opportunity for public reflection. Who the speakers are and who supports them are important factors in assessing political messages, and the motivations behind them. But how large a factor should individual identity be? After all, philosophers have battled over ideas for millennia and, while names are associated with certain schools of thought and epistemic methodologies, those names add little value to the arguments themselves. Why not also in politics? The answer should be obvious: when politicians make claims and debate them, they are not conducting a dialogue in limbo but asking for votes that provide *authority* to operate the levers of power. Sincerity and honesty also must be measured when the primary function of political debate is to provide a rationale for plans of action and the confidence that they will be carried through as promised. As we have seen, this essential vetting purpose of political free speech was widely recognized in the early Republic. Now, politicians have

---

[59] For a contrary view see *Citizens United*, at 392-93 (Justice Scalia): "The [First] Amendment is written in terms of 'speech', not speakers. Its text offers no foothold for excluding any category of speaker, from single individuals to partnerships of individuals, to unincorporated associations of individuals, to incorporated associations of individuals . . ."

opportunities to avoid Lincoln-Douglas style debates because they can speak powerfully and repeatedly through surrogates, or use the services of anonymous media experts to produce false or misleading advertising campaigns. Only by making individuals accountable for what they say, by creating a system of accountability, analogous to the personal exposure required in our courts of law, can we minimize bombastic and deceptive campaigns and achieve some useable level of political consensus.

A speaker-centered First Amendment at least creates a focus of accountability where 'no comment' or failure to debate could be politically damaging responses. In fact, the focus on the speaker actually enriches the content of speech because it puts the justification of claims on a par with the claims themselves. Of course, increased content does not directly translate into increased truth. Great volumes of speech may be refuted by a single counter example. Articulate and verbose speakers may be undermined by one salient example of hypocrisy. Rather, the demand for justification and reason-giving exposes the speaker to the risk of not being believed, and then of not being supported at the ballot box. It also empowers the listener and reader to reply and to provide public comment through opinion polling. But there is nothing in the Constitution to compel a politician to speak or to respond. One strand of free speech is the freedom against compulsory speech in the political arena. There are special circumstances prohibiting compelled speech: self-incrimination, the exempt speech of attorneys, spouses, ministers, and doctors. Though these privileges may be waived, there is no legally enforceable right for a listener to receive a better explanation from a politician seeking votes. Government compelled speech may come across as an unsavory form of compelled confession. How to get politicians to articulate, ratify, or modify policy positions is a chronic problem of modern political debate, particularly since there are so many ways to get ideas across. Some candidates (e.g., 'stealth' candidates) are selected for their attractive non-verbal traits and skimpy records to defend. In a system with a robust and widely recognized right of the public to receive information, such candidates would be at a disadvantage. However, that right is insufficiently served by the mere appearance of political debate among candidates and is more than offset by another lethal influence on democratic consensus: the great effort that goes into strategically reducing morale and turnout of opposing voters and their access to the ballot.

The original rationale for doing away with the fairness doctrine was the great increase in opportunities to speak. But that increase, which now includes media outlets devoted to just a narrow band of the political spectrum, was not matched by a corresponding increase of opportunity of listeners to directly or indirectly confront the speaker. Instead, a proliferation of speakers and channels had the result leaving the voter with little additional opportunity to witness a candidate explain in better detail, or back off from, a position that seemed so right on first impression.[60] At its extreme, speech un-responded to is just propaganda; and once well-established provides an even greater opportunity to separate and silence the listener altogether from the social dialogue required to achieve meaningful political consensus.

[60] For the importance of free speech theory for *listeners* see Jane R. Bambauer and Derek E. Bambauer, *Information Libertarianism,* 105 Cal. L. Rev. 335, 394 (2017) ("Listeners appear too infrequently in the First Amendment canon. They are increasingly important in the Internet era, where speaker and listener may be separated in time and space, unknown to one another."). Also, see Leslie Kendrick, *Use Your Words: On the 'Speech' in 'Freedom of Speech'*,116 Mich. L. Rev. 667 (2018), arguing that the communicative power of speech connecting speakers and recipients is what gives speech its special value and protected status; and Seana Valentine Shiffrin, *Speech Matters: On Lying, Morality, and the Law* (Princeton, N.J.: Princeton University Press, 2015), 14, arguing that "moral agency is a cooperative matter that depends on reliable channels of communication."

CHAPTER 7

PRIVACY, DIGNITY, INTIMACY

Elusive Zones of Privacy

Privacy, dignity, and intimacy mutually reinforce each other. Without each, the others are diminished. Throughout history we can clearly identify within nations and societies norms of privacy and intimacy regulated by law or custom; and when these norms break down, we have affronts to dignity. What we are willing to share with others of our bodily selves and our possessions vary from person to person in a given society at a given time, and also between customary practices of different societies. Is a kiss appropriate on a first date? The very question assumes that an appeal to norms and practices is necessary. But norms and practices are often also accommodations to circumstances required for living with as much dignity as could be reasonably expected. In tenement living in New York City in the eighteen nineties a small room in the hallway contained a toilet which all tenants were required to use. An access to running water and an overhead light bulb no doubt improved privacy over an outdoor outhouse. But would using such a facility be considered an affront to dignity today?

Living a life of dignity for some people would be considered for others living a life of humiliation, embarrassment, and shame. Here both law and custom struggle to find a usable point of demarcation where privacy is violated and affronts to dignity become salient enough to penalize. In the nineteenth century, garment workers, in most cases women, were crowded into factories, huddled over sewing machines in sweat-soaked dresses. At a certain point, the men who operated or managed the business recognized that these women were wives and mothers as well as employees. So, the movement for a shorter work week and workday brought with it the recognition that the law should protect dignity as well as physical well-being. Constitutional analysis of Fourth Amendment searches and seizures, whether concerning entry into private property and the home, or body cavity searches, is saturated with an implicit penumbral recognition that privacy must be taken into account and violations of intimacy avoided as reasonably as possible.

No human being can make a claim to absolute privacy. That is ruled out by their biological condition, the condition of being born connected to others and coming to be known and shaped by them. If privacy is a right to not be seen or heard in the present or revealed in thoughts or recreations of the past, then at best only a provisional privacy can be possible. Living in solitude in a remote natural world may achieve such a state for a while. The trend however is in the other direction. A legal rule of thumb in privacy law involves an expectation that what is private by custom or law should remain so. But, once we act against that course, the protection of privacy expectation is lost. The more we communicate and engage in social experience the more we narrow the sphere of privacy. The more our social experiences become an attractive data set for third-party social observation, increasingly online, the more those experiences become sources of data mining, analysis and privacy invasion. We may forget or lose interest in some of our activities, but these may be retained when we leave behind an electronic footprint. Privacy, then, can no longer have as its benefit the feeling of autonomy and security of self. That has been traded away for convenience and recapturing it all but impossible. The right to be forgotten is only marginally achievable, and increasingly less so.

Every human being has a right to at least some measure of privacy. Privacy is a precondition for personally experiencing intimacy and for socially acquiring dignity. If some privacy is to be claimed, it should be in those areas where intimacy with self or with others can be achieved, or where self-directed autonomy rises to the level of personal dignity. It is possible to live with no intimacy, and perhaps to be happy doing so, and it is even possible to live most of the time with little or no privacy, as in a prison or a military setting, but it is corrosive to the very idea of being a human person that we not be able to live at all times with our thoughts and self-awareness, these being the core of our dignity. A torture victim may retain his dignity until the point is reached when he experiences such incessant pain that causes him to lose his mind. That is a condition the torturer strives for and one we seek to avoid by banning cruel and unusual punishment. The torturer desires not only to inflict pain but to destroy dignity; that is why he focuses on creating suffering in the most intimate parts of the body.

By contrast, the civilized state is one which strives to maximize individual dignity even if that means paying a higher social cost. Laws and customs of a civilized state attempt to set the appropriate boundaries of personal sanctuary that harmonize with the demands of a given state and society. Where is the zone of privacy in a public restroom or dormitory, at the entry of the facility itself or only where showering and toilet activity occur? Even where individualism is not as valued as are social and familial relations, modesty and respect for self and others still establish zones of privacy and intimacy that can be found everywhere there is human life. The law of privacy, then, may be seen as the laboratory where these barriers are framed, tested, and reframed. One of the great tasks of law is to weigh the consequences of different scenarios where the acceptable limits of privacy, dignity, and intimacy are threatened. This work is not only accomplished in the part of the Constitution that implicates the values of privacy and bans torture, but also within the laws of ownership, trespass, assault, wiretapping, surveillance, child pornography, and of course all of the prohibitions against invasions of privacy upon the reputations of others.

Privacy Law

Harms to Privacy. Traditionally, four harms of privacy invasions have been identified in traditional tort law: (1) the appropriation of someone else's name, image or reputation;[1] (2) intentional and substantial intrusion into another's seclusion and solitude;[2] (3) publically revealing private facts

---

[1] *Robertson v. Rochester Folding Box Co.* 64 N.E. 442 (NY 1902), (lithograph print of plaintiff on commercially sold carton without permission wrongfully appropriated plaintiff's likeness); *Bullard v. MRA Holding, LLC,* 292 Ga. 748 (2013), (fourteen years old minor who was videotaped voluntarily exposing her breasts for a *College Girl's Gone Wild* production, could sue for damages when her still image from the videotaping was attached to the video box of the production without her permission).

[2] *Friedman v. Martinez,* 454 N.J. Super. 87 (2018), (privacy of sixty women employees violated when janitor placed hidden surveillance camera in company restroom, but

of another,[3] and (4) publically falsely asserting embarrassing information of another.[4] In some cases the interests of free speech and privacy are weighted against each other; in other cases, the interest of privacy and right of the public to be informed are balanced. To rise to the level of an actionable tort the injury must be serious and caused at least with a reckless disregard for the truth.

Historically, implied in the way we use the terms privacy, dignity, and intimacy is the distinction between what is public and what should be private. The common denominator is a value placed upon the *experience* of the individual that should not be made public, an experience that is unique and intimate to the individual even if it is widely experienced by others as well. My experience in a large audience still remains unique to me, an experience in which I retain a privacy interest. If I have a private business, then I have a privacy interest in my own financial books and records. No one can examine them without my consent except if the public interest overrides my privacy, and then a court-ordered subpoena would be required.

Privacy Zones. There is a threshold recognition of a 'zone' of privacy working in the background throughout American law, even where 'privacy' *per se* is not the main concern. For example, recognition of the

---

reversed on appeal for lack of sufficient evidence); *Williams v. Stoddard*, 2015 R.I. Super. LEXIS 58, (ex-wife violated ex-husband's privacy when she used a key-logger program to capture ex-husband's passwords to his private online accounts and emails.)

[3] *Smith v. Datla*, 451 N.J. Super. 82 (2017), (doctor improperly disclosed a patient's medical status to third party*); Doe v. Mills*, 212 Mich. App. 73 (1995), (publically disclosing names of patients by protesters at abortion provider clinic an invasion into private facts).

[4] *Wal-Mart Stores v. Lee*, 348 Ark. 707 (2002), (employee placed in false light as an admitted thief when he gave employer permission to search his home for missing fishing equipment after employer sent 10-15 employees and five police officers to search over seven hours and remove 400 non-fishing items to front yard which were photographed and published in newspaper.); *Strutner v. Dispatch Printing Co.*, 2 *Ohio App*. 3d 377 (1982), (publishing the names and address of criminal suspect's parent not a false-light invasion of privacy because such information is readily ascertainable from public records.)

institution of marriage has always been of primary interest to society and the nation. Legal treatises and theories unanimously proclaim its value and purpose, especially in establishing rightful ownership of property through inheritance. There was also a consensus, whether from within the Catholic or Protestant traditions, that an essential purpose of marriage was procreation. Yet, *how* people married was not rigidly regulated; and even less formal cohabiting relations under common law were often accepted. Marriage, historically, was the kind of hodgepodge of rituals and customs and, where gaps occurred, social convention or the common law would fill them in, all with a certain *laissez-faire* attitude that nature would take its course in producing commitment and children regardless of social expectations. Nonetheless, in spite of its critical high importance, no effort was ever made to establish official ceremonies or detailed contractual conditions of marital performance. There was no requirement that the marital night consummating the agreement be witnessed; and whether individual marriages were actually performing their valued social function was left to the individuals themselves. (Traditionally, it was the husband who could complain, under a claim of breach of duty, of his wife's failure to perform her marital obligations.) Day-to-day marriage, in other words, was merely assumed to be fully in effect, functioning entirely within a pervasive zone of privacy.

Polygamy. The strength of a zone of privacy was challenged when the federal government began enacting legislation outlawing polygamy. Although firmly established in the Book of Genesis, polygamy came to be seen in nineteenth-century America as monarchical and excessively patriarchal. The problem the legislators confronted was that the American law of marriage never *required* sexual relations between husband and wife; out of concerns for privacy, they were merely presumed to take place once cohabitation was authorized. So, someone challenging a law against bigamy or polygamy could argue that a man living with two women could do so without being married to either of them, let alone to both of them, and could also argue that he or she was married to one but not the other. Nonetheless, in an attempt to overcome obvious problems of proof, Congress determined that plural marriage occurs when a man holds out to society that he has several wives, that his children from several of them recognize him as their father, and that he lives in a house where one or more wives reside, eats at the table of one or more at least one-third of the time, and sleeps in the house of one or more overnight.

Polygamy prosecutions employed this definition of 'cohabitation', which did not include or reach into the zone of sexual intimacy. The anti-polygamy definition did not require direct evidence of sexual intimacy and was a roundabout way of merely *suggesting* it. The Supreme Court thought it unnecessary to "pry into the intimacies of the marriage relation" in order to establish that unlawful cohabitation. The Justices knew that the law was easy to evade by private agreement among consenting adults, and so decided that the word 'cohabitation' was given a special meaning in the polygamy statute, in contrast with prosecutions where a man lives in sexual intimacy with several women (also a crime at the time), but is not in a polygamous relationship with them. Realizing this problem of proving a polygamous *relationship*, the defendant asked how he could prove going forward that he was not violating the law. The answer given was that "he must not cohabit with more than one woman, in the sense of the word 'cohabit', as hereinbefore defined."[5] This means that he could risk prosecution if he lives with a wife and sister under the same roof. It was only due to a deep commitment to privacy that the law is made to look like a fool here. After all, methods to detect unlawful sexual contact could be easily imagined even in the nineteenth century, but only at a cost of even greater privacy intrusions.

The rationale of outlawing polygamy also seems to apply to laws against incest, laws that sweep up not only sexual relations between siblings or between parents and siblings, but also in some cases consensual relations between adult stepchildren and stepparents. In the case of step relations, we have decided that sexual relations become lawful only after the stepparent's divorce. In the case of parent and child, sexual relations are ruled unlawful as a matter of law and are not made lawful at the age of consent. Such laws are typically justified from a public policy perspective, not in terms of specific behavior and specific intent, but in consequentialist terms: incest damages the cohesiveness of the family; it has damaging psychological consequences; and it potentially produces genetically

---

[5] *Cannon v. United States*, 116 U.S. 55, 79 (1885).

damaging offspring.[6] As we ponder all of the variants of state laws against incest, we are left to wonder how clear the various interests are understood and how well the law actually protects them.

Protecting intimacy, then, has been fertile ground for non-rational law making, reflecting a desire by lawmakers to regulate private conduct without requiring the disclosure of the facts that make the conduct a crime. The primary purpose of laws against polygamy, incest, or sodomy is to discourage immoral and socially unacceptable conduct, but without imposing explicit rules of sexual conduct. If we really wanted to enforce moral norms of sexual conduct, we could easily do so by creating an affirmative obligation of sexual partners to turn each other in when their conduct transgresses the law. Yet, we at least in part embrace just the opposite by creating a husband-wife privilege of confidentiality of spousal communication on the theory that intimacy is eroded when communication between intimates may become public. All of these unusual legal maneuvers attest to the high value we place on intimacy in our social life.

Expanding Privacy

Warren and Brandeis. Intimacy may be characterized as *private* privacy; it is the privacy that does not occur in public. *Public* privacy, however, is an entirely different matter. Although we may be seen and heard in public, much of what takes place, at least traditionally, is largely anonymous and private in that sense. We are merely a fleeting face in the crowd. One of the first recognitions that privacy in public could be a problem is found in an 1890 essay by Boston attorney, Samuel Warren (1852-1910), written with his then law partner, Louis Brandeis.[7] They argue that the recognition of an expanding scope of privacy may be found in the expanding privacy protections in tort and property law. For example, hitting someone was unlawful, but at the time not swinging and missing. Then it was decided that an attempt (assault) could also be an affront to personal dignity and integrity because of the fear it creates that continues on after the swing. So too could mere words hurt, especially slanderous or defamatory words.

---

[6] See Anne C. Dailey, *The Psychodynamics of Sexual Choice*, 57 Ariz. L. Rev. 343 (2015).
[7] *The Right to Privacy*, 4 Harv. L. Rev. 193 (1890).

The history of the tort of 'alienation of affection', also noted by Warren and Brandeis, became established as a remedy against an affront against the privacy of marriage by third parties who steal away the affections of one spouse from another. The aggrieved spouse, then, sues the third party for loss of support and consortium. Ironically, the very thing that justified the tort, the loss of marital intimacy, made it difficult for courts to assess the appropriate remedy. Was the complaining spouse truly aggrieved or just out for revenge? Was there even affection in the first place? Were such suits just opportunities for juries to express their own moral disapproval? These intimate affairs of the heart seemed for many jurists and legal scholars an unbecoming subject for the public courtroom.[8]

Warren and Brandeis noted that objects of a right of privacy came to include more than land and the buildings on it; also included were works of art and science. Reputation became property as social relations increasingly took on economic significance. Intangible property like trade secrets and good will also came to be seen as adhering to the collection of assets of a creative and expressive person. But if there is a right to privacy, a right to be left alone, then damages for libel and slander could occur even without a loss of reputation, they argued. They could result merely from an invasion of privacy itself. Unless voluntarily submitted to public scrutiny, private writings or images cannot be publicized regardless of their artistic merit. Trivial scribblings in a diary and bad poetry are protected as well as great works of art. So, the only way of justifying this emerging practice in law is by recognizing that it is not a utilitarian value of work product the law protects, but the objects of personal value and the peace of mind they bring.

However, as technology increases so do the opportunities for privacy invasion. Warren and Brandeis mention the case of an actress who sued because she was photographed while performing on stage in tights. She clearly consented to be seen where and when she chose to be, but a photograph now allowed her image to be viewed repeatedly and under

---

[8] For a discussion of the decline of the tort of alienation of affection and breaches of promise to marry, see Nathan P. Feinsinger, *Legislative Attack on 'Heart Balm'*, 33 Mich. L. Rev. 979 (1935).

circumstances not of her choosing. In 1903, New York's legislature outlawed the use of a person's name, portrait, or photograph in trade or advertising without prior written consent as a violation of a "right to privacy." Upholding the law against strenuous opposition, the New York Court argued that even though ownership of photographs may be transferred to a new owner their *use* in commerce did not also transfer unless a separate right was relinquished. The basis for that right, the court argued, was "the very general sentiment which prevailed throughout the community" and a "natural a widespread feeling" that such use was "indefensible in morals and ought to be prevented by law."[9] The ultimate justification for the court was the power of the state legislature to protect morality and generally recognized practices that offend common decency.

However, the U.S Supreme Court could find no such right at the time, arguing that the federal Constitution does not "confer any right of privacy upon either persons or corporations."[10] During prohibition, wiretaps were found to be constitutional on the theory that the Fourth Amendment only applies to tangible material objects and places, not to the spoken voice whether or not transmitted over electronic media. Written words included in a sealed envelope and sent through the mail were also protected because for a while they fell under government custody. Tapping a wire was a far less intrusion than opening an envelope, the court reasoned. One dissenter in the case was Justice Brandeis who argued that the purpose of the Fourth and Fifth amendments was not to protect personal physical objects but the expressive content of them. Echoing his earlier privacy essay, he wrote:

> The protection guaranteed by the Amendments is much broader in scope. The makers of our Constitution undertook to secure conditions favorable to the pursuit of happiness. They recognized the significance of man's spiritual nature, of his feelings and of his intellect. They knew that only a part of the pain, pleasure and satisfactions of life are to be found in material things. They sought to protect Americans in their beliefs, their thoughts, their emotions and their sensations. They conferred, as against the Government,

---

[9] *Rhodes v. Sperry & Hutchinson*, 193 N.Y. 223 (1908).

[10] *Prudential Ins. Co. v. Cheek*, 259 U.S. 530 (1922).

> the right to be let alone – the most comprehensive of rights and the right most valued by civilized men.[11]

Since the Warren-Brandeis essay, greater emphasis has been placed on better identifying the zone of privacy surrounding a private dwelling. A valid search warrant would be required for both federal and state officers to enter, search and seize material; otherwise, the evidence acquired could not be used in court.[12] If a valid search warrant had been obtained, prosecution for possessing 'obscene' materials would have gone forward. But several years later the Supreme Court ruled that possession of such obscene materials in the home was an entirely private matter and no longer illegal.[13]

Under the new privacy regime, the psychic and emotional effects of law on the private lives of individuals would have to be balanced against the imposition on desired social goals. Enforcement of law always has unwanted emotional effects on transgressors. A balancing principle seems to be: the more the social goal is widely embraced the less is the weight given to these intangible collateral effects. Someone arrested and taken from his house under a lawful search warrant has little ground to complain that he has been embarrassed in front of his neighbors. So, criminals will have fewer privacy rights due to their adjudicated transgressions. But those rights will not entirely disappear. If wiretapping is allowed to catch bootleggers, why shouldn't it be authorized to catch unfaithful spouses? In the polygamy cases, the question posed was always how much intrusion into sexual intimacy is necessary to weed out lawful from unlawful marriages? If polygamous marriages are secretive, what more would be required to enforce an anti-polygamy law? Should there be mandatory paternity tests for all children? Should all cohabiting persons be required to keep a personal log of sexual encounters and be ready to disclose it to officials? Rejecting these intrusive measures as an affront to privacy, then, means that the anti-polygamy laws only ban socially manifest plural

---

[11] *Olmstead v. United States*, 277 U.S. 438, 478 (1928).

[12] *Mapp v. Ohio*, 367 U.S. 643 (1961) (seizure of obscene books and pictures).

[13] *Stanley v. Georgia*, 394 U.S. 557 (1969). The defendant had "the right to satisfy his intellectual and emotional needs in the privacy of his own home."

marriages and their official recognition by banning plural marriage licenses.

At a certain point, a threshold determination must be made by legislators through the political process, and judges through the judicial process, that the selected subject matter to be enforced invades privacy to an unacceptable degree because the means of enforcing the law are unacceptable. This is always the issue that surrounds laws with an object of enforcing strict moral standards such as the 'Sunday' or 'blue' laws discussed in chapter five. In the early Republic, some states flirted with mandatory church services for the working classes. Such laws are difficult to enforce, so it was easier to withhold the temptation by closing businesses on Sunday. But eventually that too became riddled, as we have seen, with exceptions, so that the project of moral reform was eventually dropped altogether. In the case of pornography infractions, obviously Supreme Court did not think the lewd and lascivious materials viewed in the privacy of the home were sufficiently pornographic to require legal sanction.[14]

Contraception. Until the 1960s many jurisdictions thought it necessary to promote childbirth in marriage by banning contraception. However, none took the next step of *requiring* conception outside of marriage because of the obvious invasion of privacy needed to enforce such a law. In the late nineteenth century, anti-contraception laws ('Comstock laws') were enacted as a moral tool for fighting prostitution, promiscuity, and sexually transmitted diseases. But the wider availability of latex condoms in the 1930s, also sold as a means of fighting sexually-transmitted diseases, undercut the medical rationale and opened the door fully to the question of private morality. Use of condoms explicitly to block conception was still outlawed, but how would the laws be enforced? That question was largely ignored because the seventy-five-year-old Connecticut law had only been enforced once, and condoms were readily available if not widely

---

[14] Possessing or viewing child pornography in the privacy of your home remains illegal because of the state's interest in protecting minors, who are required in the production of such materials. See *New York v. Ferber*, 458 U.S. 747 (1982) and *Osborne v. Ohio*, 495 U.S. 103 (1990). As to the First Amendment problem raised by artificially created imagery, see *Ashcroft v. Free Speech Coalition*, 535 U.S. 234 (2002).

advertised.[15] That was the question the Supreme Court finally considered in *Griswold v. Connecticut*, when the majority wrote: "Would we allow the police to search the sacred precincts of marital bedrooms for telltale signs of the use of contraceptives? The very idea is repulsive to the notions of privacy surrounding the marriage relationship."[16] Decisions about contraception were the province of married couples because they were "intimate to the degree of being sacred," the court concluded.

Soon thereafter, under the same privacy rationale birth control was extended to unmarried persons. If the basis for *Griswold* was the privacy between married persons to make their own decisions whether or not to engage in sexual relations for the purpose of conceiving offspring without regulation from the state, then either (a) privacy about sex is a privilege of married individuals alone or (b) it is a right of individuals regardless of marital status. Accepting (a) would require couples to carry around their marriage license, the way they carry their driver's license, in order to purchase contraceptives. It also would require penalizing the sale and possession of contraceptives by unmarried individuals, as well as ban agreements to enter into marriage solely for the purpose of having legally-protected sex. Since, this kind of enforcement would require a set of extremely intrusive laws and regulations, the court chose (b):

> It is true that in *Griswold* the right of privacy in question inhered in the marital relationship. Yet the marital couple is not an independent entity with a mind and heart of its own, but an association of two individuals each with a separate intellectual and emotional makeup. If the right of privacy means anything, it is the right of the individual, married or single, to be free from unwarranted governmental intrusion into matters so fundamentally affecting a person as the decision whether to bear or beget a child.[17]

As the argument is posed, the court seems to imply the existence of a fundamental right of unmarried individuals to engage in sex outside of

---

[15] The state's failure to enforce its anti-contraception law was the reason the Supreme Court declined to consider its applicability to married couples. See *Poe v. Ullman*, 367 U.S. 497 (1961).

[16] *Griswold v. Connecticut*, 381 U.S. 479, 486 (1965).

[17] *Eisenstadt v. Baird*, 405 U.S. 438, 453 (1972).

marriage (called at the time 'fornication') and even produce children that way. As the court noted, the state statute allowed the sale of contraceptives to married persons, even if they were not living with their spouses, and did not specify the authorized or prohibited uses of them. And once sold, there was no accounting for how they would be used or by whom. So, how was a marriage-only restriction to be enforced, since state laws criminalizing extramarital sex and adultery, or providing civil penalties, that remained on the books were almost never enforced?[18]

Some concurring Justices faulted the Connecticut law, not for any violation of a personal right of privacy, but because it interfered with the marriage relation in violation of the due process liberty interest protected by the Fourteenth Amendment. The stated intent of the law was to fight extramarital sex and, in the process, unfairly (over-broadly) caught up married couples in the ban as well. The two *Griswold* dissenters challenged the very idea that the Constitution protects privacy as a right, arguing that privacy is a "broad and ambiguous concept which can easily be shrunken in meaning but which can also, on the other hand, easily be interpreted as a constitutional ban against many things other than searches and seizures." "I like my privacy as well as the next one," Justice Black wrote "but I am nevertheless compelled to admit that government has a right to invade it unless prohibited by some specific constitutional provision." So, the only remedy for the people who oppose the law, he argued, would be to get their representatives to change it.[19]

Privacy and Pregnancy. The legal concept of a privacy right continued to evolve, and was soon expanded to include a zone of "personal liberty," a right to be free from government regulation in one's personal life. For a regulation to be constitutional, the social harm caused by an exercise of personal liberty must be mitigated by a minimally effective degree of state regulation.[20] In *Roe v Wade*, the Texas anti-abortion law at issue, initially

---

[18] See JoAnne Sweeny, *Undead Statutes: The Rise, Fall, and Continuing Uses of Adultery and Fornication Criminal Laws,* 46 Loy. U. Chi. L.J. 127 (2014). In *Griswold,* one dissenter admitted that the law was "silly" and "obviously unenforceable," but was still not unconstitutional. *Griswold* at 527.

[19] *Griswold* at 509-510, 530.

[20] *Roe v. Wade,* 410 U.S. 113 (1973).

enacted in 1854, did not articulate the state interests involved. The law stated that abortion was banned except to save the life of the mother. So, an interest in the health of the mother could be strongly implied. Other interests also could be implied such as raising the cost of promiscuity and saving prenatal human life. Such a sweeping law, the majority thought, infringed upon personal liberty without sufficiently specifying all the interests involved, and how they could change during the course of a pregnancy. A constitutionally acceptable abortion law would be one that calibrated the interests according to the nine-month gestation period. As the embryo grows, so does the interest of the state in protecting "health, medical standards, and prenatal life."[21] The choice of a trimester regimen was simply a way of articulating a useful rule of thumb to weigh the various interests. This rule could only be an estimate, a bench mark, due to the highly contested, and probably unresolvable, issue of when protectable life begins. The unresolvable depth of the problem, which has continued for nearly a half century, was recognized by the court at the very outset:

> We forthwith acknowledge our awareness of the sensitive and emotional nature of the abortion controversy, of the vigorous opposing views, even among physicians, and of the deep and seemingly absolute convictions that the subject inspires. One's philosophy, one's experiences, one's exposure to the raw edges of human existence, one's religious training, one's attitudes toward life and family and their values, and the moral standards one establishes and seeks to observe, are all likely to influence and to color one's thinking and conclusions about abortion. In addition, population growth, pollution, poverty, and racial overtones tend to complicate and not to simplify the problem.[22]

With all of these factors involved, a question is raised as to why there is a need to regulate abortion in the first place. Protection of infants by law is a well-grounded moral and social norm. We give serious concern and care to the process of creating human life, in part because the gestation process itself is so arduous and uncertain. Were humans to be created with the ease and rapidity of fruit flies would abortion even be cognizable under law? Is

---

[21] Ibid.,155.

[22] Ibid., 116.

a woman's privacy right to make decisions affecting her own body grounded in the facts of her difficult and solitary journey rather than in the Constitution? In spite of the many different factors complicating our views of the significance of making human life, the high court acted as a sifter of our moral stance on the value of unborn life when necessarily measured by our values of born life. By using the measure of personal liberty, the court acknowledged the tension between personal autonomy and the responsibility of the state to establish norms of public conduct. In the early stages of pregnancy, the state does not mandate that the pregnancy continue or be aborted; that is the widest zone of personal liberty. In later stages, autonomy of the pregnant woman is diminished and public interests grow.

The decision in *Roe* is predicated on a claim that there is a "guarantee of certain areas or zones of privacy" presupposed in Amendments One, Four, Five, Nine, and Fourteen. But the decision explicitly notes that the *guarantee* is not really a guarantee and is not absolute but entirely context dependent.[23] The first movements of the fetus, 'quickening', begins to erode the guarantee. We must wonder, then, whether there can be *any* limits of privacy violation from a constitutional perspective. If our privacy rights depended entirely on context, could they be whittled away with clever or even pretextual argumentation? Suppose common traffic infractions called for strip searches or body cavity searches. Could the potential danger of the infraction be articulated in such a manner as to justify that degree of intrusion? That seems to be a question that can only be answered by fleshing out the relevant context and facts, as is usually done in disputes over when interrogation ends and torture begins. We should note that while context matters, the very idea of liberty implies a resistance to external constraint, much in the same way that the First Amendment assumes dissent will occur and then seeks to protect it. Individuals who never break rules would be in no need for rules protecting their liberty. By its nature, liberty implies a struggle against non-self-imposed rules and

[23] Ibid., 152, 159 ("[I]t is reasonable and appropriate for a State to decide that at some point in time another interest, that of health of the mother or that of potential human life, becomes significantly involved. The woman's privacy is no longer sole and any right of privacy she possesses must be measured accordingly.")

some loss of control over the individual by the state and its laws. My demand for privacy requires a loss of your demand for information and control. To identify liberty with a fixed condition, such as a state of nature or a free market, is to ignore the constraining conditions found wherever there is social interaction. Liberty, then, is always in achievement that must be constantly worked on in opposition to constraining conditions. Paradoxically, my right to be left alone requires my vigilance and engagement to protect that right.

Balancing Privacy Interests

The legal balancing of individual privacy interests against various state interests crops up in many different circumstances. In such balancing, legal principles do not establish the privacy right. Instead, courts make an *ad hoc* determination based on socially acceptable norms of the day whether or not the state has overreached its constitutional authority. Examples of privacy cases include:

- A criminal suspect may not have his stomach forcibly pumped while in state custody in order to obtain incriminating evidence. *Rochin v. California,* 342 U.S. 165 (1952).
- A state may require doctors prescribing controlled substances to disclose the name and address of the persons receiving the prescription in a central database, as long as there are safeguards against the dissemination of the information and legislation is crafted through an orderly and rational decision process. The state had a legitimate interest in keeping track of such substances and doing so would not adversely impact on the freedom of the doctor to prescribe them. *Whalen v. Roe,* 429 U.S. 589 (1977).
- A city housing ordinance could not limit occupancy to single family members and could provide no rational explanation why grandchildren who were siblings were permitted but cousins were not when the purpose of the ordinance was to avoid overcrowding in housing and parking. Given the historic importance of the family in American life great deference should be given to the cohabitation decisions of a wide range of family members. *Moore v. East Cleveland,* 431 U.S. 494 (1977).

- A state may not impose a ban on the sale of nonprescription contraceptives to minors under sixteen, since minors also have some degree of constitutional privacy rights including a right to an abortion against parental wishes. *Carey v. Population Servs. Int'l,* 431 U.S. 678 (1977).
- A federal law requiring that a former president turnover to the government, for eventual disclosure to the public, papers or other materials connected to the executive function did not violate free speech, nor separation of powers, nor was it a bill of attainder. The president's personal privacy interests were outweighed substantially by the public interest, and the interest of historians to be fully informed about the workings of an administration. *Nixon v. Administrator of General Services.,* 433 U.S. 425 (1977).
- There is no expectation of privacy protected by the Fourth Amendment against a warrantless search and seizure of garbage left for collection outside the curtilage of a home. *California v. Greenwood,* 486 U.S. 35 (1988).
- Drug and alcohol abuse by railroad employees are a threat to public safety, and so compelled blood and breathalyzer tests by railroad employers on specific employees as long as conducted with careful procedural safeguards. *Skinner v. Railway Labor Executives' Association,* 489 U.S. 602 (1989).
- Releasing a person's government maintained criminal record to a news organization under the Freedom of Information Act is an invasion of privacy. *U.S. Department of Justice v. Reporters Committee for Freedom of the Press,* 489 U.S. 749 (1989).
- A State law requiring a married woman to provide a written statement to her medical abortion provider that she has notified her spouse that she is about to undergo an abortion unreasonably impairs her right to privacy. *Planned Parenthood v. Casey,* 505 U.S. 833 (1992).
- Random urinalysis of high school student athletes was not sufficiently invasive as to offset the need to control the rise of drug use and the danger of injuries to athletes using drugs. *Vernonia School District 47J v. Acton,* 515 U.S. 646 (1995).
- Releasing autopsy photos by a government agency under the Freedom of Information Act (5 U.S.C.S. § 552 (b)(7)(C)) violates the family's privacy interest unless there is a significant public interest

in the release. *National Archives and Records Administration. v. Favish*, 541 U.S. 157 (2004).

- Federal suspicionless searches at the border include authority to remove, disassemble, and reassemble a vehicle's fuel tank given the paramount interest in preventing drug importation. *United States v. Flores-Montano*, 541 U.S. 149 (2004).
- A state may subject a parolee to a suspicionless search because of the substantial legitimate public interest in reducing recidivism. *Samson v. California*, 547 U.S. 843 (2006).
- A GPS tracking device installed by law enforcement agents on the undercarriage of a vehicle without a search warrant which tracked its movement for the next twenty-eight days violates a person's reasonable expectation of privacy. *United States v. Jones*, 565 U.S. 400 (2012).
- Even detainees for minor offenses may be subject to invasive body searches because of the strong interest in maintaining security in a jail or prison. *Florence v. Board of Chosen Freeholders*, 566 U.S. 318 (2012).
- Drunk driving traffic stops do not justify an automatic blood test without a warrant obtained, based on specific facts and circumstances, given the significant constitutional protection against compelled intrusion into the human body. *Missouri v. McNeely*, 569 U.S. 141(2013).
- Taking and analyzing a routine cheek swab of any arrestee's DNA was no more intrusive than fingerprinting and photographing, as a legitimate police booking process, since there were reasonable safeguards that the information could be used only for identification purposes. *Maryland v. King*, 569 U.S. 435 (2013) (Note Justice Scalia's dissent that such a search was an unconstitutional 'general warrant'.)
- Police may not search the contents of an arrestee's digital cell phone, including historic location, without a warrant given that a cell phone is no threat to the safety of arresting officers and may contain immense storage of personal information unrelated to arrest. *Riley v. California,* 134 S. Ct. 2473 (2014).
- A motorcycle, suspected of being stolen, parked at the top of a driveway and covered with a tarp could not be searched without a warrant. *Collins v. Virginia*, 138 S. Ct. 1663 (2018).

Emerging Issues

Informational Privacy. The *Riley* case raises the troublesome issue of electronic data retrieval and storage. Should there be a legal difference between physically following somebody in a motor vehicle, and remotely extracting location information from CCTV cameras or a cell phone tower? In the first case, the data is collected in real time and in public space, where there is little expectation of privacy, for the purpose of conducting a legally authorized investigation. In the second case, CCTV imagery and cell phone location data are stored and retrievable after the fact, collecting on entire record of a person's actions to be accessed at the will of some future investigator. The privacy intrusions are greater in the second case because the data collected is better preserved, more comprehensive and accessible. Public privacy is at its maximum when a person becomes merely a face in the crowd. Facial recognition, comprehensive data collection, storage, and retrieval have the potential of reducing all degrees of anonymity to zero, something the court seemed to recognize in *Riley*.

Data Collection. How is privacy to be measured in a world where the possibilities of data collection are almost without limit? An important distinction can be made between the methods of acquiring information and the information acquired. Is it an invasion of privacy to discover innocuous facts about somebody, say, about the kind of toothpaste they use? Such information will be useful to a marketer. Suppose comprehensive toothpaste user searches are the only kind of searches permitted on the internet. In that instance, a search merely identifying the kind of toothpaste used by someone would be a minimal invasion of privacy. But suppose that information is linked up with data correlating toothpaste with economic income or political affiliation. In that instance the data set of toothpaste use can become a useful predictive tool, revealing a lot more than dental hygiene, and of powerful use in targeting political ads. In other words, the usefulness and predictive power of data increases, not only with the power to store and retrieve it, but also with the capacity to correlate and interpret it with other data sets formed subsequently. A substantial invasion of privacy that is soon perishable may be less invasive in the long run than one that is insubstantial but may be efficiently stored, retrieved and reinterpreted. A person at the checkout register obtains a great deal of visual information about a customer and their purchases, but the credit card imprint has a greater invasive potential as its digitized matrix moves through and is stored within the banking system.

Consent. Consent is another factor in measuring invasiveness. Consent may be either expressed or implied. When we leave the country and return, we consent to have our belongings searched because we enter a zone where government officials act to protect the nation's territorial borders. When we drive a motor vehicle, we do not bring with us the full expectation of privacy.[24] Even when we leave our houses, we consent impliedly to be seen and heard. When we acquire electrical service from the local utility service, we consent to have our meter read and usage monitored. In such cases, we have little if any expectation of privacy. When we check a box indicating that we consent expressly to the uses of information and privacy protections in the operations of a cell phone, we have been deemed to have actually given that express consent. Many people began using cell phones based on their understanding of what traditional phones could do, not realizing that their location may be tracked without any additional action on their part. As we have just seen, it is a primary function of the court to sift through the various interests, being guided by the Fourth Amendment's traditional partiality towards privacy. In the case of cell phone geolocations, the Supreme Court, in a close decision, has decided that extended monitoring over many days provides a detailed picture of a person private life in public: "Mapping a cell phone's location over the course of 127 days provides an all-encompassing record of the holder's whereabouts," including not just locations but whom he visited and which groups he associated with. Accessing such information, then, implicated the Fourth amendment and so required a search warrant.[25]

Intelligence Surveillance. The Foreign Intelligence Surveillance Court was set up to review the legality of surveillance of international communications obtained through the authority of the Foreign Intelligence Surveillance Act (FISA). Since foreign actors outside the United States were involved it was

---

[24] *Wyoming v. Houghton,* 526 U.S. 295, 300 (1999).

[25] *Carpenter v. United States,* 138 S.Ct. 2206 (2018).

assumed that the Fourth Amendment did not apply. However, when those actors communicated with American citizens the Amendment was implicated to some degree, so FISA rules were required to protect the latter's privacy. With national security now added to the balancing scale, it became easier to favor the national interest as against a person's privacy interest. Once electronic communication became digitized and digitized receptors (e.g., calling your bank automatic teller) were given the capabilities to redirect a sequential series of impulses generated by punching keys on a computer or icons on a cell phone (e.g., accessing your bank account by a private password) advances in technology allowed electric surveillance of the entire spectrum of a person's digital life. However, unlike the private physical contents of a home or vehicle that are inadvertently discovered in the course of a lawful search, private information from electronic surveillance could be stored for potential future investigative use.

Federal law now authorizes the collection of a series of electrical impulses specific to a given phone number, identifying the originating number or other dialing, routing, and signaling information using a 'trap and trace device'. Outgoing information using a 'pen register' device may also be authorized with or without a FISA warrant, much in the same manner as the phone company captures with your consent your phone calls for billing purposes. Asking the telephone company to install a pen register on a suspect account to obtain the calling records was deemed not a search, thereby not implicating the Fourth Amendment, because there is no expectation of privacy in billing records.[26] Nowadays, surveilling internet and cell phone data brings with it the opportunity to acquire additional content, including personal identification (pin) numbers, bank account numbers, and credit card and social security numbers. Acquiring such content information has been justified because of the difficulty of being able to segregate the impulses before they are captured and decoded. In effect, it is the digital equivalent of entering a person's house to see if a search warrant is required. Thus, the Fourth Amendment and its 'expectation of privacy' norm have been applied to searches of internet traffic even though the target of the search has little understanding of the

---

[26] *Smith v. Maryland*, 442 U.S. 735 (1979).

complexity of the processes embedding private content information. Since the complexity of the medium requires a corresponding complexity of the balancing processes, judges and legislators must acquire technical and fact-specific information on a case-by-case basis, and apply analogical reasoning from traditional Fourth Amendment jurisprudence. The sufficiency of safeguards against runaway investigations by state actors require high confidence in the ability of the branches of government to carefully reason through and balance these Fourth Amendment interests.[27] Needless to say, given the technological complexity of capturing only legally permissible data, the risk of unlawful searches is considerable.

Hacking. An even more troubling privacy issue is raised by the direct hacking by the government of third-party servers to identify visitors to the site. As encryption and anonymization tools become more widely used by the public, counteracting measures also become more sophisticated. For example, in one case in order to identify someone placing bomb threats and sending harassing emails the FBI enticed the perpetrator into linking onto an Associated Press article describing him as a tech savvy prodigy. In doing so, malware was directly installed on his computer bypassing a proxy server and his web browser security protections. An FBI agent then posed as an Associated Press editor and sent an email containing the link to the unidentified perpetrator's social media account. The malware was instructed to send back the user's IP address which the FBI then used to identify the perpetrator through his Internet Service Provider records. The question became: was the use of the malware in this case a 'search' and if so, was probable cause sufficiently determined?[28] The FBI applied for court authorization, but did not indicate the use of malware or the impersonation of a reporter. Initially the perpetrator ignored the 'editor's' request for an

[27] See, for example, *In re Certified Question of Law*, 858 F.3d 591 (2016), holding that, because of the technical difficulty of separating private content from non-private information, collecting private content without a probable-cause warrant, given the high interest when foreign surveillance is involved, does not violate the Fourth Amendment.

[28] See Jonathan Mayer, *Government Hacking,* 27 Yale L. J. 570, 574 (2018). See also https://oig.justice.gov/reports/2016/o1607.pdf.

anonymous interview and replied back "leave me alone," but with continual urging that complete anonymity would be guaranteed took the bait, clicking on the fake news article, which led to his identification.

From the government's perspective, the FBI's resort to malware resulted from the strenuous privacy protections implemented by the perpetrator, using servers in Italy and the Czech Republic. The ability to conduct unlawful activities by 'going dark' means that the probable cause and specificity requirements of the Fourth Amendment may never get formulated unless new privacy penetrating techniques also are introduced. But at what cost should these deceptive techniques be used against those not engaged in unlawful conduct, but who want to avail themselves of the highest degree of privacy protections? If the FBI had directly broken into the suspect's home and installed malware on his computer, plainly that would have been a search requiring a warrant. But in that case the suspect's identity would already be known and a standard undercover operation could go forward seeking incriminating additional evidence. Similarly, an individual's specific cell phone may be searched under circumstances allowing for the articulation of probable cause and therefore requiring a search warrant. The search warrant requirement also protects a person's computer and its data content whether or not it is located within a home.[29] But how much of what happens on the computer that continually sends and receives signals with outside sources may reasonably be expected to be private? Whenever we select a means of communication, we consent to its protocols. But does that mean we give blanket consent to make public all our information transmitted by those protocols?

The Stored Communications Act (18 U.S.C §§ 2710 -2712) (1986-2018) was designed to give constitutional protections to individuals who transmitted personal information using an Internet Service Provider (ISP), or other transmission and storage service. The Act distinguished the *content* of a communication from its 'envelope' information, and required various levels of authorization to obtain them. Information that is more intimately connected to the *expression* of a subscriber is given the

---

[29] *Katz v. United States,* 389 US 347 (1967); Fourth Amendment protections extended to a public phone booth.

highest level of privacy. An IP address, given to a subscriber, is not as private as the contents of an email itself, though since it is a unique identifier is more private than the identity of the ISP itself. The content of an email retains its protection even when stored by a third-party ISP.[30] The problem malware creates is that it can report back a suspect's IP address and other envelope data without any probable cause determination. The technology, in fact, allows for the broadcasting of many malware infections across a range of possible suspects. When the government surveilles an individual or group using eyes and ears, the information transmitted is extremely rich in human context and content and is unique to that person. Malware, on the other hand, is less specific and so less private but its method of broad dissemination may comprise the kind of unconstitutional 'dragnet' or 'entrapment' the Fourth Amendment was designed to prevent.

The very act of malware as phishing intrusion – breaking into a software regimen, extracting data from it, and sending it to a computer used by the government – has all the hallmarks of a search and seizure because it is specifically designed with the intent of carrying out a law enforcement operation where an individual's liberty is at risk. It is not the act of a business collecting records with a business purpose. Unless the suspect is identified, malware placed on a specific webpage could lead to the hacking of thousands of computers. In the case of child pornography investigations, the law stipulates that such a 'visit' to a porn site creates *per se* probable cause. This, however, is the exception. The difficulty of applying traditional Fourth Amendment analysis to malware intrusions is not that a computer can be used as an instrument for crime as an automobile can be used as a getaway car. The problem is the potential undetectability of actions the law has classified as 'criminal'. Traditionally, law enforcement quickly matched the skills of lawbreaking in ways that did not undermine Fourth Amendment protections. In the new environment, such traditional privacy protections may have to be stipulated as being waived by broad consent, expressly or constructively through legislation, as a tradeoff for access to the benefits of enhanced digital communication and networking. Will the

[30] *United States v. Warshak,* 631 F.3d 266 (2010); *United States v. Davis,*785 F.3d 498 (2015).

expertise of government legislators in drafting constitutional legislation keep pace with the technical capabilities of law enforcers and law breakers so as not to render the Fourth Amendment obsolete in the arena of digitized transmission?

Another area where informational privacy can be compromised is in the use of popular search engines like Google that also compile records of a user's mail account (Gmail). Again, by cross-referencing these data streams more and more qualitative information may be obtained about a user. If someone searches a medical question and looks for a doctor in that field, an inference may be drawn with probability greater than zero about the user's medical condition. That maybe information that is sufficient as a target for advertisers. Expanding and enriching the collection of user information, then, correlated with the expansion and quality of advertising revenue. In this expansion, privacy and consent issues were raised by users, primarily in areas such a geolocation tracking and the collection of user information using 'cookies' to bypass the privacy setting of other search engines such as Safari (Apple) and Internet Explorer (Microsoft).[31] As a result, Google was able to harvest users' information without their consent. Google also tags child pornography files uploaded to a Gmail account, and sends the files and the users IP address to the government. Since Google is a private party and not the government entity, the information it obtained from a search of a user's Gmail account was not deemed a violation of the Fourth Amendment.[32] Google and other platforms (Yahoo, Apple, Microsoft, and Facebook) also shared users' envelope and content information with the National Security Agency through a secret surveillance program (PRISM), beginning in 2007, which a whistleblower brought to light.[33]

Social Media. Facebook also has been the subject of privacy litigation for tracking users' browsing visits to third-party websites, which are then

---

[31] *In re Google Inc. Cookie Placement Consumer Privacy Litigation*, 806 F.3d 125 (3d. Cir. 2015). A 'cookie' is a small text file placed on a user's bouser by a visited web page that stores unique identifier information and user preferences when using the website pages.

[32] *United States v. Miller*, 2020 U.S. App. LEXIS 37767 (6th Cir. 2020).

[33] *Schuchardt v. President of the United States*, 802 Fed. Appx 69 (3d Cir. 2020).

compiled into a user profile and sold to advertisers.[34] The company uses 'plug ins' on its webpage (e.g., a 'Like' button) to enrich its user information profile. Facebook got its start in 2003 by asking Harvard students to submit and compare uploaded photos in a 'hot or not' popularity contest. Within hours thousands of photos had been submitted, and just as quickly the platform ran into copyright (using a Harvard student database) and privacy (posting photos without permission) problems.[35] Since then, Facebook has created a variety of ways to get users to reveal more of their preferences so as to enrich and particularize its customer base for better targeted advertising. Like Google, it also acquired competitors, such as Instagram, that would expand its customer base and provide more users to track and profile. In 2019 it invited users to post 10-year-old photos of themselves in an effort to develop reliable facial recognition technology.[36]

Big Data. The potency of the Facebook data base was seen in the way it was used by a British political consulting firm, Cambridge Analytica, and some of their clients. In 2014, the company acquired the profiles of some 87,000,000 Facebook users, which it then reconfigured into various sociological categories.[37] The information was so specific that, to test the usability of the data, a consultant made a cold call to a user in the United States, presenting himself as a pollster, and through seemingly innocent questioning, in fact, did verify that person's preferences with regard to specific TV programs and other items of interest. The data produced an accurate biographical picture of a user, where they lived, and what their interests and aggravations were. The next step was to generate political ads that would attract support for specific candidates and diminish support for their opponents. Although there was no 'I hate' button on Facebook, data analysis of user profiles could determine who, when presented with an

---

[34] *Davis v. Facebook Inc.*, (In re Facebook Inc. Internet Tracking Litigation), 956 F.3d 889 (2020).

[35] Katharine A. Kaplan, "Facemash Creator Survives Ad Board," *The Harvard Crimson* (November 19, 2003); Ellen McGirt, "Facebook's Mark Zuckerberg Hacker. Dropout. CEO," *Fast Company* (May 1, 2007).

[36] Wayne A. Logan and Jake Linford, *Contracting for Fourth Amendment Privacy Online*, 104 Minn. L. Rev 101 (2019).

[37] See, for background, Christopher Wylie, *Mindf*ck: Cambridge Analytica and the Plot to Break America*, (New York: Random House, 2019).

issue or image, would push that button and for what reasons. And from that step, it became possible to fashion advertising messages that further exacerbate feelings of hate and resentment for political gain.

The scope of big data generated by social media changed the balancing of public and private interests, typically illustrated in the above cases. Now, the balance was not between individuals and social norms reflected in law, where law served as a mediating influence. The new paradigm was able to move popular and political thought almost overnight, and do so not through the deliberations of lawmakers, but through the actions of profit seekers, political consultants, and international agents operating in the dark. For this reason, The European Union (EU) has passed legislation to curtail the freedom of online data collection. Among the change was a different definition of 'consent'. In the U.S., the Federal Trade Commission (FTC), the agency that monitors and regulates digital platforms, has used the 'notice and consent' model. A platform provides notice of the kind of data it collects, and asks the user to consent or opt out. (Usually, opting out means not using the service.) The adequacy of the notice, as in many other areas of law, determines whether the consent was informed or not. This has been the subject of continued litigation over the years. In most cases, it would take a lawyer to understand the implications of the consent given when an 'I agree' box is checked.

EU and California. The EU uses a different paradigm, starting with the notion that privacy is not something that is given away piecemeal on an *ad hoc* basis, but is instead a fundamental right. The General Data Protection Regulation (GDPR) starts with the premise that natural persons should have control over their own personal data.[38] The general thrust of the law is that data collection should not be a process of casting a wide net, and then storing it for future use. Personal data should be carefully and transparently processed and collected for specified explicit and legitimate purposes, and the extent of the collection should be no greater than the purposes required. Also, the data should be kept for a period of time no greater than required to fulfill the purpose of the collection. Data

---

[38] Regulation (EU) 2016/679 of the European Parliament and the Council of April 27, 2016.

controllers must clearly disclose any data collection, declare the lawful basis and purpose for data processing, and state how long data is being retained and if it is being shared with any third parties. Firms have the obligation to protect data of employees and consumers to the degree where only the necessary data is extracted with minimum interference with data privacy from employees, consumers, or third parties. Obviously, if the purpose is to collect all personal data and then to sell it in tranches to those who might use it for whatever reason, such a purpose would violate the GDPR norms. Owning your data means being able to review or erase, or edit it, transfer it to another platform, and monetize it yourself. Among the rights guaranteed to persons by the law, is the right to prohibit certain uses of their data, the right to know how the data is collected and processed, and the right to be notified within 72 hours of a data breach.

California, the jurisdiction of many informational privacy lawsuits, has passed its own internet privacy laws. The California Consumer Privacy Act (CCPA), which became effective January 1, 2020, requires businesses to post a clear and conspicuous link on their website's homepage stating "Do not sell my personal information," which takes the user to an opt out page. The law provides greater user protections than elsewhere in the United States. For example, Californians now have a right to access the data companies collect about them, learn which kind of companies the data is sold to, and request that the data be deleted. Personal information is defined as information that identifies, relates to, or describes and is capable of being associated with a particular consumer or household. Since the California law, unlike that of the EU, places the burden on consumers to monitor and protect their privacy, questions of its effectiveness have been raised.[39] The EU's more aggressive stance has been attributed to the earlier experiences of living in a totalitarian state. Between 1933 and 1945 the Nazis had created a total surveillance state. In France they seized the central National Security registry containing 650,000 individual records, which were then used for political control, through intimidation and the oppression, of the population. Privacy and protection of data collection also are enshrined in The Charter of Fundamental Rights of the European Union

---

[39] David Alpert, Note: *Beyond Request-and-Respond: Why Data Access Will be Insufficient to Tame Big Tech*, 120 Colum. L. Rev. 1215 (2020).

(2009), which grants to all Europeans "the right to respect for his or her private and family life, home and communications" (Ch. II, Art. 7), and "the right to the protection of personal data concerning him or her." (Ch. II, Art. 8). These EU experiences and norms push back against the transactional view, which conceives online activities as just another form of consumer interaction. They also could influence the global culture of privacy, since the regulations apply to any platform that intersects with EU territory. The Internet is a global entity and can only function, as currently configured, as such. So, in what sense should national privacy laws and standards exclusively govern national users, who might get up in the morning in New York and read online a paper in Tel Aviv?[40]

Even before the arrival of Facebook, the question was raised whether online life, that has facilitated so many useful consumer, educational, and cultural opportunities at such a rapid pace, had rendered traditional privacy norms obsolete.[41] Loss of privacy can also create social costs because privacy is part of the value that makes the internet useful. Earlier technological revolutions, such as riding on a crowded train or using a telephone requiring a switchboard operator, reduced privacy but provided a clear tangible benefit. New legal paradigms may be needed to do the work of 'notice/response' and 'reasonable expectations' models of consent. If we abandon online privacy, will it be easier to abandon offline privacy as well? Will strip searches become routine, or neighborhood dragnet home searches? Will surrendering your saliva to discover your ancestors make possible the loss of job for a grandchild as an insurance risk for medical reasons? Any restriction on data tracking and collection is bound to reduce its commercial value. On the other hand, data portability could produce newer markets to explant it. Warren and Brandeis saw the privacy value in a photo, but gave the choice of commercial exploitation to the person in the photo and not to the photographer. They reconceived privacy in a way that changed the scope of the law's protection of it.

---

[40] Michael L. Rustad and Thomas H. Koenig, *Towards a Global Data Privacy Standard,* 71 Fla. L. Rev. 365 (2019).

[41] Michael A Froomkin, *Cyberspace and Privacy: A New Legal Paradigm: The Death of Privacy?* 52 Stan. L. Rev. 1461, 1462 (2000).

Contextual Privacy. If privacy is now reconceived again, not in terms of being in public with low expectation of privacy or at home with high expectation of privacy, but in terms of the various ways of living life through various normative zones of privacy, shaped not by special location but by establishing a "foundation for policy and law expressed in terms of moral, political, and social values."[42] Privacy may be conceived as a barrier against pervasive government intrusion (big brother), as a protection of private social experience (student and medical records, club memberships), and as intrusions into private and public (public privacy) space (facial recognition, thermal imaging, CCTV). We intuitively understand that being followed in public is an invasion of privacy, even if its persistence does not rise to the level of stalking. We sense when being 'too familiar' with a causal acquaintance has breached a norm of privacy for that kind of relationship. We speak privately with our doctor but do not ask that he or she speak privately to us as well. We are comfortable with a camera in our bank, but less so with a camera pointing at our house. The same applies with giving consent to an eye scan or fingerprinting just to enter a department store. With respect to pregnancy, we try to draw a line of privacy somewhere between compulsory abortion and compulsory birth. We may tolerate a public record search when it is done by hand at the court house, but less so when it is available online for a fee. Identifying the privacy line is difficult and contextual. The line may move when a terrorist attack (handbag and backpack searches) or a pandemic (public temperature checks) is involved. Nonetheless, we function as if a line exists, and should not adopt a hard distinction between intimacy and 'anything goes', or between consent and 'anything goes'. Privacy expectation may be subjective or objective. However, even the privacy of what a reasonable person would expect, as in a phonebooth (Katz), ignores the context. In a totalitarian state it is reasonable to expect little privacy, but that does not mean that expectation *ought* to be reasonable. Privacy norms pervade ordinary life, and when violated appear to be immoral and usually illegal: "our society recognizes as wrong wealthy people buying favorable verdicts in courts of law, bosses demanding sexual favors as a condition of promotion, awarding political office on the basis of kinship, and determining wage scales by gender or

---

[42] Helen Nissenbaum, *Technology, Values, and the Justice System: Privacy as Contextual Integrity,* 17 Wash. L Rev. 119, 123 (2004).

race."[43] These violations show a link between privacy, wealth, and equality. Money buys privacy, but lack of money creates conditions for privacy intrusions, unless the law steps in to level the playing field.

Facebook's business model, in providing free online services in exchange for free use of information provided by its users, is similar to traditional hard-copy publications that would sell their mailing list, but with this difference: what print media knows about its subscribers is vastly less than what Google and Facebook can tell advertisers about you. Paradoxically, the model, then, seems to require *voluntary* discloser of *private* information, analogous to the kind of information sharing that goes on when a friendship is slowly being created, except that in the case of a two-way conversation there are many opportunities for trust to build or erode, whereas in the case of online trust, it is an algorithmic robot that is on the other side of the dialogue. The initial success of social media, again paradoxically, is that it is based on a conversational model of sharing information among trusted friends, and trusting that your own friends will make good judgments about the friends they introduce to me. The success of social media tells us what has been known for millennia, that we are social animals. But are we social animals only when we have an opportunity to create our own trusted social network one person at a time? Anti-social animals, suspicion of strangers, a need for solitude, are also part of the human experience. Private moments, moments of introspective dignity, may always remain attainable but going forward are they to be tinged with desperation and distraction?

Conclusion

At the dawn of the cybernetic era Charles Fried wrote of "insidious intrusions of increasingly sophisticated scientific devices into previously untouched areas, and the burgeoning claims of public and private agencies to personal information."[44] Such devices will soon have, he argued, the capability of monitoring and revealing to strangers, without our interest at heart, our most intimate bodily and psychological functions. So, unless

---

[43] Ibid., 145.

[44] Charles Fried, *Privacy*, 77 Yale L. J. 475 (1968).

privacy is given a presumptive and robust status in human life as the preferred default option, as the framers had intended, the alternative is a Brave New World. Privacy is not merely one of the events of social life. Without it, traditionally valued experiences of respect, love, friendship, and trust cannot be constructed. That is why "a threat to privacy seems to threaten our very integrity as persons." In Fried's view, privacy is connected to dignity and dignity to morality. When we respect a person's privacy, we are recognizing their dignity, and we do so, based on a moral judgment of their inherent value as persons with their own ends. Morality comes down to "the constraint of respect for the privacy of all, by state and citizen like," while respect is a necessary but not sufficient condition for love and friendship. Also needed is the trust building that comes from continual respect under many different circumstances. The negative connotation of privacy is secrecy and a guilty fear of disclosure. Its positive connotation, however, is autonomy and authenticity, and the means of maintaining them. If we lived a perfectly transparent life, with all facts known about our past to everyone, would we have less liberty in the future? If the answer is yes, then the social practice of the virtue of privacy can only increase the liberties of individuals to remake themselves and give greater meaning to the phrase 'pursuit of happiness'. Fried points out that the law is not merely the forum in which public and private interests are debated and balanced from a rational and consequential point of view. In its inner morality, it ought to be an institution that protects the integrity and dignity of individuals, for example, against coerced confessions and self-incrimination, against official kidnapping without access to a writ of habeas corpus, and by establishing flexible and effective standards of due process on behalf of individuals against institutions.[45]

---

[45] Ibid., 477, 480, 493.

CHAPTER 8

LAW AND POLITICS

Law and politics reciprocally interact. In this chapter the 'politics of law' refers to the ways in which politics creates and influences law, while the 'law of politics' refers to the ways in which law as 'rule of law' constrains and shapes politics. The practical interweaving of politics and law, in both how law is constituted and how it affects social life, means that morality is also affected by politics. It may not be an exaggeration to say that politics, as much as law, provides the conditions that morality requires to endure and influence that life.

The Politics of Law

Two ways in which politics creates and influences law will be considered in this section: (1) the politics that originally creates its own authority by establishing the institutions of government and law, through which politics may subsequently operate under the banner of legitimate authority; and (2) the politics that establishes the replenishing rules and procedures for the selection and appointment of judges and Justices.

Tensions between Law and Politics. What came first, law or politics? The creation myth of the nation-state is one answer: politics created law but only in the form of a new beginning on the deepest and most authentic foundation possible. But how can legitimation of authority arise without any prior commitment to certain legitimizing practices? The traditional answer to this question was: God selects the monarch, the monarch authorizes the state, and the state constitutes the law. That rubric worked well for monarchies, but not for republics. Those who have read carefully Madison's Notes on the proceedings of the constitutional Convention, or read the speeches and debates of the First Congress, when establishing the federal court system, will see at once that in the beginning there was politics; and particularly politics that was not haphazard, but rather reflected coherent social and economic interests continually operating behind the scenes. For example, we still debate today whether the Constitution established a *laissez faire* political-economic system and substantially prohibited its alteration, or whether the result of the Convention was a political stalemate over economic values that remain unresolved to this day, rather than a unified theory of government.[1] From this founding-era perspective, law originates out of politics, but once established also shapes and constraints politics. Nonetheless, the tension remains in the background and emerges when society and the body politic come under stress, in which case each may be shaken to its 'foundation'. In that case, what is considered the 'rule of law' one day is now easily overturned and replaced. What was legal precedent for a long time is suddenly out of season. The haunting question for law and politics is always: does morality bind together law and politics into some coherent whole over time, and if not, is politics capable of being sufficiently lawless to create acceptable immoral laws? These questions, as we have seen, occupied Fuller and Holmes, among others, for much of their lives.

Law and politics intersect on numerous levels. Politics creates constitutions and staffs the institutions that interpret and administer them. Political institutions and procedures select judges, often establishing their jurisdiction, and write the laws judges enforce through interpretive rulings very often using legislative history and political rhetoric for guidance. Judges, in turn, often respond to their political sponsors by supporting their political attitudes and preferences. By the time they are selected to the higher courts, they already come with a public record reflecting high-altitude political preferences and solutions for the problems of the day, often masked in abstract theoretical terms from the language of jurisprudence. The end result is that politics and law inform and influence each other, but not entirely reciprocally. Politics can exist without law, as when it suspends law and closes the courts, and the courts can do little to resist. Judges can be impeached by politicians, but only politicians can

---

[1] Stephen M. Feldman, *Is the Constitution Laissez-Faire?: The Framers, Original Meaning, and the Market*, 81 Brook. L. Rev. 1 (2015):1; and Stephen M. Feldman, *Nothing New Under the Sun: The Law-Politics Dynamic in Supreme Court Decision Making*, 2017 Pepp. L. Rev. 43 (2017); also see Sonu Bedi and Elvin Lim, *The Two-Foundings Thesis: The Puzzle of Constitutional Interpretation*, 66 UCLA L. Rev. Disc.110 (2018).

impeach each other. On the other hand, judges have a powerful weapon at their disposal: the power to respond with apparently rationally and factually based argument when hotly disputed issues become infused with popular irrationality. If politics is the Machiavellian art of convincing people to believe what is false, then the appeal by law to reason-giving and to past practice and precedent has no adequate response by politics except to meet law with threats of destruction. That is why in times of political chaos, the judges and lawyers are often the first to be killed or imprisoned.

Political Influences on Law. For the most part, however, the tension of law and politics is sufficiently elastic to adapt to large swings in political conditions and the socioeconomic forces that produce them. Any claims to the stability of legal and political institutions over long periods of time are mostly illusions created in a mirror. The foundations upon which these institutions are based are continually being dug up and replaced with new and different ones, leaving only the illusion of continuity and stability. And if the past is wholly embraced in whole cloth, it is not because it is the past *per se* but because it serves as a useful ingredient for present analysis that requires it. Consider the doctrine of *stare decisis* discussed previously – the doctrine of relying upon well-established legal precedent in order to preserve the values of continuity, stability, and rule of law – as an example of the work of politics on law. Is the doctrine simply a 'doctrine of convenience', a rationale for looking high-minded when precedent happens to be agreeable?[2] If *stare decisis* predominantly determined judicial rulings, there should be far fewer dissents and concurrences for a given court composition. In one data-set analysis support for *stare decisis* among Supreme Court Justices was found to be "extremely low."[3]

---

[2] See *Hubbard v. United States,* 514 U.S. 695, 720 (1995). (Rehnquist, C.J., dissenting) ("The principle of stare decisis is designed to promote stability and certainty in the law."). Also, *United States v. Shaughnessy* 234 F. 2d 715, 719 (1955). ("Stare decisis has no bite when it means merely that a court adheres to a precedent that it considers correct. It is significant only when a court feels constrained to stick to a former ruling although the court has come to regard it as unwise or unjust.")

[3] Jeffrey A. Epstein and Harold J. Spaeth, *The Influence of Stare Decisis on the Votes of United States Supreme Court Justices,* 40 Am. J. Pol. Sci. 971, 987 (1996).

The fact that appellate judges and Justices in the higher courts usually present, and are expected to present, reasoned analysis for their votes already diminishes the function of *stare decisis*. This practice reveals an ingrained pragmatism in American jurisprudence that is hardly noticed. An appeal to precedent provides a sound argument, but only if it is accompanied by well-reasoned consequentialist argument; otherwise, it comes across as merely nostalgic devotion. Usually appellate reasoning grows out of political and ideological attitudes about how society should function and what the proper laws within it should be. It is now commonly accepted that Justices have ideological preferences that they would prefer to implement if there are not good reasons not to.[4] But Justices are not ideological machines. They operate in a small community and often engage in the give-and-take of debate over proposed outcomes to important cases. They also think strategically, sometimes agreeing to a position, but then modifying the force of it with a carefully crafted concurrence that may better set the agenda for another day's battle. And, of course, they always have an eye on the public, the reputation of the court, and the political composition of Congress. It would make little sense for a liberal justice to overturn a law that a conservative Congress might replace with a worst one.

However, judges and justices, for the most part as we have seen, do not openly embrace an articulated political ideology, to avoid appearing to be too political. Their preferences are often contextual. If lower court judges have no interest in serving on the highest court they may be more willing to compromise; the same is true if they do not seek higher political office, or if as judges they are not accountable to the voters. In recent decades, strenuous efforts have been made, first among political theorists and economists, and then by legal scholars to identify a meaningful spectrum within which to place ideological attitudes, primarily among Supreme Court justices. The binary variables 'liberal' and 'conservative'

---

[4] Jeffrey A. Segal and Alfred D. Cover, "Ideological values and the votes of U.S. Supreme Court Justices," 83 *Am. Pol. Sci. Rev.* 557 (1989); Jeffrey A. Segal et al., *Ideological Values and the Votes of the U.S. Supreme Court Justices Revisited,* 57 J. Pol. 812 (1995); Jeffrey A, Segal and Harold J. Spaeth, *The Supreme Court and the Attitudinal Model Revisited* (New York: Cambridge University Press, 2002).

are by themselves insufficient, but are nonetheless useful in establishing trends between earlier and later court configurations, and between earlier and later votes of specific Justices. The life of a given Supreme Court composition may be studied like any other social system. Ideological clues may be found, for example, in the kind of individuals Justices select as their law clerks.[5] Conservatives like conservative law clerks, and liberals like liberal law clerks. Clerking is where the ideological work gets done in preparing arguments for or against a position on an issue. The propensity of a Justice to want to support or overturn the legislation of a liberal (or conservative) Congress is another preferential clue. Ideological extremists in the minority will sometimes leave clues in their dissents for future like-minded jurists to take up and follow.[6] A low propensity could also reveal an ideological moderate, with a lesser sense of a strategic mission to reform society according to an articulated political plan. These moderates also can turn into swing voters on the court, with a capacity to dampen ideological fervor at the extremes. However, even unanimous opinions may reveal some ideological propensities, though insufficient to override a commitment to dominant legalistic norms.[7] Another political-influence factor to be measured is the articulated support given to Supreme Court opinions and the specific votes of Justices by various constituencies: newspaper editorial boards, labor unions, Chambers of Commerce, think tanks, lobbyists, religious organizations, etc. This audience clearly is evidence of the recognized political mission of the courts. Still another factor, is the intellectual synergy among Justices, or lack thereof, which influences individual votes over time, allowing some courts to grow more liberal or more conservative.[8]

Some broad traditional political and ideological polarities have been identified: political liberalism versus economic liberalism, federalism

---

[5] Adam Bonica, et al. *Measuring Judicial Ideology Using Law Clerk Hiring,* 19 Am. L. & Econ. Rev.129 (2017).

[6] Vanessa Baird and Tonja Jacobi, *How the Dissent Becomes the Majority: Using Federalism to Transform Coalitions in the U.S. Supreme Court*, 59 Duke L. J.183 (2009).

[7] Lee Epstein, William M. Landes and Richard A. Posner, *Are Even Unanimous Decisions in the United States Supreme Court Ideological?* 106 Nw. U. L. Rev. 699 (2012).

[8] Lee Epstein et al., *Ideological Drift among Supreme Court Justices: Who, When, and How Important?* 101 Nw. U. L. Rev. 1483 (2007).

versus nationalism, libertarianism versus communitarianism, socialism versus capitalism, *laissez faire* versus regulation, property rights versus labor rights, liberty versus equality, traditional versus novel moral beliefs and social practices, big versus small government. These polarities operate in the background as lightning-quick inference generators when a dense social problem must be confronted and resolved judicially. They may also operate at an intermediate level between concrete narrowly tailored solutions and broader ideological commitments such as: 'Representative government was created by the poor (rich) to protect themselves against the rich (poor)'; or 'The Constitution leaves (no) gaps in supplying judicial answers to contemporary problems'; or 'Political authority comes (or does not come) from the consent of the governed'; or 'Political authority and human rights come (or do not come) from God'. Supreme Court opinions rarely articulate such high-altitude views lurking behind the text; and sometimes ideological preferences give way to short-term strategic calculations; so that, for example, when an opposing party holds national power political and economic minimalism may be adopted as the theory of choice until such time as power is regained. Full throated advocacy of an ideological position is rarely manifested except when the political terrain has been safely conquered. These grand ideas from the history of political theory, however, operate *sub rosa* on the high court and do not provide clearly measurable data sets for close analysis of trends and ideological shifts among Justices. The best available evidence of ideological influence has been taken from an examination of the entire institutional practice of the high court, including which cases it accepts and denies for review, which amicus briefs the court allows, and, of course, the evidence of ideological orientation in concurrences and dissents. These judicial 'events' produce a variety of numerical data that seems to correlate well with our intuitive understanding of ideology on the court.[9] Such analysis confirms our common understanding that Justices generally do hold ideological

---

[9] Andrew D. Martin and Kevin M. Quinn, "Dynamic Ideal Point Estimation via Markov Chain Monte Carlo for the U.S. Supreme Court, 1953–1999," *Political Analysis* 10 (2002): 134-153. The "Martin-Quinn scores" are now frequently used to evaluate past trends and make predictions of future ones as new members come on to the high court.

preferences, and increasingly so, as the political milieu out of which they are chosen becomes more conflicted and ideological as well.[10] There was a time when dissents were rare and justices did not wear their ideology so openly on their sleeves.[11] Nonetheless, appellate judges cannot so easily prevaricate as do politicians; their job is to resolve disputes by writing detailed opinions that identify and weigh relevant factual claims and interpret ideas and theories about those claims, all set against a backdrop of their own commitments to a legal philosophy.[12]

Judicial Selection. How judges and justices are selected also clearly reflect political interests at work. These jurists are put on the bench to carry out a mission. This has been true since the founding era, when President Jefferson added Democratic-Republican judges to the federal bench previously filled entirely with Federalist judges.[13] When the federal judiciary was first contemplated, Federalists like Hamilton wanted a judiciary with broad jurisdiction over state and national life, while Antifederalists wanted a judiciary that would restrict federal courts to impeachment and tax collection and be prohibited from overturning state legislation. Clearly at the time, Federalists and later their descendants, the Whigs and Republicans, regarded the federal judiciary as a check against the dangers of growing democratic influences, as reflected in the election of Jefferson and a continual stream of Democratic presidents thereafter. Conservatives also opposed abolishing the Electoral College, which they saw as a way of segmenting the popular vote to create opportunities to elect their candidates and get favorable court appointees. Historically, that turned out to be a good strategy, since in the few cases where the Electoral College vote exceeded the popular vote percentage wise, the conservative party prevailed.

---

[10] Neal Devins and Lawrence Baum, *Split Definitive: How Party Polarization Turned the Supreme Court into a Partisan Court,* 2016 Sup. Ct. Rev. 301 (2017).

[11] Aaron J. Ley, Kathleen Searles, and Cornell W. Clayton, *The Mysterious Persistence of Non-Consensual Norms on the U.S. Supreme Court,* 49 Tulsa L. Rev. 99 (2013).

[12] Stephen M. Feldman, *Supreme Court Alchemy: Turning Law and Politics into Mayonnaise,* 12 Geo. J. L. & Pub. Pol'y. 57 (2014); and Joshua B. Fischman and Tonja Jacobi, *The Second Dimension of the Supreme Court,* 57 Wm. & Mary L. Rev. 1671 (2016).

[13] Michael J. Gerhardt and Michael Ashley Stein, *The Politics of Early Justice: Federal Judicial Selection, 1789-1861,* 100 Iowa L. Rev. 551 (2015).

The effect of the conservative strategy to hold the high court as a check is clearly seen in the composition of the Supreme Court throughout its history. Since 1788, the two parties have fairly closely divided the popular vote, and there have somewhat more Federalist, Whig, and Republican presidents than Democratic Presidents. The number of Justices on the Supreme Court has also been fairly balanced by party. But there have been thirteen Federalist, Whig, and Republican Chief Justices and only four Democratic Chief Justices and these latter have only sat for about 67 of the 220 years of the high court's history. And since 1870, Republicans have had a court majority for more than 100 years, while Democrats have had a court majority for about 33 years – in other words, a 3 to 1 advantage when the tenures of Chief Justice and majority courts are compared.

Partisan asymmetry also has flowed through the entire process generating and replenishing the federal judiciary. At the Constitutional convention delegates debated how judges would be appointed. Some argued for direct appointment; others wanted the Senate alone to appoint them, while still others wanted the president to have a veto over a Senate nominee. The initial vote was for full Senate control, and the revote came to the same result. Although the advice and consent wording eventually was approved, Hamilton expressed his party's preference in *Federalist* No. 65, that "in the business of appointments the Executive will be the principal agent." This partisan asymmetry is especially found in judicial vacancy rates. These rates increase when a Democratic president has to work with a Republican Senate, and decline when a Republican president seeks confirmation from a Democratic Senate; and they decline even more when a Republican Senate works with a Republican President. Besides measuring vacancy rates, age of nominees shows a tendency for Republicans to select younger court nominees, which may signal that their prevailing disparity of partisan court control over time will continue well into the future.[14]

---

[14] Jonathan N. Katz and Matthew L. Spitzer, *What's Age Got to Do With It? Supreme Court Appointees and the Long Run Location of the Supreme Court Median Justice*, 46 Ariz. St. L. J. 41 (2014).

Another example of partisan asymmetry in judicial selection may be found in the fact that lawyers tend to be are more liberal than society at large, but judges tend to be more conservative.[15] Also, the President's party is more influential in judicial selection than the partisan composition of the Senate, so perhaps we may hypothesize that Republican presidents and their political advisors will at least attempt to make more partisan selections.[16] No prediction, however, of how a nominee will perform on the bench is a sure thing. Mavericks may result from poor vetting, and ideological drift is even likely as the years roll by and each Justice becomes better informed of the range of consequences that may follow from this or that ideological decision. Nonetheless, predictions are getting better because more nominees are coming from a pool of lower court judges with well understood track records.[17] Also, the vetting infrastructure is becoming more reliable both institutionally and methodologically. Even with the unexpected victory of Donald Trump, there was already a cadre of conservative nominees waiting in the wings, selected for him by conservative think tanks.[18]

The Constitution requires the "advice and consent" of the Senate for judicial candidates (Art. II, Sec. 2, cl. 2). In its modern form, the process typically begins with hearings, often televised, before the Senate Judiciary

---

[15]Adam Bonica and Maya Sen, *The Politics of Selecting the Bench from the Bar: The Legal Profession and Partisan Incentives to Introduce Ideology into Judicial Selection,* 60 J. L. & Econ.559 (2017).

[16] Christine Kexel Chabot, *A Long View of the Senate's Influence over Supreme Court Appointments,* 64 Hastings L. J.1229 (2013).

[17] Charles M. Cameron and Jee-Kwang Park, *How Will They Vote? Predicting the Future Behavior of Supreme Court Nominees, 1937-2006,* 6 J. Empirical Legal Stud. 485 (2009); and Christine Kexel Chabot and Benjamin Remy Chabot, *Mavericks, Moderates, or Drifters? Supreme Court Voting Alignments, 1838-2009,* 76 Mo. L. Rev. 999 (2011).

[18] See Lee Epstein, Andrew D. Martin, and Kevin Quinn, *Pres.-Elect Trump and his Possible Justices,* (2016), http://pdfserver.amlaw.com/nlj/PresNominees2.pdf [http://perma.cc/MA7J-GQR4]. See also Joseph Fishkin and David E. Pozen, *Asymmetric Constitutional Hardball,* 118 Colum. L. Rev. 915 (2018), discussing an organizational asymmetry in the ways Democrats and Republicans select judicial candidates.

Committee. Nominees are then questioned by members of the committee. Controversial nominees and their supporters on the committee typically try to avoid controversy by claiming that Supreme Court judicial review either involves reading and applying the text of the Constitution or statute, or else interpreting the text to extract its relevant meaning applicable today. Opponents on the committee, then, try to trap the nominee into making politically embarrassing revelations about his or her judicial philosophy. To avoid such criticism, nominees now more often claim that it would be improper to voice a general opinion about a topic without specific facts before them; and all nominees say that they would fully embrace the norm of judicial independence and deny that they will be puppets of the President or party. Responding to hypothetical questioning is a difficult problem for all nominees, since all careful judges want to have before them the actual facts that they must submit to legal analysis. It is understandable and evidence of sound judicial temperament, therefore, to withhold giving an opinion on general topics. However, non-responsiveness also is due in part to poor questioning at the hearing. Some senators want to heap praise; others want to make critical speeches and pose before the public. Even the one-on-one meeting in Senate offices prior to the hearing seems to serve little useful purpose. A better purpose might be served if nominees were given homework assignments and told to read carefully this or that opinion and the attending record and be prepared to justify this or that concurrence or descent. In fact, a good practice would be to ask nominees to present arguments *against* some of their own prior opinions, and if nominees have a record of making public speeches also to be prepared to explain in detail some of the claims made within them. Of course, there is nothing to stop nominees from arguing that such questions are slanted in such a way as to reveal how they will reason and vote in the future on a similar issue, and so decline to respond substantively here also.

Both parties play this prevarication game in judicial selection, but evidently not symmetrically.[19] Republicans and conservatives have a special claim on the value of neutrality given their interest in textualism and originalism.

[19] Carolyn Shapiro, The Language of Neutrality in Supreme Court Confirmation Hearings, 122 Dick. L. Rev. 585, 643-44 (2018).

They contend that obtaining conservative conclusions from an originalist interpretation of a text is by its nature a neutral enterprise, whereas weighing consequences and contextualizing issues is by its nature an expression of subjective and arbitrary value judgments. Meanwhile, Democrats and liberals also support this asymmetry by emphasizing that judicial review at the highest level includes solving novel problems with novel interpretations, evaluated by examining the evolution of social conditions and the court's prior response to them. Conservatives label themselves 'strict constructionists' and play upon our popular notion of the Constitution as an unconditioned foundational document similar to the Bible; while accusing their opponents of judicial activism and moral relativism. However, the dichotomy is not so clean cut. In fact, it could be argued that just the opposite might be true: Republicans and conservatives tend to embrace originalism and foundationalism because they are defending a profoundly disruptive and incessantly revolutionary economic force, capitalism, whereas Democrats and liberals embrace legal realism and pragmatism in order to maintain *traditional* moral values that are continually under assault by capitalism.

Aside from the specific political issues surrounding judicial selection, there is a deeper moral question raised when nominees hide their views with an obvious intent to deploy them later in matters that may adversely affect personal and social life. Does the public have a right to know whether they may be harmed by someone who has the authority to harm in the name of law, but does not want them to know the ways in which they may be harmed before the fact? This issue is, in part, connected to the kind of reasons we seek when we ask about the contents of salt or sugar in foodstuffs we buy. The protective values that establish product liability and habitability, and also warn against the dispersive effects of toxic substances, recognize that causation of harm is not a simple two-body problem; it is a systemic problem of pervading influences that are initially hard to detect, influences with delayed effects. It is also reflective of the paternalistic lack of full disclosure that says that some issues in the politics of law are too complicated to be understood by the average citizen, and so we must rely upon the good intentions of those who select our jurists. We are left to wonder about how much prevarication is too much for the advice and consent function to bear.

The Law of Politics

As indicated, law originates out of politics but once established also shapes and constrains politics. Once a legal regime is underway politics is constrained to work within it at least until it is modified. The difficult question, however, is whether the constraints themselves are sufficient to put limits on the way politics may modify or amend the legal order. Fuller's notion of law's inner morality is designed to place some limits on politics. Some constraints are harder for politicians to resist than others because they provide clear standards, and therefore provide signals when they are being eroded. Meanwhile vague standards may be eroded vaguely. In this section the standards to be considered, where law shapes politics, involve: amending the Constitution, apportioning population for representation, applying due process and equal protection norms to electoral procedures, partisan gerrymandering, and voter eligibility. These standards work together as in a pneumatic process, where affecting one usually affects the others.

Amending the Constitution. The Constitution sets out two fairly elaborate amendment procedures in Article V: amendments may be proposed by a two-thirds vote of both Houses of Congress; or two-thirds of the state legislatures may call a convention to propose amendments, which in either case must be ratified by three-fourths of the state legislatures or state conventions. The article also provides that state equal representation in the Senate cannot be changed by amendment without a state's consent. Although hundreds of efforts have been made to amend the Constitution, it has only been amended twenty-six times, and then only by amendments initiated by Congress. The framers were well aware that the second amending method – a vote of three fourths of state legislatures to amendments proposed by a Convention – would almost certainly be politically contentious. They directly witnessed this in the battle between Federalists and Anti-Federalists in the initial ratification process of the Constitution itself. In spite of this, the framers left it to politics to govern the formation of *state* legislatures, their composition and reelection, and the methods by which each state proposed amendments for consideration by a national Convention. They only required that state legislators take an oath to uphold the national Constitution (Art. VI). The amending process, then, was a compromise between the procedural constraints placed on the political process by the Constitution, and the freedom within those constraints of the political process to work its will.

Apportioning Representatives. The framers assumed that if the Constitution were to be amended it would, to some tolerable degree, reflect the will of the people directly or indirectly. However, the Constitution said next to nothing about the composition of individual state legislatures except, by implication, that one branch be "numerous" (Art. I, Sec. 2, cl. 1) and that the composition of the House of Representatives should in some way be proportional to the state population (Art. I, Sec 2, cl 3, and after 1867, Amd. XIV, Sec 2). *But no substantive rules of proportionality were ever provided.* In 1913, the House consisted of 435 Representatives and remains so now, even though the nation's population has tripled. Additionally, the scope of the authority of Representatives was debated and left unresolved during the founding era, some arguing that representatives were agents carrying out the instructions of their voters, and others arguing that representatives were to use their own discretion and bear the consequences at the ballot box. This created another challenge to the notion that Representatives reflected their voters' interests in addition to the apportionment problem.

The Republican Guarantee. As a result, there is nothing in the Constitution's amendment process that precludes a relatively small number of people from controlling the entire process from state legislature to convention to ratification. A small number of members composing a state legislature could vote to convene a convention in which a still smaller number of delegates could submit proposed amendments. There are no legal constraints to this process. Support for the proposed amendments during the final vote would be entirely political, but there is no guarantee that it also would be subject to republican principles of representation, raising the possibility that amending the Constitution could make it *less* representative. One possible safeguard may be found in Article IV, Sec. 4: "The United States shall guarantee to every state in this Union a republican form of government, . . ." So, if this federal guarantee applied to the states it would seem plausible that the states could not undermine the republican guarantee through the convention amending process. Here surely would be a legal constraint limiting political manipulation.

Clearly, no amendment would be constitutional which reintroduced hereditary monarchy. At the very least a republican form of government would be some form of self-government and particularly some form of popularly created government. These points were emphasized in *Federalist* No. 39, for example, where Madison defines a republican form of government as "a government which derives all its powers directly or indirectly from the great body of the people, and is administered by persons holding their offices during pleasure, for a limited period, or during good behavior. It is *essential* to such a government that it be derived from the great body of the society, not from an inconsiderable proportion, or a favored class of it." (Emphasis in original.) Although Madison's glittering standard rules out monarchy and autocracy, it does not provide any criteria for determining when popular consent has been achieved and when it has failed. If people are made fearful to speak or assemble by those seeking office, then any government that results would be something close to tyranny, and very likely would become tyranny over time. But how do we describe a form of government where political discourse and electoral practices frustrate and discourage an electorate, who then in despair or disgust simply fail to vote? Such a government would not be derived from the 'great body of the people' and would clearly fail Madison's 'essential' condition test for a properly apportioned republic. Yet, not only has that standard failed to be fully recognized, understood or applied, it has become a subject of perpetual political contest among the parties over the seemingly incidental issue of 'voter turnout'. It is a substantive standard that is overlooked much in the same way as judicial nominee prevarication is disregarded – as a standard too hard to apply or too exacting and consequential to reverse procedurally. The federal government then fails to carry out its Madisonian obligation when candidates take office as a result of low voter turnout or when legal obstacles are directly placed upon the opportunity to vote.

Electoral Procedures. Subsequent rulings of the Supreme Court interpreted the republican guarantee provision to mean that "the political department," (i.e., Congress), not the federal courts, should enforce the guarantee because, it is argued, any examination of the ways a state government organizes its elections would inevitably raise political questions.[20] Although the

[20] *Luther v. Borden*, 48 U.S. 1 (1849); *Taylor v. Beckham*, 178 U.S. 548 (1900).

Constitution allows state legislatures some leeway to determine their electoral procedures for electing members of Congress (Art. I, Sec.4, cl.1), as well as determining the manner of appointing their Presidential electors (Art II, Sec. 1, cl. 2), clearly deference to the decisions of elected state officials must have its limits. They could not, for example, decide to ban the losing party in congressional state elections from running candidates for the next ten years, or impose heavy fines on the losing party to cover the costs of conducting the election. Or, they could decide to choose their own Presidential electors in spite of delegating that authority to the voters because they thought the voters had made the wrong choice. Are these possibilities merely political questions for Congress to resolve and whatever it decides ends the controversy? What if Congress agreed to these state measures because it was controlled by the same party? The Supreme Court seems to have said that there are some legal standards above partisan politics in the Constitution and that they may be found in the due process and equal protection clauses of the Fourteenth Amendment, standards that do not require politics to explain because their violation is so immediately obvious. For example, if a state law applies to *X* but not to *Y* and there are no good reasons to explain how *X* and *Y* differ, then equal protection is violated. If a state law gives *X* an opportunity to be heard at a hearing but not *Y* and there are no good reasons to explain the difference, then due process has been violated. The Fourteenth Amendment seems to say that all that *X* and *Y* require for the Amendment to apply to them is that they be persons ("any person"). All persons are unique individuals, but every individual is fully a constitutional person. If each is a member of a class of 'persons' every other person also belongs to that class, even non-citizens. All that is required is that they be subject to the law's jurisdiction.[21]

So, if states make laws that affect persons differently, distinguishing citizens from non-citizens for example, that difference must be recognized and given some rational justification in light of the laws' overall purpose. Also, the law must be designed to achieve some legitimate public purpose without unduly

---

[21] See, for example, *Gregory v. Ashcroft*, 501 U.S. 452, 471 (1991). ("We will not overturn such a statute unless the varying treatment of different groups or persons is so unrelated to the achievement of any combination of legitimate purposes that we can only conclude that the legislature's actions were irrational.")

burdening the privileges or immunities of U.S. citizens. Suppose that to overcome congestion at the voting polls, a state was to pass a law that persons born in odd number years could only vote in odd number year elections. Such a law might not be considered a violation of the republican government guarantee because it seems to be a fair rule without regard to any status that could be easily manipulated, and would certainly be rationally related to relieving congestion. On the other hand, it would clearly be an unfair law if it worked in tandem with a law that every infant born in an even year was automatically registered as a Democrat (or Republican) and would have to vote for that party in their first two elections.

What this illustration shows is that there are assumptions buried deep in the Fourteenth Amendment that directly affect and even constrain a political distortion of the republican guarantee through voting procedures, constraints such as: (1) elections should be conducted in a fair manner without arbitrary restraints on *access* to the polls; (2) the *manner* in which elections are conducted should be subject to the electoral process as well; and (3) persons eligible to vote in state or district elections should have their votes given *equal weight* in the outcome of the election. None of these foundational democratic norms, however, can be reduced merely to a mathematical formula. They still must be implemented through decisions made in a political process, for example decisions determining whether a voting process is so onerous (e.g., allowed only between midnight and 2:00 A.M.) as to amount to disenfranchisement; or so impractical so as to hinder a sufficient number of voters from getting to a sufficient number of voting locations within a sufficient amount of time allocated for voting. Also political are threshold issues as to when disputes over voting procedures should be resolved by the voters or left to the legislature or courts, as well as issues of voting eligibility (felons?) and voting weight (one person one vote). *These three norms are as close as we may get to the moral core of the Fourteenth Amendment.* They are foundational in the sense that they serve as regulating maxims for constructing democratic consensus, while their implementation requires legislative practices subject to the integrity norms of the inner morality of law.

Section 2 of the Fourteenth Amendment does attempt to impose, in a global fashion, some constraints on abusive electoral procedures, stating that "representatives shall be apportioned among the several states according to their respective numbers, counting the whole number of persons in each state excluding Indians not taxed." This rule prohibits states from loading up on representatives to Congress by creating many small geographical congressional voting districts. It also indicates that *persons,* not eligible voters, are the relevant electoral class. The rule also seems to suggest that 'equal protection' might have a rational norm-creating function. For example, when there is a great population disparity among voting districts so that, say, a vote in one district is worth the equivalent of twenty votes in another, then the equal protection clause may be implicated.[22] But again, no mathematical guidelines have been provided and probably could not be as long as voters are assigned to unequally-sized voting districts to vote for representatives from those districts. A voter in a less populous district gets more representation per vote than one in a more populous district with the same number of representatives.

Partisan Gerrymandering. One way to tackle the problem of fair representation is to continually redraw voting districts. However, drawing compact consistently-shaped voting districts is not a simple matter of geography due to irregular popular densities within any such compact system. Nor is it a matter of empirically describing the location of undifferentiated 'persons' across a geographical terrain. These persons come with identifiable voting histories and political tendencies, as we have seen made evident in the user profiles compiled from social media. As a result, partisan gerrymandering weighs heavily as a factor in redistricting in efforts to diminish the voting strength of an opposing party by packing more of its voters into fewer districts. One obvious outcome of such a method is that the Senate could be controlled by a very small percentage of the general population. A protracted struggle for political power was behind the capping of the House of Representatives at 435 members through the Reapportionment Act of 1929, which allowed states to draw districts of various sizes and shapes specifically due to a fear of rural states that highly urbanized cities and states, with a higher

---

[22] *Baker v. Carr,* 369 U.S. 186, 254 (1962). The equal protection issue to be resolved was whether the Tennessee apportionment system was utterly a "crazy quilt without rational basis."

percentage of foreign-born inhabitants, would eventually gain control of Congress as the overall population increased.[23] These political influences and partisan gerrymandering generally challenge the notion of a republican form of government because the legislatures, whether state or federal, that typically control the formation of voting districts also are constructed out of members elected from them, making it easier to lock in partisan advantage in future elections. Special redistricting commissions may be set up to draw districts with fairly balanced populations that might do a better job in equalizing representation and enhancing competitiveness. However, even such commissions are not beyond political controversy.[24]

Drawing district maps with partisan political advantage in mind is as old as the Republic itself. The snowballing grip on power of partisan gerrymandering was well recognized at the time.[25] Each political party will opt for the means of reapportionment that produces the best political outcome in future elections. Pushed to its logical extreme, voting maps may be constructed in such a way as to preclude any possibility that the drafting authority will ever lose control of the drafting process itself. This spiral will then diminish the very conditions upon which republican government is based – that the people not only have the capacity to make choices through elections but that they be able to choose the range of choices up for a vote. In our political system that range is accomplished through the debate among political parties and the policies they propose to the voters. Partisan gerrymandering would inevitably narrow that selection because, although many different voices may present ideas for the public to consider, the opportunity for those voices to win elections to advance their ideas practically into policies will be greatly diminished. The problem is how law

---

[23] Hubert Searcy, "Problems of Congressional Reapportionment," *Sw. Soc. Sci. Q.* 16 (1935): 62; Anthony Lewis, *Legislative Apportionment and the Federal Courts,"* 71 Harv. L. Rev. 1057, 1064 (1958).

[24] See *Arizona State Legislature v. Arizona Independent Redistricting Commission,* 135 S. Ct. 2652 (2015), where Arizona's Constitution allowed the public to adopt laws directly through the initiative process and set up a redistricting commission to draw the state electoral map. Notice the liberal/conservative division in the 5 to 4 result here.

[25] *Vieth v. Jubelirer,* 541 U.S. 267, 274-78 (2004).

could deal with this potentially pernicious political influence. If the party in power also dominates the public microphone, then clearly the selections will be diminished. However, if free speech and association are zealously protected, then voters may break through regardless of party dominance. Political revolts are always possible, and our history has shown that parties could become obsolete no matter how well entrenched.[26]

An argument may be made that partisan gerrymandering exists entirely within a political process, which itself exists entirely within the ebb and flow of historical events, providing no clear standards for courts to factually measure 'fair representation' against. Many factors beyond party affiliation may go into drawing voting maps: compactness and contiguity of districts, underlying political subdivisions, and values of ensuring representation of racial constituencies. In other areas of law, courts do not shy away from multifactor analysis when determining to employ standards that are barely sufficiently clear to resolve an important issue before them, e.g., regulating child pornography while not providing a bright line test for what is pornographic in the first place. The issue of partisan gerrymandering, however, seems to be resistant to resolution using policy norms. In extreme cases, violation of standards could be in plain view. For example, how contorted is the new district relative to the old, how much does it deviate from long-established political jurisdictions, do the map drawers reveal partisan motivation?[27] The adverse consequences to republican government of not regulating district map drawing at all may be greater than the consequences of requiring map drawers to operate without predominant political motivation.

Once again Madison provides some benchmarks for us to consider. In *Federalist* No. 10 he stated: "Among the numerous advantages promised by a well-constructed Union, none deserve to be more accurately developed than its tendency to break and control the violence of faction." He believed that partisan conflict arises from the disparity of wealth and the opportunity to obtain it, and that neither morality nor religion could dampen the natural tendency of politicians to become corrupt when given

---

[26] Ibid., 287.

[27] Ibid., 321-33 (Steven's Dissent).

unfettered control of government. A well-constructed Union, then, was one in which voting districts were properly sized to contain a proportional mixture of the various conflicting interests that comprise a society. In other words, each part would be a microcosm of the whole, requiring politicians to speak to various interests when running for office and be ready to compromise. Implicit in Madison's analysis was a view that politicians should not be able to choose their own voters by altering the geographical unit of representation with partisan purpose. Though the Constitution barred the alteration of *state* boundaries except by Congress, and left to the states alterations of their voting districts, Madison's remedy for the disease of faction seems to have plausible force on the state level as well. And if that is the case, then partisan gerrymandering would, in his view, thwart a well-constructed Union.[28]

The Right to Vote. Perhaps the right to vote should be connected to the idea of equal protection of the laws guaranteed by the Fourteenth Amendment. If laws should be applied equally, one way to make this happen is to give each person subject to the laws an equal opportunity to influence what the laws will be, and more importantly *how* they will be enforced. However, this link between law formation and law enforcement is not intuitively obvious. A benevolent autocrat might assemble an equal-protection regime where all citizens suffer the same consequences for disobeying the same laws in the same manner, and all citizens benefit equally from the protection of the laws. In the real world, however, there are no philosopher kings, no benevolent autocrats. In the real world, everybody has interests that clash with everybody else's, so that equal application of the laws cannot be separated from equal acceptance of the process whereby the laws are made and enforced. Equal acceptance, however, requires an agreement

---

[28] The Supreme Court has divided along conservative-liberal lines in recognizing the potential danger to democratic norms posed by partisan gerrymandering. See Veith, 541 U.S. at 316. The same division emerges when racial gerrymandering is at issue. *Abbott v. Perez,* 138 S.Ct. 2305 (2018). When there is political disagreement over whether the Constitution embeds some norm of proportionality of representation, then it becomes all but impossible to create a standard for identifying partisan gerrymandering because that is a 'political question' rather than one over the prerequisites of democracy itself. See *Rucho v. Common Cause,* 138 S. Ct. 2484 (2019).

that the process, as clearly set out, provides the best opportunity for a fair result. 'One person, one vote' has been the slogan that seems to capture the sense of this prior acceptance. Votes should no longer be bought or sold. Voting should not be more difficult for some than others. Rules of eligibility should be clearly known, accepted, and uniformly applied. Yet, only in the twentieth century, in *Baker v. Carr*, did these norms find some recognition. Manipulating rules of eligibility could easily undermine equal protection. In 1963, in a state malapportionment case, Justice Harlan dissenting wrote: "'One person, one vote' has never been the universally accepted political philosophy in England, the American Colonies, or in the United States." A glaring example of some votes carrying more weight than others is the Electoral College, he noted. The Senate, as noted, is another example. So-called malapportionment cases are not haphazard; they almost invariably give more voting strength to rural communities, which Harlan viewed as a legitimate state interest: "a State might rationally conclude that its general welfare was best served by apportioning more seats in the legislature to agricultural communities than to urban centers, lest the legitimate interests of the former be submerged in the stronger electoral voice of the latter."[29] This view, however, was soon rejected, hence requiring substantially (i.e., less than 10% differentiated) equal population districts.[30]

The 'one person one vote' standard is also strained by the allocation of members of the House among the state populations. Some states grow faster than others and gain more representatives. Some states lose population and lose representatives. But the process is not evenly distributed across the nation. To accomplish substantial equality of representation would require drawing districts across state lines and before long would require redrawing state boundaries. The Constitution, as noted, requires apportionment of representatives "among the several states . . . according to their respective numbers." (Art. I, Sec. 2, cl. 3). This formula

---

[29] *Gray v. Sanders,* 372 U.S. 368, 386 (1963) Harlan also notes: "The Seventeenth Amendment provides that Senators shall be 'elected by the people', with no indication that all people must be accorded a vote of equal weight."

[30] Malapportionment favoring rural populations was rejected on equal protection grounds in *Reynolds v. Sims,* 377 U.S. 533, 562 (1964) ("Legislators represent people, not areas."). Also see *Evenwel v. Abbott,* 136 S. Ct. 1120 (2016).

clashes with the view that every state must have at least one representative. Suppose a state were to lose all of its population except for, say, ten persons. Those individuals, assuming eligible to vote, would have their own representative and two senators, three members being sent to Congress to represent the other seven. This *reductio ad absurdum* argument shows that when it comes to achieving a norm of 'one person one vote', apportionment among the states can only be an *ad hoc* approximation if their boundaries are to remain the same. As some states grow more rapidly than others the standard of 'one person, one vote' becomes more an unattainable ideal, raising the question of whether the republican guarantee ultimately should be accompanied by a national policy for population redistribution reminiscent of the 'Go West' policy of national development beginning in the 1790s. One consequence of the failure of the Supreme Court to put teeth in the republican guarantee provision would be realized in an election of the President in the House with "each state having one vote" (Amd. XII). This outcome could elect a President that would end up being highly unrepresentative of the general population, thus rendering the guarantee all but meaningless.[31] In the process, the representative nature of the national government would be truly transformed from a Madisonian conglomeration of diverse interests into a balkanization of highly polarized factions.

Voter Eligibility. Closely intertwined with the legal issues of apportionment and gerrymandering is that of establishing standards for voting eligibility and the right to vote. The Constitution was amended in 1971 to allow18-year-olds to vote. In 1920 women were given the right to vote. Felons have been disenfranchised in many states either temporarily or permanently. These examples indicate that there are limits to a right to vote, raising the question: could a state legislature comprising a majority of Catholics in a state comprising a majority of Catholics give to each Catholic vote a weight of, say, 1.25? Why must there be one-person-*one* vote? Or: why not correlate votes with years of education, creating in effect a system of cumulative

---

[31] *Department of Commerce v. Montana*, 503 U.S. 442 (1992). See also Jamin B. Raskin, *Taking the States' Congressional Delegations Seriously: A Twelfth Amendment and First Amendment Approach to Identifying the Worst Gerrymanders*, 59 Wm. & Mary L. Rev. Online 127 (2018).

voting, where one individual has more than one vote within each range of options? In the founding era ownership of some property was required, as was a minimum period of domicile. It was thought that a stakeholder in government was better prepared to exercise good judgment on public policy than someone with little property or was just passing through.

In focusing on voter eligibility, we may notice how the impetus to set legal standards is thwarted by political agendas. Even in the case of eligibility rules that may be clearly stated (e.g., age limits for serving in office) the method of 'becoming eligible' may be more difficult to implement (e.g., finding your birth certificate). Citizens must take certain steps in order to be eligible to vote, e.g. provide evidence they are U.S. citizens, are old enough to vote, and register in the appropriate voting district. Voting eligibility has also come into play with apportionment issues discussed previously. Some argue that apportionment should not be among the general population, but only among the eligible and registered voting population. The argument here is that in some districts with high voter registration the votes of voters in low eligibility districts are diluted by a population that either cannot vote or does not care to. At the nation's founding, when the American population was not yet neatly categorized politically, the framers decided to settle on 'inhabitants' as the units to be counted in a census and apportioned in each state. That same measure was adopted during the passage of the Fourteenth Amendment. The reasoning was that representatives of states represented the state population not just the voters who put them in office, since whether or not a person voted they were subject to the laws made by their representatives.

Historically, federal courts have had to referee issues over voter eligibility and their method of application because of the contested political questions that inevitably arise, especially from the temptation of making rules look good on paper, but which also provide loopholes for abuse in practice. Opportunity for abuse may arise from the fact that all states do not have the same uniform standards for voter eligibility, nor uniform procedures for establishing eligibility in national elections. The Constitution provides certain age, citizenship, and residency qualifications for holding office in Congress (Art. I, Sec. 2, cl. 2; Art. I, Sec. 3, cl. 3). No other eligibility qualifications were included. Madison among other framers thought it dangerous for Congress to have unfettered power to determine eligibility for office. If, for example, only persons with a net worth above 10% of the general population could run for office, they might choose policies that disproportionately increased their own worth and further aggravate class divisions. The Supreme Court has also determined that states could not add additional qualifications for serving in their congressional delegation.[32] Without that restriction, only recently established, we could imagine states adding additional qualifications. California might decide that only movie actors could run for federal office; New York might decide that only residents of New York City and who are members of the New York Stock Exchange could run. The result would be a potentially great disparity among state interests among representatives in Congress, rather than the leavening of interests Madison hoped for.

Establishing restrictive candidate eligibility requirements, then, was one way of undermining the guarantee of republican government. Narrowing the pool of potential candidates could be seen as contrary to republican values because it diminished the range of legislative voices. In *The Federalist* No. 57, Madison wrote: "Who are to be the objects of popular choice? Every citizen whose merit may recommend him to the esteem and confidence of his country. No qualification of wealth, of birth, of religious faith, or of civil profession is permitted to fetter the judgment or disappoint the inclination of the people." Madison was thinking nationally, setting up a national Congress of the people from many backgrounds. The candidate pool known as 'the people' was thought to be the most resilient and flexible and the most stabilizing across many generations. As for who should be allowed to vote, the overriding principle was that the rules of eligibility should be applied uniformly. However, articulating criteria for a set of eligibility rules does not mean that the criteria will be *applied* uniformly, or that the criteria themselves meet the deep fairness tests of the Fourteenth Amendment. If a literacy test at the polling booth is applied in the discriminatory manner by requiring only members of a certain race, and not others, to read and understand difficult or ambiguous passages from a state constitution, then its application is not uniform. And even if the same passage is given to all voters, a fair result is not guaranteed if a segment of

---

[32] *United States Term Limits v. Thornton*, 514 U.S. 779 (1995).

the population has been kept from learning to read or write by de facto force of law. If a fee of $1.50 is required for all persons to get a ballot to partially cover the cost of conducting an election, then this 'poll tax' is nondiscriminatory as written but is nonetheless much more burdensome for the poor than for the wealthy. The same applies to rules requiring a fee for a photo identification card obtained from a governmental agency in order to vote. Whether such eligibility rules are 'fair' depends on whether focus is placed upon the stated purpose of the rule or its consequences in practice. Since voting usually involves large numbers but can result in small margins of victory, the effect of either of these alternatives may come into play and be statistically significant in effecting the outcome of an election. Recognizing this and exploiting it for partisan gain is what subjects voter eligibility laws to political influence, rather than being entirely a precondition for it.

A constitutional amendment (XXIV) eliminated the poll tax in 1964 and the Supreme Court ruled it unconstitutional in state elections two years later.[33] Voting was now considered a fundamental right of U.S. citizens even though the Constitution never indicated that state residents had a right to vote in state elections for state officials. As a fundamental right, states could no longer restrict it except for compelling reasons. In the case of the poll tax, linking voting to any economic condition and to ability to pay did not meet the compelling state interest test.[34] It was invidiously designed to skim off the few individuals who had a better use for $1.50 on Election Day, it was argued. But this did not mean that the rationale for a state poll tax in state elections for state officers was now settled. Poll tax supporters argue that collecting taxes is a compelling state interest and that it is entirely rational to use an opportunity like voting to collect revenue. Tax supporters also noted that property qualifications to be eligible to vote have been in effect since the nation's founding. Justice Harlan saw no constitutional basis for eliminating the state poll tax, attributing the anti-tax view to "current egalitarian notions of how a modern democracy should be organized."[35]

---

[33] *Harper v. Virginia State Board of Elections*, 383 U.S. 663 (1966).

[34] Ibid., 671-81.

[35] Ibid., 686.

Literacy tests were banned legislatively by the Voting Rights Act of 1965. State qualification to register or vote could no longer be conditioned upon having to "(1) demonstrate the ability to read, write, understand, or interpret any matter, (2) demonstrate any educational achievement or his knowledge of any particular subject, (3) possess good moral character, or (4) prove his qualifications by the voucher of registered voters or members of any other class."[36] The Supreme Court upheld the ability of Congress to ban such tests by states through the equal protection clause of the Fourteenth Amendment (Sec. 5). So, when New York State required that voters be literate in English the court majority determined that being literate only in Spanish was not a sufficient reason to deny eligibility to vote.[37]

Since nothing in the Constitution required that voters be English speakers, some Justices believed that states were banned by the equal protection clause from setting English literacy as a voting prerequisite, while others believed that Congress had the power to ban literacy tests for all elections under the authority of the enforcement section (Sec. 2) of the Fifteenth Amendment.[38] That Amendment banned 'Jim Crow' literacy laws by protecting the right to vote by people "of race, color, or previous condition of servitude." Literacy tests had a long history of suppressing the black vote, and that was sufficient for a national ban, some Justices decided, particularly in light of the great disparity of educational opportunities for potential black voters. Yet, in spite of the unanimity on literacy tests, deep divisions remained on the court over the power of Congress to regulate state voting eligibility standards. Could states require correct answers to math problems and if so, how hard could they make the tests?

Further complicating matters, is the long-standing dispute on the Supreme Court over the *scope* of the equal protection clause in the Fourteenth Amendment. As applied to voting eligibility, was the clause intended to provide a way of assessing whether state voting laws were impermissibly discriminatory and inequitable, or was it intended only to protect the rights

---

[36] 52 U.S.C. Sec. 10501(b).

[37] *Katzenbach v. Morgan*, 384 U.S. 641 (1966) (Justice Harlan dissenting).

[38] *Oregon v. Mitchell*, 400 U.S. 112 (1970).

of freed slaves? It referred to "any person," but then did not include women. Justice Douglas argued that the Fourteenth Amendment made "vast inroads on the power of the States," while Justice Harlan argued that it said nothing about state voting requirements. "The power to set state voting qualifications," he argued, "was neither surrendered nor delegated, except to the extent that the guarantee of a republican form of government may be thought to require a certain minimum distribution of political power."[39] This last exception points to the depth of the problem we have been considering. What is a minimum distribution of political power? If it is what a state legislature says it is, then what becomes of the federal republican guarantee?

Conclusion

The reciprocity between the politics of law and the law of politics exists in dynamic tension. Politicians take oaths of office to support the Constitution. The President takes a similar oath and also vows to "take care that the laws be faithfully executed." (Art. II, Sec. 3) At times politicians operate within the law or attempt to change the law lawfully, i.e., they choose to accept and operate within established norms. At other times, they bend the law of politics, diminishing its constraints, by seeking to exploit novel opportunities that go against the spirit or original intent of the law or else introduce downright strained interpretations of existing laws and norms. They also exploit the opportunities provided by the separation of powers, sometime using the courts to achieve objectives with less exposure and fewer overt political repercussions. It is not an exaggeration to say that American political history has been laced with perverse strategies as well as with noble efforts to resist or undo them. Fuller's distinction between the inner and outer morality of law also applies to the ways in which politics interacts with law, revealing how important it is to follow certain procedural and substantive norms of behavior in political endeavors. To function properly the Fourteenth Amendment requires continual procedural efforts to achieve free and open elections, electoral processes subject to electoral review, a broad franchise, and equal weighing of votes.

---

[39] Ibid., 143, 200-201.

But in addition, adherence to substantive, or more properly *moral* norms, is required equally for politicians, candidates, and members of the judiciary, norms such as: be honest about your own motivations to yourself and to others and be prepared to explain and defend, modify, or abandon them with reasoned analysis; and determine the extent to which you are motived by personal or partisan advantage, or by the public good. To the extent that law and politics regularly deviate from these norms of good personal conduct, we cannot continually expect our multipolar system of government to always rub away the defects and dangers they produce.

We have seen how Madison linked essential attributes of a representative republic with the adherence to norms of inner morality. The powers and legitimacy of republican government, he said, must derive from the *great body* of the people and society. And yet, a well-constructed union must also constrain the inevitable impulse of politics to control government in the service of some interests over others, even if those interests were embraced by a majority of the population. Madison's solution, again, was to mix together voters with varying interests in properly-sized districts when electing representatives to represent them. Those representatives, he noted in *Federalist,* No. 10, were supposed to place "patriotism and love of justice" above special interests and strive to balance the values of public good and private rights. People should not only be given an opportunity to vote, but also to vote in meaningful competitive elections. In such a well-constructed union, then, each voting district in every state ought to be configured to reflect the variety of interests of the population of the state. Voting in those districts require, in addition to open procedures, meaningful elections where voters be presented with issues of broad significance and consequence. Striving to achieve such a norm reflects a moral commitment to the Madisonian value of fair representation. And yet, as we have seen, these norms may be systematically violated through various political practices: manipulating voting eligibility rules and access to the ballot, gerrymandering, and by giving disproportionate influence of money in political campaigns. All such practices have been vigorously defended as regular politics and justified by law since Madison's time and continue to be.

CHAPTER 9

MORALITY AND LAWS OF THE BODY

Introduction

A great deal of law involves coercive effects on the human body for the purpose of exerting social control, individually and collectively. For as long as there has been a desire to punish bad behavior, reward good behavior, and control the ways human beings experience pleasure and reproduce, law has been an important way of satisfying it. To be human is to experience pleasure and pain, but also to emotionally anticipate and later reflect upon those experiences. The sanctions of law, therefore, are designed and calibrated to work on the emotions and influence the natural intimacy between our feelings and our bodies. This intimacy is so prevalent we hardly notice it. Because we have bodies and cannot be separated from them in any manner that affects our daily lives, we carry a pervasive fear of physical and emotional damage. We fear sickness and disease; we are traumatized by serious injury and try to insure against it. The way we reproduce, even under the best conditions, is a precarious nine-month journey from the uncertainties of conception to the pains and intrusions of birth; and then birth and growth themselves become an arduous journey of coping and learning and experimenting, before arriving at some intangible degree of maturity.

Imagine how law and morality would be affected if our bodies instantly repaired themselves, and left no psychic scars. Or, imagine, at the other extreme, that our bodily lives were so fragile, that the slightest touch or taunt would instantly produce collapse and death. In the former case, there would be few if any actions and consequences for the law to protect against, or morality to blame. In the latter case, law and morality would have no purpose to serve. So, the law operates within a middle ground of attainable prohibited consequences, punishing severely the most severe, and lightly the less consequential, always weighing and evaluating. In other words, laws are made, interpreted, and enforced in a continuous state of observation of the physical conditions of individual bodies and their social interactions in order to achieve the desired control of consequences of human experience and interaction. Many areas of human life regulated by law – physical punishment, torture of enemies, sexual relations, contraception and abortion, marriage, suicide and assisted suicide, euthanasia, medical triage, public regulation of health and safety, slavery, racism, gender identity, desecration of the dead, all of the various standards and remedies of tort and penal law – are all related to the conditions of the living body, its varied attributes, and its vulnerabilities and potencies, all comprising general 'laws of the body'.

Liberty and Paternalism

Moral quandaries inevitably flow from efforts to put into practice laws of the body. Punishment is intended for the individual, but only roughly measures justice by treating that person as one among many to be punished for one of a class of crimes. A threshold question must always be asked: Is it moral to create and enforce a law of the body simply because fear, pain, and coercion are effective means of control over a person. How this question is answered distinguishes laws created under autocratic or democratic systems. Laws of the body must inevitably infringe on personal liberty. In his essay *On Liberty* (1859), John Stuart Mill, attempted to articulate some general normative principles of law governing how we ought to behave toward one another, and when bad behavior rises to the level of a legal infraction. Such principles also become a measure of how well the law serves its justifiable purpose for a given society and political community. In autocracies, the only standard the law must meet is: You are commanded by the autocrat to follow his or her edicts. Theocracies follow the same model, replacing autocratic edits with divine commands. With the rise of representative government, Mill argued, the problem of articulating a standard of law becomes much more complicated. As the institutions of self-government increase, the question becomes: what are the limits of control by the governed *over themselves*. It makes no sense to say that the governed should exercise absolute control over themselves simply because it is within their *power* to choose how they should be governed. The 'subjects' of a monarch have no such freedom of choice. However, with democratic freedom comes the responsibility of deciding how choices should be made and what they should be, and with that freedom comes a recognition that some degree of individual autonomy must be surrendered in order to have a maximally free and moral system of law.

Yet, setting up a simple rule for representative governance that 'the majority must be obeyed' also raises difficulties, specifically in the opportunity it provides for the majority to oppress the minority. This tyranny of the majority, Mill argued, is no different than the age-old oppression of a dominant religion over supposed heretics. Modern society, in Mill's case, early industrial age England, consisted of many individuals and groups with competing interests. As social life became more complex, so did the opportunities for conflict; and with conflict came a desire by a dominant group to inflict conformity upon social nonconformists. Yet, it doesn't take much imagination to recognize from the lessons of history that today's orthodoxy may be tomorrow's heresy, or that today's well-established, economically superior, classes may be overturned by the poor and thrown into the streets, as the lessons of the French Revolution had shown.

So, the best formulation of a standard for good laws and governance is one that will invite the greatest degree consent possible because it would be based on values that we all desire for ourselves: *to be free to pursue happiness in a manner that creates the greatest likelihood of success.* However, the likelihood of success, in turn, depends on a recognition that: "All that makes existence valuable to anyone depends on the enforcement of restraints upon the actions of other people."[1] These restraints, he believed, must be imposed either by law or by the dominant norms and customs of public opinion. Law is to be preferred, since dominant public opinion is usually poorly reasoned out and articulated, and invariably appears as "self-evident and self-justifying."[2] Properly constructed laws produce constraints on freedom, but also produces opportunities for greater freedom than before. Everybody recognizes the viability of that approach in their own lives. Even a person of fabulous wealth recognizes the need for a system of land recordation, a sound banking system based on fiduciary norms, and a government subject to the rule of law, in order to be secure in that wealth. Laws that provide no

---

[1] John Stuart Mill, *On Liberty,* [1859] (Indianapolis: Hackett, 1978), 5.
[2] Ibid.

constraint on individual freedom are not laws that can be relied upon for protection. The restraints the law places upon me are also placed on others. The benefit of mutually obeying traffic signals is an obvious example. Laws establishing religious toleration and freedom of speech restrict my wishes to oppose heresy or dissent, but then protect me from the same charges made by others. Laws curtailing privacy curtail my privacy. You are better off, Mill is saying, if laws prevent harm to others rather than just provide benefits to you. This "very simple" principle, more recently called the Harm Principle, provides a rational foundation for exerting legal or moral "compulsion and control" over individuals:

> [T]he sole end for which mankind are warranted, individually or collectively, in interfering with the liberty of action of any of their number is self-protection. That the only purpose for which power can be rightly exercised over any member of a civilized community, against his will, is to prevent harm to others. His own good, either physical or moral, is not a sufficient warrant.[3]

The legal system and even public opinion, Mill argued, could legitimately protect society against the actions of an individual only if the "conduct from which it is desired to deter him must be calculated to produce evil to someone else."[4] The Harm Principle mutually protects the individual who acts and those affected by the action. Although Mill does not say what he means by 'harm', he cannot mean simply physical harm (e.g., assault or killing), nor psychological harm (e.g., direct threats of imminent physical harm), nor actions that affect the interests of others, including economic interests (e.g., fraud), nor any act that has bad consequences for others.[5]

---

[3] Ibid., 9.

[4] Ibid.

[5] Mill's discussion of harm has been the subject of sustained critique. See for example: Ben Saunders, "Reformulating Mill's Harm Principle," *Mind*, 125 (2016): 1005–1032; Piers Norris Turner, "'Harm' and Mill's Harm Principle," *Ethics* 124 (January 2014): 299-326; Cass R. Sunstein, *The Storrs Lectures: Behavioral Economics and Paternalism,*122 Yale L. J. 1826 (May 2013); Arthur Ripstein, "Beyond the Harm Principle," *Philosophy & Public Affairs* 34 (Summer 2008): 215-45; Bernard E. Harcourt, *The Collapse of the Harm Principle,* 90 J. Crim. L. & Criminology 109 (Autumn 1999); Richard A. Epstein, *The Harm Principle – And How It Grew,* 45 U. Toronto L. J. 369 (Autumn 1995); Gerald Dworkin, "Paternalism," *The Monist* 56 (1972): 64-84.

Mill's Harm Principle may be regarded as a measure used to identify the costs imposed on society by a law motivated by harm-reducing policies. It asks: does the law promote adequate social self-protection by means that do not *unnecessarily* interfere with the liberty of action of individuals? It would be unreasonable for a government, for example, to spend billions of dollars to protect each house and neighborhood against a highly improbable meteorite impact. Consider, for example, a law that punishes public nudity *per se* as 'indecent exposure'. Such a law would go too far if it required a designated uniform dress code for the entire population when appearing in public. But is *any* regulation of public nudity reasonably relevant to societal self-protection and avoiding harm to others? That is really the question Mill is asking. What is the harm to others of sunbathing at the beach without a bathing suit, which is generally prohibited, as opposed to wearing a skimpy one, which is allowed? By contrast, some harm to others is foreseeable, 'calculated' to use Mill's term, as when riding on a crowded bus or attending a movie theater without clothes, and so may be deterred to some extent, say, for reasons of public health. In formulating a law on public nudity, lawmakers must explain why the means chosen are necessary to effectuate the desired end, but are also not overly restrictive. The fact that some people will be unhappy if public nudity is allowed in some circumstances by itself does not suffice to outlaw it. Maximizing personal liberty is the default rebuttable position for Mill. The law, then, must leave individuals alone if their actions do not harm others in ways that also jeopardize societal self-protection; and any human activity that involves what a person does with his own body and mind, as long as it does not cause harm to others, cannot be restrained. "Over himself, over his own body and mind, the individual is sovereign," he concludes.[6]

Laws that violate the Harm Principle, including laws that ban thoughts and beliefs, have been found throughout history. Having impure or deviant thoughts and feelings, as may arise when looking at provocative sexual imagery, entertaining heretical religious beliefs, or treasonous political beliefs, have frequently been outlawed and punished simply for experiencing them. The same applies to laws prohibiting the permanent marking with tattoos or piecing of one's own body, as well as experiencing

[6] *On Liberty*, 9.

one's own sexual self-gratification in private. Mill would regard these restrictions as violations of personal sovereignty. They would be justified only when societal survival is at risk.[7] Individual humans are all happiness seekers, every day trying to fulfill one or more objectives, no matter how poorly conceived, miserably achieved, or counterproductive. There would be little point to following the Harm Principle, if humans were incapable of making mistakes about their best interests, especially in assessing the consequences of their actions. Human beings cannot be turned into "automatons in human form" because human experience consists of a variety of choices, not all of which are within our control, and nor the consequences of those we make.[8]

Laws prohibiting drinking or dancing, or certain dietary prohibitions, or Sabbatarian laws, or Blue Laws, or zoning laws regulating the number of drinking establishments, or laws regulating the legal relationship between men and women in marriage are typically proposed *only* to advance intolerant sectarian values.[9] Even laws controlling tangible risk should not overreach. If poisons have an otherwise legitimate purpose, they should not be banned because they may be used to kill humans. Laws should not ban un-licensed procreation merely because some parents are unfit to have and raise children properly. Competitive economic practices should not be banned just because winners diminish opportunities for losers. On the other hand, gambling establishments should be regulated when they become attractive nuisances for crime, though gambling *per se* should not be criminalized. Similarly, fornication laws on the books are almost never enforced; the act of fornication itself is regarded as an utterly private matter, while brothels and prostitution, where legal, are restricted by zoning laws and tightly regulated for reasons of public health. Mill points to the United States as a nation with a proper attitude toward legislation – starting presumptively with the view of liberty of individuals and not of "paternal government" and then dialing back on liberty only to the extent necessary to identify a specific solution to a well-defined important social problem.[10]

---

[7] Ibid., 10.

[8] Ibid., 56.

[9] Ibid., 73-91

[10] Ibid., 101.

Mill's *On Liberty* has been a continual source of reflection on the limits of law and its intersection with morality. It is only the "real morality of public discussion" and "political morality," generally, that determines when coercive laws of the body should be justified, and then only through the use of reasoning designed to achieve a moral purpose. This discussion, in turn, cannot be accomplished without free expression, free democratic debate, and the disclosure and critical examination of the working assumptions of all political actors.[11] Again, the Harm-Principle standard provides a framework for evaluating the weight of laws on the scales of liberty and paternalism, and also provides a method of tracing back from legislation to its authenticating principles. In the American legal system, the touchstone of legislation is neither clearly-defined progressive liberalism of the kind Mill seems to prefer, nor a clearly-defined and systematically applied regime based on natural or divine law. Rather, legislation has been an evolving confluence of changing values and interpretations, generally trending from paternalism to liberty, but not in every case, and more importantly not of necessity. As Mill points out, as society becomes more complex and integrated, the opportunities increase for *both* paternalism and liberty, requiring that the Harm Principle be continually reapplied as new conditions arise. In the American condition, as we shall see below, the Constitution has been the focal point for resolving debates over the scope and interaction of private and public morality.

Suicide and Assisted Suicide

One of the arguments Mill makes in favor of personal autonomy is that it is impossible for individuals to express their freedom by voluntarily consenting to become slaves This is because "by selling himself for a slave, he abdicates his liberty; he forgoes any future use of it beyond that single act. He therefore defeats, in his own case, the very purpose which is the justification of allowing him to dispose of himself."[12] This remark on the contradiction of selling oneself into slavery, may suggest that Mill also would conclude that suicide can never be rationally justified. After all, how could an act of self-affirmation be justified by destruction of the

---

[11] Ibid., 14, 52; also 35, 76, 80.

[12] Ibid., 101.

self? Curiously, the issues of suicide should have been a momentous question at the center of his liberal philosophy, as it was in the daily life of Victorian England when suicide increasingly came to be looked at as a medical rather than moral issue.[13] Mill did remark that the suffering of humanity at the cruel hands of nature might become so intense that it would require "the universal & simultaneous suicide of the human race."[14] This suggests he thought suicide to be a desperate pain relieving act. But should it also be a justifiable expression of personal liberty and autonomy? And if not, should members of society stand by and allow and even facilitate the suicide of another? The law now regards self-imposed slavery a legal nullity. Clearly, Mill recognized the obligations we have as individuals and as a society to understand the difficulties others experience and to assist them in overcoming them. "Human beings owe to each other help to distinguish the better from the worst, and encouragement to choose the former and avoid the latter," he wrote.[15] But he could not bring himself to say that suicide would also be a legal nullity justifying its outright ban in every circumstance. He suggested that it could be justified on utilitarian grounds, since that theory justified not only pursuit of happiness but also the avoidance of suffering; and he believed that with the proper social reforms in education, politics, and science "all the great sources . . . of human suffering are in a great degree, many of them, almost entirely, conquerable by human care and effort." However, that still left the individual to confront the positive evils of life: "indigence, disease, and the unkindness, worthlessness, or premature loss of objects of affection," and for these afflictions suicide in practice, if not in theory, might be an option.[16]

---

[13] See Olive Anderson, *Suicide in Victorian and Edwardian England* (New York: Clarendon Press, 1987). The index to the 33 volumes of Mill's *Collective Works* does not contain an entry for suicide. *Indexes to the Collected Works of John Stuart Mill*, edited by Jean O'Grady (Toronto: University of Toronto Press, 1991). Mill himself had a close friend who committed suicide as well as a brother suffering from tuberculosis.

[14] *Collected Works of John Stuart Mill*, ed. J. M. Robson, et. al. (Toronto: University of Toronto Press, 1963-91), 14: 272.

[15] Ibid., 74.

[16] John Stuart Mill, *Utilitarianism*, (Auckland: Floating Press, 2009), 24, 27, 28. Mill experienced the premature death of an object of his affection when his wife, Harriet

In earlier centuries under English law suicide was considered a crime against God, King, and Nature, sometimes the corpse being 'punished' by hanging or torture.[17] Lacking any opportunity for an affront against a monarch, early American law downgraded the criminality of suicide to an act of moral turpitude, though still punishing those who helped someone kill themselves. The legal burden establishing suicide also shifted from assuming sanity up to the moment of death to either assuming insanity or else leaving the question of intent to a judge or jury. Even the very act of killing oneself presented difficulties of proof. Not every suicide attempt produces the intended result (e.g., by poisoning or asphyxiation), so it is hard to rule out that a person may have wanted to renounce suicide at the last moment but was too late to do so. So, the legal standard at the time was that, since the stresses of living do not lead people to kill themselves, the rarity of self-killing suggests a state of temporary insanity. Also favoring insanity was the view that no sane person with Christian beliefs would ever kill himself and therefore risk eternal damnation. Furthermore, the medication people may take in order to cope with pain, depression, or the cravings of addiction are really life-affirming acts, and also frequently produce accidental death, so that an overdose by itself could not be sufficient evidence to establish an intentional suicidal act.[18]

Attempted suicide presented its own set of proof problems. Here the person survives a botched attempt at suicide and is available to be punished. In some states attempted suicide was a crime, while in others it was not a crime because the criminal act of self-murder had never taken place. The American Law Institute's Modern Penal Code (1962) opposed criminal penalties for attempting one's own suicide and failing to achieve it, indicating that "it seems preposterous to argue that the violation of criminal sanctions upon one who fails in the effort is likely to inhibit

---

Taylor Mill, the feminist philosopher died. "Her memory is to me a religion," he wrote. *Autobiography*, (Indianapolis: Bobbs-Merrill, 1957), 156.

[17] Sir William Blackstone, *Commentaries on the Laws of England,* (Dublin, 1770) IV: 189-190.

[18] See *Coffey v. Home Life Insurance Co.,* 44 How. Pr. 481 (N.Y. 1873), and *Manhattan Life Insurance Co. v. Broughton,* 109 U.S. 121 (1883).

persons from undertaking a serious attempt to take their own lives."[19] A criminal penalty would not deter those attempting suicide since they believe they will succeed, while those who fake an attempt are not actually making an attempt in the first place.

As with suicide itself, proof problems also arose in early interpretations of assisted suicide. The public policy of criminally deterring suicide fell to punishment of the person who assisted. But is the person who furnishes a gun to a despondent person, who commits self-murder a week later, an accessory to the crime before the fact? And suppose the person who furnished the gun was told that it would be used for suicide, and then a week later the despondent person decides not to go through with it. Was this also a case of attempted assisted suicide since nothing changed from the standpoint of the assister? Suppose instead of supplying a gun someone provides a pessimistic philosophical argument of the futility of life and the utter finality of death. What form of 'assistance' would this be? To reconcile these fact patterns to norms of criminal law, some courts argued that the deceased was in fact a victim of a crime and the assister was the principal agent causing it. Others took the opposite view: since suicide was not punishable and since the assister did not directly cause the death that person should not be punished.

The conundrums of suicide law reveal the difficulties of using law to support poorly thought out moral precepts. At one time all suicide was thought to be bad, a *malum in se,* regardless of anyone's circumstances. Eventually suicide moved from the criminal to the medical realms, leading to calls for decriminalization.[20] Assisting in suicide, however, has remained a viable matter for legal debate, providing such a dense variety of circumstances, conditions, and counterfactual possibilities that jurists and legal scholars continually struggle to create a fine mesh of distinctions that allows good decisions and results to pass through and traps out the bad ones. Issues of morality are always at the heart of the debate. Some

---

[19] Modern Penal Code § 210.5 (official draft and revised comments 1980).

[20] David S. Markson, *The Punishment of Suicide –A Need for Change,* 14 Vill. L. Rev. 463 (1969); Marzen, Thomas J.; O'Dowd, Mary Kay; Crone, Daniel; Balch, Thomas J. *Suicide: a Constitutional Right?* 24 Duq. L. Rev. 1 (1985).

activities that will look well-intentioned and recognizably moral may be virtually identical to those that are not. For example, a person setting up a deadly mechanical device, e.g., a 'trap gun', to protect property from trespassers and burglars is not free of criminal liability since courts have recognized how these devices could be used to mask a murder. The same problem arises in suicide pacts that fail to be completed, raising the question of whether the survivor intended to murder the deceased.[21]

In 1997, the Supreme Court rejected a blanket due process right to physician-assisted suicide, concluding that state laws were to determine the question. Historically, states had long outlawed assisting someone to commit suicide, but in the 1970s several had defined withdrawal of crucial medical care as *not* physician-assisted suicide. So, the court had to decide whether terminally ill, but mentally competent, individuals could choose the manner of their death with the aid of a physician under the protection of the Fourteenth Amendment's liberty clause. In the deciding opinion, suicide was described as "a grievous, though nonfelonious, wrong," while assisted suicide, as a felonious crime, was "deeply rooted" in American law.[22] Many states, the opinion noted, continue to worry about the consequences of setting down on paper a statute that would allow a medicalized form of suicide. Opponents of this view argued that rejection of life-sustaining medical treatment, and choice of assisted suicide, are both manifestations of a tradition of "self-sovereignty."[23]

In *Glucksberg* the court divided over the appropriate weigh to be given to tradition. On the plus side, tradition reflects a fund of knowledge of the consequences of experiences and an opportunity to correct a law that produces bad consequences. On the other hand, the notion that past practices supported through law have become 'deeply rooted' assumes some wisdom in the past that is not available to us today, and for us to make that assumption we first must determine what is missing in our knowledge of today's proposed solution. Calling a value *deeply rooted* is the beginning of moral analysis, not its end. For one thing, as was noted

---

[21] See *In re Joseph G.*, 34 Cal. 3d 429 (1983).

[22] *Washington v. Glucksberg*, 521 U.S. 702, 714 (1997).

[23] Ibid., 724.

in *Glucksberg*, in the past most people did not die in hospitals, whereas more recently hospitals are found in many places, along with an infrastructure of ambulances and emergency rooms, and many automatic devices to sustain breathing and feed the body. The argument from tradition seems to leave out what our ancestors would have decided with the possibilities available to us today. These possibilities raise the question of privacy in a way that was seldom available previously. When a person's life has reached the point when it may only be artificially sustained and prolonged, they are typically now in a condition where they are immobilized, rendered helpless, subject to the decisions of others, including doctors who must balance the interests of the patient, family members, and the state as announced through its legislation. A right of privacy, to be left alone, at a certain point, not to be rolled and washed, and wheeled around and pricked with needles, must also be weighed in the balance. And, the argument goes, that right of privacy should not depend on the location of the state of residency but on federal constitutional rights of privacy.[24]

Since *Glucksberg,* some states have adopted physician-assisted suicide either by law or judicial decision, almost always when 'end-of-life' health issues arise. In those cases, the motivation is usually to avoid future pain and suffering, though physician-assisted suicide theoretically may be applied to any individual at any point in life, who sees no point to living even a healthy life.[25] Oregon's assisted-suicide law requires several procedural layers designed to establish patient consent, such as requiring several oral requests each separated by at least fifteen days, written requests to physicians signed in the presence of two witnesses, physician and consulting physician requirements to inform the patient of feasible alternatives to assisted suicide, such as hospice care and pain control.[26]

---

[24] See Erwin Chemerinsky, *Washington v. Glucksberg was Tragically Wrong,* 106 Mich. L. Rev. 1501 (2008).

[25] https://euthanasia.procon.org/view.resource.php?resourceID=000132. For a debate summary see Browne Lewis, *A Deliberate Departure: Making Physician-Assisted Suicide Comfortable for Vulnerable Patients,* 70 Ark. L. Rev. 1 (2017).

[26] Oregon Revised Statutes 127.800 et. seq; ("Death with Dignity Act"). See also Charles H. Baron, et al. *A Model State Act to Authorize and Regulate Physician-Assisted Suicide,* 33 Harv. J. on Legis. 1 (1996).

Sense could not be made of these precautions absent recognition that even a dying person should be regarded as a self-determining being, as Mill had urged, to the greatest extent possible even at the last stage of life.

Assisted Dying, Triage, and Euthanasia

Unlike physician-assisted suicide, where patient consent is preeminent as an expression of self-determination and self-control, assisted dying, triage, and euthanasia operate along a spectrum where the expression of consent is problematic at best, and often entirely unavailable. What is to be done with a living person with little or no capacity to make informed decisions about their health? Healthcare directives work best when a patient sets the range of preferred options just before undergoing risky surgery, and also are meaningful when terminal illnesses first become known. Paradoxically, these practices accept the autonomy of an individual under stressful conditions to make decisions about their death, but deny it to individuals who ask for physician assistance in a similar context. Autonomy is valued, but only up to a certain point. A paralyzed patient may give consent to end their lives by blinking their eyes in response to questions, but that consent is not accepted when a patient asks in a fully articulated way for physician assistance. Instead, an individual must travel to a country like Switzerland for assistance in dying. The current limit of autonomy in the United States seems to be the right to refuse or withdraw life support as long as there is clear evidence that is what the patient desires.

When it comes to life-or-death decisions, the ultimate guardian is the state that sits as an institutional factfinder and adjudicator without private interest or gain.[27] This view raises the following questions: if competent individuals have an absolute right to refuse treatment no matter how benign or invasive and 'let nature takes its course', is that right lost once competency is lost? Are constitutional rights protected only when an individual may assert them and does assert them? Do such rights exist while a healthy person is asleep? If a constitutional right of autonomy and privacy, including a right to be free of searches or intrusions, protects a sleeping person from the state, why not also a dying person? In *Cruzan,* the

---

[27] *Cruzan v. Director of Missouri Department of Health,* 497 U.S. 261 (1990).

majority maintained that the Constitution had nothing to say about an incompetent person refusing or withdrawing critical medical treatment when life is in the balance; that is left to the states to decide the kind of evidence required, in this case clear and convincing evidence, to show that the patient would have requested withdrawal of treatment were she competent to make such a request before such treatment can be withdrawn. In this case, a thirty-year-old woman, without a living will, was rendered incompetent and in a vegetative state as a result of an auto accident. The dissenters maintained that the state's interest in keeping her alive in order to 'protect life' could not be balanced against the patient's interest, since she no longer had an interest in living with an atrophied brain, and was in no way capable of even possessing interests.

The difficulty of resolving disputes over assisted dying, at least in part results from disagreements over the origin and purpose of life. Laws applying to all are drafted embracing values not shared by all. One such value is the claim that God created us to live out his plan regardless of our own will. This is a distinctly shared theological perspective, subject to many conflicting interpretations. Neither the Constitution nor the states, however, explicitly incorporate this purpose as a rationale for life-ending laws. Instead, they give high priority to individual autonomy, but only if the individual adopts certain pre-conditions, such as placing a living will in their medical file, often drafted at an earlier time when most people would not want to focus on their incapacitation and death. Courts and legislatures struggle when they attempt to give high value to autonomy, and at the same time maintain their traditional role in protecting life in general. That role is well-established when life is threatened by criminal behavior; it is less well defined when life is threatened by terminal diseases or catastrophic accidents.[28]

Nonetheless, the institutions in charge of resisting morbidity and mortality on a day to day basis cannot afford to ignore or be evasive about the intractable problem of dying. Triage involves a prioritizing of scarce resources under time constraints to achieve desired ends. The typical setting

---

[28] See for example, Megan S. Wright, *End of Life and Autonomy: The Case for Relational Nudges in End-Of-Life Decision-Making Law and Policy*, 77 Md. L. Rev. 1062 (2018).

is the emergency room, where people are processed in the order of arrival but cared for in the order of greatest need. Triage is a rule-based system permeated with moral assumptions. Even using a sorting rule like 'first come first treated' is a value choice. Traditional battle field or mass-casualty triage procedures typically follow a different rule: 'treat those likely to survive first and among those treat those who will benefit the most from immediate care first'. Stopping severe bleeding is an example of the latter situation. Early evaluation of medical needs by those committed to following the rules is critical. A triage nurse who lets a neighbor jump the line is not following the rules, raising the question of how fairly the rules should be followed. A wounded President almost certainly would jump the line, which raises the question of whether triage rules are embedded in another set of background priority rules such as 'treat Very Important Persons first' or 'treat persons with the greatest ability to pay, all other things being equal'. These kinds of question gave rise to a nationally mandated form of triage found in the Emergency Medical Treatment and Active Labor Act (EMTALA) passed by Congress in 1986. The Act required hospitals receiving federal Medicare funds to assess all emergency room patients regardless of citizenship or ability to pay. The hospital "must provide an appropriate medical screening examination within the capability of the hospital's emergency department," or otherwise must provide transportation to another hospital.[29] EMTALA was passed to avoid 'patient dumping' and the harsh visuals of the sick congregating and dying at the front doors of hospitals, and to make sure pregnant women having contractions are always admitted. However, whether patients receive 'appropriate' screening and their condition is 'stabilized' becomes a question of whether prevailing and customary medical procedures have been followed and appropriate judgments exercised.

Discussions of assisted suicide and assisted dying appear to embed assumptions about the conditions of life, as a form of social triage. Human adult life at every stage is seen as an investment in care and resources no matter how debilitated. That view, however, is predicated on the assumptions that human life is still scarce enough to require preserving and that social efforts must be made to accomplish this. Were there an overabundance of living humans relative to scarce resources intentional

[29] 42 U.S. Code § 1395dd (a).

dying might be valued and even encouraged. There has always been a correlation between life-sustaining conditions and an acceptance of dying. Under conditions of extraordinary social stress, intentional dying, whether as suicide, assisted suicide, or assisted dying, gains acceptance as a preferable social option. The Masada suicides of ancient Judaism, the suicides of the Japanese at Okinawa, and the Germans under Russian assault in World War II, the Buddhist Monk suicides during the Vietnam War, the religious suicides of Jonestown and Heaven's Gate, all illustrate the correlation between social triage and suicide acceptance.[30] When the elderly recognize that their share of food may create starvation in the young, cultural norms blurring suicide and euthanasia gain acceptance. In subsidized health care, the advanced elderly no longer receive certain subsidized and expensive preventative procedures, partly due to the risk associated with intrusive procedures, but also on a triage theory that by the time a disease progresses to threaten life the patient most likely will have already died.[31]

Though the line can be blurred between intentional dying, triage assessments, and euthanasia, there are clear examples of each activity. Euthanasia, 'good death', involves administering a painless death to end the suffering of the sick with little or no hope of recovery. It may be voluntary, non-voluntary, and involuntary. Voluntary euthanasia is simply some form of suicide whether self-induced or assisted, while non-voluntary and involuntary euthanasia lack even implied consent by the person being euthanized. Euthanasia in these latter cases also differs from suicide in so far as it is administered as a result of a program with standards and procedures applicable to anyone whose condition meets them. The program itself must be formulated; its application assessed in particular cases and then carried out by decision makers holding some form of official authority. Whereas suicide results from a specific unique decision, and assisted suicide from a unique collaboration of decision makers, non-voluntary and involuntary euthanasia result from a policy decision of officials. Voluntary euthanasia,

---

[30] David R. Beisel, "The German Suicide, 1945" *Journal of Psychohistory,* 34 (2007): 302-313.

[31] Adam Powell, et. al., "Rates and Correlates of Potentially Inappropriate Colorectal Cancer Screening in the Veterans Health Administration," *Journal of General Internal Medicine,* 30 (2015): 732-41.

then, is simply a form of assisted dying, especially since such dying is usually designed to be painless, while euthanasia as involuntary painless dying is almost universally thought to be murder.

No uniform standards of morality apply universally to the law of non-natural death. They differ from country to country and state to state. The only constant seems to be that the law has something to say about all forms of non-natural death, from premeditated physical murder to involuntary euthanasia to assisted suicide to voluntary and non-voluntary assisted dying. However, no legal norm so far has even embraced the idea that the cost of continued living to the individual and to society should be identified and measured at some acceptable standard when it comes to questions of non-natural death. Such a standard would run headlong into the various modern formulations of the Hippocratic Oath, admonitions that physicians should use their abilities and available modern technologies always to preserve and enhance the health of their patients. By contrast, a more realistic and accurate *cost-benefit* approach would place reasonable time limits on recovery so that seriously compromised individuals, with little prospect for self-administered care, would be euthanized. Imagine a state law that reverses the evidentiary standard accepted in *Glucksberg,* for example, by establishing a presumption in favor of non-voluntary or involuntary euthanasia for patients who do not show progress within a specified time. Since, according to *Glucksberg,* there are no federally enforceable end-of-life rights, such a triage law would appear to be perfectly constitutional, particularly where laws are enacted after extensive public discussion over proper due process procedures. If this is a repulsive notion to a modern sensibility revealing why would be an important and needed exercise in moral reasoning. By themselves, mere slippery-slope warnings are insufficient as technology opens a wider horizon of possible states between life and death. [32]

---

[32] Margaret P. Battin, *Physician-Assisted Dying and the Slippery Slope: the Challenge of Empirical Evidence,* 45 Willamette L. Rev.91 (2008), and Penney Lewis, "The Empirical Slippery Slope from Voluntary to Non-Voluntary Euthanasia," *Journal of Law, Medicine. & Ethics,* 35: 197-210 (2007); also Mason L. Allen, *Crossing the Rubicon: The Netherlands' Steady March Towards Involuntary Euthanasia,* 31 Brook. J. Int'l L. 535 (2006), and Neil M. Gorsuch ,*The Legalization of Assisted Suicide and the Law of*

Marriage and Parenthood

Historically, marriage in the Anglo-American tradition has been seen as a social status designed to protect or create rights primarily based on gender. Gender determined the array of unmarried rights that could be transformed by marriage. English law contained many rules regarding who could marry. It was made treason to marry certain designated royal descendants without permission of the monarch. A woman of nobility did not lose her status when she married a commoner, but if she acquired nobility by marrying a nobleman, she lost it when the marriage ended. A woman always acquired the legal domicile of her husband. Until the Deceased Wife's Sister's Marriage Act of 1907, it was unlawful to marry your deceased wife's sister or half- sister. In America, state law comingled with common law to create a variety of marriage laws tied to local conditions. For example, if a spouse deserts for seven years, the marriage ceases, allowing subsequent valid marriages in some states, but not in others, while in most states children of those marriages were usually deemed legitimate. Upon marriage, a woman became entitled to a portion of her husband's or his family's property at his death (a dower) held in trust for her future support. This practice was later replaced by inheritance laws. As for a woman's property upon marrying, the Supreme Court set out the rule in a famous 1819 case: "A man has just as good a right to his wife, as to the property acquired under a marriage contract. He has a legal right to her society and her fortune; and to devest [sic] such right without his default, and against his will, would be as flagrant a violation of the principles of justice, as the confiscation of his own estate."[33] At common law, however, the husband also acquired the debts of his wife, unless state law exempted him from them.[34] If a wife, however, acquires property

---

Unintended Consequences: a Review of the Dutch and Oregon Experiments and Leading Utilitarian Arguments for Legal Change, 2004 Wis. L. Rev. 1347 (2004).

[33] *Dartmouth College v. Woodward,* 17 U.S. 518, 697 (1819). See also James Kent, *Commentaries on American Law,* 12th ed. (Boston: Little Brown, 1896) I: 557.

[34] *Pitkin v. Thompson,* 30 Mass. 64 (1832). Kent, *Commentaries,* II: 186 ("The general rule is, that the husband becomes entitled, upon the marriage, to all the goods and chattels of the wife, and to the rents and profits of her lands, and he becomes liable to pay her debts and perform her contracts.")

during the marriage, it is not conveyed to her husband, but to a trustee to be held for her use as separate property. However, both parties were allowed by law to enter into a prenuptial agreement as to the disposition of their property, which would override the general rules of common law marriage as long as the purpose of the agreement is not to evade creditors and is made to support the social purposes of marriage.

Publicly solemnized marriage stood in contrast with common-law marriage, where a man and woman privately agreed to live as husband and wife and hold themselves out to the public as married, but with no publicly established ceremonial act. Kent defined marriage as "the only lawful relation by which Providence has permitted the continuation of the human race," and defined its purpose as the creation, sustenance, and education of offspring. Since common law marriage could have the same purpose in practice as official marriage, it was necessary that it be lawful as well. We are all familiar with marriage rules still in effect today for age limitations (previously fourteen for boys, twelve for girls), parental consent, mental incapacity, dissolution, as well as tax and property ownership rules. Previously, marriage could be dissolved only for bad behavior, but now no-fault dissolutions are routinely granted. In the early nineteenth century the only grounds for divorce in New York was adultery. In some states, divorces could only be granted by a vote of the legislature.[35] Previously, spouses could sue seducers of their spouses for alienation of their affection but such legal recourse has since been abolished.

In marriage law, background moral and religious norms are rarely expressly articulated. The law is simply presented as what the nature of things requires. For Kent, since monogamy was "founded on the precepts of Christianity, and the laws of our social nature," cultures that practiced polygamy were uncivilized.[36] Patriarchal authority of the household was also based on natural law: "In the case of the death of the father during the minority of the child, his authority and duty, by the principles of natural law, would devolve to the mother."[37] Justice Story also supported a natural

---

[35] Kent, *Commentaries*, II: 76, 282, 108,146, 148.

[36] Ibid., II: 112.

[37] Ibid., II: 307.

law view of marriage. Marriage, he argued in 1832, "promotes the private comfort of both parties" by promoting peace in society, a control over coveting another's spouse, stability for child rearing, incentives for work and self-improvement, and an over-all benefit to society and the state.[38]

Compare Kent and Story's views with those of American pragmatist and lawyer, Nicholas St. John Green (1830-1876). Writing in 1871, he argued that marriage was entirely a social institution that slowly evolved from the outright capture and later purchase of women to their more recent patriarchal economic domination, at each point the status quo being justified by reference to the 'laws of nature'. He noted a new British law (the Married Women's Property Act of 1870) that for the first time gave working women direct rights to the money they earned from wages or rent, or from an inheritance and investments, a first step to reforming marriage as "the last vestige of slavery."[39] Nonetheless, the natural law view of marriage has persisted in opposition to more non-sectarian views of domestic relations. It is reflected in Catholic doctrine and in many scholarly debates over birth control, abortion, *in vitro* fertilization, anti-miscegenation law, and same-sex marriage.[40] Interracial marriage, for example, was banned on theistic natural law grounds. The lower court ruling that led to the overturning of Virginia's anti-miscegenation law stated: "Almighty God created the races white, black, yellow, malay and red, and he placed them on separate continents. And but for the interference with his arrangement there would be no cause for such marriages. The fact that he separated the races shows that he did not intend

---

[38] Joseph Story, "Natural Law" (1836) reprinted in *The Journal of Christian Jurisprudence* , 7 (1988): 31, 34.

[39] *Married Women,* 6 Am. L. Rev. 57, 73 (1871).

[40] See encyclicals of Pope Pius XI ("Casti Connubii," 1930) and Pope Paul VI ("Humanae Vitae," 1968). See also, for example, pro and con natural law issues in Joseph W. Hovermill, *A Conflict of Law and Morals: The Choice of Law Implications of Hawaii's Recognition of Same-Sex Marriages,*53 Md. L. Rev. 450 (1994); Ronald R. Garet, *Deposing Finnis,* 4 S. Cal. Interdisc. L. J. 605 (1995); Perry Dane, *Natural Law, Equality, and Same-Sex Marriage,* 62 Buff. L. Rev. 291 (2014); and Christopher R. Leslie, *Dissenting from History: The False Narratives of the Obergefell Dissents,"* 92 Ind. L. J. 1007 (2017).

for the races to mix."[41] The Virginia statute in *Loving* stated: "If any white person intermarry with a colored person, or any colored person intermarry with a white person, he shall be guilty of a felony and shall be punished by confinement in the penitentiary for not less than one nor more than five years." Sixteen states had similar penal laws. Laws containing racial classifications, the Supreme Court argued, needed to advance a beneficial social purpose in order to justify restriction on the freedom to marry, since marriage was "one of the vital personal rights essential to the orderly pursuit of happiness by free men." Racial purity was the state interest at issue and anti-miscegenation laws were thought to be the means of accomplishing it, even though racial sexual relations had continued to produce offspring since before the founding of the Republic. As a practical matter, to achieve racial purity would have required a complicated system of Nürnberg-style race and ancestry laws and the systematic extermination of mixed-race children, something no state has ever implemented or even contemplated. To the Supreme Court in *Loving,* Virginia's inter-racial marriage expressed a state interest in advancing White Supremacy that was outweighed by the social value of promoting marriage based on love and personal choice.[42]

Same-sex marriage was approved in 2015, using the same *Loving* analysis: since states exclusively regulate and record marriages by granting marriage licenses, they cannot deny those licenses on the basis of the gender of the parties requesting them, particularly in the light of recent decisions decriminalizing homosexual acts.[43] Although states have an interest in the kind of values described by Story, they do not *require* partners to pledge to have children or withdraw the marriage license from childless couples; nor do states ban adoptions. Rather, marriage in American life is now regarded as a private matter of personal choice, part of the liberty interest protected

---

[41] *Loving v. Virginia,* 388 U.S. 1, 3 (1967); pre-*Loving* see *State v. Gibson,* 36 Ind. 389, 404 (1871) ("The natural law which forbids their intermarriage and that social amalgamation which leads to a corruption of races, is as clearly divine as that which imparted to them different natures."), and *Naim v. Naim,* 197 Va. 80 (1955).

[42] *Loving 388 U.S. at 5, 11.* Also see Keith E. Sealing, *Blood Will Tell: Scientific Racism and the Legal Prohibitions against Miscegenation,* 5 Mich. J. Race & L. 559, 560 (2000).

[43] *Obergefell v. Hodges,* 135 S. Ct. 2584 (2015). On decriminalizing homosexuality compare *Bowers v. Hardwick,* 478 U.S. 186 (1986) and *Lawrence v. Texas,* 539 U.S. 558 (2003).

by the Fourteenth Amendment. Further, where married same-sex couples are allowed to adopt children or enter into contracts with surrogate mothers the state interest in procreation can be advanced in same-sex marriages as well. While the majority in *Obergefell* looked at the evolving social conditions of marriage as allowed and actually practiced today, the dissent focused more on its procreative function.[44]

The definition of marriage has also been modified by the acceptance of surrogacy and *in vitro* fertilization. Throughout history, orphaned children have been cared for by relatives and friends. Can we measure the quality of that affection and differentiate its origin or legitimacy as something uniquely 'natural'? If biological procreation is supposed to contain unique attributes, why are so many families lacking them? Traditional natural law has focused on the family and protected its institution by supporting laws against divorce or adultery simply because there were no other acceptable procreative alternatives. Now birth control, surrogacy, fostering, adoption, freezing embryos, and *in vitro* ferlilization provide a wider range of choices to fit procreation to people and their circumstances. With its emphasis on human flourishing, modern natural law theory moves the area of debate from past practices to future consequences, moving the question from how to maintain existing social forms to how to produce as many fulfilled human lives as possible. This is both an empirical and moral question, and the way we answer it in the future will challenge traditional notions of what it means to be a family or parent.[45]

Birth Control and Sterilization

At what point in the history of human life a connection was first made between sexual intercourse and conception may never be finally pinned down. Whenever that point was, folk remedies to frustrate conception invariably also came into practice. Techniques of population promotion or limitation were critical to early nomadic and farming communities, and

---

[44] *Obergefell* 135 S.Ct. at 2613.

[45] See Michael J. Higdon, *Constitutional Parenthood,* 103 Iowa L. Rev.1483 (2018); Ayelet Blecher-Prigat, *Conceiving Parents,* 41 Harv. J. L. & Gender 120 (2018); and Douglas Nejaime, *The Nature of Parenthood,* 126 Yale L. J. 2260 (2017).

first established the nexus between conception and politics. The Book of Genesis fixated on conception of offspring by patriarchal elites for purposes of social dominance and political advantage. Ancient Greeks and Egyptians used pessaries and animal skins to neutralize or block insemination. Using marriage and conception to create opportunities for future alliances was a constant preoccupation of blood, and later economic, royalty well into modern times. Birth control has profound consequences for the creation of citizens and military fighters, as well as for the liberty of women, and so was identified long ago as a point of vulnerability in the nation state, requiring legal regulation.[46]

In the 1870s, laws against dissemination of birth control information were passed by the federal government and many states denominated as laws against "obscenity" or "offenses against morals." The federal Comstock Act (1873-1957) banned advertising, use of the mails or transport across state lines, of any instruments or materials intended to prevent conception or induce abortion.[47] Such laws were said to counter the growing trade of romance and sexually suggestive literature and imagery (e.g., *Venus's Miscellany*) that, for example, had been mailed to soldiers at the front lines of the Civil War. Birth control methods at the time included sponges, douches, condoms, abstinence during periods of presumed fertility, and complete or partial withdrawal. Folklore and folk remedies were the rule. Some believed that a woman could not conceive without having an orgasm. A high demand for accurate information was met with a focused effort to limit, but not entirely shut off, such information. Doctors could not disseminate such information in public, yet such anti-obscenity laws stayed clear of private patient-doctor conversations. Advertising 'secret drugs' for use by women was banned, but not substantially similar discussions in medical schools or standard medical books.[48] Scientific studies of

---

[46] Linda Gordon, *The Moral Property of Women: A History of Birth Control Politics in America* (Urbana: University of Illinois Press, 2002).

[47] 17 Stat. 598. The Comstock Law for the District of Columbia and some states referred instead to "unlawful abortion."

[48] *Commonwealth v. Tarbox*, 55 Mass. 66 (1848). See Janet Farrell Brodie, *Contraception and Abortion in Nineteenth-Century America* (Ithaca, N.Y.: Cornell University Press, 1994).

conception were also exempted as non-obscene. In fact, the very notion of an obscene purpose was left unclear, leading a Kansas judge to observe that without a clearly articulated purpose, application of the law would be "largely haphazard and capricious."[49]As a result, pornographic materials were successfully suppressed as were pro-contraception advertisements, but the flow of information and materials to the public continued.[50]

Anti-birth control laws suffered the same difficulty as would laws against pornography years later: criminalizing the same behavior in public that was tolerated in private would eventually undermine the laws, and the rule of law, as being hypocritical. In reality, there was no driving national consensus on the immorality of birth control. After World War I, scientists responded to a request by social reformers, like Margret Sanger (1879-1966), for more reliable methods of birth control that would lead to the contraceptive pill. Since the goal was control of conception, research was largely funded in the United States, but carried out in Great Britain.[51] In 1930, a federal appeals court ruled that contraceptives could be sold to wholesalers and druggists who supplied doctors; and in 1936 the same court ruled that a gynecologist could lawfully import birth control pessaries for use in her practice because the Comstock Act banned only immoral conduct, not medical care.[52] Some state courts took the Comstock wording literally and ruled that contraceptives were *per se* illegal no matter their source or purpose.[53] Legal commentators pointed out the inconsistence in the application of these various laws. They noted that one problem was that a complete ban on contraceptives was impossible to enforce because 'contraceptives' could be any lawful substance that thwarts conception; and a partial ban was even easier to subvert. Inconsistency was also found in the view that contraception thwarted the will of God and

---

[49] J.C. Ruppenthal, "Criminal Statutes on Birth Control," *Journal of Criminal Law and Criminology*, 10 (1919): 48, 51.

[50] Andrea Tone, "Black Market Birth Control: Contraceptive Entrepreneurship and Criminality in the Gilded Age," *Journal of American History* 87 (2000): 436-59.

[51] For historical background see Merriley Borell, "Biologists and the Promotion of Birth Control Research, 1918-1938," *Journal of the History of Biology* 20 (1987): 51-87.

[52] *Youngs Rubber Co., v. C.I. Lee*, 45 F.2d 103 (CA2 1930); *United States v. One Package*, 86 F.2d 737 (CA2 1936).

[53] *Commonwealth v. Gardner*, 15 N.E.2d 222 (Mass. 1938).

natural law, but that sterilization laws were widely acceptable. Critics also argued that Comstock laws violated a liberty interest of individuals to have the best available health care options.[54]

Finally, in 1965 birth control for married couples was legalized on a national scale. In the *Griswold* decision, discussed previously, access to birth control was considered a privacy right supported by the Constitution.[55] The Connecticut law overturned fines or imprisonment for using "any drug, medicinal article or instrument for the purpose of preventing conception," with similar penalties for doctors. The court majority decided that the law "operates directly on an intimate relation of husband and wife and their physician's role in one aspect of that relation."[56] Seven years later, the law was extended to unmarried persons on privacy and unenforceability grounds.[57]

Sterilization laws, which may be regarded as state-sponsored birth control, were in effect in the United States roughly between 1907 and 1963, primarily driven by the eugenics movement to improve the physical and mental attributes of the general population. Compulsory sterilization was first adopted in Indiana and made applicable to "confirmed criminals, idiots, rapists and imbeciles" in state custody as long as a board of physicians and experts determined that their condition was 'unimprovable'. The 1907 law was overturned because sterilization (by vasectomy) could be ordered against someone, without proving notice and opportunity to be heard.[58] Even when due process was provided, a state sterilization law was upheld in state court, arguing that sterilization was not a punitive act but a legitimate act of police power to protect public health and morals. That ruling subsequently was upheld by the Supreme Court, where Holmes made a eugenic argument in favor of regulated

---

[54] *Note: Some Legislative Aspects of the Birth-Control Problem,* 45 Harv. L. Rev.723 (1932); and *Note: Contraceptives and the Law,* 6 U. Chi. L. Rev. 260 (1939).

[55] *Griswold v. Connecticut,* 381 U.S. 479 (1965). The author of the opinion, Justice William O. Douglas, had a made a similar argument in his dissent in *Poe v. Ullman,* 367 U.S. 497 (1961).

[56] *Griswold,* 381 U.S. at 482.

[57] *Eisenstadt v. Baird,* 405 U.S. 438 (1972).

[58] *Williams v. Smith,* 190 Ind. 526) (1921).

sterilization:[59] *Buck* is still good law, though its state-law progeny has been refined to include, in many cases, a higher burden of proof (clear and convincing evidence), court adjudication, and a "best interest" of the subject standard. Nonetheless, in cases where involuntary sterilization is allowed, using a court best-interest finding by clear and convincing evidence, the risk of discriminatory abuse is still ever present. This danger was recognized fifteen years after *Buck* when the Supreme Court ruled that compulsory sterilization laws were required to meet a high constitutional burden because the right to create offspring was a fundamental liberty right of individuals.[60]

Sexual Activity and Experience

Sexual activity had always been subject to cultural norms. Their violation has been the disproportionate focus of the Old Testament and ancient Greek dramas. The Seventh Commandment outlawed adultery, but not fornication because concubines were permitted. Nor could a neighbor's wife be coveted, but her unmarried daughter might be. The distinction between adultery and fornication is paradoxical. The distinction is not in the act itself, but in the norms they violate. Adultery violates an existing vow of marriage, while fornication was thought to diminish the vow of a future marriage. In that event, fornicators were often obligated to marry

---

[59] *Buck v. Bell*, 143 Va. 310 (1925); *Buck v. Bell*, 274 U.S. 200, 207 (1927). For some subsequent commentary on the case, see Harry Bruinius, *Better for All the World: The Secret History of Forced Sterilization and America's Quest for Racial Purity* (New York: Knopf, 2006). See also Stefan Kühl, *The Nazi Connection: Eugenics, American Racism, and German National Socialism* (New York: Oxford University Press, 1994) discussing the interaction between eugenics in the United States and in Nazi Germany.

[60] *Skinner v. Oklahoma*, 316 U.S. 535, 541(1942). ("The power to sterilize, if exercised, may have subtle, far-reaching and devastating effects. In evil or reckless hands it can cause races or types which are inimical to the dominant group to wither and disappear.") See also, Mindy K. Fersel, *Note: Liberty and Justice for All? Protecting the Right of Privacy for Incapacitated Individuals: The Need for Comprehensive Sterilization Legislation in All Fifty States*, 20 Cardozo J. L. & Gender 827 (2014); and Michele Goodwin and Erwin Chemerinsky, *Book Review: Pregnancy, Poverty, and the State, The Poverty of Privacy Rights*, by Khiara M. Bridges, Stanford University Press, 2017, 127 Yale L. J. 1270 (2018).

their sexual partner, in which case it is the law that creates the marriage obligation not the vow itself. One option, of course, is to sever fornication and marriage altogether by regarding them as different types of human sexual interaction. Early American law struggled to weigh the appropriate sanction for each, and it was usually a court specializing in disputes over intimate human affairs like divorce or adoption (a 'court of equity' or Chancery Court) that had to do the balancing of rights and injuries. In 1787, New York established divorce for the first time and made adultery the only grounds for it. In New Jersey, a court determined that a married man did not commit adultery with an unmarried woman. In Vermont, unmarried fornicators were subject to fine and imprisonment. In Massachusetts, a woman could divorce her adulterous husband even though he had condoned her own adultery, while continuing to cohabit with an adulterous spouse became a bar to a divorce. A husband, who successfully induced someone to seduce his wife, also could not divorce for adultery. Strengthening marriage and confining sexual relations within it was the stated purpose of these laws. However, soon enough nineteenth-century courts realized that adulterous conduct was not the only way to destroy a marital contract, and so allowed divorces for desertion, extreme cruelty, incest, bigamy, impotency, alcoholism, or spousal imprisonment.[61] Today prosecutors virtually ignore fornication or cohabitation as crimes. Although some of these 'dead laws' remain on the books, most last enforced in the 1950s and 1960s, some groups continually hope to revive them.[62] Meanwhile, the Supreme Court has never expressly decided that fornication or cohabitation was a fundamental right.[63]

Not only was the line between adultery and fornication difficult to sustain judicially, so was the line between heterosexual and homosexual sodomy.

---

[61] Kent, *Commentaries*, 12th ed. II: 98, 99, 101-102, 106. See, for example, *Cumming v. Cummings* 135 Ma. 386 (1883). In some states, adultery remains a basis for divorce, often requiring proof by clear and convincing evidence; recently in Kentucky a man could divorce his wife for a single act of infidelity, while the wife could only divorce her husband if he engages in more than one act, and "lives in adultery." *Griffin v. Rice*, 381 S.W.3d 198 (2012).

[62] JoAnne Sweeny, *Undead Statutes: The Rise, Fall, and Continuing Uses of Adultery and Fornication Criminal Laws*, 46 Loy. U. Chi. L. J. 127 (2014).

[63] See *Carey v. Population Services International*, 431 U.S. 678 (1977).

In the close ruling in *Lawrence v. Texas* five Justices determined that a Texas law against homosexual conduct defined as "deviate sexual intercourse" with a member of the same sex was unconstitutional.[64] It was evident to at least five of the Justices that homosexual men were being prosecuted for acts commonly carried out by heterosexual couples as well; and though historically anti-sodomy laws had included heterosexual conduct, they were not enforced uniformly. The case, however, was not based on a lack uniform application of sodomy laws violating equal protection, but rather because such laws reached private conduct between consenting adults regardless of sexual orientation.

Years earlier the Supreme Court confronted the question of whether solitary sexual experience *per se* ought to be criminalized. The court decided that private sexual experience by adults aided by sexual imagery was not illegal.[65] However, materials that are not obscene when viewed in private became obscene if given public exposure or imported into the country.[66] In these and similar cases, courts struggle to identify exactly what is criminal about possessing obscene materials. Is it the arousing effect of the materials, in which case the same effect might result from viewing a medical textbook or clothing catalogue? Is it the effect on others, including exposure to children? Is it merely the *content* of the imagery whether or not it produces sexual feelings and emotions, or whether or not it is viewed in private or in public? The definition of 'obscenity' does not include a requirement of actual social and public exposure, but it does require a certain prohibited kind of arousal: "(a) whether 'the average person, applying contemporary community standards' would find that the work, taken as a whole, appeals to the prurient interest; (b) whether the work depicts or describes, in a patently offensive way, sexual conduct specifically defined by the applicable state law; and (c) whether the work, taken as a whole, lacks

---

[64] *Lawrence v. Texas*, 539 U.S. 558 (2003). Texas defined "deviate sexual intercourse" as "(A) any contact between any part of the genitals of one person and the mouth or anus of another person; or (B) the penetration of the genitals or the anus of another person with an object." Texas Penal Code, Title 5, Ch. 21, § 21.01 and § 21.06.

[65] *Stanley v. Georgia*, 394 U.S. 557 (1969). (Mere possession of adult films at home with no evidence of intent to sell, expose or circulate them is protected by the First Amendment.)

[66] *United States v. 12 200-Ft. Reels of Super 8mm Film*, 413 U.S. 123 (1973).

serious literary, artistic, political, or scientific value."[67] As it functions in law, the expression "prurient interest" appears to describe, by definition, an attraction to obscene materials when a deviant group experiences it, while 'atypical' sexual proclivities of the non-deviant group do not, presumably, rise to the level of obscenity.[68] Even depictions of 'normal' sexual acts may engender prurient interest from someone who has a deviant interest in the content of the imagery. However, it is legally impossible, the Supreme Court seems to argue, for a jury to decide that a bare midriff was "patently offensive," and so could never create prurient interest, at least until a state mandates full covering at the beach and elsewhere.[69]

The architecture of First Amendment obscenity law seems to rely upon circular standards and definitions as to what an 'average' person is, and what community standards are, with respect to sexual experience. The legal acceptance of sexual experiences in privacy zones like the home goes against the long history of disapproval of private masturbation as an impermissible form of self-abuse. The analogy to birth control cannot be missed. Here a private practice facilitated by aids that may be found in most drugstores, gains widespread if tacit public acceptance and yet remains subject to continual debate over the scope of its legality. Given the weight of this history, ambiguity seems to mark the law's stance on private masturbation as still being connected with unnatural acts of bestiality or the expression of excretory obsessions.[70]

---

[67] *Miller v. California*, 413 U.S. 15, 24, 25 (1973); for example, "(a) Patently offensive representations or descriptions of ultimate sexual acts, normal or perverted, actual or simulated. (b) Patently offensive representations or descriptions of masturbation, excretory functions, and lewd exhibition of the genitals." See also 18 U.S.C. Sec. 1461.

[68] *United States v. Petrov*, 747 F.2d 824, 830 (2nd. Cir. 1984), involving bondage and bestiality; ("material appealing to atypical sexual proclivities may be found 'obscene' only when its dominant theme appeals to the prurient interest of members of a 'clearly defined deviant sexual group'.")

[69] *Jenkins v. Georgia*, 418 U.S. 153, 161 (1974).

[70] An historical survey is provided by Geoffrey P. Miller, *Law, Self-Pollution, and the Management of Social Anxiety*, 7 Mich. J. Gender & L. 221, 289 (2001). Legal ambiguity

A better alternative to proscribing certain personal sexual experiences as inherently bad, is to put the emphasis on *social* conduct such as acts of cruelty or harming others without their consent or their ability to give it, as in the case of minors. The state interest that more consistently requires protection is in punishing personal interaction with, or the dissemination of materials to, others, who do not wish to interact or receive them, or would predictably be offended, fearful, or embarrassed by making public certain matters that should remain private. This norm applies to the regulation of sexual conduct in relation to minors, FCC rules about what may be said or depicted in mass media, or the much more intrusive sexual norms associated with the Code of Military Justice, where even consensual sexual conduct normally accepted in civilian life may be violations of the Code.[71] It may also apply to more challenging environments, such as prisons or group homes for the disabled or elderly. In these environments, privacy jurisprudence breaks down because, generally, people from the 'non-deviant' community are being asked to become asexual creatures.[72] Privacy consent jurisprudence also is strained in the modern variants of the age-old quasi-contractual request 'I'll show you mine if you show me

---

may result from the view that "masturbation and spermatorrhoea threatened to upset the reliability and predictability of the law, given that these conditions were universally acknowledged to be extremely widespread." Justice Scalia's dissent in *Lawrence* has been called "opaque" because although he does not come out and say it, he seems to assume that states may legitimately criminalize private masturbation *per se*. Robert E. Rains, "The Future of Justice Scalia's Predictions of Family Law Doom," 29 BYU J. Pub. L. 353, 376 (2015). See also for example *United States v. Guthrie*, 720 Fed. Appx. 199, 203(5th Cir., 2018) ("Guthrie points to no case law holding a video of an adult man masturbating to ejaculation cannot be obscene as a matter of law" i.e., appearing to say, obscene 'in and of itself, regardless of use or purpose'.)

[71] Walter T. Cox, III, *Consensual Sex Crimes in the Armed Forces: A Primer for the Uninformed*, 14 Duke J. Gender L. & Pol'y 791 (2007).

[72] See such issues raised by Joanna E. Saul, *Of Sexual Bondage: The 'Legitimate Penological Interest' in Restricting Sexual Expression in Women's Prisons*, 15 Mich. J. Gender & L. 349 (2009); and Richard Guidice Jr., *Procreation and the Prisoner: Does the Right to Procreate Survive Incarceration and Do Legitimate Penological Interests Justify Restrictions on the Exercise of the Right*, 29 Fordham Urb. L. J. 2277 (2002). Also, Natalie M. Chin, *Group Homes as Sex Police and the Role of the Olmstead Integration Mandate*, 42 N.Y.U. Rev. L. & Soc. Change 379 (2018).

yours', e.g., in consensual teen sexting, and in forms of bondage/role playing sexual experiences where simulating consent refusal in the moment is part of the agreed upon general rules of the game.[73]

Abortion

In Chapter Seven, we considered the abortion issue in the context of a right to privacy. In *Roe,* the majority decided that the Texas ban on all abortions, except to save the life of the woman, did not take into consideration any of a variety of other interests that come into play during pregnancy. The health of the woman, the viability and health of the fetus, whether the pregnancy resulted from sexual contact with a spouse, a brief acquaintance, a blood relative, or a rapist were all issues a woman was entitled to weigh in her decision to continue or terminate a pregnancy. All of these interests were said to affect, in various ways, the woman's liberty interest because they fell within a zone of privacy. But as noted in that chapter, liberty implies the existence of a constraint against it. With absolute freedom and autonomy, the question of a liberty interest would not arise. Pregnancy, however, is one of the most interactive processes of nature and social life due to its complexity and multidimensionality. Pregnancy is complex due to its long gestation period and the many risks associated with it. It is multidimensional because *biologically* it involves the pregnant woman, fertilization from another person known or unknown, and usually assistance from medical providers, but in addition *psychologically* it raises worries during pregnancy and increasingly afterwards regarding the responsibilities of caring for a new helpless human being; and also *socially, politically, economically,* and *morally* it raises a cluster of questions regarding the responsibilities of raising a child and what ought to be done to preserve or change the surrounding world to reduce the prospects of needless suffering by that child. Historically, attitudes toward abortion reflect the

---

[73] See for example Kacey Jones, *On Idaho: Teenage Sexting Statutes: A Critical Examination of Idaho Code 18-1507A and an Argument against Criminalization of Consensually Shared Sexts,* 54 Idaho L. Rev. 644 (2018); Derek E. Bambauer, *Exposed,* 98 Minn. L. Rev. 2025 (2014); and Elizabeth Mincer, *Fifty Shades and Fifty States: Is BDSM a Fundamental Right? A Test for Sexual Privacy,* 26 Wm. & Mary Bill Rts. J. 865 (2018).

degree to which the environment may sustain life. Abortions have been disfavored when human life was scarce (e.g., in Visigoth law), but the opportunity to gain from new human life was considerable, while, we may predict, it would be favored in a world of food scarcity, economic collapse, or widespread political violence.

Most of the issues in this chapter will focus on the legal response to abortion as a prolonged and complex bodily event in the life of individual pregnant women. If gestation lasted only a day and was not restricted to one gender the abortion debate would take on a different focus and raise different issues. The same would be true if the entire gestational process were conducted outside any living person, with each process of cell division initially 'edited' genetically, and then carefully monitored and adjusted to achieve the creation of a viable and healthy neonate or 'test tube baby'. Besides the multi-faceted complexity noted above, there are an array of moral and philosophical questions in the abortion debate that cannot be answered without well thought-out moral stipulations, issues such as 'When does life begin?' or 'What is a person and is a fetus one of them?' or 'Is a high tech biologically-based 'test-tube' baby also a person with rights, and could the same be said for silicon-based robots that repairs and reproduces themselves'? The notion that there is a clear distinction, both in thought and in reality, between a traditionally formed human being and these other greater or lesser 'artificial' creatures has been continually undermined by science since the nineteenth century. Presumably, robots are constructed, while human beings grow and develop on their own, but we distinguish the two only as a result of our ignorance of how things grow and develop, not because of any difference in kind we can clearly point to. To say that one has a soul and the other does not is not an explanation, but a shorthand way of describing the limits of our knowledge and technical capabilities up to this point. The Fourteenth Amendment refers to "all persons born or naturalized" simply because when it was written the termination of a pregnancy by birth was the natural starting point of personhood. For much of human history, the explanation for the uncontrollable events we care deeply about, like conception and death, but cannot always micro-manage, was that they were in the hands of some super rational higher being sympathetic to us. In the case of pregnancy, the higher being is said to select beforehand discrete specific persons to become created. Hence, within that framework of assumptions, abortion is thought to interrupt supernatural agency, and each actually living adult may imagine that *they* would not exist, but for an earlier choice not to abort them. Nothing we know about the fine-grained details of biological generation, however, supports such an expansive teleological hypothesis. To say that *this person* (e.g., Einstein) came from *that fertilized egg* is to ignore a multitude of intervening factors that influenced Einstein's development at conception and *in utero*, creating an illusory sense of causal inevitability.

Defining something as a 'person' is also a strand of the complexity of abortion debates. We may ask: Is this an empirical issue or a purely moral one, an issue decided by finding facts or one by making value judgments? The two questions may be interrelated. We reserve the category of *persons* to thinking and speaking beings capable of communicating with us. The fact that we name ships as if they are persons does not make them persons. Instead, persons are thought to have a cognitive 'life' that can be detected by their use of language. So, we interpret electrical impulses in the fetus as a 'heartbeat' though not yet of a heart, and physical movement in the womb as if it were *expressive activity,* perhaps an expressive response to pain. By this standard, however, the entire kingdom of nature from viruses and bacteria to mammals must also be classified as proto 'persons' in various forms and in various stages of evolutionary development. In 1884 Justice Holmes, sitting on the Massachusetts Supreme Court, had to decide whether an infant spontaneously born after only four or five months' gestation, as a result of the woman's injury, and then died after ten to fifteen minutes, was sufficiently a person the woman could be compensated for, as if the loss of a child. Holmes decided the woman could not be compensated for that part of her injuries because "the unborn child was a part of the mother at the time of the injury," could not live independently, and so was not a person as the statute authorizing recovery for injury assumed.[74] This ruling contained a mixture of empirical observations and legal norms. You could have no legal standing in court, Holmes was saying, unless you were a living human organism with a reasonable likelihood *at birth* of continuing life even if only briefly. However, as our knowledge of fetal development increased and with it our ability to medically treat the

---

[74] *Dietrich v. Northampton*, 138 Mass. 14, 17 (1884).

fetus *in utero,* we have come to include within the scope of viability later prenatal life, and with it, protection of the law.[75]

It is important to recognize that when people typically argue over the status of what is in the process of being born (zygote, fetus, embryo, unborn baby, unborn child, or person) they are not expressing disagreement over biological facts. Historically, Anglo-American law has dealt with these 'category' problems by setting down a variety of *ad hoc* rules. At one time, killing or harming a pregnant woman that also resulted in the death of her growing embryo that has 'quickened' was not considered murderous infanticide, but rather manslaughter. (Quickening was the initial signs of fetal movements typically after fifteen weeks of pregnancy.) At a later time, the offense was reduced to a "heinous misdemeanor." However, once there is a live birth the offense becomes murder if the child then dies as a result of the woman's injuries. Also, an anticipated unborn child may be considered an heir along with other already born brothers and sisters, but only if "its continuance in life may be reasonably expected."[76]

In *Roe,* the majority argued that when the Fourteenth Amendment was drafted the word 'person' did not include prenatal life as evidenced by the general acceptance at the time that abortion was not murder. As a result, a prenatal right to life could not have been within the protection of that amendment.[77] In response to this view, a 'personhood movement' sprang up after *Roe* to give embryos the full status as persons. In 1986, Missouri passed a law stating that "the life of each human being begins at conception" and that "unborn children have protectable interests in life, health, and well-being." But the law also stated that "nothing in this section shall be interpreted as creating a cause of action against a woman for indirectly harming her unborn child by failing to properly care for herself or by failing to follow any particular program of prenatal care."[78] The law would have effectively banned abortion, some methods of birth control,

---

[75] *Bonbrest v. Kotz,* 65 F. Supp. 138 (D.D.C. 1946).

[76] William Blackstone, *Commentaries on the Laws of England in Four Books,* edited by William Draper Lewis (Philadelphia: Rees Welsh, 1915), I: 118-119; IV: 1595.

[77] *Roe v. Wade,* 410 U.S. at 156.

[78] Missouri Statutes, Title I, Ch. 1, § 1.205(1)-(4); *Webster v. Reproductive Health Services.,* 492 U.S. 490 (1989).

and would have impacted on assisted reproductive technologies.[79] However, while the Missouri abortion law asserts prenatal personhood in its preamble and requires doctors to make viability assessments, it did not give the prenatal person equal protection of the law by virtue of its non-viable circumstance. Prenatal persons, for example, could not sue their mother for neglect or for inflicting prenatal alcoholism on them.

Is the abortion debate so intractable because it sits at a crossroads of deeply conflicting theological and secular value systems, or because it raises moral difficulties even within each system?[80] For example, Catholic theologian St. Thomas Aquinas would not have accepted Missouri's theology because he accepted abortion before forty days after conception, while most secularists would recoil from abortion at the end of a full-term pregnancy, except under extreme circumstances. *Roe* weighed the moral implications of the empirical reality of fetal viability against the moral values of maternal privacy, dignity and health. If a strictly secular and utilitarian standard had been used, preserving the life of the unborn child over that of a woman at end-stage cancer would have been justified because the former would produce more opportunities for happiness in the future. Most women in such a situation would gladly sacrifice themselves for the life of their offspring. However, the pragmatic orientation of the *Roe* framework would have presumptively given that decision to a woman, not the state. That is because *Roe* starts its analysis with the existing human person and her liberty to be a person and to act as a person in a society reflecting the values embodied in the Fourteenth Amendment. In this case, prenatal life is at a

---

[79] See Greer Gaddie, *Note: The Personhood Movement's Effect on Assisted Reproductive Technology: Balancing Interests Under a Presumption of Embryonic Personhood*, 96 Tex. L. Rev. 1293 (2018).

[80] *Webster*, 492 U.S. at 565. (Justice Stevens: "There is unquestionably a theological basis for such an argument, just as there was unquestionably a theological basis for the Connecticut statute that the Court invalidated in *Griswold*. Our jurisprudence, however, has consistently required a secular basis for valid legislation."). The Christian dualism of body and soul sits at the heart of the abortion debate for many, and raises questions for others, such as, for example, if embryos have souls, when do they acquire them, and what becomes of them if they spontaneously abort, as many do? See, for example, David Albert Jones, *The Soul of the Embryo* (New York: Continuum, 2004).

dispositive disadvantage. Thus, "only personal rights that can be deemed 'fundamental' or 'implicit in the concept of ordered liberty', . . . are included in this guarantee of personal privacy."[81]

Two views of liberty seem to be working in *Roe:* (1) I am free to operate within and only within the bounds of legislative norms set by the state; or (2) I am free unless the state has compelling reasons to limit that freedom in specific circumstances, and then only by well- recognized constitutional norms. The first gives the state the final word on all questions; the second presumes liberties retained by individuals and places the burden on the state to say why and how they should be curtailed. This philosophical distinction, however, is not useful in resolving disputes like those raised in the abortion debate because there is simply no societal agreement about the best sources of morality governing abortion law. Is the authority to be found in a Texas statute passed by a democratic process, or in the cryptic wording of the Ninth Amendment, or in the densely interpreted wording of the Fourteenth Amendment? As the dissent in *Roe* points out, can the Supreme Court really say that the state can have no interests to assert under any circumstances against an abortion decision in the *first* trimester? *Roe's* analysis assumes that the state's interest in potential life increases during gestation. Even without believing that the embryo carries a promissory note from God to become ensouled, does this view reflect an anthropomorphic bias against the tiny embryo merely because it is not readily recognizable as a mature form of human life? Although small in size, the embryo is a marvel of genetic bioengineering undergoing vast exchanges of energy and information at every moment. We cannot say that it possesses less potentiality than at any other later stage in the process of gestation.

The conundrum posed by *Roe* is that it attempts to balance irreconcilable interests in protecting potential human life. The interests of the pregnant individual are the liberty interests of privacy, autonomy of choice and self-determination, and of being a beneficiary of constitutional protections, especially freedom from state sectarian laws. The interests of the state have been described as minimizing the offense many citizens feel about terminating potential human life, promoting population expansion to

---

[81] *Roe,* 410 U.S. at 152-53.

sustain or increase national economic and cultural vitality, and seeing to it that individuals make informed and considered judgments when initiating or terminating pregnancy.[82] As we have seen, calling privacy a fundamental unenumerated right never means privacy in every conceivable circumstance. On the other hand, claiming, as *Roe* dissenters do, that the decision was "wrongly decided," cannot mean that privacy cannot be a factor in balancing interests. Calling something a fundamental right cannot simply mean that it is 'rooted' in evidence of past traditions and conscience; it also means that current law should be carefully scrutinized for excessive intrusion into the privacy interests of living persons. Unfortunately, there does not seem to be a deeper set of constitutional norms to resolve this broad disagreement.[83] One side argues that restrictive state laws must be closely scrutinized to justify their privacy intrusions; the other is satisfied if the state merely articulates some reasons for its restrictions. One side relies wholly upon the Constitution; the other believes that the Constitution requires that the people of the states have wide latitude to decide how, if at all, they want to regulate abortion.[84] In the latter case, a state need only *say* that regulating abortion is an important state interest and then make any law of its choice – whether by specifying the period during which a legal abortion may be obtained, or by punishing abortion providers, etc. – that is rationally related that interest. *Ultimately, these disagreements cannot be resolved through empirical inquiry because all crucial facts are essentially contested.* At the heart of the intractable abortion

---

[82] These competing interests are described by Justice Stevens in *Planned Parenthood v. Casey*, 505 U.S. 833, 914-917 (1992).

[83] The dissent in *Casey* seems to admit this. ("[W]e referred to a 'principle of justice so rooted in the traditions and conscience of our people as to be ranked as fundamental'. These expressions are admittedly not precise, but our decisions implementing this notion of 'fundamental' rights do not afford any more elaborate basis on which to base such a classification."). Ibid., 951.

[84] Justice Scalia in dissent writes: "The States may, if they wish, permit abortion on demand, but the Constitution does not require them to do so." Ibid., 979. Scalia argues that the Supreme Court should not be in the business of micro-managing State abortion laws. Ibid., 996. The background influence of religious views on abortion law is discussed by Barbara Pfeffer Billauer, *Abortion, Moral Law, and the First Amendment: The Conflict between Fetal Rights and Freedom of Religion*, 23 Wm. & Mary J. Women & L. 271(2017).

debate lies a status problem. Some issues of legal status may be resolved by definition (e.g., marital status), or by factual debate (minimum voting age). In the case of the human reproduction no set of facts can be agreed upon from which to debate, weigh, and reason upon.

Punishment

Inflicting pain and restraint on the human body has been an age-old method of social and political control. Every warm-blooded creature has a pain threshold. It is the cost we pay for having a central nervous system. Without pain, our laws would be very different and so would our methods of enforcing them. Here our focus will be on the elaborate apparatus of state sanctioned punishment for crime, asking under what circumstances is the state justified in inflicting pain, how much, to whom, and by whom? These are questions most intimate to the law of the body, and central to the interaction of law and morality. From a purely *legal* point of view, we must not lose sight of the fact that there is nothing prohibiting the reintroduction of public hangings or dismemberments, if authorized by accepted norms of the constitutional and legal system; only a moral infrastructure holds that back. Saying, for example, that the punishment must fit the crime says very little, unless we have a settled agreement of the dangers posed by committing it. Our idea of danger, in turn, depends on our expectations in daily life about our own safety. In a world about to be obliterated by an asteroid or mega nuclear warfare very little else that happens would be dangerous, while just about anything else has the potential of being dangerous that disrupts a secure and orderly happy life. In other words, for almost any activity an argument may be made that light punishment is insufficient, even justifying the death penalty for jay walking, if, for example, done as an act of defiance against faltering state authority in a dangerous world.

In asking what the appropriate punishment should be we are also asking what a *just* or *fair* punishment is. Aristotle seems at times to argue that returning to the *status quo ante* after a bad act would produce a fair result.[85]

---

[85] See Ernest J. Weinrib, *Corrective Justice in a Nutshell,* 52 U. Toronto L. J. 349 (2002); and Thomas C. Brickhouse, "Aristotle on Corrective Justice," *The Journal of Ethics,* 18 (2014): 187-205.

This view, *corrective* justice, may work for economic crimes under some circumstances. Thieves or embezzlers must return to their victims the value of what has been taken from them in the form of restitution. But is a fair result achieved when a thief steals $1000, invests that money to make $500 more, and then returns the initial amount to the victim, along with maybe a small additional amount of lost interest? Such a measure correcting a two-party transaction seems to leave out the interests of other parties, including family members and those of the public with a general interest in crime prevention. So, although the ingenuity of the thief produced economic value for himself and possibly others, the surplus also would likely be forfeited to the state as 'ill-gotten' gains. This reasoning also applies to a notorious criminal who is not allowed to profit from publishing a book about his crimes. Corrective justice, applied to non-economic crimes, is even more difficult to calculate. The pain of a torture victim may not be replicated on the body of a sociopath, who actually may feel vindicated by it. Raping the rapist also may not achieve a satisfying result. Punishment, then, it is thought by some, should include besides restitution also some amounts of pain for retribution and for deterrence. At the other end of the spectrum, advocates of *restorative justice* see a futility in identifying justice simply with pain infliction ordered in a courtroom setting. They place a focus on helping victims recover from trauma, and on reducing recidivism by getting wrongdoers to see the harm they have done, take responsibility for it, and experience remorse.[86]

Theories of punishment, then, may be regarded as a search for a clear moral standard to determine the appropriate amount of punishment, no more nor less. In our current system of justice, the sentencing phase of a trial consists of weighing aggravating and mitigating circumstances relating to the crime, the victim, and the defendant. The process itself, however, is not a search for truth, but a clarification of accepted values, keeping in mind that with different values the punishment might be greater or lesser for the same crime committed by a very similar defendant. It is also possible for a system of

---

[86] Olivia Levinson, *Reconciling Ideals: Restorative Justice as an Alternative to Sentencing Enhancements for Hate Crimes*, 105 Minn. L. Rev. 209 (2020); and Lynn S. Branham, *"Stealing Conflicts" No More?: The Gaps and Anti-Restorative Elements in States' Restorative-Justice Laws*, 64 St. Louis L. J. (2020).

punishment to dispense entirely with a state obligation to implement it. Punishment could be left to the victims or their families, or to public opinion; or perhaps it is possible to imagine no state sanctioned system of punishment at all, merely letting the adjudicated wrongdoer go free with a reprimand and a reminder never to do it again. Imagining such a system of mercy reminds us of how embedded in any theory of punishment are traditional ideas and judgments about actions deemed 'evil'. Traditionally, those who are adjudged to have committed bad and evil acts, should never get off without some form of punishment. Doing so would constitute a terrible forfeiture of the rule of law, or so it is argued. Yet, we also ban placing the accused in double jeopardy by retrying him for the same crime (Amend. V), which allows a crime to go unpunished as a price for maintaining a lawful state. And we also give the President and state governors various degrees of power to pardon punishment for crimes committed or charged; and although the pardon power does not extend to future crimes, it has been thought to pardon crimes that *may have been* committed within a certain timeframe.[87] Pardons and commutations of sentences clearly violate the rule that there should be a just fit between the punishment and the crime.

In order to decide how much punishment is enough, too much or too little, theories of punishment provide reasons to justify the 'correct' answer. A correct punishment, then, is one that meets the standards set out by the theory. For example, if the purpose of punishment is to deter the future conduct of the criminal or of others, then the correct punishment should be one that has sufficient deterrent effect. If the purpose of punishment is retribution in response to evil and immoral conduct because of a felt belief that mercy or indifference is an insufficient response, then the appropriate punishment must satisfy the emotional demands of that felt belief. Unfortunately, there is a gap between the theory and practice of punishment. There are many ways to achieve deterrence: public executions, placing the chastised in pillory, castration of rapists, forfeiture

[87] (Const, Art II, Sec. 2, cl. 1). For discussion of the extent of the pardon power, see Aaron Rappaport, *An Unappreciated Constraint on the President's Pardon Power,* 52 Conn. L. Rev. 271 (2020); and Paul F. Eckstein and Mikaela Colby, *Presidential Pardon Power: Are There Limits and, if Not, Should There Be?* 51 Ariz. St. L. J. 71 (2019). See also *Ex parte Grossman,* 267 U.S. 87 (1925).

of all wealth and property of embezzlers and other financial criminals, punishing their family members and associates as well, etc. And, there are many ways to punish evil and immoral acts. Theories that measure punishment by the severity of the consequences of the harmful conduct upon a victim and society, as well as theories that measure punishment by the severity of moral duties breached by the perpetrator, (i.e., consequentialist and deontological theories), do not get us very far, and for two reasons: (1) most of the theoretical work is constructed out of already accepted value norms, norms defining or illustrating what is excessive or insufficient punishment, and (2) the theory is of such a level of generality that it provides little actual guidance in the workaday world for punishing individuals. Even a practical way of determining the optimally best deterrent punishment, by measuring rates of recidivism, may vary over time with social and economic conditions, themselves not causally related to criminal behavior itself. In a violent crime-ridden world, incarceration may be a refuge and violent public torture the only sufficient method of deterring further crime.

A characterization of punishment as "cruel and unusual" also is not a very helpful standard because what shocks the conscience and is deemed cruel varies over time and circumstance. The phrase itself is ambiguous and its meaning is still debated well into the twentieth century. Does it mean that punishment could be cruel as long as it is not unusual? It may be that the Eighth Amendment framers intended punishment to be less cruel and unusual than that practiced by Europeans in the past, though a standard of how much less, and by what measure, is difficult to determine. In the earliest Eighth Amendment case, the Supreme Court decided that although the cruel and unusual standard was imprecise, capital punishment by hanging or firing squad was constitutional, but death by torture was not.[88] Here the standard seems to be that inflicting pain is acceptable but prolonging it should be avoided. Yet by this standard beheading by the guillotine should be preferred to hanging, or death by firing squad over lethal injection, both of which are less easily botched. A decade later the Supreme Court determined that electrocution, even though novel and highly unusual for its time, was constitutional as

---

[88] *Wilkerson v. Utah*, 99 U.S. 130 (1879).

long as it did not amount to torture or result in a lingering death.[89] The framers did not want punishment to be an act of torture intentionally carried out as a prolonged defilement of the prisoner's body, especially in public.[90]

So, is pain reduction, then, at least one standard embedded in the Eighth Amendment, even if not an entirely clear one? No, because there is no state obligation to seek the least painful alternative method of punishment, for example, in the protocols for administering lethal injections. If such injections were an improvement over hanging, firing squads, or the electric chair, which were not deemed cruel and unusual, then *any* protocol that was not specifically and intentionally designed to cause additional substantial and unnecessary pain to carry out a death sentence also would be constitutional.[91] Yet, it is difficult to know what protocol is done simply for pain reduction, and what protocol is selected to achieve a satisfying level of retributive cruelty, since different theories of punishment weigh the pain of punishment on different scales of justice. Advocates of deterrence and retribution seem to tolerate and even welcome more pain than do advocates of penal reform or restorative justice. The Supreme Court has attempted to provide a fixed and clear standard for acceptable pain, arguing that the Eight Amendment prohibits states from inflicting gratuitous suffering, while at the same time rejecting a claim that states have an affirmative duty to seek less painful alternatives. Instead, the burden is placed on the prisoner to show that an alternative method is "feasible and readily implemented" and would "significantly reduce a risk of substantial pain and that the State has refused to adopt without a legitimate penological reason." However, the court rejected the view that a

---

[89] *In re Kemmler,* 136 U.S. 436, 447 (1890). See also, *Louisiana ex rel. Francis v. Resweber,* 329 U.S. 459 (1947). (Failure of the electrical device was not torture, the court determined, because the amount of mental anguish or physical pain was no greater than would be experienced in a cell block fire.)

[90] See John F. Stinneford, *The Original Meaning of 'Unusual': The Eighth Amendment as a Bar to Cruel Innovation,* 102 Nw. U.L. Rev. 1739, 1745 (2008). ("As used in the Eighth Amendment, the word 'unusual' was a term of art that referred to government practices that are contrary to 'long usage' or 'immemorial usage'.)

[91] *Baze v. Rees,* 553 U.S. 35, 86 (2008).

prisoner's specific medical condition would cause more pain than is constitutionally permitted.[92]

The subjective and *ad hoc* dimension of the conceit of 'fitting' punishment to crimes is clear in the systematic disparities in punishment in different states for very similar crimes. The standard solution to what looks like manifest injustice is that the punishment should have its own trial, separate from that of determining guilt. In a penalty phase trial, the state is required to set out procedures for weighing individualized aggravating and mitigating factors in the hopes that reasoned judgment rather than blind revenge would prevail.[93] The criminal history of a defendant, if any, is one such aggravating or mitigating circumstance. Punishment can be enhanced for prior crimes, making punishment fit the criminal rather than the crime. For example, three separate small fraudulent financial transactions could lead to life imprisonment without parole through a state recidivist statute.[94] However, even without having a criminal history, punishment cannot be challenged as excessive since the Supreme Court has determined that standards of proportionality cannot be read into the Eight Amendment.[95] We must ask in debating the question of fitness if there is nothing but perhaps a natural desire for leniency to *legally* prohibit a life sentence for repeated parking violations.[96] At some point, the recidivist gets punished more harshly for repeatedly flaunting the law, not for violating it on several discrete occasions.

If fines could be 'excessive' under the Constitution should not some forms of corporeal punishment also be? Some Justices believe the answer lies in the punishment practices in effect at the time the Constitution was ratified, and should be assumed to be acceptable today, unless the people through their legislatures say otherwise. Others believe that modern views of penology should prevail, including eliminating the death penalty altogether as a "pointless and needless extinction of life" with very little if

---

[92] *Bucklew v. Precythe*, 139 U.S. 1112, 1125 (2019).

[93] *Gregg v. Georgia*, 428 U.S. 153 (1976); *Lockett v. Ohio* 438 U.S.586 (1978).

[94] *Rummel v. Estelle*, 445 U.S. 263 (1980).

[95] *Harmelin v. Michigan*, 501 U.S. 957 (1991).

[96] *Rummel*, 445 U.S. at 288.

any deterrent influence; and that the courts with an eye on fundamental constitutional protections of the dignity and physical integrity of the individual are in the best position to make such a decision.[97] Although, the court has asserted that the Eight Amendment bars states from expressly choosing a method of execution for its pain enhancing effects, it still defers to state methods that may be shown to be pain enhancing in any case. So, in theory, a method that creates pain that is "substantial when compared to a known and available alternative," would be excessive. However, in practice, reference to actual empirical data of pain thresholds in determining what is or is not excessive is not dispositive.[98]

Whether measured against the standards of the framers or of settled practices, the Supreme Court so far has never told a state its method of execution was unconstitutional. In leaving punishment to the state legislatures, subject to an obligation that they provide penological reasons and penalty trials, our Eight Amendment jurisprudence allows laws that respond to strong public opinion and produce troubling inconsistent results. Cruel times may demand cruel punishment and be satisfied with it. An act of faith sits at the heart of the confidence that democracy will fit correctly the punishment to the crime. A question of consistent penal standards is reflected, for example, in the narrower issue of corporal punishment in public schools. Common law and some states by law require that punishment fit the purpose of education, i.e., advance the goals of discipline required for effective education. However, Justices debate whether the Eight Amendment ought to apply to state action that is not specifically criminal in nature. The present answer is that it does not, leaving it to legislatures or school officials to decide how much punishment is necessary to make an effective lesson out of breaches of school discipline.[99]

---

[97] See *Glossip v. Gross*, 135 S. Ct. 2726, 2749-50 (2015) (Scalia: "Capital punishment presents moral questions that philosophers, theologians, and statesmen have grappled with for millennia. The Framers of our Constitution disagreed bitterly on the matter. For that reason, they handled it the same way they handled many other controversial issues: they left it to the People to decide.")

[98] *Bucklew*, 139 S. Ct. at 1125. (See Breyer's dissent.)

[99] *Ingraham v. Wright*, 430 U.S. 651, 685 (1977). See dissent: "if it is constitutionally impermissible to cut off someone's ear for the commission of murder, it must be

Conclusion

Mill attempted to formulate a rule to guide legislation for a pluralistic, tolerant, complex, and progressing society consisting of members with diverse interests. The Harm Principle best summarized that rule, he thought, because it produced the best overall outcomes for both individuals and society in the long run. Those who wanted to use law to hyper-manage the experiences and interactions of members of society would be disappointed, and so would those who wanted little or no legal constraints whatsoever. His primary insight was that our individual desire for privacy and autonomy in our feelings, thoughts, and aspirations requires our recognition and acceptance that such liberty may only be practiced where there is some degree of limited paternalistic restraint upon acts that harm others. In creating such a system, however, we adapt to the biological reality that every individual starts life with "the fact of living in society," where the inevitable conflicts of interests are already in effect.[100] Since it is in law that the primary work of balancing interests is done for a society under its jurisdiction, it is imperative that law develop the kind of procedural norms of inner morality later identified by Fuller.

Fuller thought that Mill's theory of liberty placed too much emphasis on autonomous individuality, not recognizing sufficiently the significance of an ordering and coordinating mechanism for competing interests provided by law and morality. Against Mill, Fuller wrote: "The complex network of institutional ways by which the bulk of our energies is directed and channeled is not an unfortunate limitation on freedom. It is essential to freedom itself;" and: "The choices a man can make without requiring collaborative social effort for their realization are trivial." Specifically, "freedom requires a congenial environment of rules and decisions."[101]

---

unconstitutional to cut off a child's ear for being late to class." See also Patrick Lenta, "Corporal Punishment of Children," *Social Theory and Practice* 38 (2012): 689-718.

[100] *On Liberty*, 73.

[101] Lon L. Fuller, *Freedom – A Suggested Analysis,* 68 Harv. L. Rev. 1305, 1311, 1312, 1314 (1955). Fuller refers to "On Social Freedom" attributed to Mill in late life as evidence that Mill changed his view of liberty. (Ibid., 1312). Apparently that essay was not from Mill's pen. See G. W. Smith, "J.S. Mill on Edger and Réville: An

However, Mill was, in fact, aware of the need for law and morality to nurture and sustain liberty in a social setting, writing: "Whenever, . . . there is a definite damage, or a definite risk of damages, either to an individual or to the public, the case is taken out of the province of liberty and placed in that of morality or law."[102] What he advised was that we take a close look at our laws, particularly those that impinge on our physical capabilities, to see if they only contain definite harms and risks of harm; and then when we do, recognize our historically slow but steady rejection of overly restrictive laws in favor of greater privacy and autonomy. Indispensable to this recognition, Mill believed, is a process of moral dialogue and political debate, always asking questions like: Are these still good laws in spite of the costs they incur? Good for whom and bad for whom and why? Are they properly reasoned out with evidence when enacted and enforced? In asking these questions, two forms of paternalism are at play: the paternalism of a law's effect on those who must obey it, and a paternalism of the manner in which the law was created in the first place. The former is a measure of the degree to which liberty and constraint can be rationally reconciled; the latter is a measure of the degree to which all stakeholders have had an opportunity to be heard in making and remaking the law.

Our survey of some of the laws of the body has revealed glaring failures of consistency and proof under critical examination. Suicide laws start as an affront to a Creator and end up being unenforceable altogether as a crime. Marriage is a legally created compact, but then we recognize marriages without one because we have to recognize the reality of enduring familial bonds. A decision to passively withhold end-of-life care is no less a consequential decision than one to affirmatively terminate end-of-life care. We invariably accept living wills written years before without asking for any evidence that the patient would ratify its terms under current conditions. A legal ban against a plural marriage can only be realistically enforced as a ban against a plural marriage license. Laws against adultery, fornication, cohabitation, contraception, and miscegenation cannot be effectively enforced because we cannot clearly demarcate the conduct or

---

Episode in the Development of Mill's Conception of Freedom," *Journal of the History of Ideas* 41 (1980): 433-449.

[102] *On Liberty*, 80.

the harm protected against. Homosexuality has been banned for conduct that went unpunished in heterosexual relations. In the abortion controversy, the terms 'life' and 'person', which have always been loose terms of art in science or philosophy, are used uncritically to introduce *ad hoc* assumptions into law as if they had precisely delineated meanings. The same applies to 'obscenity' in laws that attempt to regulate sexual experience. Confusing subjective legal fictions like 'cruel and unusual' punishment dominate Eight Amendment jurisprudence, and yet punishment never actually 'fits' the crime, nor the specific criminal; and nor do theories of punishment give precise instructions in concrete cases, raising questions of their usefulness. Use of tenuous analogies and vague penal standards probably explain why the Supreme Court has never rejected a state's method of execution as unconstitutional.

The bottom line is that all laws of the body may be formulated and interpreted in such a way as to produce cruel and invasive results. They only require politicians and jurists who are adept at explaining away the moral norms of fairness and equal protection embodied in the Fourteenth Amendment. In all of the areas where law regulates, restricts, or punishes individuals through control of what they may see, feel, or experience, or how long they may live, our legal history often supplies only vague and poorly reasoned themes that make possible a wide range of *ad hoc* interpretations disconnected from actual harms. To counter these oppressive interpretations, Mill insisted on the political morality of open public discussion focused on the processes that make and enforce our laws, while Fuller adds to this how law itself can continually reform itself from within by adhering to the norms of inner morality.

www.ingramcontent.com/pod-product-compliance
Ingram Content Group UK Ltd.
Pitfield, Milton Keynes, MK11 3LW, UK
UKHW041643031026
15587UKWH00001B/462